Agrarian Change,
Gender and Land Rights

Fatma Gül
Umail

Spring 2004

Amherst

Agrarian Change, Gender and Land Rights

Edited by

Shahra Razavi

Blackwell Publishing

9600 Garsington Road, Oxford OX4 2DQ, UK
350 Main Street, Malden, MA 02148-5018, USA
550 Swanston Street, Carlton South, Melbourne, Victoria 3053, Australia
Kurfürstendamm 57, 10707 Berlin, Germany

First published 2003 as *Journal of Agrarian Change* Special issue 3(1&2) by Blackwell Publishing Ltd

Library of Congress Cataloging-in-Publication Data has been Applied for

British Library Cataloguing in Publication Data has been Applied for

ISBN 1-4051-1076-7 (paperback)

Set in Hong Kong
by Graphicraft Ltd
Printed and bound in the United Kingdom
by Cambrian Printers

For further information on
Blackwell Publishing, visit our website:
http://www.blackwellpublishing.com

Contents

The **United Nations Research Institute for Social Development (UNRISD)** is an autonomous agency engaging in multidisciplinary research on the social dimensions of contemporary problems affecting development. Its work is guided by the conviction that, for effective development policies to be formulated, an understanding of the social and political context is crucial. The Institute attempts to provide governments, development agencies, grassroots organizations and scholars with a better understanding of how development policies and processes of economic, social and environmental change affect different social groups. Working through an extensive network of national research centres, UNRISD aims to promote original research and strengthen research capacity in developing countries.

Current research programmes include: Civil Society and Social Movements; Democracy, Governance and Human Rights; Identities, Conflict and Cohesion; Social Policy and Development; and Technology, Business and Society.

A list of UNRISD's free and priced publications can be obtained by contacting the Reference Centre, UNRISD, Palais des Nations, 1211 Geneva 10, Switzerland; Phone: (41 22) 917 3020; Fax: (41 22) 917 0650; E-mail: info@unrisd.org; Web: http://www.unrisd.org

UNRISD thanks the governments of Denmark, Finland, Mexico, the Netherlands, Norway, Sweden, Switzerland and the United Kingdom for their core funding.

Preface

Over the past two decades processes of agrarian change in developing countries have been deeply influenced by neo-liberal policy prescriptions that have taken the form of exchange rate devaluations, the reduction of trade barriers, and cutbacks in public expenditure outlays on agriculture. This has coincided with deflationary macro-economic policies that have had a negative impact on formal employment, and pushed the bulk of the population, especially women, into the casual agricultural workforce and/or into taking up precarious forms of self-employment in informal trade and services. The contributions to this volume explore how the deflationary macro-economic policies and processes associated with economic liberalization are impacting on rural livelihoods and agrarian change in diverse political economies, focusing in particular on the gender specificities of these impacts. This is the general background against which this volume's analyses of gender and land tenure reform must be read.

The problems that women encounter in accessing land have tended to remain on the margins of policy deliberation, both nationally and globally, despite the growing presence and voice of gender policy advocates in some contexts. Where the issue has been raised, it has tended to attract "one-size-fits-all" policy pre-scriptions, in the form of individual land titling, private ownership and the like. By bringing together situated analyses of the gender/land interface from highly diverse agrarian economies, this volume provides a more complex and differen-tiated picture. The challenges that rural women confront in political economies as diverse as Tanzania, Uzbekistan and Brazil in accessing land and constructing livelihoods—both as wives/daughters within male-dominated households *and* as members of vulnerable social classes and communities that face the risk of land alienation and entitlement failure in the context of liberalization—require far more nuanced and contextualized analyses and policy responses than are currently on offer. By highlighting the inadequacies of blanket policy prescriptions, and pro-viding a textured analysis of the differentiated landscape in which the gender/land nexus is situated, this volume takes a step in the right direction.

Thandika Mkandawire
Director
United Nations Research Institute for Social Development (UNRISD)

Editors' Introduction

We are delighted to publish this double special issue, guest-edited by Shahra Razavi, on *Agrarian Change, Gender and Land Rights*. In it, recent shifts in policy thinking about land rights – in general and specifically as they relate to women – are juxtaposed against developments in land tenure arrangements in selected regional contexts. Leading feminist scholars in the field provide searching treatment of the long-neglected matter of gender and access to land.

The articles are incisively introduced and contextualized, and their arguments and findings woven together, by Shahra Razavi. After Shahra Razavi's introductory paper, there comes an article in which Utsa Patnaik provides a searching examination of global capitalism, the neo-liberal policy agenda and its deflationary effects upon those countries that have experienced structural adjustment and trade liberalization. With that context of agrarian crisis and its roots powerfully established, there follow articles by Ann Whitehead and Dzodzi Tsikata, in which policy discourses on women's land rights in sub-Saharan Africa are comprehensively treated; by Cherryl Walker, on gender policy and land reform in South Africa; by Dzodzi Tsikata, on land tenure reforms and women's interests in Tanzania; by Bina Agarwal, on new prospects with respect to gender and land rights in India; by Deniz Kandiyoti, on agrarian reform and its impact on women in Uzbekistan; and by Carmen Diana Deere, on rural social movements and women's land rights in the Brazilian land reform.

This is a timely collection, in which careful empirical analysis is presented with considerable analytical power and great clarity. The papers are refreshingly original, always richly informative, sometimes provocative, and unfailingly of absorbing interest.

H.B.
T.J.B.

1
Introduction: Agrarian Change, Gender and Land Rights

SHAHRA RAZAVI

Neo-liberal economic agendas are impacting on rural livelihoods and people's attachment to, and functions of, land in rural and non-rural household economies differently in diverse contexts; the present collection of papers explores the gender specificities of these impacts. With the deceleration of more formal forms of employment, the diversification of rural livelihoods, and the intensification of women's unpaid and casual labour in agriculture and the informal sector, the land question has taken on a new urgency and needs to be posed in a new light. Given women's centrality to diversified livelihoods, and their increasing political agency, their interests in land (both as wives/daughters within male-dominated households and as members of vulnerable social classes and communities that face the risk of land alienation and entitlement failure in the context of liberalization) are more politicized today as well as being more contested. The interface between gender and land is contextually specific and cannot be adequately addressed through all-purpose global policy prescriptions.

Keywords: gender, land tenure, livelihoods, diversification, neo-liberalism

BACKGROUND

The past two decades have witnessed significant shifts in global development agendas and policies, marked by a resurgence of *laissez-faire* orthodoxies and a marked ambivalence, if not outright hostility, towards the 'heavy-handed' developmental state. The debt crises of the early 1980s and the subsequent multilateral lending programmes provided a decisive opening for the international financial institutions (IFIs) to impose a neo-liberal agenda of fiscal restraint, open trade and capital accounts, and privatization on indebted developing countries.

The author would like to thank Terry Byres for extensive comments, advice and support in bringing together this special issue; Ann Whitehead, Deniz Kandiyoti and Cherryl Walker for their helpful comments on the Introduction; Caroline Danloy for excellent research assistance; and all contributing authors for agreeing to make numerous rounds of revision. Funding for the UNRISD project 'Agrarian Change, Gender and Land Rights' was provided by Sida, UNDP, FAO as well as the governments of Denmark, Finland, Mexico, Netherlands, Norway, Sweden, Switzerland and the United Kingdom which provide UNRISD's core funds.

Issues of agrarian change and rural development have been a palpable part of these policy shifts. The neoliberal attack on the post-World War Two consensus was built on a deep aversion to state-led import substituting industrialization, while agriculture featured as the centrepiece of the narrative in national economies where agriculture formed a high proportion of GDP. Here alleged 'urban bias' was to be corrected by 'getting prices right' through various measures, such as exchange rate devaluation, abolishing export taxes and reducing trade barriers, while tenure insecurity was to be tackled through land titling (e.g. World Bank 1989). These standard measures, it was argued, would restore agricultural export growth and improve rural incomes and livelihoods. At the same time, cutbacks in public expenditure outlays on agricultural input subsidies, marketing boards, and research and extension services (representing an inflow of resources into agriculture that was largely ignored by proponents of 'urban bias') were prescribed and justified on the grounds that state expenditure needed to be significantly lowered and that the benefits were, in any case, either being captured by big farmers or squandered by state officials. Ironically, these public expenditure outlays were eroded at a time when they were most needed – when developing countries were being urged to open up their economies to global agricultural markets by intensifying their export thrust and exposing themselves to imports from countries that often provide generous agricultural subsidies to their farming sectors.

Gender concerns have made a shadowy, and less than satisfactory, appearance in these global policy debates. In the early 1980s, as a result of criticisms by feminists that structural adjustment policies were failing to recognize social reproduction as a set of activities that were essential to the economy, some attention was paid by gender specialists within the World Bank to women's role in the reproductive economy. Later, the focus shifted to women's role in production at the household level in sub-Saharan Africa, in what has become known as the 'gender efficiency argument' (Razavi and Miller 1995). This shift in focus – from women's role in reproduction to that in production – coincided with the growing concerns about the lack of agricultural supply response in Africa.[1]

One strand of thinking, which has been taken up by mainstream policy institutions, uses neo-classical micro-economic analytical tools to argue that the structure of male and female incentives in farm households leads to 'allocative inefficiencies' and a muted agricultural supply response (e.g. Udry et al. 1995; Blackden and Bhanu 1999).[2] In these arguments gender is thus effectively about inequality in resource allocation. These analyses have been abstracted from a set

---

[1] I am grateful to Ann Whitehead for pointing this out to me.
[2] For a critical assessment of this literature see Whitehead (2001) and Whitehead and Kabeer (2001). As Ann Whitehead (personal communication, April 2002) further notes, these arguments have been widely taken up by the mainstream policy establishment, in part at least, because this kind of analysis is compatible with the overall orthodox neo-classical position on African agriculture which sees the absence of a land market (and other ways in which the economy is less than fully commoditized) as the source of inefficiencies in resource use.

of empirical accounts of agricultural production in sub-Saharan Africa. One important resource constraint to which they draw attention is women's inadequate access to land – attributed to patriarchal land tenure institutions – while disregarding other constraints (such as inadequate command of labour and capital, and inaccessible markets) which tend to be far more debilitating as far as women smallholders in the region are concerned (Whitehead 2001).

The 1990s have also been a period of monumental political transformations. The collapse of authoritarian regimes in the Soviet Union and Eastern Europe, Latin America and sub-Saharan Africa, has given issues of rights and democracy a major impulse (Molyneux and Razavi 2002). The decade saw the growing size and influence of an international women's movement, linked through sub-regional, regional and international networks and able to collaborate on issues of policy and agenda setting. This has coincided with the revival of national women's movements, which in post-authoritarian settings in particular have found themselves in a position to press for political and legal reforms. An important component of these broader processes of democratization have been political and institutional reforms such as decentralization, which have revived and strengthened the institutions of local governance. While in some countries this has brought more women into government structures, questions remain as to how local, and indeed national, power relations feed into these local and community-based structures.

Inspired by these democratizing impulses, a wide range of feminist groups and networks, operating at national, regional and international levels, and influenced by the increasing use of rights language and instruments, have drawn attention to unequal land rights as an important mechanism through which female poverty and subordination is sustained and reproduced. Whether in the context of national debates on land tenure reform, rural social movement activism or the political dynamics associated with decentralization and the competing claims over resources that this has given rise to, women's interests in land have emerged as a contested issue. In some country contexts, tensions and divisions have emerged within civil society ranks: while some policy advocates have been pushing for women's unambiguous rights to land as a 'good' policy intervention (because it is presumed to enhance their intra-household bargaining power, irrespective of broader contextual forces), others have opposed women's land rights categorically because it is seen as the thin end of the wedge used by pro-liberalization lobbies to open up 'customary' systems of land management to market forces and foreign commercial interests.[3] This is a dangerous dichotomy which precludes the kind of nuanced and conceptualized analysis that is needed to identify situations where inadequate access to land constitutes a serious constraint on women's agricultural enterprises. Nor can it facilitate appropriate policy suggestions to enhance greater justice with respect to resource allocation for rural women – both as wives/daughters within male-dominated households *and* as members of vulnerable social classes and communities that face the risk of land alienation and entitlement failure in the context of liberalization.

[3]   For an illustration of this point in the case of Tanzania, see Tsikata's contribution to this special issue.

The contributions to this special issue critically reflect on the broad set of issues that have been raised in both the academic literature as well as in policy debates on the interface between gender and land. Different aspects of the gender and land question are explored by the contributing authors. The analysis that they bring to bear on the subject is informed by different understandings of gender relations and the most important arenas within which those relations operate. Yet despite their crucial conceptual and methodological variations, and their different entry points, together they constitute a strong statement on the importance of taking the *contextual specificities* of the gender and land question seriously. They also agree broadly on the inadequacies of policy prescriptions that rely on the magic of 'the market' and downplay the role of the state, while underscoring the crucial task of making the state more democratic and account-able to all its citizens irrespective of gender and class.

ORGANIZATION OF THE SPECIAL ISSUE

The contributions to this special issue fall under two parts. The first part includes two broad-ranging articles, which provide an empirically grounded and theoret-ically informed engagement with some of the principal themes of the special issue – neoliberal macroeconomic policies, agricultural liberalization and the re-form of land tenure institutions. The second part consists of country case studies, examining the diverse ways in which gender structures are implicated in the reproduction of the rural economy and the transformation of land tenure ar-rangements in the different settings.

The special issue opens with two panoramic papers, by Utsa Patnaik, and Ann Whitehead and Dzodzi Tsikata, respectively. The contribution by Utsa Patnaik analyses the neoliberal policy agenda and its deflationary impacts on the large number of countries which have undergone loan-conditional structural adjust-ment and trade liberalization over the past two decades, by theoretically situating the recent period of neoliberal ascendancy (1980–2002) with respect to the his-torical experience of deflationism of the inter-War era (1925–35). The histor-ically informed analysis of neoliberalism is juxtaposed against the present day impacts of liberalization and adjustment on rural livelihoods, land use and food security based on a country case study of India. While not directly concerned with the gender-differentiated impacts of neoliberal macroeconomic policies, the paper's analysis of deflationism and liberalization provides the essential background for understanding the broader macroeconomic policies and forces that are shaping rural livelihoods and land tenure arrangements in developing countries.

The paper by Ann Whitehead and Dzodzi Tsikata is a study of policy discourses about land tenure in sub-Saharan Africa – a continent where the IFIs have made policy interventions of unparalleled range and depth over the past two decades, based on a rather thin understanding of the social and economic institutions that they have set out to 'adjust' and 'reform'. It is the specificities of African land tenure arrangements and their very particular implications for women's land access that the authors are at pains to highlight. They are deeply apprehensive about one-size-fits-all gender and development prescriptions that still advocate a blanket policy of ensuring women's land access through titling, without any reference to these African specificities. The paper provides a brief account of how African land tenure arrangements have changed and been transformed in colonial, post-colonial and current settings in the context of rapid socio-economic change and policy interventions by an array of international, national and local actors and interests. Throughout, the authors highlight and explore historical shifts in thinking and the evidential and theoretical, as well as political and ideological, factors affecting these shifts. They examine an emerging consensus among policy advocates from very different political and ideological positions, that rejects the older idea of making a complete rupture with 'customary' systems of land tenure, and instead stresses building on 'the customary'. Drawing on other feminist literature on women and the state, they discuss some of the potential problems that such a return to 'the customary' will pose for contemporary African women.

The second part of the special issue consists of five country case studies from diverse regional contexts – sub-Saharan Africa (South Africa, Tanzania), South Asia (India), Central Asia (Uzbekistan) and Latin America (Brazil). They provide situated analyses of agrarian change, land tenure reform and gender structures, but their contours and entry points are different, reflecting the particular agrarian histories, current processes of land tenure reform and the on-going preoccupations of women's movements and advocates in the different countries.

Tables 1 and 2 provide a rough comparative picture of the significance of the agricultural sector to the national economies of these five countries: the contribution of the agricultural sector to GDP (Table 1), and the percentage of the economically active population in the agricultural sector (Table 2). At one end of the spectrum are South Africa and Brazil, where the agricultural sector today makes a relatively small contribution to GDP (3.2 per cent and 7.4 per cent, respectively), while Tanzania appears at the opposite end with the agricultural sector contributing a far more significant share of GDP (45.1 per cent). Uzbekistan and India (with 34.9 per cent and 24.9 per cent, respectively) fall somewhere

Table 1. Percentage of GDP from agriculture

	1980	*1990*	*1999*	*2000*
South Africa	6.2	4.6	3.4	3.2
Brazil	11.0	8.1	7.2	7.4
India	38.6	31.3	26.2	24.9
Uzbekistan	–	32.8	33.5	34.9
Tanzania	–	46.0	44.8	45.1

Source: The World Bank, Country at a Glance Tables, www.worldbank.org/data/, accessed on 11 March 2002.

Table 2. Percentage of employment in agriculture

	1980	1990	2000
South Africa	17.29	13.49	9.59
Brazil	36.67	23.28	16.69
Uzbekistan	–	–	27.65
India	69.53	64.02	59.64
Tanzania	85.78	84.41	80.45

Source: FAO, FAOSTAT Agriculture Data, www.fao.org, accessed on 21 March 2002.

in-between the two extremes. The labour force statistics produce a roughly similar ranking of the country case studies. Corresponding to agriculture's relatively small contribution to GDP, South Africa and Brazil also have the lowest proportion of economically active population engaged in the agricultural sector (9.59 per cent and 16.69 per cent, respectively), while Tanzania has the highest proportion (80.45 per cent). Again, Uzbekistan (27.65 per cent) and India (59.64 per cent) fall in-between the two extremes. However, while the agricultural sector contributes a higher proportion of the GDP in Uzbekistan than it does in India, it seems to absorb a lower share of the economically active population in Uzbekistan compared to India.

In her contribution to this special issue, Cherryl Walker examines the disjuncture between high-level policy commitments to gender equality in South Africa's on-going land reform programme, and weaknesses in translating these lofty policy principles into vigorous action on the ground. The South African agrarian scene is deeply marked by a brutal history of colonial forced dispossession in the eighteenth and nineteenth centuries and the ferocious racial inequalities of land dispensation put in place by successive minority white governments after 1910. This was accompanied by a programme of spatial control, which forcefully re-settled more than 3.5 million black people out of what were deemed 'white' areas and into labour reserves, or 'bantustans'. For much of the twentieth century, the bantustans served as labour reserves for the mining and industrial centres of the country, whereby government policies targeted men as migrant labourers and women as the reproducers of an impoverished subsistence economy within the reserves. The land reform programme that emerged out of the constitutional negotiations and policy debates of the early 1990s attempted to combine a strong commitment to the goals of social justice and redress – including an explicit commitment to gender justice – with the principles of market-led land reform. Yet, a decade later it can be argued that the commitment to gender equity has operated mainly at the level of lofty principle – a kind of 'piety in the sky'. To explain the disjuncture between high-level policy principles and on-the-ground action, Walker's account examines the wide range of factors – macroeconomic, socio-political, institutional and conceptual – which have shaped and constrained government policy *vis-à-vis* land.

Land tenure in Tanzania also bears the imprint of colonial policies character-istic of 'Africa of the labour reserves' (Amin 1972)[4] in the form of massive land dispossession and a pro-white settler policy. However, given the much earlier establishment of independent African rule together with the particular character-istics of Tanzania's road to modernization, agrarian relations and land tenure arrangements present an altogether different scenario to that found in South Africa. Despite considerable regional and ethnic heterogeneity, Tanzania has been described as a nation of predominantly 'peasant farmers, who, virtually without exception, endeavour[ed] to provision their own staple food needs' (Bryceson 1993, 2). Post-colonial agricultural policy, in the form of *Ujamaa* or 'African socialism', entailed extensive state intervention in the agricultural sector. In addi-tion to state attempts to accelerate industrialization, this involved 'villagization' or the physical relocation of the mass of the rural population into concentrated village settlements where they were supplied with basic social services, while at the same time marketing boards, crop authorities and cooperatives were also extended to these settlements for the supervision and control of peasant agricul-tural production (Gibbon 1995). As far as land tenure was concerned, the post-colonial government did not pursue the route of individualization, titling and registration, as occurred in Kenya and some other countries. In the 1980s, how-ever, the government's commitment to the policy of 'villagization' was reversed and the conditions were created for the increasing liberalization of agriculture. This has also coincided with a process of democratic opening. It is within this contentious liberalizing context that the policy proposals on land tenure reform were developed and debated beginning in 1992. In her contribution to this spe-cial issue, Dzodzi Tsikata documents and analyses the debates and controversies between government officials, academics, and various activist groups and net-works around land tenure reform, focusing in particular on how women's inter-ests in land were understood and debated by these actors. Some of the key themes and questions that emerge from the Whitehead and Tsikata contribution – the reappraisal of 'customary' laws, the limits of statutory interventions, local level land tenure institutions as a site of unequal social relations – are explored further in the light of Tanzania's agrarian economy and the recent land policy debates.

Echoing Patnaik's analysis of the general stagnation of rural non-farm em-ployment in India in the post-reform period, Bina Agarwal argues that for women the slowing down of rural non-farm employment opportunities in recent years has been dramatic. In other words, as more men shift to urban or rural non-farm employment, while non-farm employment opportunities for women stagnate, an increasing number of households will become dependent on women bearing

---

[4] According to Samir Amin (1972), what defined 'Africa of the labour reserves' was the fact that capital at the centre needed to have a large proletariat immediately available. This was because there was great mineral wealth to be exploited. In order to obtain the necessary labour, the colonizers dispossessed the African communities (sometimes by violence) and drove them deliberately into small, poor regions with no means of modernizing and intensifying their farming.

the larger burden of cultivation and farm management. This in turn means that the issue of secure land rights for women is becoming even more important, for both productivist and equality reasons that are examined in her article. What then are the prospects for enhancing women's land access? Agarwal explores the three main sources of arable land in India today – the state, the family and the market – and, in relation to market access, she makes a departure from current discussions by focusing on various forms of collective investment and cultivation by women, mediated by NGOs. It is argued that these institutional innovations, which have helped landless women use subsidized credit to lease-in or purchase land in groups and cultivate it jointly, can provide the basis for reviving land reform in a radically new form.

In the case of Uzbekistan, as Deniz Kandiyoti illustrates, it was not merely the stagnation of non-farm employment, but the virtual collapse of public sector employment and wages due to the crisis in public finance following the break-up of the Soviet Union, which has had important repercussions for the agricultural sector. Labour retrenchment in social services, rural industries and collective farming enterprises has pushed the bulk of the rural population into reliance on the smallholder economy (composed of household and subsidiary plots) and precarious forms of self-employment (in informal trade and services) for their subsistence. The agricultural sector has in effect acted as a 'shock absorber', providing livelihoods for an increasing number of people. At the same time, the state's continued dependence on cotton as the major export crop and the stake it retains in the maintenance of existing export revenues has made the shift away from the institutional structures of the command economy very difficult. The smallholder economy is thus effectively acting as a social safety net, but exists in a symbiotic relationship with an export sector (in the form of 'independent farms' and restructured collective enterprises) that is in turn tied to the state procurement system. However, as Kandiyoti shows, a thorough understanding of the actual workings of this mutual dependency – between smallholder agriculture and the export sector – reveals the marked feminization of labour in both sectors, whether as family or casual labour.

Agricultural reforms in Uzbekistan are sometimes compared to the Chinese agrarian reforms initiated more than two decades ago under the Household Responsibility System (HRS). However, while the shift from work brigades to 'family leaseholds' in Uzbekistan was modelled on the Chinese HRS, it has not granted farmers the decision-making freedom that was a key element of China's agrarian success in the 1980s. State dependence on cotton exports in Uzbekistan is the main factor inhibiting agricultural liberalization, while in China state-owned industrial enterprises were the state's 'cash cow' during the early period of reform (Pomfret 2000, 274), thereby reducing the state's dependence on surplus extraction from the agricultural sector. The diversification of livelihoods in the two contexts has also taken very different routes, given the dynamic rural industrialization process in China compared to the stagnating non-farm sector in Uzbekistan. While women's informal activities in rural Uzbekistan generally constitute survivalist, low-return strategies in an overcrowded informal sector,

Chinese household diversification strategies in the 1980s, which involved women taking up wage work in township and village enterprises (TVEs) and other non-farm enterprises, contributed to processes of accumulation.

If the state is resistant and reluctant to carry out agrarian reforms, the issue can still be kept on the agenda and in the public eye if there are dynamic social movements pressurizing for it 'from below'. This has certainly been the case in Brazil, particularly since the democratic openings of the 1980s. But the question that Carmen Diana Deere poses is why in the midst of some of the most radical and dynamic rural social movements to be found in Latin America, the evolution of the demand for *women's* land rights in the process of agrarian reform in Brazil has been so slow. This question is explored by examining the manner in which women's land rights occasionally surfaced in some of the leading rural social movements (the landless movement, the rural unions, the autonomous rural women's movement), but remained marginal to their main demands and struggles. Where rural women's demands were clearly articulated and persistently pursued, these concerned their labour and social rights (paid maternity leave, entitlements to retirement benefits, and so on); these issues apparently were of interest to all rural women independent of their class position and thereby united the hetero-geneous membership of the unions and the autonomous women's movement. However, what the article goes on to document is a more recent change in priorities as it has become increasingly clear that the marginalization of women's land rights can be detrimental to the development and consolidation of the agrarian reform settlements, and thus the landless movement itself. This realization has grown as a result of the territorial consolidation of the landless movement and the surge in the number of land occupations.

Having briefly sketched out the organization of the special issue, in the fol-lowing pages we shall consider the cross-cutting issues that emerge from the different contributions in order to place them in a broader policy context. The discussion is organized under four sections: (1) neoliberal globalization, gender and agrarian change; (2) agrarian transitions, diversified livelihoods and the place of land; (3) land tenure arrangements: institutions, reforms and constraints; (4) joint or individual titles: rethinking the agrarian household. The concluding section then briefly draws together the special issue's main findings.

NEOLIBERAL GLOBALIZATION,[5] GENDER AND AGRARIAN CHANGE

The economic agenda imposed by the IFIs on indebted developing countries since the early 1980s tends to embrace a number of orthodox policies, such as exchange rate devaluation, cuts in public spending, wage restraint, tariff

---

[5] 'Globalization' has become a catch-all term for many different trends; it is therefore crucial that we clarify what we mean by it. Here we are concerned with economic globalization, which is taken to mean greater openness of economies to international trade and capital mobility.

reduction and open capital accounts. Together these measures have had a deflationary impact on the economies undergoing reform, which has prevented governments from dealing effectively with unemployment and underemployment. The main targets of macroeconomic policy have been low inflation and balanced budgets, regardless of their impact on social development – and indeed, on economic growth.[6] While the disruptive social consequences of deflationary macroeconomic policies, marked by rising levels of social inequality and marginalization, have been widely recorded and commented upon, it is becoming increasingly clear that the orthodox policies have been far from successful in generating even moderate rates of economic growth. Economic growth has slowed dramatically over the past two decades (1980–2000), especially in the less developed countries, compared with the previous two decades (1960–80) (Weisbrot et al. 2000, see also Table 1 in Patnaik, this issue).

Patnaik's contribution to this special issue provides a penetrating analysis of the political forces underpinning neoliberal deflationary policies of the past two decades. Deflationary macroeconomic policies combined with the removal of all national barriers to the free movement of finance capital constitutes the core of the policy agenda of finance capital – a narrow but powerful interest group which has moved into a position of global dominance since the late 1970s. One of the central arguments of her paper is that the current global crisis of livelihoods is of a scale and magnitude which is unprecedented since the run-up to the Great Depression 70 years ago, and furthermore, that the 1920s too, like the current era of neoliberal prescriptions, was a period when finance capital was dominant.

Two questions are of particular interest to this special issue. First, how are deflationary macroeconomic policies impacting on livelihoods in the rural areas of developing countries? It is the changing nature of rural livelihoods that will affect the processes driving attachment to, and functions of, land in rural and non-rural household economies. Second, are deflationary macroeconomic policies gendered in their content and impact? Patnaik's contribution provides an answer to the first question, by outlining two powerful mechanisms at work. First, as a result of cuts in state spending, economies have become demand-constrained in the present era; in the case of India, which is her main point of reference, the post-1991 cuts in the state's development expenditures to contain the budget deficit have caused the collapse of rural non-farm employment (which in India refers to all forms of work other than crop and livestock production, and covers a vast variety of possible activities, both formal and informal) and rural wages, and a consequent decline in mass incomes.

---

[6] As Elson (2002) rightly argues, very high rates of inflation can indeed be an important problem for poor people, but so are very low rates of inflation, which generally come with stagnant employment opportunities. Moreover, inflation can be brought under control through a number of different mechanisms, with a varying balance between cutting expenditure on public services important to poor people and raising taxation on the incomes of rich people.

Agarwal's account complements Patnaik's by providing the gender content of this collapse for India. The current employment figures suggest that 58 per cent of all male workers, but 78 per cent of all female workers, and 86 per cent of all rural female workers are in agriculture; and it is astonishing that for women this percentage has declined less than four points since 1972–3. Moreover, while Agarwal confirms that the absorption of women and men into the non-agricultural sector has slowed down since 1987–8, and especially since 1991, for women the deceleration has been dramatic. The figures are worth re-citing: the compound growth rate of female non-agricultural employment fell from 5.2 per cent over 1978–88 to 0.2 per cent over 1988–94, and during the latter period while 29 per cent of rural male additions to the labour force in the over 14 age group were absorbed into non-agriculture, less than 1 per cent of the additional female workers were so absorbed. There is then a marked gender difference in non-farm employment, which means that increasing numbers of women are crowded into the agricultural sector and/or are taking on precarious forms of work in the informal sector that are not picked up by the employment statistics.

The second mechanism through which deflationary macroeconomic policies contribute to the livelihoods crisis in rural areas is the liberalization of agricultural trade. In the context of deflationary macroeconomic policies, Patnaik suggests, trade liberalization contributes to the collapse of primary commodity prices and the build-up of stocks. For the developing countries as a whole, the 1980s brought a sharp fall in the dollar price of their primary commodities, and after a brief price upsurge for some commodities in the late 1980s and early 1990s, the decline in commodity prices continued at an accelerated pace in the second half of the 1990s. UNCTAD asserts that the breadth and depth of the commodity price decline since 1998 have been unprecedented and have exerted a significant squeeze on the economies of many developing countries (UNCTAD 1999). As Patnaik shows, the extent of the price fall for many primary commodities between 1995 and 2000 has been as great as it had been in the period 1925–30. In both periods, she asserts, it is not temporary 'overproduction' that is causing the falling prices, but the cumulative demand deflation.

Again in the case of India, which is explored at length by Patnaik, substantial shifts in cropping patterns occurred as trade was liberalized; it is estimated that seven million hectares were diverted from food crops to export crops by the mid-1990s. This had negative implications for per capita foodgrain availability,[7] given the fact that the export thrust took place in a contractionary context marked by investment cuts in agriculture. At the same time, it exposed farmers to new sources of risk, given the volatility of international commodity prices. In the subsequent period, as global commodity prices collapsed, farmers who had switched to cotton found themselves enmeshed in mounting debt.

---

[7]   It is difficult to know whether the ensuing food insecurity has given rise to gender-differentiated nutritional outcomes, especially in view of the fact that much of the earlier micro-level research found inconclusive evidence of anti-female bias in nutritional status (Harriss 1990; Saith and Harriss-White 1999).

The account of post-socialist agricultural reforms and livelihoods crisis in Uzbekistan that is provided by Deniz Kandiyoti provides both parallels and contrasts with Patnaik's account. In Uzbekistan, too, the post-Soviet stabilization programme has been deflationary. Non-agricultural occupations – in teaching, health services and rural industries, which represented significant employment opportunities for women in particular – have been major casualties of the post-Soviet recession. Many of the rural industries have either closed or operate with a reduced workforce that receives irregular wages or payments in kind. Moreover, labour retrenchment in social services and rural industries is happening in parallel with labour retrenchment on collective agricultural enterprises. These collective farming enterprises (the former *sovkhozes* and *kolkhozes* which have been restructured into Joint Stock Companies or *shirkats*) continue to occupy the bulk of irrigated land and produce more than half of the country's agricultural output. The restructuring of these collective farming enterprises, initially from work brigades to family leaseholds and finally to *shirkats*, has represented a progressive retrenchment of labour – a process that is acknowledged by many to disproportionately affect women. The female workers who are made redundant tend to crowd into the casual agricultural work force and/or to take up precarious forms of self-employment in informal trade and services.

Uzbekistan remains dependent on cotton exports and, like other countries relying on primary commodity exports for its foreign exchange earnings, has suffered from the fall in international cotton prices since 1995, which has deepened the crisis in public finance. However, in contrast to the situation in trade-liberalized India, where an increasing acreage of land was being switched from food crops to cotton in the late 1980s and early 1990s (prior to the price collapse of 1995), in the case of Uzbekistan, the disruption of Soviet trade links in fact forced the government to expand the acreage of land devoted to wheat (the main food crop) through state procurement quotas,[8] and to increase the size of private plots that the population is entitled to. By 1998 the country had achieved the goal of drastically reducing grain imports. The expansion of household plots has entailed an intensification of women's agricultural labour, especially as women substitute their own labour wherever possible for expensive agricultural inputs (fertilizers, machines, pesticides). At the same time, as a result of both growing unemployment and of changing cropping patterns and technology,[9] there has been an increase in labour-intensive operations using casual agricultural labour, which is heavily feminized.

---

[8] The decisions concerning land use of collective enterprises and *shirkat* are made administratively from the top and get passed down to all the localities which receive a plan concerning what acreage will be planted with which crops.

[9] Unlike cotton, wheat makes it possible to plant other crops after the harvest in June. The introduction of polythene covers (which helps protect cotton from late frost) lengthens the growing season and necessitates back-breaking work, since hoes can no longer be used for weeding and thinning (women have to bend low under the polythene covers and weed with spoons).

As for sub-Saharan Africa (SSA), there are strong indications that both export crop and food crop sectors have performed poorly in the 1980s and 1990s, rather than any massive crop-switching taking place (along the lines suggested by Patnaik for India). Throughout the 1980s and 1990s, SSA has witnessed the steady decline of its agricultural exports as a share of the world's agricultural trade, as well as dramatic surges of agricultural imports, notably food, into the continent (Bryceson 1999).[10] In fact, as we noted earlier, much of the debate on structural adjustment policies (SAPs) and African agriculture has been about the muted supply response to price changes. By the mid-1990s, the World Bank had come to admit that African agriculture's response to SAPs had been disappointing, which compelled the organization to ask 'What nonprice factors are still constraining the supply response: Does the sector have adequate capacity to adjust to changing incentives?' (World Bank 1994, cited in Mkandawire and Soludo 2000, 53–4) – questions that critics of SAPs had been raising over the years.

These critics have argued that the objective of getting prices right was far from adequate under the prevailing African conditions. The excessive focusing on prices, they claim, took attention away from other problems and constraints, such as the feebleness of commodity and financial markets, structural bottlenecks, the immense climatic uncertainties and the low levels of irrigation and fertilizer use (Binswanger 1989; UNCTAD 1998; CUTS 1999; Mkandawire and Soludo 2000). Moreover, SAPs largely dismantled African marketing boards and parastatals, which had serviced smallholders' input requirements, provided marketing channels to geographically dispersed and under-capitalized farmers, and enforced commodity standards (Wold 1997; Bryceson 1999; MAFF 1999; Oxfam-IDS 1999; Deininger and Olinto 2000; Winters 2000). The private traders that have come to replace them vary in their performance through time and space, but mounting evidence suggests that, with their patchy marketing services, they have not lived up to the hopes vested in them by the IFIs (Wold 1997; Bryceson 1999; MAFF 1999; Oxfam-IDS 1999; Deininger and Olinto 2000; Winters 2000).

It is in the context of these debates that the micro-economic gender literature, referred to briefly in the Background section, has come to identify the intra-household structure of male and female incentives in African farm households as a major source of 'allocative inefficiency' and the muted supply response of African agriculture to price changes.[11] But, as Whitehead (2001) argues, the evidence and arguments that are presented by this set of literature are not very convincing as accounts of the economic imperatives and constraints that exist for both women and men smallholder farmers in SSA. Not only do some of the

---

[10] It is noteworthy that countries like Nigeria departed from the standard SAP package prescriptions by banning staple food imports (in the early stages of SAP implementations and again more recently). This in turn provided an opportunity for domestic food producers to sustain their production for the urban markets without the threat of being undercut by cheaper foreign imports (Bryceson 1999).

[11] Whitehead (2001) provides what is probably one of the most up-to-date and comprehensive analyses of the empirical studies on which the more abstract modelling exercises have been built.

empirical studies adopt a very narrow focus (e.g. treating the production of a single crop in isolation from the farming and livelihood system as a whole), but with their attention focused on the intra-household structure of incentives (e.g. women's poor incentives arising out of separate resource streams in farm households) as the explanation for a muted supply response, they effectively exclude from consideration a much more important set of constraints that are to be found in women's difficulties in accessing resources, especially their weak command of labour, their severe capital constraints, as well as their difficulties in accessing markets. 'Here again, the literature picks out land rights as highly significant, but this emphasis seems to be grounded in theoretical rather than empirical considerations' (Whitehead 2001, 26–7).

From these brief observations, we can then draw out a number of feasible gender implications. First, the evidence cited above seems to suggest that deflationary macroeconomic policies can have a particularly detrimental impact on the formal employment opportunities for women; in both Uzbekistan and India the retrenchment of employment has disproportionately affected women. As Elson and Cagatay (2000, 1355) observe more broadly, the deflationary bias of macroeconomic policy has 'a disproportionately negative effect on women . . . Women in the formal sector tend to lose their jobs faster than men, and usually have worse access than men to social safety nets. They crowd into the informal sector, driving down earnings there'. These two authors also draw attention to a second source of gender bias in deflationary macroeconomic policies which is not highlighted by our case studies, namely the intensification of women's care work as a result of cutbacks in public expenditure outlays on social services which forces women to become the 'unpaid provisioners as of last resort' (Elson and Cagatay 2000, 1355).

But as far as the impacts of trade and agricultural liberalization on export performance are concerned, our country case studies provide diverse scenarios. Some countries have accelerated their agricultural export thrust (e.g. India) at the expense of domestic food crop production and food security, with dire consequences as farming households have become exposed to the vagaries of world commodity markets in a deflationary context. In some of the other case studies, agricultural supply response has been sluggish at best, if not downright negative. In many sub-Saharan African countries, agricultural exports have performed rather poorly, while food crop production has also suffered as a result of import liberalization and multiple infrastructural and institutional inadequacies. Here women smallholders continue to encounter severe constraints on their agricultural operations, although the nature of those constraints is the subject of controversy. We shall return to this question below, when we look at the debates about African land tenure arrangements and women smallholders. In Uzbekistan, abrupt change in the external environment – the decision to accelerate wheat cultivation as a result of the sudden disruption of Soviet trade links – affected agricultural production. Here there has been an intensification of female labour in the subsistence sector (the expanded household plots) as well as in the export cotton sector.

AGRARIAN TRANSITIONS, DIVERSIFIED LIVELIHOODS AND THE PLACE OF LAND

An important view emerging from both Marxist and non-Marxist analyses of successful capitalist transformation, and indeed one important requirement of successful agrarian transitions, is the shift of labour from agriculture to industry.[12] The historical record of advanced industrialized countries certainly confirms this view, even though the paths taken have been significantly diverse. But what is striking about the contemporary record of structural change as it is unfolding in the developing countries is the limited extent to which capitalist industrialization, even where it is proceeding, is able to absorb labour, as well as the disproportionate weight assumed by the heterogeneous category of 'services' (Byres forthcoming). This clearly marks a significant departure from the historical record, and it can be taken to suggest 'an unresolved agrarian question: in terms of social property relations in the countryside that, unlike those experienced historically, or more recently in Taiwan and South Korea, have blocked a sufficient contribution to capitalist industrialization by agriculture' (Byres forthcoming). In other words, very unequal forms of land distribution in the countryside have blocked agriculture's potential contribution to capitalist industrialization. This is one interpretation of contemporary agrarian change – a view that is supported by comparative analyses of successful 'late industrialization' in East Asia with less successful attempts in Latin America (Kay 2001) and South Africa (Hart 1996, 2001).[13]

But an important feature of agrarian change and industrialization in contemporary developing societies – which is not problematized by the classical Marxist model of agrarian transition, and is perhaps buried under the inflated figures for 'services' – is the growing prevalence of livelihood diversification, defined as 'the process by which rural families construct a diverse portfolio of activities and social support capabilities in their struggle for survival and in order to improve their standard of living' (Ellis 1998, 4). As Ellis goes on to argue, and as is evident from the contributions to this special issue, making any generalizations about the meaning of diversification is hazardous, since the forces underpinning it and the outcomes flowing from it are both extremely diverse – depending on geographical location, assets, income, opportunity and social relations.

---

[12]   In addition to labour contributions, the other important contributions that agriculture can make to economic growth and industrialization are: (a) capital and entrepreneurs (i.e. landlords or capitalist farmers who then become industrialists and merchants); (b) agricultural commodities as cheap food and other wage goods; and (c) a domestic market for industrial commodities.

[13]   Kay (2001) and Hart (1996) emphasize different aspects of this question. Kay argues that the relatively equitable income distribution in East Asia, as a result of land reform in the countryside, widened the size of the domestic market for industrial commodities, which is particularly important in the initial stages of industrialization. In Latin America, however, the limited extent of agrarian reform coupled with the fact that it was implemented several decades after the onset of industrialization, denied the region this potential widening of the domestic market and created a distorted and inefficient industrial structure. Hart's focus, as the following paragraphs illustrate, is on the contribution that agriculture (and redistributive land reforms) can make to the 'social wage' and the satisfactory reproduction of labour as a precondition for successful industrial accumulation (Hart 2001).

Diversification thus refers to several different economic processes and its blanket use to describe all forms of non-farm employment hides important differences. It is particularly important, from the point of view of thinking about how to lift farming households out of poverty, to distinguish between diversification as a survival strategy and diversification that feeds into a process of accumulation (Hart 1994; Whitehead and Kabeer 2001). One finding that emerges from some of the contributions to this special issue is the tendency for women to be confined to the less lucrative segments of the non-farm sector, in the form of survivalist strategies, which do not offer good long-term prospects. This seems to be the case in both India and Uzbekistan.

In the case of India, Agarwal argues that women tend to be largely concentrated in the low-and-insecure-earnings end of the non-farm occupational spectrum, which she attributes to their domestic work burden, lower physical mobility, lesser education and fewer assets. Similarly, Kandiyoti's research in rural Uzbekistan shows that women are crowded into precarious forms of self-employment in informal trade and services, which have a very limited market since there is an oversupply of such services. While there are exceptions, such as the more lucrative cross-border trading operations, this avenue is open to a small minority of women with 'courage, wit and resourcefulness'. In conclusion, she thus notes that whereas some skilled men may achieve more sustainable forms of self-employment, women's survival strategies in rural Uzbekistan have involutionary properties that do not offer good long-term prospects.[14]

Under what circumstances then can a more dynamic interaction between the agrarian and industrial sectors be created? China is often singled out as a country where such positive synergies were successfully forged. Here the diversification of income-earning opportunities for rural residents has taken the form of both farm-based businesses and non-farm employment (in TVEs and foreign-owned export-oriented industries). While the land reforms under HRS boosted incomes from farming in the first half of the 1980s, the TVEs and other non-farm employment provided the main stimulus to rural incomes afterwards (Summerfield 2002). These activities seem to have provided an avenue of accumulation for rural residents, *including women*, even though gender inequalities in wages and work conditions persist. Nevertheless, both employment in TVEs and the setting up of some forms of off-farm sidelines seem to have added substantially to women's incomes and exerted a positive impact on their intra-household position (Summerfield 2002).

Summerfield (2002) argues that it was the higher incomes from farming, brought about as a result of the HRS, which initially provided the necessary investment funds for enterprises run by townships and villages. In addition, some villages had retained funds from the collective period, which they invested

---

[14]   A recent review of the literature on the non-farm sector in sub-Saharan Africa reached similar conclusions, namely that the non-farm sector is segmented by gender and that women tend to be crowded into the low-profit niches of trading and services (Whitehead 2001).

in TVEs. Later, a substantial inflow of funds came through foreign direct investment (FDI), much of it from overseas Chinese. However, as Chris Bramall
(2000) has convincingly shown by analysing the experience of four very different
regions of China, these external sources of growth (i.e. FDI and growing exports) were far less significant than is often claimed, while domestic sources,
including financial flows from agriculture, have been crucial to Chinese accumulation.[15] In turn, the cash income from non-farm employment is invested in
other household activities, including green revolution agricultural technology
and animal husbandry (Bramall and Jones 2000).

It has been argued that successful industrialization in the East Asian countries
of Taiwan and China was built on changes in agrarian property relations in the
form of highly redistributive land reform programmes. Agriculture was thereby
able to provide both a broad basis for industrial growth by making the necessary
contributions (of labour, cheap food) and providing a domestic market for industrial commodities. Hart (1996) draws attention to a rather different aspect of
the agro-industrial linkages in these East Asian success stories, which highlights
the inter-connections between three crucial sets of issues: land reform, industrial
accumulation and restructuring, and livelihoods diversification.

Since the 1960s, much of the growth of small-scale, labour-intensive industry
in Taiwan, as well as in post-reform China, has been located in rural areas, and
industrial accumulation has effectively benefited from, and been subsidized by,
the population's broad-based access to land for their subsistence (Hart 1996).
Hart's own research in northwestern Kwazulu Natal (South Africa), by contrast,
reveals that Taiwanese industrialists who, over the past decade, have invested
directly in the clothing industry in this district, have encountered intense difficulties in recruiting labour. One of the reasons why these garment factories
operate so problematically in South Africa, she argues, is to be found in the
conditions of social reproduction, which in this case primarily turns on lack of
access to land. In sharp contrast with conditions in Taiwan and China, where
subsistence guarantees in the form of broad-based access to land guaranteed
workers' livelihoods by underwriting the money wage, in South Africa the
workforce has been constituted through a particularly brutal process of land
dispossession (i.e. very unequal property relations).[16] In other words, low wages
in rural industries are not backed up by systems of support from household
subsistence production as part of the overall livelihood strategy, as they are in
East Asia. This understanding of agro-industrial linkages and the 'social wage' in
turn has major implications for how land reform is understood.

Instead of focusing primarily on small farmers and agriculture, land reform
needs to be understood as a means to create conditions in which people can

[15]   Moreover, as Hart (1995) argues, the foreign-owned, export-oriented industries located in the
southern coastal provinces of China profit directly from the social investments made during the
communist era, while running these investments down.
[16]   On the continuing (and increasing) importance of land as social insurance after the dissolution of
the communes in 1983 and the reduction in the role of the state, see Bramall and Jones (2000).

construct livelihoods from a variety of sources, both agricultural and non-agricultural, in more effective and productive ways. East Asian experience suggests that land reform capable of supporting multi-livelihoods calls for *access to small plots of land in close proximity to other sources of income and services*. A very small but well-watered piece of land that can support intensive cultivation and is close to other income opportunities is likely to be far more useful for large numbers of poor families – and particularly women – than becoming a farm household wherever land happens to become available through the market. (Hart 1995, 46)

In this kind of diversified livelihood strategy, access to land therefore assumes a new strategic significance.

In some areas of sub-Saharan Africa, primarily South Africa, historically constructed and very unequal land relations have affected the conditions of reproduction of many households who pursue diversified livelihoods in which some income is derived from wages, some from the informal economy and some from subsistence production for which access to land is needed. As Walker (this issue) explains, access to land remains critically important in people's livelihoods, and is often combined with wage labour and state pensions. Land, she argues, has value not only for food and market crops, but also for the non-commoditized resources it offers people, such as housing, firewood, grazing, building and craft materials and so on.

Yet it is important to underline that these multiple, diversified, spatially extended livelihood strategies are not peculiar to South Africa. While it is true that for historical reasons agriculture plays a minor role in the South African national economy (as Table 1 shows, agriculture now contributes under 4 per cent of South Africa's GDP), research findings from other parts of Africa, where agriculture retains much greater weight in terms of its contribution to the GDP, attest to the fact that diversification is proceeding apace across the continent. Based on detailed survey findings from seven sub-Saharan African countries, Bryceson (1999) reports a surge in non-agricultural income sources over the past 15 years as structural adjustment policies have been implemented.[17] The vast majority of households in the surveyed countries have one or more non-agricultural income source, 'be it active participation in trade, service provisioning or craft work, or more passive receipt of a transfer payment in the form of a state pension or remittances from relations' (Bryceson 1999, 11). The state's withdrawal from the agricultural sector during the SAPs era has entailed rising input costs and poor market prospects; this is leading to the relocation of land and labour away from commercial agriculture (Bryceson 1999). These changes combined with the rising cash needs of household reproduction, due to the

---

[17] These findings are synthesized from the De-Agrarianisation and Rural Employment (DARE) Research Programme (Africa-Studiecentrum, Leiden), which includes extensive field research in the following countries: Congo-Brazzaville, Ethiopia, Malawi, Nigeria, Tanzania, South Africa and Zimbabwe.

imposition of 'user fees' at health centres and schools as well as rising food prices, have intensified households' diversification strategies and the proliferation of income earners within the rural household.

Most of this livelihood diversification is for 'survival' rather than 'accumulation', which is another way of saying that these households are not meeting conditions of social reproduction. Importantly though, these are not areas where households lack access to land. What they lack are the resources to work the land, and also the institutional and infrastructural support that would enable them to take advantage of prices for agricultural products (although there are questions as to whether the terms of trade in a globalized economy are ever going to enable them to make a living out of selling agricultural commodities). This then raises the general argument for SSA about what is the role of land as a site of food production and as a site of income production in households that are pursuing these multiple, spatially extended livelihood strategies. And what are the effects as other more powerful interests start alienating this land (for tourism, for highly commercial forms of agriculture, for dams, for industrial production) – the predation that is referred to in the Whitehead and Tsikata contribution?

In the very different political economy of Uzbekistan, where public-sector employment and wages have collapsed, Kandiyoti documents a dual process of demonetization and re-agrarianization as the rural population falls back on household and subsidiary plots for self-subsistence. But, at the same time, it is important to underline that while in the face of stagnation or collapse of non-farm employment, land remains (or becomes) critically important for household re-production, land is not the single most important basis for livelihoods. Nor does the process of re-agrarianization in Uzbekistan mark a re-turn to the old subsistence farming – state pensions, other social benefits and social assistance continue to play an important role in people's livelihoods, and people scramble for a place in the over-crowded informal sector of trade and services. Kandiyoti is emphatic that the cry for land in rural Uzbekistan must be understood as the product of a very specific conjuncture – when rural inequalities in access to land are not curbed by significant mechanisms of rural out-migration, receipt of migrants' remittances, or diversification into off-farm employment. Women's current land hunger thus encapsulates both a wish to reinstate the terms of their former social contract with the collective enterprises (which included access to subsidiary plots), and their despair in the face of the apparent lack of any other alternative.

The second important implication, and indeed question, emerging from the East Asian experience cited above, concerns the gender sub-text of how the agrarian question is resolved. If the logic of accumulation and labour mobilization in the Asian success stories was based on a patriarchal social structure which still managed to provide subsistence guarantees in the form of *broad-based* access to land – through a highly egalitarian distribution of use rights among, though not within, households (Hart 1996, 258) – then what is this reading of East Asian experience saying about women's likely place in the changes in the links between agrarian and industrial sectors taking place elsewhere? More specifically, what are the gender dynamics of these processes – both in terms of women exercising political pressure for access to land, and in terms of women being able to sustain that pressure and maintain their own (independent?) access to land? It is to these questions that we now turn.

LAND TENURE ARRANGEMENTS: INSTITUTIONS, REFORMS AND CONSTRAINTS

In recent years, increasing emphasis has been placed, by academics and a wide range of development practitioners, on secure property rights (through gender-equitable land titling) as a solution to women's unequal access to land, female poverty and women's subordination.[18] This emphasis on the importance of land rights for women raises two sets of issues. First, the diagnosis that the absence of secure property rights for women is the cause of unequal gendered access to land is often premised on the assumption that individual legal ownership is an automatically better way of guaranteeing claims to subsistence resources – an assumption that is questioned by several contributions to this special issue.

As is well known, access to land can take different forms, non-alienable individual ownership rights being only one possible way (and not a very equitable, nor necessarily efficient, one) of establishing such access. In post-reform China, for example, while the collective agricultural enterprises have been gradually dismantled, the village collectives (or village cooperatives) have retained ownership rights to the land, while they have leased use rights to households, rather than opting for individual ownership. Individual ownership has in any case not been supported by rural residents (Summerfield 2002). Should this route be taken, and full-fledged land markets be developed, many fear that this is likely to lead to even more marked social inequalities, with politically destabilizing implications.

In the case of sub-Saharan Africa, Whitehead and Tsikata contend that land has been historically subject to multiple uses and multiple users, which recognizes the presence of different interests and claims in land vested in different persons. While individual and family access to land under indigenous tenure has become more exclusive, in many places these claims fall short of private property rights in land. Moreover, it is now widely recognized that individualization and titling, which were major components of free market modernizing approaches to rural economic development in many African countries (especially Kenya), produced highly inequitable outcomes, 'because those with money, information and power grabbed land titles' while the more vulnerable groups experienced a weakening of their claims. These findings are borne out by studies that have looked at the specific impacts of registration and titling on women's land access. They find overwhelming evidence of women losing access, while male household heads have strengthened their hold over land by registering their claims on

[18]   See especially Agarwal (1994) for a scholarly analysis of the gender and land question in South Asia.

land as being 'ownership'.[19] It is in recognition of the huge constraints that women as *individuals* would face in purchasing, leasing and cultivating land that Agarwal (this issue) proposes various forms of collective investment and cultivation by women, with institutional support from NGOs.

The second question that is raised implicitly by the growing emphasis on the importance of strengthening women's land rights (through titling and forms of private ownership) concerns women's access to land in indigenous systems of land tenure. Have indigenous systems of land tenure been uniformly discriminatory towards women, denying them access to land? There is a fairly widespread understanding, reflected in the contributions by Agarwal and Deere in this special issue, that indigenous land tenure arrangements in much of South Asia and Latin America have been constructed on a unitary household model marked by unequal gender relations which casts the male household head as the breadwinner–subject–citizen and thus the legitimate claimant of land, while women (along with children) are subsumed as 'dependents' who are, by definition, less-than-complete subjects or citizens. In traditional family farming in India and Brazil, therefore, men have appeared as landowners, tenants and leaseholders, while women have tended to be subsumed under the ubiquitous label of 'family labourers' with tenuous claims to the 'household' land. The critique that is levelled at the state, and even at 'progressive' political parties and social movements in India and Brazil by these authors is that they are predisposed to replicate this male breadwinner–female dependant model through public policy (e.g. Operation *Barga* in West Bengal) and in bottom–up land invasions and the setting up of agrarian reform settlements (e.g. by landless movements).

Whitehead and Tsikata point out the danger of extending analyses and arguments from these rather different socio-economic contexts to sub-Saharan Africa, where considerable land scarcity is developing in some countries. Sub-Saharan African women tend to have claims to land independent of their husbands, and even those through their husbands are much stronger than conventional accounts imply. Women's claims to land, however, are not identical to men's claims, and have been weakening for complex reasons explored in their paper. The misrepresentation of women's land claims as secondary to men's arises out of a widespread mis-construction of indigenous concepts that express multiple uses embedded in social relations (where alienability is not a property of the land–person relationship). For example, the notion of multiple land claims seems to have produced the widespread description of land in African tenure systems as subject to a 'bundle of rights'; this idea, which was used in the colonial period to underline the different character of various kinds of land claims, is modelled on the distinction made in Western jurisprudence between use rights and ownership

---

[19] Nor have processes of land registration and titling and the development of land markets enhanced agricultural investment and productivity (see sources cited in Whitehead and Tsikata, this issue), even though secure individual tenure and a land market have been promoted in the belief that they will lead to higher levels of agricultural investment and productivity, while customary land management has been perceived as an obstruction to capitalist agriculture.

rights. But the use of this distinction both in colonial times and today is misleading. Currently, a major contestation is between those who use the term 'bundle of rights' to describe multiple claims in land, and see them as being hierarchically ordered and gendered (with women having the weaker 'use rights', while men or lineages have the stronger 'ownership' or 'control' rights), and others who, while arguing that there are multiple claims, reject the core distinction between primary and secondary rights and also the idea of a hierarchical ordering of claims. The latter authors stress instead the negotiated dynamic and fluid nature of the tenure relations and tenure claims and treat their socially embedded nature in radically different ways.[20]

There is, however, no doubt that women are losing out as land scarcity bites, but how this is happening needs to be fully understood. Discriminatory inheritance laws and poor land access constitute significant constraints on the agricultural operations of some rural women in the region, but elsewhere inability to get access to land is rarely a major factor constraining women's agricultural output and income and thereby a cause of female poverty (Whitehead and Lockwood 1999; Whitehead 2001). 'There are a number of areas of Africa where this is certainly not the case and where although land is not "abundant" the main constraints in farming and on incomes remain lack of capital to invest in farming and lack of labour too' (Whitehead and Tsikata 2001, 16). This is an important observation to bear in mind.

The three factors highlighted above – women's relatively strong claims to land in indigenous African land tenure systems; the gender-inequitable outcomes of land titling and registration in modernist African states; and the fact that the main constraints on female farming in the region stem from capital, labour and marketing constraints, rather than land constraints – underpin Whitehead and Tsikata's discomfort with many gender and development policy documents that still advocate a blanket global policy of ensuring women's land access through private property rights and titling, without reference to these African specificities.

Does this mean that public policy in the region should not concern itself with land tenure arrangements – thereby allowing existing indigenous land tenure arrangements to evolve at their own pace? Their answer to this question is clearly and vehemently negative: the rural customary, they argue, cannot be left to muddle along without widening the gap between men's and women's land access; it is necessary to manage and direct change in order to produce greater gender justice with respect to resource allocation for rural women. This in fact constitutes the second pillar of their argument, and the point is forcefully made because such a *laissez-faire* position (trust 'customary law' and 'the local') does seem to be emerging from policy institutions across the political spectrum (Land Policy Division of the World Bank, OXFAM-Great Britain, International Institute for Environment and Development – IIED). The emerging consensus maintains that the local/indigenous land tenure institutions and arrangements should be

---

[20] See Whitehead and Tsikata (this issue) for references.

left to manage land disputes and land claims on their own, because they can do the job more cheaply, more flexibly, more effectively, and by provoking less conflict.

Subsidiarity and Devolution

For policy advocates such as OXFAM and the IIED, and the National Land Forum in Tanzania (discussed in Tsikata, this issue), subsidiarity and devolution are key objectives in current land reform policy. Given the history of political abuse and processes of land alienation and 'land grabbing' facilitated by national political elites, they claim that it is best that decisions on land management and control be taken at the lowest levels possible, 'closer to home' in the words of the Shivji Commission in Tanzania. 'The local' is thus seen as a site of resistance against the state (and international capital). This approach fits their general support for participation, building of local capacities, and local-level democracy. But there is very little discussion by these groups as to how the proposed local level systems might work in practice, including their capacity to deliver more equitable (and especially gender-equitable) resource allocation. The main problem, as Whitehead and Tsikata remind us, is that women have too little political voice at all the decision-making levels that are implied by the land question: not only within formal law and government, but also within local level management systems and civil society itself.

Ironically, some of the social movements that are struggling for land redistribution at the local level are often more aware of the importance of having the weight of the federal government behind them, and also more attentive to the risks and dangers of local government capture by powerful vested interests. One of the initiatives of the government of Fernando Enrique Cardoso in Brazil has been to decentralize agrarian reform, devolving greater responsibility for its planning and execution to state and local governments. But there has been very little follow-up to this initiative, primarily because of the resistance of the rural social movements to decentralization (Deere and León 1999). The rural social movements were reportedly worried that the federal government would abdicate responsibility for leading the cause of agrarian reform, and that the power of landlords at the local level would be sufficient to stop any significant redistribution of land from taking place if the initiative was left to the state and local governments (Deere and León 1999).

In other contexts there is serious apprehension about the place that is going to be given to 'culture' and 'traditional authorities' in rural local government. This question emerges forcefully from Walker's account of the political dynamics surrounding land reform at The Gorge in KwaZulu Natal. At the heart of this land redistribution project there has been an ambiguity about the residents' status as beneficiaries of the project in relation to the claims of the neighbouring Tribal Authority which regards the land and the people on it as its domain. This ambiguity is in fact rooted in ANC's attempts since 1994 to accommodate some of the demands of IFP (Inkatha Freedom Party), which is the ruling party in KwaZulu

Natal, on the place of traditional authorities in rural local government. Given the fact that the traditionalism that is espoused by IFP and many of its adherents in the Tribal Authorities is deeply patriarchal, Walker (1994, this issue) maintains that these political manoeuvrings have effectively blunted ANC's commitments to gender equity in rural affairs. Whitehead and Tsikata voice similar concerns about the political dynamics that are being unleashed by the return to 'customary law', the revival of 'traditional' authorities and the renewing of chieftaincy in many parts of SSA – warning that these trends could have highly disempowering implications for rural African women and their claims on resources.

Questions regarding traditional authorities aside, there are many warnings across the literature that 'the local' is a site of unequal rural social relations, with crucial implications for women. And even more problematically, stark inequalities and grave injustices can exist without being openly contested by those who are the victims. This last point, which has been the subject of on-going feminist debate (Kandiyoti 1988, 1998), is brought out in Walker's contribution to this special issue, where she looks at women's involvement in the three land reform projects in KwaZulu Natal. The demand-driven nature of the South African land reform programme, and the fact that officials from the Department of Land Affairs (DLA) were working with already-constituted social groups and existing power relations between men and women, ensured that initially very little attention was paid to gender equity – in the words of one DLA official 'it (gender equity) did not even emerge as an issue'. As Agarwal (this issue) notes in response to those who argue that policy priorities should be identified on the basis of expressed wants, in situations of deprivation people often adapt their preferences and felt needs to what they see as attainable. Women, in particular, may be so thoroughly subordinated that they are unable to recognize any injustice in the prevailing order. Even though such a statement edges disturbingly close to notions of 'false consciousness', it has been an indispensable component in feminist thought (Phillips 2002).

On the positive side though, what we see from Walker's account is that the constitutional commitments to gender equity in land reform have created some space and provided some institutional mechanisms for gender issues to be brought in by the DLA – though unevenly across the three land reform projects, depending on how active DLA staff have been around gender issues, as well as the presence of external agencies such as land rights NGOs. This seems to have encouraged community debate on the subject, even though the results to date are modest. Women's presence on land reform committees, which is considered as DLA's most tangible achievement in relation to women's land rights, is itself not a guarantee that women's specific concerns and demands will necessarily be voiced. The fear of ridicule for stepping outside their socially designated roles is cited as one of the main reasons why women committee members have kept a low profile. Yet from informal discussions it is clear that women recognize their vulnerabilities in relation to their husbands, and are interested in exploring ways in which their rights and interests can be made more secure (more on this further below). But as Walker rightly warns, 'social process' work is difficult, time-consuming and expensive, and yet essential if the DLA's gender policy is to serve more than a largely rhetorical function.

In Brazil, for example, even though constitutional guarantees of women's land rights (in 1988) were combined with pressure from below in the form of women's active involvement in dynamic rural unions and in the nascent landless movement to create what would appear to be highly propitious circumstances for the substantiation of women's land rights, the outcomes have been far from automatic. By the mid-1990s, rural Brazilian women constituted what is, by regional standards at least, a very modest proportion (12.6 per cent) of the beneficiaries of agrarian reform. Deere identifies a number of factors to explain why it took so long (almost 12 years) for organized rural women to even demand effective recognition of their land rights, and even longer for these voiced demands to find meaningful representation in the rural social movements.

Even if women's demands are being promoted by powerful and dynamic social movements, having the weight of the state behind the agenda for gender justice is a *sine qua non* for its realization. The central instrument for the protection of rights has been, and must remain, the state (Molyneux and Razavi 2002). Hence the role of the state in raising such issues and providing the institutional mechanisms and macroeconomic and statutory frameworks for their realization is highly significant. Whether states advance or curtail women's rights cannot, of course, be explained in terms of any single variable, although democratic institutions and procedures are generally assumed to allow greater voice and presence to social forces pressing for reform (Molyneux and Razavi 2002), assuming that democratic processes and institutions are 'thick', and that they adequately engage with issues of gender equity.[21]

Statutory Interventions

There are plenty of examples across this special issue documenting both the considerable progress that was made throughout the 1980s and 1990s in making formal laws more gender-equitable (e.g. Hindu and Muslim laws pertaining to land in India, gender-egalitarian constitutional principles in Brazil and South Africa, and so on), as well as evidence of repeated failures in making these statutory interventions 'real'. The reasons for failure are legion – from budgetary constraints arising from government fiscal discipline, to administrative and institutional weaknesses within government in the management of gender policy, and weak political accountability for gender policy within parliament and/or civil society. The legal domain itself, with its implicit gender-biased assumptions and discourses, such as the unencumbered individual of contract theory and the notion of individual rights, and its inaccessible institutions and mechanisms, has not been a comfortable terrain for women to operate within. There are then

---

[21] Peter Evans (2002) makes the distinction between 'thin' and 'thick' democratic processes; the former refers to having leadership succession determined by a regular electoral process, while the latter means having continuous deliberative involvement of the citizenry in the setting of economic and social policies and priorities.

many deep-seated reasons why gender-progressive laws do not deliver gender justice when they intersect with decision-making processes and rural (or urban, for that matter) power relations.

The fundamental question, however, as Tsikata puts it, is whether these difficulties in implementation have rendered statutory law, whatever its purpose and character, totally pointless? In other words, is there any purpose to be served by legislation? The answer that seems to be emerging from this special issue to the last question is a qualified yes. Yes, because it sets a benchmark against which progress can be measured; and because it provides discursive resources that can be capitalized upon by rural women and their advocates to establish their access to material resources, be it through courts or through informal processes of dispute settlement. But a qualified yes, because it is one among many resources that women will bring to their daily struggles for access to resources, in what is arguably a messy reality wherein individuals use different dispute settlement fora and deploy different arguments (whether grounded in 'customary' or 'modernist' principles), whichever is to their advantage. Ultimately, what determines outcome is to a considerable degree the power relations at stake, within an overall context of inequality.

JOINT OR INDIVIDUAL TITLES? RETHINKING THE AGRARIAN HOUSEHOLD

Where land titling is an appropriate way of improving women's land access, there is little consensus among the contributors to this special issue as to whether individual titles or joint titles would serve women's interests better. For Agarwal, joint titles (in the Indian context, at least) present problems: it makes it difficult for women to gain control over the produce, to bequeath the land as they want, and to claim their share in case of marital conflict. Individual titles provide women with more flexibility in pursuing their own agendas. However, given some of the problems that resource-strained women smallholders with individual titles might confront – for example, their lack of investible funds, and the difficulties of investing in capital equipment if the farm is small – for Agarwal, the optimum institutional arrangement would be some collective form of investment and cultivation that would bring women smallholders together, thereby cutting across households (rather than being based on the household unit itself). Individual titles for women thus need to be pursued in tandem with institutional innovations to forge new forms of collective investment and cultivation that reduce the risks of individual enterprise for women, and yet provide mechanisms for their greater independence and autonomy from male-dominated households. Such institutional innovations are premised on the prior existence of active and well-funded NGOs that can act as facilitators.

Reflecting on the South African context, where the first phase of land reform has failed to deliver individual rights to women because the land reform programme has been based, implicitly at least, on a model of a relatively homogeneous community made up of stable and implicitly egalitarian households, Walker admits that even where women have been listed as independent household heads and as beneficiaries in their own right, their access to land has been mediated overwhelmingly through their membership in patriarchal households. Nevertheless, rather than endorsing individual rights as the solution (which is a component of the new land reform policy, 'Land Redistribution for Agricultural Development' or LRAD, issued in November 2000), she thinks that there needs to be deeper appreciation of the importance of household membership in poor women's lives, and thus the importance of ensuring women's rights to household resources. Had the LRAD framework, with its emphasis on individual rights, been in place from the start of the land reform programme, she argues, very few, if any, of the women in the present beneficiary communities would have been able to access land through it – they are simply too poor, too isolated and too dependent on male authority to be able to establish individual rights to land. Moreover, many women beneficiaries endorse the household model implicit in DLA's work, and some have struggled very hard to secure household interests. While a minority seemed interested in the idea of individual titles, de-linked from that of their husbands or families, few saw this as the solution to their problems. They were more interested in mechanisms that would secure and extend their rights to household resources (through joint titles, and copies of title deeds). Moreover, given the weak presence and patchy coverage of land rights NGOs in KwaZulu Natal, it is rather difficult to imagine that they would be able to provide, on a sufficiently large scale, the kind of institutional experimentation suggested by Agarwal.

It is clear from the above statements that the question about joint or individual titles is in fact not as straightforward as it appears. Implicitly, it is a question about the conceptualization of conjugal relations and the forces that bind agrarian households together. The two positions, by Agarwal and Walker, in fact bring to the fore some of the tensions within the current, second-generation feminist (F2) conceptualizations of the household, where the first-generation feminist critique (F1) has established, in both theoretical and empirical terms, serious flaws in the previously dominant unified household paradigm.[22] While most feminists would agree that households are sites of struggle and inequality (as per F1), there is currently far less agreement as to how the given inequalities and tensions, as well as common interests and cooperative behaviour, should be understood and conceptualized. Do conflictual and bargaining models sufficiently capture the *common* interests that all household members have in the overall economic success of their households? What makes women and junior men stay inside the patriarchal household, even though they are allocated fewer resources and enjoy less leisure time? Is it really pure despotism on the part of the male household head, and 'false consciousness' on the part of the junior household members, that binds the household together (Whitehead and Kabeer 2001)?

---

[22]   My distinction between first-generation and second-generation feminist conceptualizations of the household should not be confused with the distinction between first wave and second wave feminism used historically.

These are not questions to which any definitive answers can be given. But there are powerful arguments for seeing households as 'maximizing a *range* of utilities – these might include capacity for diversification, flexibility in the case of agro-climatic shocks, other kinds of risk spreading (against illness and death, for example), long term investments, social reproduction and so on and so forth' (Whitehead 2001, 19). It is within this broader understanding of households and their positioning within the social economy that the 'woman and land' question needs to be placed. In some contexts and for some groups of women, mechanisms that secure and extend women's rights to household land can provide appropriate forms of access and entitlement, yet without having to venture down the risky path of individual rights where rural power relations are stacked against them. In other contexts, where rural class structures and power relations are less menacing, it may be more feasible to experiment with alternative institutional arrangements that require (and enhance) women's greater autonomy from male-dominated households.

GENDER AND LAND: TOWARDS A MORE CONTEXTUALIZED ANALYSIS

This special issue highlights the importance of posing the gender and land question within its broader context. This in turn requires moving beyond the 'critical assumption that gender power relations at the local level are embedded in conjugal intra-household relations alone' (Sen 1999, 691). As the contributions to this special issue make clear, the structures of power that women confront operate at multiple levels (global, national, local) and within diverse institutional arenas (communities, social movements, markets, states, kingroups, households and so on).

The special issue has discussed how the deflationary macroeconomic policies and processes associated with economic liberalization are impacting on rural livelihoods and agrarian transitions differently in diverse contexts and has emphasized the gender specificities of these impacts. The deceleration of more formal forms of employment is accompanied by the diversification of household livelihoods, and the intensification of women's unpaid and casual labour in agriculture and the informal sector. These are the stark effects at the level of individual well-being of the fiscal crisis of the nation state and its retreat from development and welfare provision, as well as the imperatives of flexible accumulation and global competition (Hart 1996, 269). In this context the land question has taken on a new urgency and needs to be posed in a new light. Land reform needs to be understood as a means to create conditions in which people can construct livelihoods from a variety of sources, both agricultural and non-agricultural, in more effective and productive ways. Given women's centrality to these diversified livelihood strategies, as well as their increasing political agency (thanks to processes of democratization which have entailed some engagement, though uneven, with issues of gender equity), their interests in land are more politicized today than they were two decades ago.

And yet, while the trends towards democratization have revitalized the national debate on agrarian reform in a number of countries, and provided greater voice to women's advocates, the dominant anti-state rhetoric does not bode well for women, nor are there any reasons to believe that, in such a climate, processes of devolution and decentralization will necessarily enhance equity and gender justice in access to resources. These trends raise many urgent questions about power configurations at the local level, and the political and institutional obstacles to ensuring greater gender equity in access to resources, including land.

Finally, several contributors to this special issue emphasize the importance of taking seriously the contextual and institutional specificities that shape women's access to resources, including land. There are numerous warnings about the dangers of 'downloading' all-purpose gender and development (GAD) analytical frameworks and blindly reproducing policy prescriptions developed with other contexts in mind. This de-contextualized approach to 'doing gender' is in fact part of a broader problem that currently afflicts gender policy, as GAD tool kits, planning modules and institutional blueprints are carelessly replicated across diverse contexts. While there may be some vague benefits to institutional learning, the dangers of 'institutional monocropping'[23] (Evans 2002) in the field of gender and development need to be taken far more seriously.

REFERENCES

Agarwal, B., 1994. *A Field of One's Own*. Cambridge: Cambridge University Press.

Amin, S., 1972. 'Underdevelopment and Dependence in Black Africa – Origins and Contemporary Forms'. *The Journal of Modern African Studies*, 10 (4): 503–24.

Binswanger, Hans, 1989. *The Policy Response of Agriculture*. Report No. 14355. Washington, DC: World Bank.

Blackden, M. and C. Bhanu, 1999. 'Gender, Growth and Poverty Reduction: Special Programme for Assistance to Africa'. Status Report on Poverty in sub-Saharan Africa. Washington, DC: World Bank.

Bramall, C., 2000. *Sources of Chinese Economic Growth: 1978–1996*. Oxford: Oxford University Press.

Bramall, C. and M.E. Jones, 2000. 'The Fate of the Chinese Peasantry Since 1978'. In *Disappearing Peasantries? Rural Labour in Africa, Asia and Latin America*, eds D. Bryceson, C. Kay and J. Mooij, 262–78. London: ITDG.

Bryceson, D.F., 1993. *Liberalizing Tanzania's Food Trade: Public and Private Faces of Urban Marketing Policy 1939–1988*. Geneva: UNRISD.

Bryceson, D.F., 1999. 'Sub-Saharan Africa Betwixt and Between: Rural Livelihood Practices and Policies'. ASC Working Paper 43. Leiden: Africa-Studiecentrum.

Byres, T.J., forthcoming. 'Structural Change, the Agrarian Question, and the Possible Impact of Globalization'. In *Globalization, Structural Change and Income Distribution*, eds C.P. Chandrasekhar and J. Ghosh. Delhi: Tulika.

---

[23] Evans defines 'institutional monocropping' as the imposition of blueprints based on idealized versions of Anglo-American institutions, whose applicability is presumed to transcend national cultures and circumstances.

Consumer Unity and Trust Society (CUTS), 1999. 'Conditions Necessary for the Liberalisation of Trade and Investment to Reduce Poverty'. Final Report to DFID.

Deere, C.D. and M. León, 1999. 'Towards a Gendered Analysis of the Brazilian Agrarian Reform'. Occasional Paper No. 16. Storrs/Amherst: Center for Latin American Studies.

Deininger, K. and P. Olinto, 2000. 'Why Liberalization Alone has not Improved Agricultural Productivity in Zambia: The Role of Asset Ownership and Working Capital Constraints'. Working Paper 2302. Washington, DC: World Bank.

Ellis, F., 1998. 'Household Strategies and Rural Livelihood Diversification'. *Journal of Development Studies*, 35 (1): 1–38.

Elson, D., 2002. 'Gender Justice, Human Rights and Neo-liberal Economic Policies'. In *Gender Justice, Development, and Rights*, eds M. Molyneux and S. Razavi, 78–114. Oxford: Oxford University Press.

Elson, D. and N. Cagatay, 2000. 'The Social Content of Macroeconomic Policies'. *World Development*, 28 (7): 1347–64.

Evans, P., 2002. 'Beyond "Institutional Monocropping": Institutions, Capabilities, and Deliberative Development'. Berkeley, CA: University of California, mimeo.

Gibbon, P., ed., 1995. *Liberalised Development in Tanzania: Studies on Accumulation Processes and Local Institutions*. Uppsala: Nordiska Afrikaninstitutet.

Harriss, B., 1990. 'The Intra-family Distribution of Hunger in South Asia'. In *The Political Economy of Hunger: Volume 1, Entitlement and Well-being*, eds J. Drèze and A. Sen, 351–424. Oxford: Clarendon Press.

Hart, G., 1994. 'The Dynamics of Diversification in an Asian Rice Region'. In *Development or Deterioration?: Work in Rural Asia*, eds B. Koppel, J. Hawking and W. James, 47–71. Boulder, CO: Lynne Reinner.

Hart, G., 1995. 'Clothes for Next to Nothing: Rethinking Global Competition'. *South African Labour Bulletin*, 9 (6): 41–7.

Hart, G., 1996. 'The Agrarian Question and Industrial Dispersal in South Africa: Agro-industrial Linkages through Asian Lenses'. *Journal of Peasant Studies*, 23 (2/3): 245–77.

Hart, G., 2001. *Reworking Apartheid Legacies: Global Competition, Gender, and Social Wages in South Africa, 1980–2000*. Geneva: UNRISD, mimeo.

Kandiyoti, D., 1988. 'Bargaining with Patriarchy'. *Gender and Society*, 2 (3): 274–90.

Kandiyoti, D., 1998. 'Gender, Power and Contestation: Rethinking Bargaining with Patriarchy'. In *Feminist Visions of Development*, eds C. Jackson and R. Pearson, 135–51. London: Routledge.

Kay, C., 2001. *Asia's and Latin America's Development in Comparative Perspective: Landlords, Peasants, and Industrialization*. The Hague: Institute of Social Studies.

Ministry of Agriculture, Food and Fisheries (MAFF), 1999. *Strategies for Increased Food Security and Rural Incomes in the Isolated Areas of Zambia*. Lusaka: Zambia.

Mkandawire, T. and C.C. Soludo, 2000. *Our Continent, Our Future: African Perspectives on Structural Adjustment*. Dakar/Ottawa/Asmara: CODESRIA/IDRC/Africa World Press.

Molyneux, M. and S. Razavi, 2002. 'Introduction'. *Gender Justice, Development and Rights*, eds M. Molyneux and S. Razavi, Oxford: Oxford University Press.

Oxfam/IDS, 1999. 'Liberalisation and Poverty: Zambia Case Study'. Report to DFID.

Phillips, A., 2002. 'Multiculturalism, Universalism, and the Claims of Democracy'. In *Gender Justice, Development, and Rights*, eds M. Molyneux and S. Razavi, 115–38. Oxford: Oxford University Press.

Pomfret, R., 2000. 'Agrarian Reform in Uzbekistan: Why Has the Chinese Model Failed to Deliver?' *Economic Development and Cultural Change*, 48 (2): 269–84.

Razavi, Shahra and Carol Miller, 1995. 'From WID to GAD: Conceptual Shifts in the Women and Development Discourse'. Occasional Paper No. 1. Geneva: UNRISD.

Saith, R. and B. Harriss-White, 1999. 'The Gender Sensitivity of Well-being Indicators'. *Development and Change*, 30 (3): 465–97.

Sen, G., 1999. 'Engendering Poverty Alleviation: Challenges and Opportunities'. *Development and Change*, 30 (3): 685–92.

Summerfield, G., 2002. *Gender and Agrarian Reform in China*. Geneva: UNRISD, mimeo.

Udry, A., J. Hoddinott, H. Alderman and L. Haddad, 1995. 'Gender Differentials in Farm Productivity: Implications for Household Efficiency and Agricultural Policy'. *Food Policy*, 20 (5): 407–23.

UNCTAD, 1999. *Trade and Development Report*. New York/Geneva: United Nations.

UNCTAD, 1998. *Trade and Development Report*. New York/Geneva: United Nations.

Venkateshwarlu, D. and L. Da Corta, 2001. 'Transformations in the Age and Gender of Unfree Workers on Hybrid Cotton Seed Farms in Andhra Pradesh'. *Journal of Peasant Studies*, 28 (3): 1–36.

Walker, C., 1994. 'Women, "Tradition" and Reconstruction'. *Review of African Political Economy*, 61: 347–58.

Weisbrot, M., D. Baker, R. Naiman and G. Neta, 2000. *Growth May Be Good for the Poor – But are IMF and World Bank Policies Good for Growth: A Closer Look at World Bank's Most Recent Defense of Its Policies*. Washington, DC: Centre for Economic and Policy Research.

Winters, L.A., 2000. *Trade, Trade Policy and Poverty: What are the Links?* Background Study for World Bank's World Development Report 2000/01.

Whitehead, A., 2001. 'Trade, Trade Liberalisation and Rural Poverty in Low-Income Africa: A Gendered Account'. Background Paper for the UNCTAD 2001 Least Developed Countries Report. Sussex, mimeo.

Whitehead, A. and N. Kabeer, 2001. 'Living with Uncertainty: Gender, Livelihoods and Pro-Poor Growth in Rural Sub-Saharan Africa'. IDS Working Paper 134. Brighton: Institute of Development Studies.

Whitehead, A. and M. Lockwood, 1999. 'Gender in the World Bank's Poverty Assessments: Six Case Studies from Sub-Saharan Africa'. Discussion Paper 99. Geneva: UNRISD.

Whitehead, A. and D. Tsikata, 2001. 'Policy Discourses on Women's Land Rights in Sub-Saharan Africa'. Geneva: UNRISD, mimeo.

Wold, B., 1997. *Supply Response in a Gender Perspective: The Case of Structural Adjustment in Zambia*. Oslo: Statistics Norway and Lusaka: Zambian Central Statistical Office.

World Bank, 1989. *Sub-Saharan Africa: From Crisis to Sustainable Growth*. Washington, DC: World Bank.

2

Global Capitalism, Deflation and Agrarian Crisis in Developing Countries

UTSA PATNAIK

Periods of economic crisis for agriculture in developing countries have been marked in history by declining incomes and worsening employment possibilities, resulting in adverse outcomes of loss of land rights against debt and declining nutrition levels for the poorer majority of populations. This paper argues that a similar conjuncture of agrarian crisis has become visible in recent years, as had been seen in the prelude to the inter-War Depression, owing to the income-deflation inherent in current macroeconomic policies driven by the dominant global neo-liberal agenda. The argument is illustrated primarily with reference to the experience of India under economic reforms. The question of land rights and gender equity are strongly affected by the dominant policy regime; hence the paper, while not addressing these questions directly, seeks to contextualize them through its critique of the dominant neo-liberal policy regime.

Keywords: globalization, deflation, agrarian crisis, land reforms, cooperation

INTRODUCTION

The issue of land rights and that of gender equality, are both strongly affected by the prevalent economic and social policy regime, both at the national and at the global level. The prevalent, dominant policy regimes decide to what extent movements for securing land rights or gender equality encounter favourable conditions and have some hope of securing positive gains, or the converse. This paper will not directly address the question of either land rights or gender, but will seek to analyze the nature of the economic policy regimes associated with globalization, and thereby seek to contextualize the issues of land rights and gender in the present era. It will illustrate the main arguments with reference to the experience of India in the last decade.

This paper is divided into four main parts. The first part deals with the deflationary impact of global finance capital on the large number of developing countries that have undergone loan-conditional structural adjustment and trade liberalization under the guidance of the Bretton Woods institutions (BWI) during the last two decades. These outcomes, driven by neo-liberal ideas, are theoretically situated with respect to the historical experience of deflationism in the inter-War period in the second part, which discusses the crisis induced by the prolonged fall in primary product prices. In the third section, the arguments are illustrated in terms of the Indian experience with reference to food security and employment. The fourth section attempts to explore the contours of possible strategies for protecting rural livelihoods.

THE INCOME-DEFLATING RESULTS OF THE GLOBAL DOMINANCE OF FINANCE CAPITAL

A great deal has been written regarding the emergence and dominance of highly mobile and fluid global finance capital in the wake of the oil-shocks of the 1970s, and the subsequent, largely successful attempts of this finance capital in moulding economic policy agendas across the globe in its own interests (Baker et al. 1998; Halevy and Fontaine 1998; *Monthly Review* July–August 1999). Our concern is with the economic agenda of finance capital, in so far as it impacts on and affects the livelihoods of the millions of people, mainly in the rural areas of developing countries, who make up the poor of the world. The implementation of this agenda is exercising profound effects, both on land rights and on gender equity in developing countries.

The interests of capitalists who deal in money to make profit have always been substantially different from the interests of capitalists who are engaged in material production for profit on the basis of borrowed money. Financiers are creditors, and creditors wish, above all, to prevent inflation, which erodes their returns, to maintain high real interest rates, and to have complete freedom to move their finance in and out of countries in search of the highest profits, which are mainly speculative in nature. Further, rather than accumulation through the route of productive investment, the rapid centralization of capital via takeovers and acquisition of cheapened foreign assets is the preferred route for finance capital, which is achieved through periodic asset-deflation along with income deflation in those developing countries that have opened themselves fully to the destabilizing effects of these flows.

Deflationary economic policies combined with removal of all national barriers to the free movement of finance capital thus forms the core of the policy agenda of finance capital. The dominance of finance capital over all other types of capital, and the systematic implementation of its deflationary agenda in dozens of countries across the globe through the weapon of external debt used by the international lending agencies, has brought about the present global crisis of livelihoods. This crisis is of a scale and magnitude that is unprecedented in the post Second World War era and indeed has not been seen since the run-up to the Great Depression seventy years ago.

In many ways the causes are similar, for the 1920s were also a period of dominance of finance capital (although its nation-based character then demarcates it from the more fluid, globalized capital of the present). Finance Ministers of all capitalist countries rigidly adhered to the dogma of balanced budgets and deflationary solutions to balance of payments problems, regarded as 'sound finance' at that time. As agricultural prices fell from the mid-1920s, all big exporters of primary products, which included Germany and USA, found their trade balances moving towards or into the red and a fall in customs and other revenues. Empire and dominion countries similarly affected were advised by the British Treasury to immediately cut public expenditures and balance budgets, and all countries did precisely that. Incomes were thereby reduced by a multiple of the initial cuts, demand for internal goods as well as capacity to import in each country fell, affecting incomes of trading partners, feeding back in turn into further falls in output and trade. Keynes' warnings, based on his revolutionary theory of income determination (which rightly held that governments should be spending more, not cutting effective demand by reducing expenditure) fell initially on unheeding ears. What started as an agricultural recession deepened into a downward spiral of output and trade, into the Great Depression, largely owing to the wrong policies of reducing effective demand.

Something very similar is happening at present under the rigid implementation of the neo-liberal dogma of reduction of fiscal deficits through cuts in public spending even in the face of mounting unemployment. The term 'dogma' is used advisedly, for there is no objectively acceptable theoretical basis to these prescriptions: they reflect the narrow self-interest of a politically dominant minority. Halevy and Fontaine (1998) contains a number of studies on the way economies have become demand-constrained systems in the present era. The difference from the 1920s is that these policies have been in operation for two decades and the current agrarian crisis is the end-result, not the beginning, of the consequent global slow-down. The theoretical similarity, indeed identity of inter-War deflationism and current neo-liberal economic prescriptions, is discussed in more detail later for the lessons they hold for the present era.

In the era of globalization, over the last two decades of the twentieth century, there has been a halving of the world's GDP growth from 4.0 per cent in the 1970s to 2.1 per cent in the 1990s (Table 1). While growth in the Advanced Economies slowed from 3.5 to 1.9 per cent, the slowdown has been relatively sharper in all Developing Economies, from 5.3 to 2.9 per cent. If we exclude China, the only large sovereign area in the world not subordinated to deflationary neo-liberal policies, the developing economies have even lower growth than are indicated by these figures. Given their much lower initial income base, the impact on developing country populations of the deceleration in their per capita income growth is more severe.

More than 80 countries in the world were implementing loan-conditional deflation under 'structural adjustment' as well as trade liberalization in the decade of the 1980s. Table 2 summarizes an IMF study of the six main policy instruments used in 78 countries that were implementing Fund-guided structural adjustment in the 1980s. These included cuts in Government expenditures, tight money and caps on money wages. It is clear enough that the policies are deflationary, for they add up to consistent macro-economic contraction, and that the intersection set of countries implementing at least four contractionary policies at the same time was very large.

Table 1. Decade trends in GDP growth per annum

	1970s	*1980s*	*1990s*
Advanced economies			
Overall GDP	3.5	3.1	1.9
Agriculture	3.7	1.9	0.0
Industry	3.4	0.9	2.3
Services	3.6	4.5	1.8
Per capita GDP	2.7	2.4	1.5
Population	0.8	0.7	0.5
Developing economies			
Overall GDP	5.3	3.1	2.9
Agriculture	2.8	3.4	1.5
Industry	5.6	2.9	3.4
Services	6.0	3.1	3.1
Per capita GDP	3.0	1.0	1.2
Population	2.3	2.1	1.7
World			
Overall GDP	4.0	3.1	2.1
Agriculture	3.1	2.9	1.1
Industry	4.1	1.5	2.5
Services	4.0	4.2	2.0
Per capita GDP	2.1	1.4	0.6
Population	1.9	1.7	1.5

Source: Mohan Rao and Storm (2002, from Tables 1a, 1b, 1c).

Most of the 46 countries of sub-Saharan Africa were under structural adjust-ment programmes from the late 1970s or early 1980s, which entailed either negative, or negligible (± 0.4 per cent), per capita investment and GDP growth in the majority (Cornia 1987, 16–18; Pinstrup-Andersen et al. 1987, 76). World Bank data covering 1980–9 show that out of 33 adjusting countries, nine coun-tries, with 40.4 per cent of the region's population, had annual per head real GDP decline in excess of 2 per cent. Another 12 countries, with 40.8 per cent of the total population, registered decline ranging from 0 to 2 per cent (Cornia 1987, 16–18; van der Hoeven 1994). The per capita real GDP of the region fell over the 1980s at an average rate of 1.1 per cent. Food security was adversely affected: annual per head output of the food staples (including tubers and plan-tains) fell from 156 kg in 1980 to only 137 kg by 1988–91, and availability per head dropped despite food aid.[1] The six most populous countries of the region were all under structural adjustment. They saw, per head of population, a 33 per

---

[1]   For per head food output, calculated from UNDP (1992) data, see Patnaik (1996), and for per capita calorie decline see Patnaik (1999b). *Africa Recovery* 16, 3, October 2001, mentions 1999 poverty estimates.

Table 2. Fund-guided policies implemented in 78 countries in the 1980s

Type of policy	Percentage of total number of countries implementing policy
1. Restraint on central government expenditure	91
2. Limits on credit expansion	99
3. Reduction in budget deficit/GDP ratio	83
4. Wage restraint	65
5. Exchange rate policy	54

Source: Constructed from data in Cornia (1987, 11).

cent fall in cereals output and a 20 per cent fall in all food staples output in the 1980s, at the same time that cash crop export volumes were being pushed out at the annual rate of 6.5 per cent (Kenya) to 13.9 per cent (Sudan), despite falling unit dollar prices (data: UNDP 1992). All except one country suffered a decline in average calorie intake, even after food imports are taken into account (Patnaik 1999b). No doubt falling nutrition has been unequally distributed within affected households, with women suffering the largest declines.

The devastation of the HIV epidemic might not perhaps have been as great without the accompanying falling nutrition levels during this period. During 1990–9 per head GDP fell by a further 6 per cent and the number of persons in absolute poverty (less than one US dollar a day) rose from 300 to 380 million. The richest African country, South Africa, is now firmly and officially under the domination of neo-liberal deflationism and is seeking to cut already very low budget deficits despite a 35 per cent unemployment rate for the black majority and opposition from the unions.

Many countries in Latin America under BWI-guided structural adjustment also saw substantial real income decline in the 1980s. Summarizing a number of IMF studies, van der Hoeven (1994) finds that, taking all countries that implemented adjustment and liberalized between 1980 and 1990, the per capita GDP declined by 9 per cent, the minimum wage fell by 31.7 per cent and the agricultural wage fell by 26.5 per cent. The absolute numbers of people in poverty, taking all Latin American countries, rose from 91.4 to 132.7 million over the decade (World Bank 1992).

In the course of the 1990s, mass income deflation has become generalized to ever-larger areas of the globe. In the first half of the decade, the Soviet Union's break-up and 'shock therapy' to usher in market reforms under the advice of Western 'experts' saw a catastrophic absolute collapse of GDP in Russia and the Ukraine to half the 1990 level by 1996 and a large rise in the male death rate. All constituents of the CIS also saw similar orders of GDP decline, except Georgia, which was worst-off with 82 per cent decline, and Uzbekistan, which was the best-off with 'only' 17 per cent decline (UNDP Poverty Report 1998, 47).

This region had been a large importer of temperate food grains and tropical products – both were severely affected.

This was followed by the 1997 crisis of the former Asian 'tigers', soon after they had unwisely fully opened their economies to speculative financial flows, and both asset deflation and income deflation were seen in those economies over the next three years. Through trade linkages, the collapse of those of the erstwhile Asian tigers, which were closely integrated with other economies, affected export incomes elsewhere, notably in Brazil, while Argentina is in acute crisis, with loans drying up and widespread social unrest against the implementation of harsh deflationary measures by successive governments to satisfy international creditors.

From 1991, after taking a US$4.8 billion IMF loan, India has also been implementing mass income deflationary policies, though much less intensively than other countries, owing to domestic opposition from the very beginning. Nevertheless, given its low initial income, the impact of these policies on the poorer majority of the population has been severe, the most important aspects being a collapse of rural employment and a large fall in per head food availability (Sen and Patnaik 1997). These outcomes are discussed in greater detail in the last section.

China remains the only large area of sovereign economic policy in the world where 'reforms' – whatever their independent merits or demerits might be – have been internally determined, were not the outcome of the debt-conditional internalization of a finance capital-driven global neo-liberal agenda, and hence have not been mass demand-deflating in character but rather have been associated with high growth rates until recently.

We believe that it is a grave mistake to think that adjustment can ever have a 'human face'. On the contrary, since the basic agenda is reduction in mass incomes along with a large rise in income inequality, neo-liberal reforms always imply a welfare worsening for the most vulnerable and push down hitherto viable producers into the mire of unemployment, indebtedness, and asset loss. It is not correct to say that IMF and World Bank policies 'have failed', as many writers have put it, after looking at all the evidence that shows a rise in poverty and de-industrialization. On the contrary, we believe that the BWI have *succeeded* to a remarkable extent in what they were actually trying to do, namely deflate mass incomes and open up third world economies in the interests of global finance capital (Patnaik 1999a). They continue to implement the same agenda today.

RECOLLECTING SOME LESSONS OF HISTORY

The Importance of Land Reforms and a Wider Social Base of Investment in Stabilizing and Improving Livelihoods

The problem of archaic semi-feudal relations and tenures has been tackled historically in different countries through two main, much discussed alternative paths or strategies: *landlord-dominated redistribution* and *peasant-dominated redistribution*, respectively. In the first, more conservative path, there is no radical takeover of landlord land by peasants; the landlords continue to monopolize land and may give up only a part of it against compensation; but they may begin themselves to turn into capitalist producers, evicting their former tenants and employing them as hired workers. In the second, more democratic and revolutionary path, the land is seized *without compensation* from the landlords and distributed to the landless and land-poor peasants, while the rural capitalists are thrown up in large numbers from the ranks of the well-to-do sections of the peasants themselves. The first path preserves land monopoly, the second abolishes it. In the Asian context we may characterize the conservative path as the Meiji Japan path, and consider as illustrative of the second, more democratic path, that followed in the same country itself after the Second World War, and also in China after Liberation.

Thus, in Japan after the 1868 Meiji restoration, the high nobility – the *daimyo* – were compensated heavily with bonds for loss of their feudal revenues. Little land went to the actual tillers, for in 1873, over most of the land, ownership certificates (*chiken*) were issued to village-level non-cultivating landlords. Under this conservative, landlord-dominated reform, small tenancy grew rapidly to cover over half of the rice area (Norman 1940), and high rents along with tenant insecurity became such a fetter on productivity that rice output started stagnating. Japan turned to colonized Korea, which by 1937 was made to supply 65 per cent of the increasing rice imports (Penrose 1940; Grabowski 1985; Hochin Choi 1988). By contrast the post Second World War land reform in Japan itself was a radical redistribution in which the ceiling for the landlord's personal ownership was only 1 *cho* or 2.45 acres, while the remainder, making up one-third of total cultivated area, was given to the tenants. The data show that as tenant area fell to below 5 per cent of total cultivated area, rice yields spurted upwards (Nakamura 1981).

In China, an even more comprehensive peasant and landless-dominated redistribution took place. An estimated 43–45 per cent of total cultivated area passed from the landowners to the landless and land-poor, creating a highly egalitarian distribution (Hinton 1968; Lippit 1987). Cooperatives in the 1950s, and later the communes, permitted underemployed surplus labour to be mobilized for capital formation on a massive scale, especially in water management (Nickum 1974), while non-farm enterprises and basic health and education also spread rapidly in villages, mainly through the strategy of such decentralized, local cooperative effort, aided where necessary by supplementary central grants. Much of China's good growth, reduction in rural poverty and excellent performance on the human development indicators can be traced to the initial egalitarian land reform and its consolidation through the decentralized units like cooperatives and the later commune system up to 1980.[2]

[2] Allegations of 30 million famine deaths during the Great Leap, 1958–61, have been examined in my paper (Patnaik 2002c). Nearly 20 million of those alleged to have died were not born in the first place. The demographers (Coale 1984; Banister 1987) talk of high 'famine mortality' on the basis of some very creative statistical manipulations: they construct an arbitrary new total of deaths over the inter-censal period 1953–64, then arbitrarily allocate this total over particular inter-censal years, and finally fit linear time trends to deaths derived from a variable – the death rate – which always behaves non-linearly.

In India land reforms can also be usefully analyzed in terms of the two-paths conceptualization. In all states, the conservative path of landlord-dominated redistribution has prevailed, with the sole exception of Punjab, where the peasant element was strong. When intermediary tenures (*zamindar, jagirdar*) were abolished, it was the powerful former intermediaries who got automatic ownership rights over the land they claimed as *khud-kasht* (own-cultivated) while being compensated with cash and bonds for the small part of their estates they surrendered. Their former tenants, however, had to purchase ownership rights, which most were too poor to do. Some land in excess of statutory 'ceilings' on landholding was also taken over. An estimated maximum of about 12 per cent of total cultivated area has been redistributed at the all-India level in the four decades of reform from 1950 to 1990 through the market mechanism.

Those developing countries that do not tackle the question of archaic agrarian relations and effectively abolish land monopoly soon find that their development strategy runs aground on account of an insufficiently expanding internal market, which only a prospering peasantry can provide. Preserving land monopoly entails preserving the fetters on productivity growth within agriculture itself, for those monopolizing land will not have an adequate incentive to invest and those forced to lease in land or to labour for hire, do not have the means to invest. All the painful aspects of high-caste domination and discrimination against the *dalit* (literally 'ground-down') population are also preserved. Second, it means that mass incomes hardly grow, the market for manufactures of mass consumption becomes near stagnant and companies start looking to the external market through collaboration with foreign companies.[3]

These problems of the *dirigiste* development strategy in India led to a naïve belief amongst many that economic liberalization would solve growth problems and they initially looked hopefully upon the successful attempt by the BWI, using the Gulf War conjuncture in 1991, to impose through a minority government and a pliant Finance Minister, a neo-liberal programme of structural adjustment (Patnaik and Chandrasekhar 1995). This was followed by incessant pressure to liberalize trade completely, especially under the WTO regime after 1995. Starting in 1997, by April 2001 all quantitative restrictions on imports had been removed. As predicted from the beginning by the prescient critics of liberalization within India, the result has been to turn problems which could have been tackled into a crisis of unprecedented dimensions, in which employment growth has collapsed and the purchasing power and food security of the poorer majority of the population have been severely eroded.

Agrarian Crisis, Inter-War Deflationism and its Present-day Variant

The second important lesson to be learnt from history relates to the dangers of following deflationary policies in a recession-hit world economy, as was the case

---

[3]   I have discussed some of these issues in a paper on 'The Agrarian Question and the Development of Capitalism in India', reprinted in Thorner (2002).

during 1925–35, and as is the case today. An agrarian crisis is currently unfolding in India and in a large number of developing countries, involving a collapse of employment growth, falling export prices and a rising spiral of farm debt. The crisis is directly linked to the contractionary fiscal stance of governments undertaking neo-liberal reforms, and to trade liberalization against the background of world recession.

The global conditions of trade in primary commodities are extremely unfavourable at present. It is significant that the World Bank's price projections to 2005, made in a 1993 Report, are not being borne out by the actual price trends experienced so far. The World Bank had projected quite steeply falling prices for non-grain products exported by developing countries, while projecting firm, even rising, prices for the food and feed grains whose global sales are dominated by the USA and West Europe. The price projections were for real prices, viz. the particular primary product price divided by an index of manufactured goods prices.

Actual price trends have been very different: after a brief upsurge in the early 1990s, prices of primary products mainly exported by developing countries have indeed crashed. But contrary to all projections, prices of cereals exported by developed countries have also crashed.

Declining from 1996, five years later food and feed grain prices remain depressed to about half of earlier levels. With the removal of quantitative restrictions and the opening up to global trade, developing country farmers who are engaged in growing the exported cash crops like tea, coffee, rubber, cotton etc. are suffering, but also millions of food-grain producers are facing the threat of the undermining of their livelihoods through import of exceptionally low-priced foreign grain. *By liberalizing agricultural trade, the depression in the global markets is being imported into the Indian economy and into other liberalizing countries.*

Table 3 shows that all commodities, whether temperate cereals or tropical crops, have declined strongly in price between 1995 and 2001, the extent of decline ranging between over one-third to over one-half. The exceptions are jute and groundnut oil, which have declined to a smaller extent, and the edible oils, which have declined more strongly than average. Most prices are substantially lower in 2001 than even as far back as 1988. Some of the oils by 2001 had only 12–15 per cent of the unit value of 1995. A halving of the price of the major staples like rice, wheat and maize has very serious implications for the incomes of producers, not only of the exporting countries, but also of countries that are now forced to become cereal importers owing to the removal of protection. Farm debts are rising, and developing country farmers in particular are getting caught in a spiral of escalating indebtedness and land loss, just as was the case in the inter-War period.

For those who know something of capitalism's history, the situation is strongly reminiscent of the run-up to the inter-War Great Depression. Four years before the famous stock market crash of 1929, from 1925 onwards, all primary products prices started falling combined with the build-up of stocks. It is argued that this took place owing to over-production relative to demand, in a number of large

Table 3. Prices of some important globally traded primary products, in US dollars

	1988	1995	1997	2000	2001 (Jan.)	Per cent change 2001 over 1995
Wheat (US HW)	167	216	142	130	133	−38.2
Wheat (US RSW)	160	198	129	102	106	−46.5
Wheat (Argentine)	145	218	129	112	118	−45.9
Maize (Argentine)	116	160	133	88	80	−50.0
Maize (US)	118	159	112	97	92	−22.0
Rice (US)	265.7	–	439.0	271	291	−33.7
Rice (Thai)	284	336	316	207	179	−46.7
Groundnut oil	590	991	1010	788*		−20.5*
Palm oil	437	626	93.5	74.7*		−88.1*
Soyabean oil	464	479	625	71.4*		−85.1*
Soyabean seed	297	273	262	199	178	−34.8
Sorghum seed	110	156	111	102	99	−36.5
Sugar	10.2	13.3	11.4	10.2	9.2	−30.8
Jute	370	366	302	276*		−24.6*
Cotton	63.5	98.2	77.5	66	49.1	−50.0

Sources: *Food Outlook*, Statistical Supplement, 1986 and 1996, and various issues from 1999 to 2001; and *Monthly Commodity Price Bulletin* (Food and Agriculture Organization, Rome).
Note: For the cereals, edible oils and seeds, the unit is USD per ton; for cotton and sugar, US cents per lb; and for jute, USD per metric ton.
* Relates to 1999, and per cent change is 1999 compared to 1995.

producing countries (Timoshenko 1953). Up to 1929, the agricultural recession was just that, and there was no premonition that generalized deep economic depression was to follow. To this day, some analysts maintain that the industrial depression was independent of the prior agricultural depression. But such a position appears to be unrealistic, when we consider the policies that were followed systematically by all primary product exporters as revenues fell.

Kindleberger (1987) draws the connections between agricultural depression and industrial depression, precisely, through the deflationary policies, especially expenditure cuts, universally implemented by governments wedded to the then-dominant ideas of 'sound finance', i.e. balanced budgets. It is essentially the working out of the Keynes–Kahn multiplier in reducing incomes by a multiple of initial expenditure cuts, with cumulative adverse effects on employment and trade, which we see detailed in his account of the impact of deflationary policies followed in various countries (Kindleberger 1981, chapters 4 and 8). With falling export earnings, the major primary products exporters experienced strong pressure on their currencies and tax revenue decline. Maintenance of sterling exchange parity had 'almost mystical force' (Kindleberger 1981, 85) so balance of payments and fiscal deficit problems were addressed solely through deflation.

With their thinking confined in the iron grip of the dogma of balanced budgets, a dogma upheld and promoted by financial interests in the City of London (the main centre of the financial world at that time), Finance Ministers in all countries reduced spending (today, they 'cut the fiscal deficit') and, through multiplier effects, income in each country was reduced to a much greater extent than the initial cuts, thus reducing importing capacity and resulting in lower export incomes of trading partners. These affected countries in turn deflated their economies when faced with the external imbalance and falling revenues. A mutually reinforcing deflationary spiral resulted, demand for manufactured goods fell and unemployment rose steadily as, worldwide, income growth slowed down or there was absolute decline. Massive gold losses by deficit countries eventually forced countries off gold either before or following Britain's departure from gold in 1931, but the ensuing competitive devaluations helped nobody.

According to data in Triantis (1967), there were only seven other countries in the world that suffered larger export earnings fall than India. The colonial government, responding to falling revenues, cut spending sharply. Outlays on roads, irrigation and railways fell from 27 to 18 per cent of (declining) public expenditures, comparing 1937–8 with 1927–8 (Thavaraj 1960; Bagchi 1972). As peasants, no longer able to make ends meet from cultivation, threw themselves on the labour market, their employment prospects were worsened with these spending cuts. By the 1931 Census, 38 per cent of all rural workers were returning themselves as relying on wage-paid labour compared to only 26 per cent in 1921. A great deal of mortgaged land changed hands and landlessness increased. During the inter-War period, per capita food availability fell by 29 per cent in British India, and by as much as 38 per cent in Bengal, with a slightly lesser order of fall in per capita calorie intake (Blyn 1966). We have elsewhere argued that this prior fall in nutrition levels affected the extent of the toll in the great Bengal famine of 1943 (over 3 million people died), although inflationary War financing was the proximate cause of the famine (Patnaik 1991).

In 1929, Lloyd George in Britain had put forward a suggestion of public works to create employment when the unemployment rate was 10 per cent (it was to double to 20 per cent later), supported by Keynes in a pamphlet titled *Can Lloyd George Do It?* (Keynes and Henderson 1929). The mere suggestion of expansionary policies caused consternation in the City. The Treasury, articulating financial interests, hurriedly brought out a White Paper in the same year to counter Lloyd George, titled 'Memorandum on Certain Proposals Relating to Unemployment'. This argued that in an economy at a point of time there is a fixed pool of savings, and spending more on public works would simply reduce private domestic investment or foreign investment and have no net positive impact on employment. Today, the neo-liberal deflationists put forward the same argument using slightly different jargon – that increased public expenditure will 'crowd out' private investment. Exactly as in the Treasury view, they assume a fixed savings pool.

A rigorous formulation of the counter-argument, with which Keynes was familiar, was provided by his young pupil, Richard F. Kahn, who exposed the fallacy of the Treasury view in a paper published in late 1931, which has deservedly become a classic (Kahn 1931). Kahn's argument was fundamental, and simple enough for any informed lay person to understand. He pointed out that total savings in an economy depended on total income and – unless income itself cannot be increased because there is already full capacity utilization and full employment of labour – there is no reason to think that savings cannot increase. There is thus no given, fixed savings pool as the Treasury view assumed.

If there is already full employment, then public works are unnecessary anyway. If there are unemployed resources and manpower owing to lack of aggregate demand, as was actually the case, then expenditure on public works would result in employment and income rising through successive rounds of spending (the multiplier) until precisely that amount of extra income resulted, which would give the extra savings for financing the initial extra expenditure. The Treasury economists were thus fallaciously using an argument requiring the assumption of full employment in order to oppose measures to combat actually existing unemployment. Kahn's concept of the multiplier was central to Keynes's *General Theory*, which said that savings did not determine investment, but on the contrary autonomous expenditure determined savings via the rise of incomes by a multiple of the initial expenditure.

These ideas were diametrically opposed to the concepts driving economic policy and leading countries into depression. In Germany, grossly inappropriate deflationary policies in the face of farm crisis and rising industrial unemployment produced a disastrous outcome by 1931, for they aided the collapse of the Weimar republic and the rise to victory of fascism. Bruning implemented punishing contractionary policies as late as 1930–1, when unemployment was already high (earning the nickname of the hated 'Hunger Chancellor'), in the attempt to please Germany's international creditors and end loan-financed reparations.

Orthodox economics professors supported Bruning on grounds of sound finance, and opposed a proposal in 1930 by W. Lautenbach, an official in the Economics Ministry, to undertake bank credit-financed public works to reduce unemployment. This was the German equivalent of Lloyd George's proposal. A similar proposal for reducing unemployment was formulated for the trade unions by W. S. Woytinsky, along with two others, in 1931 and published by the German Federation of Unions the next year (Kindleberger 1981, 171–2), but they were all dismissed by the deflationists. Had these intelligent schemes for creating employment actually materialized early enough, the history of Germany and of Europe might perhaps have taken a different course.

Joan Robinson referred to 'the humbug of finance which Keynes first attacked' (Robinson 1962, 95). The humbug of finance has a way of reasserting itself, however, whenever financial interests dominate policy, and we have seen in recent years this humbug reasserting itself in the face of all logic, all reason and indeed in subversion of the humanism which had informed the intellectual efforts of its critics seven decades ago. The theory of income determination based on the Keynes–Kahn multiplier has been in every economics textbook for half a century, yet today's neo-liberal deflationists try to pass off an old fallacious argument assuming a fixed savings pool, as newly minted wisdom. Using the power of their status as creditors, they enforce deflationary policies in the face of unemployed resources, and thereby condemn millions of people to declining income, asset loss, nutrition decline and even starvation. Today, in India, for example, enormous food stocks in excess of 65 million tonnes coexist with falling average nutrition and starvation deaths, but all suggestions for a massive food-for-work programme are being dismissed by the deflationists, expressing the BWI view, on the same fallacious ground that it would 'increase the fiscal deficit and crowd out private investment'. The manner in which neo-liberal deflationist dogma is leading to these anti-humanist outcomes in India – the case with which I am most familiar – is discussed in the third section. But this adverse welfare outcome can already be seen in all its starkness in sub-Saharan Africa.

Returning to the present, we find that the extent of price fall between 1995 and 2000 has been as great for many primary commodities as it had been in the period 1925–30. For example, at that time, the price index of wheat (with base 1929=100) had declined by 43 per cent, cotton by 42 per cent and sugar declined as wheat did, by 43 per cent (these figures are quoted from graphs by Timoshenko and the League of Nations, reproduced in Kindleberger 1981, 76–7). As Table 3 shows, the decline for prices of these crops during 1995–2001 has been of a similar order, by 46, 50 and 31 per cent, respectively.

What is the reason for the recent prolonged decline of prices, especially of those crops traded by the advanced countries? An important difference in the global situation now, compared with the 1920s, is that we have seen an even more prolonged dominance of neo-liberal orthodoxy – similar in essentials to earlier balanced budget doctrines – which has been effective in imposing loan-conditional income deflation across the globe for over two decades, since the late 1970s. This global dominance of finance capital has meant a ruthless imposition, through the international lending institutions, of effective demand-contracting economic agendas on dozens of countries, entailing cuts in fiscal deficit, high interest rates, caps on wages, reduction in priority sector lending, cuts in social subsidies, retrenchment of workers from enterprises, and so on. The impact of these policies in deflating mass incomes has been briefly detailed earlier. Further, the 1990s have seen a generalization of deflation over larger areas of the world, with the GDP collapse and demographic decline of the so-called 'transitional economies' and with the East Asian crisis dating from 1997, which has sharply reduced trade growth. Among advanced economies, the Japanese economy is still contracting, the US economy is in recession, as is that of Germany.

It is perhaps hardly surprising that the end-results of two decades of the globalization of deflationism are now becoming visible as price declines of the major commodities. Our argument has been that it is not temporary 'overproduction', but cumulative demand deflation that lies behind these declines, hence we cannot expect a sustained upturn unless the basic deflationary macroeconomic policies are reversed. In an earlier, more detailed examination of the behaviour of output, price and stocks of a number of primary commodities taken individually, I have showed that the recent price falls are combined with, and are in spite of, *rising global stocks* in each case, indicating that price slippage would have been even greater without stocks accretion – just as was the case in the 1920s (Patnaik 2002a). Stocks cost money to hold, and how much longer this can go on, with little prospect of a major revival in global demand, is a moot point: whether another 1931 is in the making already, with further price declines in store, deepening the crisis of third world peasantries, is the question.

The supply side of the picture as regards the temperate exportable products is also important. Very large subsidies are given by advanced countries to their farming sector – including the giant agro-business corporations – in order to capture global markets and maintain corporate profits. Every episode of falling global food and feed-grains prices leads to subsidies being increased, further sending the wrong signals. Instead of a cutback, over-production is promoted and we see even more aggressive attempts to penetrate external, developing country markets. While lecturing the developing countries on the iniquity of their meagre subsidies, the advanced countries, under the pressure of their farm lobbies, keep further raising their own subsidies.

Thus, during 1980–6, as cereal prices fell by a quarter to a third, the US had increased producer subsidy equivalent (PSE) as a percentage of its total value of agricultural output, from 9 per cent to an astronomical 45 per cent. All European countries did the same: the average rise for ten EC countries was from 25 to 66 per cent, while Japan raised it from 71 to 93 per cent (Ingersen et al. 1994). A part only (termed the 'aggregate measure of support') of these highly inflated mid-1980s subsidy levels was then made the base, from which a mere one-fifth cut was undertaken by advanced countries in compliance with the Agreement on Agriculture of GATT 1994.

Following only two or three years of reducing subsidies in compliance with the WTO, as soon as prices started falling, from 1996 large increases in transfers have been effected. The US increased total farm transfers, from US$71 billion to US$96 billion, or by 35 per cent, in just two years, 1997–9. The share of transfers to agricultural output, which had fallen in the US to 34 per cent by 1996, has again risen to over 50 per cent, and for the OECD 24 group, to nearly 60 per cent (OECD 1998, 2000). These annual transfers to a few million farmers by the USA or Japan exceeds the entire GNP of the majority of developing countries. While some analysts are inclined to think that it is these subsidy increases which are contributing to the global price fall of temperate commodities as a worked-out strategy of capturing external markets, we disagree. In our view, as discussed earlier, it is the income-deflationary trends inherent in neo-liberal policies that have affected global demand, causing the stocks build-up combined with price fall, and it is in response to price declines that the farm and corporate lobbies have mounted successful pressure on their governments for increasing cash bail-outs. On 13 May 2002, President Bush signed a new farm bill, which raised US crop and dairy subsidies by a massive 67 per cent, ensuring an additional US$52 billion in transfers over the next six years, and ending five years of annual ad hoc increases since 1998, totalling US$30.5 billion.

Such large, over-compensatory rises in farm transfers every time there is a fall in prices merely compounds the problem of excess supply in advanced countries and induces, as already seen in Philippines and in India, very strong pressure by advanced countries to prise open developing country markets to their grain and dairy products exports, years before they were required to do so under the WTO. This in turn, by undermining the incomes of local farmers, contributes to the vicious circle of economic distress.

Those researching issues of land rights and gender should expect to see several adverse outcomes in developing countries most affected by the economic forces discussed so far. These may include: increasing loss of land by poorer farmers under the pressure of debt, falling female work participation rates, increased destitution-induced migration, rising school drop-out rates for girl children in particular, perhaps also increased infanticide among the poorest in South Asia, sales of persons into servitude as well as a rise in prostitution and beggary. In India, agrarian distress is manifesting itself in increased enmeshing of producers in unrepayable debt, and in extreme cases large numbers of farmer suicides as well as sales of bodily organs for transplant purposes. The policies that have led to these outcomes are discussed in the next section.

THE INDIAN EXPERIENCE

Effects of Liberalization and SAP on Employment and Food Security in India

We will be mainly concerned here with the impact of liberalization and adjustment on rural livelihoods, land use and food security in India, considered as a case study. While some developments may be specific to India, the general thrust of the policy impact in deteriorating employment and food security is common to most developing countries.

Analysts of long-term trends in India find a sharp contrast between the pre-reform 1980s and the 1990s, which started with income-deflating economic reforms. The Seventh Plan period, 1975–80, had seen public expenditures on rural development, employment generation and infrastructure rise to 13.2 per cent of GDP, almost double the earlier level. The minor drought of 1987 gave an impetus to employment-generating schemes in particular. A number of state governments, especially the South Indian states and West Bengal, had extended the Public Distribution System (PDS) of food grains and other necessities to villages and had given an additional subsidy, out of local budgets, over and above the central food subsidy to keep basic staples affordable for the poor. Rural employment was diversified as state development expenditures rose, such that 29 per cent of rural workers were reporting non-farm employment by 1990 compared to 25 per cent five years earlier (Bhalla 1996, 1997; Sen 1996). Real wages in crop production also rose by half following the increase in alternative employment. A fairly sharp fall in measured rural headcount poverty in rural areas resulted,

Table 4. Poverty estimates, 1978–1998 (percentage of poor in total population, headcount)

NSS round	Period	Rural poverty headcount				Urban poverty headcount		
32	Jul 77–Jun 78	50.60				40.50		
38	Jan 83–Dec 83	45.31				35.65		
42	Jul 86–Jun 87	38.81				34.29		
43	Jul 87–Jun 88	39.60				35.65		
44	Jul 88–Jun 89	39.06				36.60		
45	Jul 89–Jun 90	34.30				33.40		
46	Jul 90–Jun 91	36.43				32.76		
47	Jul 91–Dec 91	37.42				33.23		
48	Jan 92–Dec 92	43.47				33.73		
50*	Jul 93–Jun 94	38.74				30.03		
43**	Jul 87–Jun 88	39.23				36.20		
50**	Jul 93–Jun 94	36.66				30.51		
		Gupta	Datt	S–T	Gupta	Datt		S–T
51	Jul 94–Jun 95	38.0	41.0	43.6	34.2	33.5		34.1
52	Jul 95–Jun 96	38.3	37.2	40.1	30.0	28.0		28.7
53	Jan–Dec 97	38.5	35.8	38.3	33.9	30.0		31.0
54	Jan 98–Jun 98	45.3	NA	44.9	34.6	n.a		31.8

Sources: Sen (1996), quoting, 'A Database on Poverty and Growth in India', World Bank January 1996, for all estimates up to the 48th Round.

* For the 1993–4 estimate, exactly the same method as rest of series applied to the 50th Round NSS data by Sen (1996).

** In World Bank (May 1997), this same series is reproduced with one change for the 1987–8 Round, and an estimate for 1993–4. See also Datt (1999) for this series. The three estimates for Rounds 51 to 54 are summarized from Sen (2000), and include Gupta (1999), Datt (1999) and Sundaram and Tendulkar (2000).

from about 45–50 per cent in the late 1970s, to about 35–36 per cent by 1990 (Table 4).

All these positive trends came to an end and were reversed as the temporarily abnormal situation associated with the 1991 Gulf War's impact on India was used to take an IMF-extended financing facility loan of US$4.8 billion in 1991 with the commitment to liberalize and implement SAP. Advised by the Fund-Bank, the newly elected minority central government from July 1991 immediately slashed development expenditures to contain the budget deficit and made it more difficult for state governments to borrow. From 13.2 per cent, rural development expenditures, including spending on infrastructure, fell to only 7.8 per cent of GDP by 1992 and has stagnated since then. All-India poverty rose sharply by

Table 5. Annual growth rates of food-grains production in India (index-based). Base triennium ending 1981–2=100

Period	Wheat	Rice	Coarse grains	Total cereals	Pulses	Food grains
1979–80 to 1989–90	4.24	4.29	0.74	3.63	2.78	3.54
1989–90 to 1998–9	3.62	1.60	−0.48	1.88	1.19	1.80

Source: *Economic Survey 1999–2000* (Govt. of India), rearranged from Table 8.6.
Note: Exponential functions using least squares have been used to obtain the compound growth rates.

1992 according to all estimates (to 42–44 per cent in rural areas in three independent estimates, a level not seen for a decade, and to 48 per cent in the fourth estimate).[4] *The crude death rate rose in a number of states in 1992, as did the Infant Mortality Rate.* Poverty rose because non-farm jobs were at once badly affected, the proportion of workers in lower-return farm work rose again, and earnings fell (Bhalla 1996, 1997; Sen 1996).

The rate of agricultural growth slowed down very markedly, at the same time that there was a marked shift in the land use and cropping pattern towards export crops at the expense of food grains consumed by the local population. The food grains growth rate halved and, at 1.8 per cent, fell below the population growth rate (even though the latter was itself falling) in the 1990s, for the first time in 30 years (Table 5).

On the industrial front, as imports were allowed the pent-up demand of the top 10 per cent of the population for modern consumer durables kept activity levels in this segment high for a few years, but as this one-time stimulus played itself out, both displacement of domestic manufacturing by freer imports and a marked industrial stagnation set in from 1996. The industrial recession and the collapse of agricultural growth are reflected in the latest employment data for 1999–2000 (55th round of NSS, Table 6). While high agricultural output growth in the late 1980s was matched by employment growth of 2.01 per cent, the output growth collapse under reforms is reflected in the abysmally lowered growth of employment (0.58 per cent). This growth rate would be even lower if we measured it from 1991 rather than 1993, for the sharpest macroeconomic contraction actually came in 1991–2 and 1992–3. The slowing down of manufacturing growth is reflected in lower growth of urban employment in the last period even though its terminal year precedes the period of the full impact of the recession.

Low growth rates of employment impact in two ways: first, via a rise in the rate of unemployment and second, via some *decline in the work participation rate.* When job opportunities are fewer, many workers, especially women, simply

---

[4]   The three estimates agreeing about a rise to 42–4 per cent were Gupta (1994); Sen (1996); Ravallion and Datt (1996), updated by Datt (1999). The fourth was by Tendulkar and Jain (1995).

Table 6. Annual rate of growth of total employment (per cent)

Period	Rural	Urban
1983 to 1987–8	1.36	2.77
1987–8 to 1993–4	2.03	3.39
1993–4 to 1999–00	0.58	2.55

Source: National Sample Survey Rounds 55th Round, discussed in Chandrasekhar and Ghosh (2001).

Note: The periodization is dictated by the five-year intervals at which large-sample surveys are conducted, which are more reliable than the small-sample surveys of intervening years.

drop out of the workforce. The data confirm both these tendencies. The current daily status unemployment rate rose between 1993–4 and 1999–2000 for rural males, rural females and urban males (urban females were the only exception), the rise for rural males being the steepest (29 per cent). If we use the more stringent concept of weekly-status unemployment (i.e. a person belonging to the workforce who did not work for even one hour on any of the seven days preceding the date of the survey), we again find a 40 per cent rise comparing 1993–4 and 1999–2000 for rural males, and a two-thirds rise for females. Between 1994 and 2000 there was a decline in the worker/population ratio for all categories. Taking both males and females, the decline was from 444 to 419 per thousand in rural India and from 347 to 337 per thousand in urban India. Taking both urban and rural India together, the decline was from 418 to 395 per thousand.

Many micro-studies have established the increasing casualization and feminization of the manufacturing and service sector workforce in the era of reforms (see Bose 1996; Ghosh 1999, 2001; Papola and Sharma 1999; Ramaswamy 1999). This is the outcome of a number of processes: large enterprises in the organized sector are subjected to male workforce retrenchment; output subcontracting to the informal sector increases, which uses female labour; and substantial job losses occur in traditional areas like hand-woven and power-loom woven textiles, where escalating costs under liberalization and reforms have forced closure and the desperate search for casual work by women.

Declining employment opportunities are reflected in the trend of the head count poverty ratio. The rural poverty ratio fell sharply until the end of the 1980s, after which the decline stopped and there was a sharp increase, as already noted, by 1992–3. There was again a slow fall as more expansionary policies were followed, but poverty incidence still remained much higher in 1998 than in 1987–8 (see Table 4). The decline in urban poverty, which again was quite sharp in the 1980s, has continued into the 1990s, though at a lower rate. Taking rural and urban India together, the 'reform and liberalization' years have been bad for poverty, and especially so for rural poverty.

Table 7. Per capita annual net output and availability of food grains for human consumption, 1989–90 to 2000–2001 (in kg)

	Per capita net output (kg)			*Average population (m)*	*Per capita net availability (kg)*		
	Cereals	*Pulses*	*Food grains*		*Cereals*	*Pulses*	*Food grains*
1989–90 to 1991–2	159.9	14.4	174.3	850.7	159.3	14.2	173.5
1992–3 to 1994–5	162.2	14.0	176.2	901.02	156.5	13.6	169.7
1995–6 to 1997–8	157.3	13.0	170.3	950.07	156.6	12.7	170.4
1998–9 to 2000–01	157.6	12.1	169.7	1008.14	147.3	11.8	157.2

Source: Basic output, trade and stocks data from Reserve Bank of India, *Reports on Currency and Finance*, (1995–6, 1998–9) and Govt. of India, *Economic Survey* (1999–2000, 2000–2001). The 1991 and 2001 Population Census estimates give a population growth rate of 1.89%, which has been applied to obtain the population for inter-Censal years. These estimates are compared with pre-Independence levels in Patnaik (2001).

Note: Net output is defined in official data sources as gross output minus one-eighth on account of seed, feed and wastage. Additionally, we have deducted estimated commercial feed demand for cereals, taking the estimate corresponding to the median growth rate in Bhalla et al. (1999). Availability is net output plus net imports minus addition to government stocks.

Cropping Pattern Shifts, Price Volatility and Suicides

A substantial shift in the cropping pattern occurred as trade was liberalized. Seven million hectares of food-crop land was diverted to export crops by the mid-1990s, during which primary export growth was high. The main crops that saw an area expansion or export thrust were cotton, soyabeans, sugarcane, horticulture and floriculture, and prawn fisheries, which displaced paddy production in some coastal areas. As global recession took hold, the primary export thrust tended to peter out and some land has reverted back to food crops, but with exports picking up again the net displacement by 2001–2 was eight million hectares compared to 1990–1, amounting to 6.3 per cent of the initial food-grains area and 22 per cent of the initial non-food-grains area. The cropping pattern shifts in India have been analysed in detail elsewhere (Patnaik 2001). We have long pointed out that an inverse relation exists in *all* developing countries between primary export thrust and domestic food availability, because the export thrust takes place in a contractionary milieu of *investment cuts* in agriculture. Thus, the required degree of productivity rise does not take place for sustaining both larger exports as well as maintaining domestic food availability. Just as had occurred historically under completely trade-liberalized colonial systems, in the present era of liberalization the primary export thrust is also at the expense of declining nutrition levels for the mass of the population. This is a strong and categorical argument, which has been developed elsewhere, and the evidence will not be repeated; the interested reader is referred to these previous papers (Patnaik 1996, 2002b).

The per capita annual net food-grains output for human consumption has fallen by 4.6 kg comparing beginning and end of the decade, but net annual availability has fallen by a record 16.4 kg per head, owing to the massive build-up of stocks, reflecting the deflation in mass purchasing power (Table 7). The risk factor for farmers has increased greatly with the new export orientation, since international prices are notoriously volatile and, with a short-term global price rise, unsustainable credit-financed expansion of a cash crop, glut and price crash takes place, aided and abetted by export agents.

The story of cotton and crisis encapsulates the problems with unregulated primary export thrust and is worth a brief retelling. *The fastest growing individual crop, displacing food grains, was raw cotton, which had seen a violent export thrust from 1990 onwards.* Thus exports jumped from an annual average of 35,000 tonnes during the four years before 1990–1 to more than ten times this amount at 374,000 tonnes in that year and, while fluctuating, maintained a high average of 200,000 tonnes in the next three years. Owing to this sudden jump in exports, there was a domestic raw cotton famine, open market yarn price trebled, and many thousands of handloom and power-loom weavers were badly hit; the former were forced to take consumption cuts and the latter lost jobs as smaller enterprises closed down. Indian cotton yarn using the domestic raw material remained internationally competitive, and the quantum index of yarn exports grew sixfold between 1990 and 1998.

The problem was further compounded in a particular state, Andhra Pradesh, whose government has entered into a state-level Structural Adjustment Programme under the advice of the World Bank. Under this, in order to reach 'market rates' for power, the power tariff has been hiked fivefold, driving textile producers to the wall. In the handloom centre of Sircilla in Andhra Pradesh, dozens of weavers, unable to feed their families any longer, have been committing suicide. Most suicides are males, but in a few cases entire families facing starvation have killed themselves. These cases are too recent to have been studied by academics; investigative journalists' reports are available (e.g. *Frontline* 27 April 2001). Other indicators of distress, highlighted by NGOs working in the area, are an increase in the sale of children to adoptive agencies (especially from the tribal communities) and an increased incidence of prostitution by women as normal sources of incomes dry up.

If it is ruining textile weavers, did the raw cotton export boom at least benefit the farmers growing the crop? The spate of suicides of cotton farmers in Andhra Pradesh, northern Karnataka and in hitherto prosperous Punjab since 1998 provides the answer. Over 1000 farmers, swamped by mounting debt, have committed suicide – usually by ingesting pesticides – and in Andhra Pradesh alone the numbers exceed 600 according to official estimates, while the actual figures are many more (Table 8 details the statistics for Andhra Pradesh).

The risk of producing a commercial crop, which is borne entirely by the grower, is greatly increased when the crop is grown for export, which induces price volatility. The Indian farmer is highly price-responsive and has been since colonial times. As the world cotton price improved in the early 1990s and un-regulated exports were permitted many hundreds of thousands of small farmers, hoping to improve their economic position, rapidly expanded the area sown to cotton by diverting it from millets, taking large cash advances from traders and commission agents and loans from banks to meet the extra seed and input costs on 1.5 million hectares of rain-fed land, mainly in Andhra Pradesh and Maharashtra. The squeeze on lower-cost bank and cooperative credit, caused by the economic reform policies, meant greater reliance on higher cost private credit. Both dealers in uncertified seed and in sub-standard pesticides have a field day under such boom conditions of rapid area expansion with no state supervision, as everything is left to the allegedly 'efficient' market.

The trinity of commission agent/moneylender/fly-by-night pesticide dealers and seed-suppliers all had a role to play in the debacle, as farmers purchased uncertified seed, spent large sums of borrowed money applying sub-standard pesticides to their pest-affected crop on the advice of the pesticide dealers, but often could not save the crop. Had they grown their traditional drought- and pest-resistant local *jowar* (sorghum) and *ragi* (finger millet), they would have had something to eat. With reliance on cotton, they had neither anything to eat nor any prospect of clearing the large debts already incurred, because globally cotton prices started declining from 1995 and by now are at less than half the previous level (Table 3). Hundreds of hopelessly indebted farmers have been driven to the extreme step of ending their lives, leaving their families to face a harsh neo-liberal world.

A small sample survey of 30 families of suicides, carried out in two *mandalas* or administrative divisions (Venkateswarlu 1998), found that 73.4 per cent of the cases reported debt and another 16.7 per cent reported family tensions as the cause of suicide. In only one case was the suicide a woman who ran her own farm, while the remaining 29 were men. It also found that a large number of farmers had switched from food crops and were growing cotton for the first time, and applied inputs mainly with the advice of pesticide suppliers.

For every suicide, there are thousands of farmers enmeshed in escalating debt owing to the shift to a fickle export crop from hardy local food grains. Other farmers have been selling bodily vital organs: a kidney fetched Rs. 40,000 in 1998, but the price has declined as agrarian distress intensifies. After the illegal operation, for which farmers are taken by touts working for the large private super-speciality hospitals, they are unable to do a full day's work. In families which had been sufficiently viable earlier for the women not to work for wages, women reported seeking wage-paid work, any work at all, including stone-breaking, which involves hard physical labour, to make ends meet (oral evidence of farmers at a tribunal in Bangalore, September 2000). Such a crisis of mounting indebtedness and despair is unprecedented in independent India and it is the direct result of trade liberalization, exposure to global volatility and resulting

Table 8. Suicides of farmers in Andhra Pradesh – District-wise numbers, 27 January 2002

Sl. No.	District	1998	1999	2000	2001	2002	Total
1.	Warangal	77	7	7	28	1	120
2.	Ananthapoor	1	1	50	50	10	112
3.	Mahaboob Nagar	14	2	25	10	–	51
4.	Karim Nagar	31	10	6	30	3	80
5.	Guntur	32	10	1	6	–	49
6.	Khammam	20	5	3	6	2	36
7.	Medak	15	3	2	8	–	28
8.	Adilabad	9	8	5	13	–	35
9.	Nalgonda	5	1	10	11	8	35
10.	Nizamabad	9	1	–	11	–	21
11.	Ranga Reddy	5	–	3	6	–	14
12.	Kurnool	4	4	2	4	–	14
13.	Chittoor	3	–	–	2	–	5
14.	Krishna	4	1	1	3	1	10
15.	Prakasham	1	3	–	2	–	6
16.	West Godavari	1	–	–	5	–	6
17.	East Godavari	–	–	1	2	–	3
18.	Sreekakulam	–	1	–	–	–	1
19.	Cuddapah	–	–	–	4	–	4
20.	Visaka Patnam	–	–	–	1	–	1
	Unknown	2	1	–	–	–	3
	Total	233	58	116	202	25	634

Source: Table supplied by Kisan Sabha (Peasant Union) at symposium on farmer suicides, held at Hyderabad, Andhra Pradesh, on 3 February 2002 and attended by the author.

price crashes. The state government has taken a cynical decision a year ago to stop making any *ex gratia* payments to families of farmers committing suicide, as it had initially done, on the grounds that it 'encouraged' suicide. The maximum number of suicides in recent years have taken place after this decision.

The plight of cotton growers has been quickly exploited by TNCs like Monsanto, which has carried out trials of its genetically modified BT Cotton in India and is attempting to carve out a market for it by claiming that the farmer will never face attacks of pests if they plant the expensive seed they exclusively supply.

The Social Irrationality of Mounting Grain Stocks and Increasing Hunger

At the time of writing, more than 65 million tonnes of food grains are lying in the government storehouses and are covered by tarpaulins in the open, while unemployment and hunger increases and starvation deaths take place, among tribal populations in particular. The stocks in excess of buffer norms are at least 40 million tonnes, and are likely to exceed this by mid-2002. The FCI (Food Corporation of India) is now refusing to procure from farmers because it has no storage capacity, leading to unprecedentedly low farm-gate prices. Paralyzed by the neo-liberal dogma that raising state expenditure is a sin, and bowing to IMF warnings that the fiscal deficit must be cut, the central government refuses to intervene to launch a massive food-for-work programme, as is being demanded by all thinking people of nearly every political persuasion within the country. This outcome in India today is driving home the irrationality and the sheer immorality of the agenda of globalization as nothing else could.

The coalition led by the BJP, which, cobbled together in 1998, precariously won the elections of 1999, doubled issue prices of food grains in order to cut food subsidy, and sales from ration shops dropped, while a continuation of a record run of good monsoons and procurement from farmers has led to a continuous build-up of stocks. In a decade when the food output growth rate has halved, and per head food production has fallen, the mountains of unsold food grains today stand testimony to the extent of cut in mass purchasing power brought about by the deflationary macroeconomic policies detailed earlier. In addition, the transition from a universal coverage system to targeting from 1997 onwards has worsened the situation considerably, because large numbers of those actually in poverty are not identified as such and are not issued ration cards, which would enable them to access cheaper grain.[5] Consequently, the per capita availability of food grains for human consumption has declined, since 1990–1, by a massive 16 kg to only 157 kg in the triennium centred on 1999–2000 (Table 7), which incidentally, is the same level that had prevailed 70 years ago, in the hungry 1930s (Blyn 1966). It is clear from Table 7 that four-fifths of the decline has taken place since targeting was introduced in 1997. Obviously, since the well-to-do have maintained their consumption, the decline must be even greater for the lowest deciles ranked by income. The government is again trying to export food grains, but can do so only by subsidizing exports, as the world price has crashed.

The Bretton Woods institutions have always pressed for *targeting the food subsidy* in every indebted country implementing neo-liberal economic reforms under their guidance. In abstract, it is difficult to oppose targeting because it sounds reasonable that subsidy should be concentrated on the poor. Why then have the targeted schemes usually misfired? The reason, we believe, is bad faith: international lending institutions arguing for targeting and their domestic adherents are theoretically committed to the free market, to the idea of no state intervention at all in the food economy, to winding up the existing PDS completely

---

[5] The criteria used for identifying households as 'below the poverty line' (BPL) and entitled to subsidized grain are arbitrary, leading to large errors of wrong exclusion of the poor (see Swaminathan 2002, for an excellent discussion). In India's largest slum, Dharavi, with a population of half a million persons, only 151 BPL cards had been issued in 1997.

sooner or later. What they therefore want initially is a *change* in the earlier universal access system, because change is the first step, the thin end of the wedge, with which the state's role in the food economy can be levered out completely within a few years. This has happened already in a number of countries like Sri Lanka and the Philippines, whose functioning systems of grain procurement and distribution have been destroyed.

Once the principle of change is accepted, however, more things change than only the beneficiary group: the consumer subsidy itself is drastically cut, reducing the entitlement of the poor compared to what it was under the earlier universal system. In 1997, in India, in the name of better targeting, an absurd principle of calculating grain requirements for the PDS was introduced, by taking the average of the past ten years of actual sales of grains from the fair-price shops. A decade ago the population requiring ration grains was smaller by 160 million people. The actual off-take during five years out of the ten (1991–6) had been reduced by excessively raising the grain price and pricing out the poor from the ration shops even while a strongly contractionary fiscal policy stance was being implemented, to the extent that the crude death rate, as well as the infant mortality rate, had actually risen in a number of regions in 1992. The only possible objective of the dishonest principle of taking the past 10 years' abnormally low average off-take was evidently to reduce the food subsidy further. Under the new scheme, the grain allocation in 1997 from the central pool to the PDS of the poorest state in India, viz. Orissa, was reduced in the case of rice from over 100,000 tonnes to hardly a third of that level, 34,000 tonnes, and in the case of wheat it was reduced from 50,000 tonnes to zero!

A great deal of public noise is made about the 'large' and 'unsustainable' food subsidy by the BWI and the domestic Finance Ministry – which is packed with ex-BWI employees. Yet the total central food subsidy for a country and population the size of India is minute – at present about US$2.5 billion, or only 0.5 per cent of the nation's income, which is being transferred to benefit many millions of the poor. We may evaluate the size of India's food subsidy against the fact that over seven times as much, 38 per cent of the entire revenue expenditures in India (nearly 4 per cent of GDP), is given as *interest payments* every year to the tiny minority of the well-to-do in the country from whom the government has preferred in the past to raise money in the politically easy form of borrowed funds, rather than as taxes.[6]

---

[6]   In the 1997 Budget, lower income tax rates gifted away more than twice as much as the food subsidy bill, or an estimated 120,000 million rupees (US$3000 million) to the income-tax payers in the country who number only 12 million, the top 1.2 per cent of the population. There are only eight other countries out of 80 reporting countries in the world that, in 1996, taxed less than India, which ranked ninth from the bottom in the lowness of its central tax to GDP ratio of only 10.3 per cent (World Development Report 1998–9. Data for central tax/GDP but not total tax/GDP across countries are available in this annual publication of the World Bank). By 2001 the central tax /GDP ratio has fallen further to 8.5 per cent and the total tax/GDP ratio has also declined. If the present course of belligerent armament continues unchecked, the already low funding for the social sectors and for poverty alleviation will be further reduced in *de facto* terms.

Public-interest litigation has been initiated on behalf of the starving poor by progressive groups demanding the right to food: the Supreme Court has directed the government in November 2001 to distribute the excess food stocks (excess over buffer norms) of 40 million tonnes in order to alleviate hunger. For a long-term restoration of badly eroded purchasing power, it is essential to follow boldly expansionary policies, which the existing excess food stocks would permit without any inflationary pressures. As has been repeatedly and correctly argued by a number of economists in India, a large-scale investment and employment-generating effort in rural areas in the form of food-for-work is required, directed towards building up productive assets which will enhance growth (of which irrigation, soil conservation and afforestation are the most important). The matter has been discussed in detail in Patnaik (2000), who concludes that: 'To argue against the mitigation to human suffering that an increased fiscal deficit can provide is therefore bad theory, the sheer "humbug of finance".'

Concrete proposals for countering industrial recession have been formulated, keeping in view rising unemployment and excess capacity combined with excess liquidity in the banking system. It is argued that at least Rs. 160 billion can be safely raised annually through bond issues to finance a programme of infrastructure development, namely railways, roads, irrigation and power (Shetty 2001). These proposals are in substance similar to the proposal for credit-financed public works in Britain and Germany during 1929–30, except that the huge food stocks and deepening agrarian distress in India make these proposals even more urgent, as well as more feasible in terms of implementation.

The die-hard deflationists of neo-liberal persuasion have immediately warned the government against any increase in expenditures for public works in villages, or indeed for any purpose at all, which according to them will increase the fiscal deficit (recalling exactly similar deflationism in Britain, Germany and the capitalist world in 1929–31). The cash component of a bold programme of employment generation and asset creation using food stocks would in fact pose no problems, as initially it will result in matching reduction in the costs of holding the stocks, and subsequently savings would be generated from rising incomes as employment rises through the multiplier effects of expenditures. If such a programme could have been carried out after the 1987 drought, there is no reason why a much larger programme cannot be carried out now, given the more massive wage-goods stocks available.

It is socially irrational, and politically dangerous, to let grain rot while employment falls and more people go hungry. No amount of apologetics by way of academic arguments that Indians do not need as much food as others do, or – based on NSS consumption data – the argument that nothing is wrong on the nutrition front because the poor are 'diversifying' their diets away from cereals to animal products, is going to remove the fact that, according to the same data source, per capita *total* calorie intake has been falling in rural areas everywhere from levels that were already inadequate (except in two states, Kerala and West Bengal: Swaminathan 2000).

The government has so far, under pressure from the courts, taken only such small and hesitant steps with respect to food-for-work as will make little impact on the problem, especially given the barriers erected by the endless partitioning of the beneficiary population under many petty schemes. It seems to be completely paralyzed as regards any bold measures because its thinking appears to be locked in the iron vice of deflationary dogma based on the incorrect concept of a fixed savings pool.

The visiting BWI economists propagate and repeatedly reinforce these dogmas through their advice, ignoring all thought of mass welfare and solely in the narrow interest of finance capital. On a visit to India, the first Deputy MD of the International Monetary Fund, Anne Krueger, in a meeting with India's Finance Minister on 20 December 2001, is reported to have warned that 'India will have to address its deficit for fiscal sustainability because deficit financing is going to crowd out private investments'.[7] One can hardly ask for a clearer restatement of the fallacious, 70-year-old Treasury view that increasing public expenditure will reduce private investment. In the face of rising unemployment, mountainous food stocks and increasing hunger, the representatives of finance capital argue for caution and cuts in expenditure. Feasible and obvious measures for reducing unemployment and lifting the economy out of deepening recession are thereby prevented, much as the implementation of the fallacious Treasury view had prevented counter-depression measures in time. Moreover, it is one thing to propagate logically wrong arguments in 1929–30, when there was much genuine confusion; it is a different matter altogether to put forward these same arguments today, when the theory exposing the fallacy of deflationism, has been in every economics textbook for at least 50 years. It will be a tragedy a second time, and not a farce, if all the bitter lessons of past history and present developments are ignored, and 1931 is re-enacted.

STABILIZING LIVELIHOODS: BOTH MACROECONOMIC POLICY CHANGE AND DECENTRALIZED COMMUNITY INITIATIVES ARE REQUIRED

The story of economic reforms in India detailed so far can be replicated with variations for a large number of developing countries that have seen the adverse effects of deflationary policies, unregulated trade, social subsidy cuts and privatization of state-owned enterprises. The question arises, are there ways in which people can counter the attack on their livelihoods inherent in globalization? What are the policy measures that would be conducive to a stabilization of rural livelihoods, particularly when producers are exposed, without protection, to the volatility of global prices?

These are big questions, and we believe they have to be answered at the level of the macro-economy as well as at the level of the peoples' cooperative

---

[7]   Reported in *The Hindu* (21 December 2001, p. 16).

organization and community action for protecting and improving their livelihoods. The importance of overall macroeconomic policies arises from the fact
that the forces which are continuing to push for deflationary globalization are too
centralized and too ruthlessly pursued by powerful international organizations
acting concertedly to be tackled at a decentralized rural level alone. It is only state
action through public expenditure that can immediately revive mass demand on
a large scale. Therefore, it is imperative for the individuals and organizations
concerned with peoples' welfare to mount pressure on the nation state to undertake boldly expansionary policies to generate employment and incomes and to
finance such expansion, preferably not mainly through internal borrowing which
raises the future interest burden on the people, but mainly through taxation
of those who can afford to pay. But in the face of unemployed resources and
contracting effective demand, even credit-financed expenditure is infinitely preferable to inaction.

Both the need to raise the tax/GDP ratio and the need to launch a comprehensive food-for-work programme linked to creating rural assets, are measures that
the thinking public of almost every political persuasion agree upon in India
today, for example, whereas advocacy of these same policies by prescient critics
of reforms had found few takers in the early years of neo-liberal hegemony. The
change has come about because all initial wishful thinking and euphoria has
evaporated, and the people can now see before their eyes the socially irrational
outcomes of following these policies.

It is naïve to imagine that all attempts to alter the policies followed by national
states are completely hopeless, however much such states might appear to be
subordinated to the agenda of international finance capital today. Public opinion
and pressure expressed through the media and all the various fora open to civil
society does make a difference to governments, which exist and run ultimately
because of the peoples' mandate under democratic systems. Conversely, we see
governments in developing countries politically committed to implementing deflationary policies advised by the BWI, attempting to curtail the parliamentary
system, centralize political power and curb civil freedoms, because in the long
run these are incompatible with these deflationary policies, which harm the people.

The longer-run problems of rural livelihoods that existed before the inception
of the neo-liberal agenda have been aggravated acutely with the implementation
of this agenda. These relate to land distribution and to the control of land, water
and credit resources. There are systematic attempts in developing countries to
allow TNCs and local big business engaged in agro-business and the global food
chain to have access to agricultural and tribal land by altering the laws that
hitherto hindered such access. In India, for example, maximum limits or 'ceilings' on landholdings are sought to be raised and bans on non-farmers acquiring
land done away with under the pressure of agro-business corporations in a number
of states, and in some (Karnataka, Maharashtra) the laws already have been rolled
back. The retention of such laws becomes a site of struggle for the people. The
implementation of existing laws relating to security of tenure and redistribution
of land, wherever these exist, is very important and can make a great deal of

difference, even in situations where radical redistributive peasant-dominated land reforms on the model of post-War Japan, Korea or China may no longer be politically feasible. There have been substantial cuts in low-interest bank credit to rural areas under financial sector reforms, which raises the problem of supply of credit. We briefly discuss the experience of tenancy reform, revival of the *panchayat* system, land rights to women and credit supply in West Bengal, India as a case study of the possibilities of positive developments even in the era of globalization.

Elements of Stabilization of Rural Livelihoods: West Bengal

In May 2001, the people of this state, overwhelmingly so in the villages, voted back a Left Front government to power with an absolute majority, in the face of a determined united assault by all opposition parties, for a sixth term (possibly a world record), ensuring continuous rule by the same coalition since 1977, which will last at least until 2006. The reason they did so was because this is a state that, from experiencing a colonial state-made famine which killed over 3 million people in the Second World War and rendered millions destitute, is one which has achieved the highest rate of agricultural growth in general, and food-grains growth in particular, in the whole of India in the course of the 1980s, extending into the 1990s, and has the second highest rate of reduction in rural poverty. While in every other state the per capita cereal intake, as well as the per capita total calorie intake, has fallen in rural and in urban areas according to National Sample Survey data on consumption, in two states only – West Bengal and Kerala – both have risen in each sector, during 1977–93.

Independent academic analysts of the causes of the good performance of West Bengal under Left Front governance focus on the important institutional changes brought about by two complementary sets of policies: Operation Barga, which started in 1978, and the revival of the *Panchayat* (decentralized local government) system in the 1980s. *Barga* means 'share', and the *bargadar* was a small tenant sharecropper on an oral lease with no security of tenure. Such tenancy accounted for a third to two-fifths of the area under cultivation: the landowner-rentier had no incentive to invest because he got a high income without doing anything at all, amounting to 50–60 per cent of the crop, while the *bargadar* was squeezed dry and had nothing left to invest.

The importance of Operation Barga lay precisely in the fact that it gave owner-like security to the mass of poor tenants by recording them and making eviction difficult, and fixed fair limits to the share of crop payable as rent. There was no distribution of ownership to the tenant and the title remained with the landowner, who could freely transfer the land. But the tenants, after recording, acquired a legal existence and did not face the threat of arbitrary eviction as earlier; they could only be evicted if there was due cause (non-payment of rent etc.).

Implementation of fair rents (varying according to extent to which the landowner shared costs) meant that some income remained with the tenant to be used for shifting to a higher-value cropping pattern and for tube-well investment, helped by the spread of institutional credit. Doctoral research studies of the early 1990s have shown that in some 80 per cent of leases in the sampled villages the legal rental share was actually paid and in the remainder it was somewhat higher than the legal share, but considerably short of the half-share or more which was prevalent earlier. Without the effective revival of the institutions of democratized local government through regular elections to *panchayats* it would have been impossible to enforce legal shares in the villages.

The results with regard to production have been quite outstanding. From a situation of low growth up to 1980, West Bengal in the last 20 years has seen a steady spread of HYV-fertilizer use aided by shallow tube-well investment, over the rice areas cultivated by newly recorded and empowered tenants. An estimated 2.5 million of the formerly landless and land-poor have obtained 1.04 million acres of redistributed ceiling-surplus land, making up nearly a fifth of the all-India total (Mishra and Rawal 2002). Banks were directed to give priority to rural areas, and the rapid extension of institutional credit has financed input loans to poorer cultivators taking land on seasonal lease, enabling them to employ the new technology. Analysis of the output data show that for 18 years, starting in 1977–8 and ending in 1995–6, the growth of yields per acre of all crops has been maintained at an annual compound rate of 5 per cent, higher than anywhere else in India. The yield per acre growth for food grains has been even higher at 5.7 per cent annually and therefore, despite some fall in area, the food-grains output has been growing at 4.6 per cent annually, more than double the population growth rate, in sharp contrast to other states where per head output has been falling. This is not accidental: production and cropping-pattern decisions, where small producers are free to make them, will preserve food security to a greater extent than where large commercial farmers dominate. Yet non-food grains have not suffered and have grown at 4.7 per cent annually. Analysts have traced a major role for Operation Barga, combined with the spread of institutional credit and the dynamic role of the revived, democratized *panchayat* system (local self-government bodies) in unleashing the latent production potential of the rural economy (Sanyal et al. 1998).

There are case studies in West Bengal of landless persons who, after acquiring small pieces of redistributed ceiling-surplus land, decided to pool their efforts and cooperatively operate their land for growing vegetable and fruit crops for the local urban markets, with great success with respect to raising and stabilizing their incomes, to the extent where reliance on daily work on wages dropped to zero. Others engaged successfully in cooperative aquaculture. A permissive environment of encouragement from the democratized local bodies and easy access to credit helped this process. On the other hand, similar successful cooperative effort by large numbers of hitherto landless labourers in a Gujarat village to whom ceiling-surplus land was distributed, and who grew profitable *papaya* for local urban markets winning freedom from daily wage labour, invited the wrath of their former employers, high-caste Rajput landlords who, faced with labour shortages, razed the orchards and physically attacked the erstwhile labourers, while the local administration did nothing (this incident relates to 1991). Thus the question of an enabling environment and defence mechanisms provided by democratized local bodies becomes crucial for the preservation of the gains of such self-help efforts on the part of the disadvantaged.

In the past, the dimension of gender equality had not been explicitly addressed, but this has been remedied and Bengal now leads in implementing land rights of women. Registration of titles to redistributed land used to be in the name of the male of the family and an exception was only made for female-headed households. After representations by women's organizations on the gender discrimination involved, the decision was taken by government to issue land registration (*patta*) jointly (Gupta 2000). About 425,000 new redistributed land titles have been registered to date, either by giving joint *pattas* in the name of both spouses or solely in the name of women (Mishra and Rawal 2002). The principle of natural justice demands that women should enjoy the same legal rights as men, but it is not enough to amend the legal provisions alone to permit registration in the name of women heirs by bringing agricultural property in line with the provisions relating to urban property. The persistence of social attitudes determined by the centuries-old habits of gender discrimination in a patriarchal society imply that extra effort has to be put in by women's organizations and bodies of local administration to raise the level of informed consciousness regarding women's rights. There are many other areas where the performance of the state can be bettered, especially with regard to rural health care and education, where it is far behind Kerala.

CONCLUDING REMARKS

There is a new awareness that has emerged over the years, which sees the way forward in the cooperative effort of households and communities to conserve resources, improve productivity, empower women and educate children. Unregulated capitalist exploitation of bio-resources by big landlords, rich farmers and town contractors has produced a crisis for the rest of the village people through deforestation, the lack of firewood, falling subsoil water tables and acute scarcity of drinkable water (in India these features are most evident in states like Rajasthan, Gujarat, Maharashtra and Andhra Pradesh, where a large number of districts are now classified as 'drought-prone'). On this has been superimposed the additional factors of falling non-farm work as governments windup employment-generating programmes, and these income-deflating policies combined with export thrust lead to a progressive exclusion of the poor from access to basic food grains, detailed earlier as the direct and indirect result of neo-liberal reforms.

Albeit in an inchoate and unsystematic way, people affected by such crises are arriving through their own experience to much the same model of cooperative effort which over 40 years ago allowed the poverty-stricken villagers in China to lift themselves out of the slough, invest jointly in water and land conservation, build up basic health care and primary education facilities and begin to address gender inequalities. In India by now there are a fair number of highly successful village-level examples of joint community effort to invest especially in drought-proofing and integrated watershed management, afforestation, aquaculture and diversifying activities within a voluntary cooperative framework, thereby preserving livelihoods and giving enough income and manoeuvrability to hitherto poor households to allow them to remain in the villages rather than migrate seasonally to cities, and to allow their children to go to school rather than work to support themselves. This, we believe, is also the way forward in most third world developing countries. It will not be easy where local government institutions have not been democratized and where state support is lacking; this way often encounters resistance because better incomes and empowerment of the disadvantaged may be seen as a real threat to their domination by local landed employers. Where there is at least a minimal level of state support and activism against deflationary globalization, however, it can be generalized to a relatively successful stabilization of livelihoods.

REFERENCES

Bagchi, A.K., 1972. *Private Investment in India*. Cambridge: Cambridge University Press.

Baker, D., G. Epstein and R. Pollin, eds, 1998. *Globalization and Progressive Economic Policy*. Cambridge: Cambridge University Press.

Banister, J., 1987. *China's Changing Population*. Stanford: Stanford University Press.

Bhalla, G.S., P. Hazell and J. Kerr, 1999. *Prospects for India's Cereal Supply and Demand to 2020*. Discussion Paper 29. Washington, DC: International Food Policy Research Institute.

Bhalla, S., 1996. 'Workforce Restructuring, Wages and Want: Recent Events, Interpretations and Reanalysis'. Presidential Address to the 37th Annual Conference of The Indian Society of Labour Economics. *Indian Journal of Labour Economics*, 39 (1): 1–22.

Bhalla, S., 1997. 'The Rise and Fall of Workforce Diversification Processes in Rural India'. DSA Working Paper, 12 August. Centre for Economic Studies and Planning, Jawaharlal Nehru University.

Blyn, G., 1966. *Agricultural Trends in India 1891–1947: Output, Area and Productivity*. Philadelphia: University of Philadelphia Press.

Bose, A.J.C., 1996. 'Subcontracting, Industrialisation and Labouring Conditions in India: An Appraisal'. *Indian Journal of Labour Economics*, 39 (1): 145–62.

Chandrasekhar, C.P. and J. Ghosh, 2001, 'Rural Employment in the 1990s'. Available at www.macroscan.org

Coale, A.J., 1984. *Rapid Population Change in China 1952–1982*. Washington, DC: National Academy Press.

Cornia, G.A., 1987. 'Economic Decline and Human Welfare in the First Half of the Eighties' and 'Adjustment Policies 1980–85'. In *Adjustment with a Human Face Vol. 1*, eds G.A. Cornia, R. Jolly and F. Stewart, 9–47 and 50–72. Oxford: Clarendon Press.

Datt, G., 1999. 'Has Poverty Declined Since Economic Reforms? Statistical Data Analysis'. *Economic and Political Weekly*, 34 (5): 3516–18.

FAO (Food and Agriculture Organization), 1996. *Food Balance Sheets 1992–94*. Rome: FAO.

Frontline, 2001. 'Despair and Death'. *Frontline* 27 April 5–24, Chennai.

Ghosh, J., 1999. 'Macroeconomic Trends and Female Employment: India in the Asian Context'. In *Gender and Employment in India*, eds T.S. Papola and Alakh N. Sharma, 318–50. New Delhi: Vikas Publishing House.

Ghosh, J., 2001. 'Urban Indian Women in Informal Employment: Macro Trends in the 1990s'. In *Informal Sector in India: Problems and Policies*, eds A. Kundu and A.N. Sharma, 301–10. New Delhi: Institute for Human Development.

Government of India, 1999–2000; 2000–2001. *Economic Survey*, Annual publication of Economic Division, Ministry of Finance, Delhi: Government of Inida.

Grabowski, R., 1985. 'A Historical Reassessment of Early Japanese Development'. *Development and Change*, 16 (2): 235–50.

Gupta, J., 2000. 'Women, Land and Law: Dispute Resolution at the Village Level'. Occasional Paper 3. Calcutta: Sachetana Information Centre.

Gupta, S.P., 1994. 'Recent Economic Reforms and their Impact on the Poor and Vulnerable Sections of Society'. Paper presented to IDPAD Seminar on 'Structural Adjustment and Poverty in India', The Hague, November.

Gupta, S.P., 1999. 'Trickle-down Theory Revisited: The Role of Employment and Poverty'. V.B. Singh Memorial Lecture, Indian Society of Labour Economics, 18–20 November.

Halevy, J. and Jean-Marc Fontaine, eds, 1998. *Restoring Demand in the World Economy*. Cheltenham: Edward Elgar.

Hinton, W., 1968. *Fanshen*. New York: Vintage Books, Random House.

Hochin Choi, 1988. *The Economic History of Korea, Part Six – The Collapse of Feudalistic Society – The Period of Japanese Colonialism*. Seoul: Sekyungsa.

van der Hoeven, R., 1994. 'Structural Adjustment, Poverty and Macroeconomic Policy'. Paper read at international seminar on Structural Adjustment and Poverty in India, The Hague, November. Stated as due to be published in *The Poverty Agenda – Trends and Policy Options*, eds G. Rodgers and R. van der Hoeven. Geneva: IILS, 1995.

Ingersen, K.A., A.J. Rayner and R.C. Hine, eds, 1994. *Agriculture in the Uruguay Round*. London: St Martin's Press.

Kahn, R.F., 1931. 'The Relation of Home Investment to Employment'. *Economic Journal*, 41 (2): 193–8.

Keynes, J.M. and H.D. Henderson, 1929. *Can Lloyd George Do It?* London: The Nation and Athenaeum.

Kindleberger, C.P., 1987. *The World in Depression 1929–1939*. London: Pelican Books.

Lippitt, V., 1987. *The Economic Development of China*. Armonk, NY: M.E. Sharpe.

Mishra, S.K. and V. Rawal, 2002. 'Agrarian Relations in Contemporary West Bengal and Tasks for the Left'. In *Agrarian Studies: Essays on Agrarian Relations in Less-Developed Countries*, eds V.K. Ramachandran and M. Swaminathan, 329–55. Delhi: Tulika.

Mohan Rao, J. and Servaas Storm, 2002 (forthcoming). 'Agricultural Globalization in Developing Countries: Rules, Rationales and Results'. In *Globalization, Structural Change and Income Distribution*, eds C.P. Chandrasekhar and J. Ghosh. Delhi: Tulika.

Monthly Review, 1999, 'Capitalism at the End of the Millennium – A Global Survey', *Monthly Review*, 51 (3), July–August.

Nakamura, T., 1981. *The Post War Japanese Economy – Trends and Structure*. Tokyo: University of Tokyo Press.

Nickum, J.E., 1974. *A Collective Approach to Water Resource Development – the Chinese Commune System 1962–1972*. Ph.D. thesis, University of California, Berkeley.

Norman, E.H., 1940. *Japan's Emergence as a Modern State. Political and Economic Problems of the Meiji Period*. New York: Institute of Pacific Relations. Reprinted in John W. Dower, ed., 1975, *Origins of the Modern Japanese State – Selected Writings of E H Norman*, 110–316. New York: Pantheon Books. Republished in 2000 with accompanying essays on Norman's work, as *Japan's Emergence as a Modern State. 60th Anniversary Edition. Political and Economic Problems of the Meiji Period*. Vancouver: University of British Columbia Press.

OECD, 1998. *Agricultural Policies in OECD Countries – I. Monitoring and Evaluation. II. Measurement of Support and Background Information*. (2 volumes). Organization for Economic Cooperation and Development: Paris.

OECD, 2000. *Agricultural Policies in OECD Countries – Monitoring and Evaluation*. (Parts I–III) Organization for Economic Cooperation and Development: Paris.

Papola, T.S. and A.N. Sharma, eds, 1999. *Gender and Employment in India*. New Delhi: Vikas Publishing House.

Patnaik, P., 1999a. 'Capitalism in Asia at the End of the Millennium'. *Monthly Review*, 51 (3): 53–70.

Patnaik, P., 1999b. 'On the Pitfalls of Bourgeois Internationalism'. In *The Political Economy of Imperialism – Critical Appraisals*, ed. R.M. Chilcote, 169–80. Massachusetts: Kluwer Academic.

Patnaik, P., 2000. 'The Humbug of Finance'. *Chintan Memorial Lecture*, delivered on January 8, at Chennai, India. Available at www.macroscan.org

Patnaik, P. and C.P. Chandrasekhar, 1995. 'The Indian Economy under Structural Adjustment'. *Economic and Political Weekly*, 30 (47): 3001–13.

Patnaik, U., 1991. 'Food Availability and Famine – A Longer View'. *Journal of Peasant Studies*, 19 (1): 1–25. Reprinted in Patnaik U., 1999. *The Long Transition – Essays on Political Economy*, 323–50. Delhi: Tulika.

Patnaik, U., 1996. 'Export Oriented Agriculture and Food Security in Developing Countries and in India'. *Economic and Political Weekly*, 31 (35–37): 2429–49. Reprinted in Patnaik, U., 1999. *The Long Transition – Essays on Political Economy*, 351–416. Delhi: Tulika.

Patnaik, U., 2001. 'Food and Land Use: Sustainable Development in India in the Context of Global Consumption Demands'. Paper read at Symposium on Population, Life Support and Human Development, Indian Institute of Management, Kolkata, 5–6 February.

Patnaik, U., 2002a. 'Deflation and Déjà Vu'. In *Agrarian Studies – Essays on Agrarian Relations in Less Developed Countries*, eds V.K. Ramachandran and M. Swaminathan, 111–43. Delhi: Tulika.

Patnaik, U., 2002b (forthcoming). 'On the Inverse Relation between Primary Exports and Domestic Food Absorption under Liberalized Trade Regimes'. In *Globalization, Structural Change and Income Distribution*, eds C.P. Chandrasekhar and J. Ghosh. Delhi: Tulika.

Patnaik, U., 2002c. 'On Famine and Measuring Famine Deaths'. In *Thinking Social Science in India – Essays in Honour of Alice Thorner*, eds S. Patel, J. Bagchi and Krishna Raj, 46–68. Delhi: Sage.

Penrose, E., 1940. 'Rice Culture in the Japanese Economy'. In *The Industrialization of Japan and Manchukuo*, ed. E.B. Schumpeter, 131–53. New York: Macmillan.

Pinstrup-Andersen, P., M. Jaramillo and F. Stewart, 1987. 'The Impact on Government Expenditure'. In *Adjustment with a Human Face Vol. 1*, eds G.A. Cornia, R. Jolly and F. Stewart, 73–89. Oxford: Clarendon Press.

Ramaswamy, K.V., 1999. 'The Search for Flexibility in Indian Manufacturing: New Evidence on Outsourcing Activities'. *Economic and Political Weekly*, 34 (6): 363–8.

Ravallion, M. and G. Datt, 1996. 'India's Checkered History in the Fight against Poverty: Are There Lessons for the Future?'. *Economic and Political Weekly*, 31 (35–37): 2479–85.

Reserve Bank of India, 1995–6; 1998–9. *Report on Currency and Finance.* Mumbai Reserve Bank of India

Robinson, J.V., 1962. *Economic Philosophy.* London: C. A. Watts & Co.

Sanyal, M.K., P.K. Biswas and S. Bardhan, 1998. 'Institutional Change and Output Growth in West Bengal Agriculture'. *Economic and Political Weekly*, 38 (47–48): 2979–86.

Sen, A., 1996. 'Economic Reforms, Employment and Poverty: Trends and Options'. *Economic and Political Weekly*, 31 (35–37): 2459–77.

Sen, A., 2000. 'Consumer Spending and its Distribution – Statistical Priorities after 55th Round'. *Economic and Political Weekly*, 35 (51): 16–22.

Sen, A. and U. Patnaik, 1997. 'Poverty in India'. Working Paper, Centre for Economic Studies and Planning, Jawaharlal Nehru University; also presented as country study on India in International Workshop on Poverty, UNDP, New York, 21 September 1997.

Shetty, S.L., 2001. 'Reviving the Economy – Some Explorations'. *Economic and Political Weekly*, 36 (30): 2824–30.

Sundaram, K. and S. Tendulkar, 2000. 'Poverty in India: An Assessment and Analysis'. Mimeo. Delhi School of Economics.

Swaminathan, M., 2000. *Weakening Welfare – the Public Distribution of Food in India.* Delhi: Leftword.

Swaminathan, M., 2002. 'Excluding the Needy: the Public Provisioning of Food in India'. *Social Scientist*, 30 (3–4), 34–58.

Tendulkar, S.D. and L.R. Jain, 1995. 'Economic Reforms and Poverty'. *Economic and Political Weekly*, 30 (23): 1373–7.

Thavaraj, M.J.K., 1960. 'Capital Formation in the Public Sector in India: A Historical Study 1898–1938'. In *Papers on National Income and Allied Topics*, Vol. 1, eds V.K.R.V. Rao et al., 215–30. London: Asia Publishing House.

Thorner, Alice, ed., 2002. *Land, Labour and Rights.* Delhi: Tulika.

Timoshenko, V.P., 1953. *World Agriculture and the Depression.* Ann Arbor: University of Michigan Press.

Triantis, S.G., 1967. *Cyclical Changes in Trade Balances of Countries Exporting Primary Products.* Toronto: University of Toronto Press.

UNDP (United Nations Development Programme), 1992. *African Development Indicators.* Washington, DC: World Bank.

UNDP (United Nations Development Programme), 1998. *Overcoming Human Poverty.* New York: UNDP Poverty Report.

Venkateswarlu, D., 1998. *Cotton Farmers' Suicides in Andhra Pradesh.* Mimeo: A study commissioned by BASIX, Hyderabad. E-mail: basix@hd1.vsnl.net.in

World Bank, 1997. *India – Achievements and Challenges in Reducing Poverty.* Report No. 16483-IN, May. Washington, DC: World Bank.

3

Policy Discourses on Women's Land Rights in Sub-Saharan Africa: The Implications of the Re-turn to the Customary

ANN WHITEHEAD AND DZODZI TSIKATA

This article examines some contemporary policy discourses on land tenure reform in sub-Saharan Africa and their implications for women's interests in land. It demonstrates an emerging consensus among a range of influential policy institutions, lawyers and academics about the potential of so-called customary systems of land tenure to meet the needs of all land users and claimants. This consensus, which has arisen out of critiques of past attempts at land titling and registration, particularly in Kenya, is rooted in moderniz-ing discourses and/or evolutionary theories of land tenure and embraces par-ticular and contested understandings of customary law and legal pluralism. It has also fed into a wide-ranging critique of the failures of the post-colonial state in Africa, which has been important in the current retreat of the state under structural adjustment programmes. African women lawyers, a minority dissenting voice, are much more equivocal about trusting the customary, pre-ferring instead to look to the State for laws to protect women's interests. We agree that there are considerable problems with so-called customary systems of land tenure and administration for achieving gender justice with respect to women's land claims. Insufficient attention is being paid to power relations in the countryside and their implications for social groups, such as women, who are not well positioned and represented in local level power structures. But considerable changes to political and legal practices and cultures will be needed before African states can begin to deliver gender justice with respect to land.

Keywords: land tenure reform, women's land interests, customary law, legal pluralism, Africa

INTRODUCTION

This paper examines the content of some contemporary policy discourses about land tenure reform in sub-Saharan Africa, in general and specifically as it relates

The research on which this paper is based was part of the UNRISD project on Agrarian Change, Gender and Land Rights.

This paper has benefited from discussions with many people, including Jo Beall, Yao Graham, Elizabeth Harrison, Ambreena Manji, Marjorie Mbilinyi, Shahra Razavi, Alex Shankland, Camilla Toulmin, Gavin Williams and Ingrid Yngstrom. Many thanks to them for their comments and to Iman Hashim, Kirsty Millward, Dinah Rajek and Stephen Whitehead for assistance.

to women's interests in land. We identify a developing debate about the potential of so-called customary systems of land tenure to meet the needs of all land users and claimants of land use rights and go on to examine the implications of this return to the customary for achieving gender justice with respect to land. Local populations all over Africa are being affected by pressure on land resources. In most cases this represents a historical shift from relative land abundance to relative land scarcity, a change that has occurred, or is occurring, throughout the sub-continent. Although there are still some rural regions where suitable land is not all under agricultural use, these tend to be areas poorly served by markets and where the commercialization of agriculture is low. African countries differ widely with respect to contemporary levels of land scarcity. In the context of an absolute rise in total populations, the severity of land scarcity depends on a country's particular experiences of the colonial appropriation of land, of the commercial development of agriculture and the nature and degree of urbanization. This paper is heavily weighted towards British post-colonial states and confines itself to rural land issues. Many regions are experiencing growing conflicts between land users and they, together with national and international policy makers, are increasingly concerned with growing land access problems and land conflicts all over the continent. A burgeoning policy debate about land tenure issues – described by Quan as reforms 'which change tenurial relations between land owners and land users without necessarily altering land distribution' (Quan 1997, 1) – is evident. Recent land tenure reform has been undertaken, or is underway, in a number of countries, including Tanzania, Uganda, Malawi, Cote d'Ivoire, Niger, Ghana and Zimbabwe, and international donors have been heavily involved in the design of these reforms. In many countries, government proposals have sparked off considerable NGO and civil society activity about land issues, which has been picked up and commented upon by international NGOs. In some cases land is an important focus for radical and democratizing struggles, as land scarcity bites and land conflicts take on an international character, as for example throughout the 1990s when land was annexed for tourist enterprises and extraction.

An important minority voice in these national debates are African feminists and women's advocates and international gender and development experts and advocates, who have long sought to promote better and more secure land access for rural African women. Most rural African women play a substantial part in primary agricultural production, making the complex of local norms, customary practices, statutory instruments and laws that affect their access to and interests in land very significant (not only to them, their dependants and their male relatives, but also arguably to levels of agricultural production). Although there are discernible common features, local level empirical studies demonstrate great diversity and complexity in women's land interests and in the factors affecting these. In addition, norms and practices about women's land access, as well as who gets land, how much and from whom, are not static but have changed and are changing over time. Our primary concern is not with this level of analysis, although as a setting for our discussion, the next section considers, through a gender lens, some of the main features of rural land access and use. After this, the policy discourses of some of the main protagonists in current debates about tenure reform are then explored. We consider first, the World Bank and discuss documents from its Land Policy Division and from several of its gender specialists and second, OXFAM Great Britain (OXFAM GB) and International Institute for Environment and Development (IIED), as two UK-based organizations that have been very active for a number of years on land policy issues. Third, we consider the approaches and discourses of African and Africanist feminist legal specialists. Throughout these accounts, we highlight and explore historical shifts in thinking and the evidential and theoretical, as well as political and ideological, factors affecting these shifts. These sections demonstrate a developing consensus amongst the non-gender specialists towards encouraging the evolution of customary practices to deal with conflict and disputes over land access. Gender specialists are divided. Some argue that a reformed and strengthened customary law is in women's interests, but the majority reject this and instead argue for women's land and property rights to be enshrined in statutory law. In the final section of the paper, we examine the idea of reforming and building on customary law from the perspective of gender justice, outlining some important problems that we think the return to customary law will pose for contemporary African rural women.

AFRICAN LAND ACCESS AND USE: A GENDERED DISCUSSION

The scholarship on land issues in sub-Saharan Africa is both deep and wide, with developed and sophisticated literatures from several disciplinary perspectives and a large policy literature.[1] None of these can be read simply or innocently. They diagnose and describe circumstances of profound and complex change, on the basis of empirical evidence that has been produced out of the negotiations between actors with widely different access to the political, economic and technical resources required to record history. Most of the historical evidence about the local level was collected after rural localities had been affected by colonialism, as had the research and official communities that played a large part on the production of the written records. The recent writings of anthropologists and historians have emphasized the ways in which the perspectives, concepts and meanings attached to African forms of land tenure arise as much from the framework of colonial history and the forms of evidence this produced, as from the nature of land holding itself. These kinds of nuances are rarely found in the policy-focused writings of land tenure experts. As a result many implicit and explicit contestations over meaning run through the literatures.

---

[1] Basset and Crummey (1993), Berry (1992, 1993), Bruce and Migot-Adholla (1994), Chanock (1991b), Deininger and Binswanger (1999), Downs and Reyna (1988), Falk-Moore (1998), Feder and Feeny (1991), IIED (1999), McAuslan (1996), Mackenzie (1998), Migot-Adholla et al. (1991), Okoth-Ogendo (1989, 1998), Platteau (1996), Shipton and Goheen (1992), Toulmin and Quan (2000a).

'Individual' Land Access and Kenya's Experience of Registered Individual Titles

Today, most rural areas of the subcontinent have active land markets, although it is important to distinguish between formal market transactions, where titled land is bought and sold, and other kinds of informal transaction, which form the bulk of land transfers. All the sources agree that the growth of land markets has not and does not require formalized property rights and they also document the multiple, though often limited, forms of local land markets (Reyna 1987; Shipton 1988; Bruce and Migot-Adholla 1994; Heck 1996; Platteau 1996; Toulmin and Quan 2000a). Informal transactions can include a wide variety of loans, leases, sharecropping contracts, exchanges and pledges, while in some places, forms of sale take place in the absence of registered title (Bosworth 1995). These kinds of transaction have a long history under so-called customary systems of tenure, but they are interpreted in very different ways in the literatures. Bosworth, who in the mid-nineties studied land transactions in south Kigezi in Uganda, where population densities are very high, warns against seeing them as the emergence of individual rights (Bosworth 1995). She is at pains to distinguish herself from authors such as Feder and Noronha who see individual rights as a long-established feature of African land holding systems and informal market transactions as evidence of these individual rights (Feder and Noronha 1987).

These contestations about whether individual rights exist outside registered titles, and their longevity, pivot around perspectives on 'the evolution' of African land tenure, a language which also has a long history in this context and which has been particularly powerful in policy. Chanock, in an account of the development of colonial property law in Africa, argues that from early on, British colonial administrators developed a common framework for understanding tenurial systems that dominated the colonial period, 'fitting like a grid over events' (Chanock 1991a, 73). In this evolutionary framework, indigenous African land holding was viewed as 'communal', and individual proprietary ownership was interpreted as a more developed form of land tenure linked to the development of market exchange (see, for example, Lugard 1922, 280–1, quoted in Chanock 1991a).[2] In British colonial administrative discourse, societies were understood to have progressed on a grand and rather long-term scale from communal to individual forms of land holding; conversely, the type of land tenure of particular colonial societies was thought to indicate the level reached within this evolutionary progression. Bassett argues that early British colonialists used this idea of the communal nature of African land tenure to gain ultimate control over land, establishing the legal right to alienate land by creating Crown land and by declaring that 'vacant' lands belonged to the State (Basset 1993). Cultivators were dispossessed in Eastern and Southern Africa, where European settlers and companies were provided with land to farm, on which Western property categories

---

[2]   Chanock suggests that the central idea of the communality of earlier resource access rules owed much to the British Colonial Service's familiarity with the work of nineteenth-century legal theorists, such as Maine.

of freehold and leasehold were conferred. Formal legal pluralism, with customary and statutory law established and constructed as two separate systems was an
essential element in these policies. Basset also argues that up until the 1930s,
colonial authorities did not wish to transform communal to individual tenure for
Africans, but wanted to preserve what they described as customary rights in the
interests of political stability, which was the paramount colonial objective. When
in the 1930s colonial administrators became more interested in developing African
agriculture, this self-same colonially constructed customary tenure 'was increasingly viewed as an impediment to growth' and 'a major obstacle to realizing
production goals', and they began to promote land tenure reform on the basis of
individual ownership in African held land areas (Basset 1993, 12). At this point,
individual land tenure became firmly embedded in modernizing discourses about
agricultural intensification and economic growth. The more developed form of
land tenure – freehold tenure and individual property – offered 'the most propitious conditions for agricultural investment' (Basset 1993, 12) (see footnote 8).

In a further, latter-day evolutionary model, extensively discussed by Platteau
(which he calls The Evolutionary Theory of Land Tenure, ETLT), modernizing
discourses and the evolution of individual land tenure are also closely linked
(Platteau 1992, 1996, 2000). The ETLT, prominent in policy discussions from
the 1980s onwards, contends that population pressure, together with commercialization of agriculture, puts great pressure on land resources and leads to increased individualization of land access, increased conflicts between land users
and a growing demand from them for more formal property rights (i.e. from
'below'). In response, states step in to initiate formal systems of registered individual ownership. In the ETLT, this in turn promotes greater security, reduces
the incidence of conflict and sets in train a number of economic benefits – the
accelerated development of the land market, investment in land and in agriculture, reallocation to more efficient producers and ultimately greater capital accumulation and government revenue.

The most important case-study of the link between individual titled ownership and positive economic effects is Kenya, where the registration of rights for
Africans to land in individual freehold title began in the 1950s and continued to
be official policy until very recently. Several commentators on the history of
Kenya's land tenure policy suggest that the highly influential Swynnerton Plan
for Kenyan agriculture (Swynnerton 1954), which set in motion colonial land
tenure reform, was concerned not only with the benefits of formal titling for
improving agricultural productivity, but also, and perhaps equally, the potential
of these economic policies to undermine the widespread political instability (Heyer
and Williams no date; Platteau 1996).[3] Heyer and Williams argue that land tenure
reform in Kenya was part of a plan to create a new agricultural class of yeoman
farmers as a response to the rebellions in Central Province in the 1950s. After

[3]   The main outlines of Swynnerton's blueprint for Kenya are reproduced in a subsequent policy
document covering East Africa as a whole (EARC 1955).

independence, the new government was equally attached to a modernizing agenda. Registration and titling continued throughout the 1960s and 1970s, as part of agricultural and land policies justified on almost identical grounds as those of the colonial state (Platteau 1996; Okoth-Ogendo 2000).

As registration of titles proceeded, concern about their effects grew and many case studies in the 1980s found bountiful evidence to criticize free-market modernizing approaches to tenure reform (Haugerud 1983; Bruce 1986; Green 1987; Shipton 1988; Barrows and Roth 1989).[4] A repeated finding was that land registration had promoted inequality and enhanced insecurity: '. . . land titling can be said to supply a mechanism for transfer of wealth in favour of the educated economic and political elite . . .' '. . . land titling opens up new possibilities of conflict and insecurity' (Platteau 2000, 68). This finding from Kenya is supported by Atwood's wider overview, which concludes that, wherever it has been introduced in sub-Saharan Africa, titling *creates* greater uncertainty and conflict (Atwood 1990). '. . . [W]omen, pastoralists, hunter-gatherers, and low-caste people, former slaves and people belonging to minority tribes etc.' (Platteau 2000, 66) were particular groups whose customary claims were denied recognition during registration processes (Green 1987). Vulnerability increased as land access became much more insecure (Platteau 2000; Quan and Toulmin 2000). On the other side of the coin, research on the economic effects is summarized by Platteau as showing 'no clearly discernible impact on investment behaviour' (Platteau 2000, 57). Far from getting greater efficiency, the absentee owners and urban educated elites who scrambled for titles in the early period of registration 'farm inefficiently and under-cultivate the land' (Platteau 2000, 57) and there had been paradoxical effects with respect to credit (Platteau 2000, citing Green 1987; Shipton 1988; Barrows and Roth 1989).

Land in Post-Independence States

The considerable continuity between colonial and post-colonial land and agricultural policies found in Kenya is much more widely applicable. Most post-independence governments in ex-British and French colonies continued the land policies of their previous regimes. 'Nationalization in the early years is followed by a set of policies to grant private title and redistribute land' and more recently, to 'decentralize' land management and grant some form of recognition to customary rights' (Toulmin and Quan 2000b, 11). Few, if any, relinquished the states' rights to land appropriated to establish and maintain colonial political sovereignty, nor could they resist the appeal of the wide-ranging potential for political patronage (Mamdani 1996; Shivji 1998; Alden-Wiley 2000; Lavigne-Delville 2000; Okoth-Ogendo 2000; Toulmin and Quan 2000b; Moyo forthcoming). Land remained and remains a significant weapon in power struggles within many

---

[4]   Sorrenson (1967) is one of very few commentators on the Kenya experience of titling who is positive about it.

African states (Platteau 1996). In the first decades of independence, many governments seized land for infrastructure development and state-owned agricultural projects – a period also marked by land grabbing by political and economic elites.[5] These processes were aided by very poor and inefficient land administration, with many opportunities for abuse and corruption, offered by the postcolonial systems of statutory land law and administration, which Okoth-Ogendo describes as poorly understood, especially in their differences from those in the ex-colonial metropoles (Okoth-Ogendo 2000).

The Kenya experience also throws the spotlight on how the relation between statutory and customary law worked in practice and the extraordinary complexity of the legacy of the pluralistic legal orders as post independence unfolded. Some of the problems in Kenya were that formal land registration did not work very well in tandem with local practices. It was time-consuming and costly, so that as time went on, the land registers became increasingly at variance with possession and use '. . . a gap developed between the control of rights as reflected in the land register and control of rights as recognized between most local communities' (Barrows and Roth 1989, 7, cited in Platteau 2000, 61). Confusion was created and the land law 'failed to gain popular understanding and acceptance'. Moreover '. . . the state has decided to retreat from radical interpretations of freehold tenure and to revert to some customary principles' (Platteau 2000, 63). Haugerud (1989), Mackenzie (1993), Pinckey and Kimuya (1994) all suggest that land boards 'are frequently reluctant to permit transactions that would leave families and their descendants landless and destitute' (Platteau 2000, 63). Despite the existence of registered titles, access to the majority of plots was through inheritance or non-registered sales, lending and gifts (Haugerud 1983; Green 1987; Shipton 1988; Barrows and Roth 1989; Mackenzie 1993).

This interpenetration of statutory and customary systems at the local level is borne out by studies of the effects on women's land access of the introduction of registered title and the new systems of land administration (Mackenzie 1990, 1993; Haugerud 1989; Davison 1988a; Karanja 1991; Fleuret 1988; Shipton 1988). Although Lastarria-Cornhiel summarizes that 'usually women lose access or cultivation rights while male household heads have strengthened their hold over land' (Lastarria-Cornhiel 1997, 1326), Mackenzie's historical study of the different ways in which the land reform of the 1950s had affected patrilineal Kikuyu women's land claims in Central Province gives a more detailed and nuanced picture (Mackenzie 1990, 1993, 1998). Women's claims to use land as wives and as daughters were becoming insecure as the area was experiencing severe land shortage and land was becoming commoditized. Some of her cases showed that

---

[5]   Several authors have noted how new sprees of land grabbing by urban elites emerged in different states and in different periods, especially when state funds were being spent on agricultural modernization. See, for example, Goody (1980) and Shepherd (1981) who describe the rash of absentee landowners on land being used for commercial rice-growing in Ghana's Northern Region in the 1970s. These were mainly southern-based state employees and entrepreneurs who persuaded local chiefs to give them access to so-called customary land.

lineage land given to men on marriage was still managed on a day-to-day basis by women, but it was now registered in the name of the husband who thereby gained more exclusive rights over its disposal. As the married couple purchased land out of their joint efforts, this land too could be registered in the name of the husband. The strength of the claim that wives had to land through marriage was implicitly diminished, especially in the light of the difficulties that a small group of elite women faced trying to purchase land in their own names. Although the land reforms could support daughters' inheritances within their patrilineages, these practices were coming under growing pressure from the sub-clan, which wanted to consolidate land interest within their own groups. Mackenzie thus concludes that land reform had increased men's resistance to women's control over land, while increasing women's insecurities. Registration and titling diminish women's land access in this example by encouraging a single registered owner, and providing a new legal arena for gender conflicts, but it did not extinguish customary claims on land. But in addition it gave a new context for claims in the language of custom and 'men found they were able to manipulate the historical precedents of "custom" to exercise greater control over land to the detriment of women' (Mackenzie 1993, 213; see also Yngstrom forthcoming).

Legal Pluralism and 'Customary' Tenure

There now exists a considerable debate within the academic literature on law and legal theory about the nature of Africa's legal pluralism (Woodman 1985; Manuh 1994; Griffiths 1997, 1998, 2001; Manji 1999; Wilson 2000). Woodman (1985) points out that there is a dominant centrist legal conception that views statutory law as a proper and higher form of law and customary law as a residual subordinated category.[6] Woodman describes this as 'lawyers' customary law' and contrasts it with 'sociologists' customary law' 'the former referring to that law applied within the state courts, the latter to that which is socially recognized outside' (Manuh 1994, citing Woodman 1985, 215). African states are routinely described as legally pluralist and customary law as constructed, but sources differ widely in what they mean by this. Much rural land holding is characterized by informal local-level practices and normative principles, usually called customary tenure arrangements.[7] These coexist within the nation state with others that are guaranteed by statutory law and in some states with other legal orders based on religious law. Colonial legal pluralism consisted of a formal, and sometimes constitutional, recognition of customary practices, in which these practices were systematized and placed within a framework of recognized institutionalized dispute

---

[6]　Interesting insights into this process are to be found in Griffiths's account of the discourses of othering and difference present in the historical devolution of these conflicts to a realm of custom (Griffiths 2001).

[7]　Lavigne-Delville (1999, 2) provides an interesting discussion of what these should be called. 'Researchers prefer to talk about local landholding systems, conforming to . . . socially determined land use rules . . . There is no system that is traditional or customary in itself, but there are forms of land management based on custom'.

settlement procedures.[8] In many of today's national legal orders, the constitution and statutory law *prescribe* the nature and broad competencies of the customary system, specifying the scope of its practices and processes. For legal centrists, customary law may be constructed, but there is nothing wrong with that. After all, its contemporary existence is palpable and sculptured and guaranteed by the statutory.

However for many other commentators, there are more broad-ranging and significant differences between the customary and statutory systems. The formal system of local dispute settlement fora, together with a body of rules about the principles of adjudication, introduced by colonial states, was far from a simple formalization of existing local-level practices. Formalizing its content also changed it. 'Despite official interest in preserving "native law and custom" the interpretation of customary tenure was quite narrow, influenced as it was by European notions of proprietary ownership. The search for individual landowners, the redrawing of community boundaries . . . created new rights and conditions of access that became the subject of considerable dispute' (Berry 1997). Many of the supposed central tenets of African land tenure, such as the idea of communal tenure, the hierarchy of recognized interests in land (ownership, usufructory rights and so on), or the place of chiefs and elders, have been shown to have been largely created and sustained by colonial policy and passed on to post-colonial states (Okoth-Ogendo 1989; Berry 1992, 1993, 2000; Shipton and Goheen 1992; Bosworth 1995; McAuslan 1996; Lavigne-Delville 1999; Yngstrom 1999; Heyer and Williams no date). In addition, the content of so-called customary rules reflected only some of the voices of indigenous society. In Chanock's well-known interpretation, what came to be the content and procedures of customary law were generated out of a compromise and uneasy alliance between the power holders of African indigenous societies and colonial powers (Chanock 1985).

In centrist models of legal pluralism, customary law comes not only to have a static and over systemic character, but also an *overly legal* one. Many legal specialists see the customary as a separate system that has rules of adjudication and other features similar to those in the statutory system (Griffiths 2001). Many terms with distinct meanings in Western law are then used to describe characteristics of customary systems. The model is one of dualism, albeit of an unequal kind. This dualism, in which customary law is seen as a different kind of primarily legal system carrying out many of the same functions as formal law, is one of the most common modalities in which policy advocates describe customary systems. For example, Bruce and Migot-Adholla say: 'in land tenure . . . two sometimes conflicting sources of legitimacy, philosophy and rules have come to govern land tenure' (Bruce and Migot-Adholla 1994). An example here is the use

---

[8]   In writing in this very general way on the basis of sources which seek to generalize, we are conscious of Anne Phillips's caution about the dangers of producing a much too coherent account of what was often a very messy and contradictory set of policies. As she notes, colonial policy was 'necessarily makeshift' (1989, 11) and so different in different states, despite recourse to often highly uniform analyses of the economic, social and political situations of particular states.

of rights language to describe land claims in indigenous systems. 'Generally, individual families enjoyed fairly clearly defined spatial and temporal rights of use over different parcels of cultivated land. Such family rights were transmitted to succeeding generations in accordance with prevailing rules of succession' (Migot-Adholla and Bruce 1994, 5). By using the term rights, Migot-Adholla and Bruce imply that the claims made by persons against each other with respect to land are strong and unambiguous.[9] For anthropologists and historians, local level systems of dispute settlement are not really 'law' at all, but practices which are processual as well as being socially embedded. They use more circumspect language, implying, for example, that the language of 'rights' may be inappropriate. Translating local-level ideas into the term 'rights' gives an erroneous impression that the claims are similar. In this vein, Bosworth, referred to earlier, argues that there is no Bakiga word corresponding to the English word 'rights' (Bosworth 1995).

The Implications of Social Embeddedness

Many of the differences between African local-level legal processes around land claims and statutory processes arise from the socially embedded nature of land access. Continent-wide, socio-legal practices with respect to land and modes of gaining access to it are very diverse, although there is broad general agreement within the historical and anthropological literature that African systems of land access were socially embedded, created by use and negotiated, and that to some extent they remain so today.[10] Although overwhelmingly individuals and households got access to land through intergenerational succession, most claims were claims to use and community-level patterns of land use were not rigid, but flexible and negotiable.[11] Control and ownership rights in which land could be alienated from the social groups with claims to use it were limited. Within kinship groups and households, claims to use were made by men and women for land inherited within these social groups, while between them, claims could also be made on a number of bases. Pawning, pledging and loaning provided access to land for use without undermining the flow of land through inheritance and most communities also had ways in which in-migrants could make claims to land that was not already assigned. The land as a natural resource also provided different kinds of utility, often for different groups of people. In all these cases the claims to use and dispose of land arose out of social relations – out of

---

[9] See Whitehead (1984) for a discussion of how to conceptualize the subjects of resource claims in pre-modern kinship systems.

[10] Land access is used here in the loose sense of the ability to make claims on land and not in the narrow sense of the character of a particular interest acquired in a piece of land.

[11] This is attributed to the relative land abundance that characterized much of sub-Saharan Africa in the past. This land abundance is closely linked to agricultural technology and practices. Examples of areas with forms of intensive land use of relatively long duration include the dry zones of Northern Nigeria and some of the areas of the Barotse plain. In both cases more restricted kinds of land use access came in (Gluckman 1941; Hill 1972).

relations between people, rather than out of property relations – relations between people and things.

Multiple socially embedded land claims have produced the widespread description of land in African tenure systems as subject to a bundle of rights, but this designation is coming under increasing scrutiny in recent historical and anthropological scholarship. The description of African land tenure as a bundle of rights, used in the colonial period to underline the different character of various kinds of land claims, is modelled on Western jurisprudence.[12] One distinction often made is between land ownership and various categories of use rights, with use rights defined as belonging to members of a land-owning group and ownership as vested in political leaders on behalf of their groups. This formulation, which was in the past embedded in ideas of communal ownership, generated conflicts between political leaders and persons with use rights.[13] The different kinds of interests between use and disposal in African land tenure do not properly correspond to the Western jurisprudential distinction between ownership and usufruct and the collapse of these differences in colonial anthropology and today is misleading. A significant contestation in current policy discourses is between those who describe multiple claims in land as a bundle of rights that are hierarchically ordered, in which some are primary and some secondary (especially the distinction between claims to cultivate, or otherwise use, as against claims to alienate, or otherwise control), and those who, while arguing that there are multiple claims, reject the core distinction between primary and secondary claims and their hierarchical ordering. These latter authors stress instead the negotiated dynamic and fluid nature of the tenure relations and tenure claims and treat their socially embedded nature in radically different ways (Falk-Moore 1975; Berry 1989; Okoth-Ogendo 1989; Moore and Vaughan 1994; Lavigne-Delville 1999).

Women's Land Claims

Whether land is subject to hierarchically ordered claims and the meaning of social embeddedness are very important in understanding the gender aspects of land access. Women have long had access to land in sub-Saharan Africa, but men and women have rarely, if ever, had identical kinds of claims to land, largely because the genders have very differentiated positions within the kinship systems that are the primary organizing order for land access.[14] It is striking that there

[12] Western jurisprudential ideas were a strong influence also on anthropological accounts of law in the colonial period – for example, Meek (1946), Gluckman (1943, 1965), Fallers (1969).
[13] Mamdani (1996) argues that control over land was an important area of struggle between the colonial state and the kinship/chieftaincy-based political institutions. He argues that there were differences in the outcomes of these struggles for various societies and suggests that in a large number of cases, kin groups succeeded in maintaining their control over land, marginalizing the state.
[14] For discussions of gender aspects of land interests see Jacobs (1991), Moore and Vaughan (1994), O'Rourke (1995), Fortmann et al. (1997), Rocheleau and Edmunds (1997), Schroeder (1997), Davison (1988b), Kevane and Gray (1999), Manuh et al. (no date).

is no recognized formal category for the particular character of women's land access. Marriage is one important site for women's claims to land and many authors report that husbands devolve land to their wives for farming. However, other authors find that it is from the husband's kin groups that wives get land and it is this kin group that may in some circumstances protect her claims. Women often also retain some residual land claims in their own kin groups as well as frequently obtaining land by loan or gift from a wider circle of social ties. That women get land through many social relations bears emphasis because some policy discussions assert that women get access to land as wives and go on to argue that their claims are weak because of this.

Several recent studies of gendered land access that have examined land disputes and court cases suggest not only that women's claims to land are much more diverse, but also that women's claims to land are much stronger than usually represented (Cheater 1982; Moore and Vaughan 1994; Bosworth 1995; Yngstrom 1999, forthcoming). Ironically, for those who link social embeddedness with women's *weaker* claims, the empirically demonstrated strength of women's claims seems to lie precisely in their social embeddedness.[15] These authors contest the idea that women's indigenous land claims are secondary, or amount simply to a use right contrasted with a control right. They also suggest that women's claims to land are not justified solely through the recognition of their obligations in food production, but that local-level land-management fora make moral and material evaluations of inputs and behaviour between male and female household members over a very wide spectrum when adjudicating land claims (Bosworth 1995; Kevane and Gray 1999; Yngstrom 1999).

These more recent studies represent an important break with the interpretation of the difference in women's land claims from men's as necessarily implying their claims are weaker. Nevertheless, the key issue remains what happens to men's and women's historically constituted land interests with economic transformation, especially where land has become scarce as new economic uses for land have developed. Several studies show that with changing uses for land, particularly with new crops and forms of agriculture, contestations take place between men and women (Davison 1988b; Carney and Watts 1990; Moore and Vaughan 1994). Although there are examples where women do maintain their land access in these contestations, the weight of evidence suggests that economic changes have resulted in women's diminished access to land. But what are the factors and processes at work?

One set of factors lying completely outside the issue of gendered land tenure is the distribution of economic resources required successfully to work the land in the context of present-day agriculture. Although they do farm much less land than men do, this is not usually because women are prevented from getting

---

[15]   Lavigne-Delville (2000) and Leonard and Toulmin (2000) point out that as both men and women acquire land through social relations, this is not an explanation for the respective strength of their claims.

land, but because they lack working capital, inputs, extension access or credit.[16] This point is analogous to one made by Lastarria-Cornhiel (1997), who has examined the continent-wide evidence for the effects of land privatization, finding that simple titling and land registration do not transform a customary tenure system into a freehold one; other changes in the commercialization of agriculture and the development of a land market are needed. She concludes that the general processes of privatization and concentration affect women's land and property rights negatively, rather than national land registration schemes per se. In the development of private property regimes of any kind, sub-Saharan African women tend to lose the rights they once had. This is because women suffer systematic disadvantages both in the market and in state-backed systems of property ownership, either because their opportunities to buy land are very limited, or because local-level authorities practise gender discrimination, preventing women from claiming rights that are in theory backed by law.[17] Women also encounter problems in both the statutory and customary systems for resolving land struggles and disputes – who does the adjudicating and how – or in wider aspects of gender relations. In Kenya, as new economic uses for land developed, men's and women's historically constructed claims to land use were always potentially in conflict and titling 'provided a new institutional arena for existing struggles and debates to be played out' (Yngstrom forthcoming), but women could not translate resources for negotiating informal access into negotiating registered ownership. Carney (1988) and Carney and Watts (1990) have documented a particularly visible example of gender conflicts over land in the Gambia, where men re-labelled as 'household' land, farms that had once been women's 'private' fields, thereby wresting control from women of rice lands for a new irrigation project. Here men use the language of custom to dominate a new economically rewarding form of agriculture. The remainder of this paper examines this theme on a wider canvas, as we turn to modern uses of the language of custom in the field of land tenure policy-making, in the gendered processes of claiming land and in the politics of state and society in Africa.

POLICY DISCOURSES

Land tenure reform has become a significant area of policy-making in many African states in the last ten years and international organizations have been heavily involved. This section focuses on the policy discourses of three sets of significant agents: The World Bank, OXFAM Great Britain and the International Institute for Environment and Development (IIED) and African women lawyers.

---

[16] See Whitehead (2001a) for a more extended discussion of this point.
[17] These findings are important because many gender and development policy documents still advocate a blanket policy of ensuring women's land access through titling, without any reference to the specificities of the sub-Saharan African situation.

The World Bank 1970–2001

'The approach of the World Bank to the issue of land reform has not always been without ambiguities and (at least) potential contradictions. Nor has it remained constant' (Platteau 1992, 7).

The World Bank's interpretation of macro-economic processes and development and its evaluations of the nature of African societies, states and economies has been of profound importance in the last 20–25 years, in which African countries have become heavily aid-dependent and indebted, with the World Bank and IMF particularly significant donors and creditors. Their strongly top–down analysis and policy prescriptions are allied with interventions of unparalleled range and depth. The World Bank, however, is a large and complex organization and, despite heavy orchestration to produce a strong orthodoxy in its analyses,[18] its many separate divisions have different kinds of policy focus and make a range of thematic arguments, no more so than with respect to land and gender issues, where the Bank's separate sections have very different levels of expertise.

Land Policy Division and the Evolution of its Land Tenure Policy for Africa

Changes in the World Bank's thinking between 1975 and 2001 about land reform are well documented by their own land and agriculture specialists. A series of papers has commented on the empirical bases for these changes and on the implications for approaches to productivity and growth in African agriculture (Deininger 1998; Deininger and Binswanger 1999; World Bank 2001). The Land Policy Division (LPD) is the major unit charged with formulating land policy. From being centrally concerned with freeing land into individual ownership through the introduction of 'modern' registered freehold titling, the LPD has moved against registered titling as the necessary precondition for agricultural investment and growth (World Bank 2001). Although still dominated by an orthodox modernizing position that land markets and individual tenure are essential if individuals are to be willing to invest in land in order to raise its productivity (cf. Quan 2000, 34), the LPD's current thinking is influenced by recent evolutionary theories of land tenure that see privatization developing from below, in response to population pressure and commercialization (Platteau 1996). By the late 1980s, it had become ambivalent whether and when states should kick in to support these processes and increasingly developed a more positive view of the capacity of African customary systems of tenure to change in the 'right' directions.

The landmark policy statement was a 1975 Land Reform Policy Paper from the LPD (World Bank 1975). Quan summarizes this as recommending 1) 'formal

---

[18] See Whitehead and Lockwood (1999) for a description of this process with respect to the World Bank's Poverty Assessments.

land titling as a precondition of modern development, 2) the abandonment of communal tenure systems in favour of freehold title and sub-division of the commons, 3) widespread promotion of land markets to bring about efficiency-enhancing land transfers, and 4) support for land redistribution on both efficiency and equity grounds' (Quan 2000, 38). In addition to its concerns with equity and the highly political nature of land distribution, land reform had wider development implications because of its role in wealth creation and accumulation. Tenure reform was seen as central to promoting agricultural growth, with private freehold tenure an essential step to a modernized agriculture, promoting investments and providing incentives to adopt new technologies.

Platteau argues that land tenure reform in the World Bank was seen as primarily relevant to Latin America and Asia throughout the 1970s, on the widespread understanding that sub-Saharan Africa was a land-abundant continent characterized by extensive agriculture (Platteau 1992, 5–6). All this changed in the 1980s, when the food crises and famines of different regions led to a renewed focus on agricultural productivity and the conditions for agricultural growth in Africa. This coincided with the adoption of highly interventionist structural adjustment lending, and economic reform aimed at removing rigidities and promoting markets and the 1980s saw a series of developing critiques of Africa as a land-abundant continent. As early as 1982, a highly authoritative report on agricultural development in sub-Saharan Africa pointed to land as a growing constraint and recommended greater attention to land use and land tenure issues (Eicher and Baker 1982). An equally influential account emphasized the growth of land sales and the impediments afforded to a free market in land by post-colonial states. Feder and Noronha suggest that some post-colonial states were creating considerable problems of land access by continuing the colonial prohibitions on land sales and denying that land markets were growing (Feder and Noronha 1987). The informality of what was in reality a thriving land market, involving informal and disguised transactions all over Africa, led to distortions in the market, they argued. Continuing to prohibit land sales had allowed politically influential groups, such as chiefs and civil servants, to accumulate and become economically distinct from their subjects.

These developments are readily apparent in the 1989 Report, *Sub-Saharan Africa: From Crisis to Sustainable Growth*. It was manifestly concerned about growing land scarcity and rising population and with environmental and sustainability crises arising because land fertility was no longer sustained by long fallow periods (World Bank 1989).[19] It argued that increased agricultural productivity required new technologies and the incentives to adopt them, to be provided by tenure security through land titling. Land rights secured by titles would also help rural markets in credit and land to develop. Customary or local-level systems of

---

[19] In an extensive discussion Williams (1994) argues that this report has many similarities with British colonial policies towards the end of the colonial period, especially the content and approach in the Swynnerton report and its implementation plans. See also Heyer and Williams (no date).

resource allocation, in contrast, led to poor incentives, did not stimulate land and credit markets and hence prevented the distribution of land to the most efficient users.

This report, with its marriage of liberalization and neo-Malthusianism, was a high level macropolicy document (cf. Williams 1994) and very influential, but the LPD itself had meanwhile become more concerned with the growing evidence that registered individual title had not brought the predicted economic benefits (Feder and Feeny 1991). In the early 1990s, new studies were undertaken or funded by the World Bank on the supposed link between the security of freehold tenure and improved agricultural productivity (Bruce and Migot-Adholla 1994). Among the countries studied was Kenya, and here the findings confirmed earlier research. No differences in the productivity and investment of lands held in freehold title compared with those held in customary tenure were found (Migot-Adholla et al. 1994b). Companion studies in other countries concluded that many farmers without formal title perceived that they had rights to continuous and unchallenged use of agricultural land (Migot-Adholla et al. 1994a). Customary tenure systems appeared to offer sufficient security of tenure for farmers to invest in land, although the lack of formal title meant they had no automatic rights of disposal (Bruce 1993). There seemed to be no compelling economic justification for replacing customary land law with state-guaranteed titles.

This important set of studies led Bruce et al. to re-evaluate customary systems and their capacity for change and flexibility and to downplay the role of state-backed formal systems of individual titling (Bruce et al. 1994). They forecast: 'a market economy will eventually produce a land tenure system that, while not identical, will bear a strong family resemblance to the Western concept of ownership' (Bruce et al. 1994, 262). They therefore recommended incremental approaches to policy, adapting and not replacing existing land management practices, with the role of the state to provide the legal and administrative environment that will support and promote evolutionary change. The heavy financial costs of introducing and maintaining systems of registered title are further reasons cited for the policy sea-change.

In a 1999 presentation, Migot-Adholla summarized the World Bank's current position: the circumstances in which land titling is 'an optimal solution' are 'much more limited'; 'communal' tenure systems can provide 'a more cost-effective solution', 'if transparency and local accountability can be assured' (Migot-Adholla 1999). The World Bank is now promoting reforms that will eliminate conflicts between parallel sets of rights and is setting up pilot programmes to register and adjudicate customary rights, to provide titles on a community basis and to redistribute land through negotiation and the market (Quan 2000). This consolidates the shift away from the 1975 document in the attitude towards customary systems of tenure. From being one of the greatest obstacles to agricultural modernization and enhanced productivity, in this new analysis they emerge as flexible and locally managed systems for guaranteeing secure land access on owner-occupied farms. The LPD has recently posted a 2001 policy statement on the net that says quite unequivocally that there is now a consensus for the legal recognition of customary tenure and in favour of building on these (World Bank 2001).[20]

As statements about the policy approach taken to land tenure reform in particular African states, however, these documents from the LPD have to be treated with caution. The policy drivers in the constituent parts of the World Bank are by no means the same. The nuanced, self-critical and empirically foregrounded approaches of the Land Policy Division, with a new stress on the evolution of local-level practices are not necessarily shared elsewhere. One competing set of discourses comes out of the Bank's divisions working on the environment and sustainability where there is a long-held view that communal forms of property ownership lead to over-exploitation. Cleaver and others take a very strong line on the need for individual land rights to prevent land degradation (e.g. Cleaver and Schreiber 1993). Many macro-economists also support this position, although for rather different reasons. A free-market philosophy and an agenda of economic growth through further market liberalization, even when accompanied by poverty-reduction objectives, are responsible for the almost routine way in which reform to individual land titling appears in many country-level documents.[21] The World Bank continues to offer substantial support to governments establishing land tenure reform with individual registered titles.[22]

World Bank Gender Specialists

The LPD identifies its new policy directions as positive for women, although the Internet responses point out the brief and ill-developed nature of the gender analysis in its recent draft policy document (Hanstat 2001; Quan 2001). Beyond the LPD, there are discernible and sharp differences among gender specialists. Within the Africa Division, for example, some gender specialists have put considerable work into looking for synergies between better outcomes for women, poverty reduction and overall economic growth (Blackden and Morris-Hughes 1993). Centred on the growth-efficiency model and taking a modernizing approach, the 1998 SPA report stresses the need for top–down reform to give women better land rights and secure their access to land (Blackden and Bhanu 1999). In contrast, the Gender and Law Reform in Africa (GLRA) group within the Africa Division emphasizes that state reform involving titling and ownership has been negative for women and is much closer to the Land Policy Division in arguing that customary systems have some merit.

---

[20] This statement is the equivalent of the 1975 LPD paper. It represents the outcome of the kinds of shifts and assessment of empirical evidence that we have described in this section. However, it came out only when this paper was in its very final stages and hence we do not consider it fully.

[21] For example, in its Country Assistance Strategies, which are largely written from a macroeconomic perspective (World Bank 2000c).

[22] See, for example, World Bank (2000d), where it is stated that one of the components of phase 1 of the Land Administration Programme would be sub-pilot projects in systematic land titling and registration. The World Bank is financing US$25 million of the US$40 million estimated cost of the project.

This group has been very active throughout the region, providing support for various networks of feminist lawyers and sponsoring in-country and cross-country studies, workshops and networks. It operates against a backdrop of the rights-based approaches, symbolized in CEDAW,[23] which have come to dominate international discourses on gender and development and in which legal reforms and statutory law are a major means for women to achieve rights denied them through custom and tradition. Much of the discussion in the conference proceedings on *Gender Discrimination in Francophone sub-Saharan Africa*, which was promoted and funded by GLRA, uses the language of rights to address discriminatory practices in customary systems. Publications authored by the GLRA itself, in contrast, take a more positive approach to the customary, and often criticize formal law as a means of achieving gender equity in Africa (World Bank 1994). Gopal suggests that reformed customary law has the potential to promote women's land and property issues, at the same time as acknowledging that land allocation is for the most part based on customary practices that deny women control over land (Gopal 1998). For them, these customary practices need to be understood as colonial constructs, and as not fixed. As socio-economic conditions changed, the implementation of customary law as a fixed body of rules or practices, largely misunderstood by colonial regimes, has been very disadvantageous to women.

Elsewhere, Gopal criticizes colonial and post-colonial modernist legal reforms more elaborately (Gopal 1999). Legal reform 'introduced personal laws that were based on a vision of personal relationships that bore little connection to the reality in these countries' (Gopal 1999, 22) and simultaneously undermined existing systems of claims and dispute settlement, 'leaving women in the unenviable position of being unprotected in either legal system'. Drawing an important distinction between the premises underlying customary law and the forms of customary law and practice prevalent in African states today, they promote the idea of basing change on the reformed customary. She argues forcibly that women must participate in legal reform and that this participation will be strengthened when women get better access to wider economy (Gopal 1999, 22).

These differences between World Bank gender specialists in the late nineties, which appear to reflect the degree of institutional commitment to growth and efficiency models and of appreciation of the potentials and pitfalls of legal reform and of the customary, are also apparent in some uneasiness about land issues in a recent important gender and development policy document (World Bank 2000b). This analysis owes a good deal to the newer poverty frameworks (for example, in the 2000/2001 World Development Report), which while remaining committed to growth, now stress institutions and rights, emphasizing the role of the state in institutional reforms and the use of law to promote governance objectives (World Bank 2000a). In their analysis of gender and development issues and policy priorities, Mason and King give high priority to transforming the institutional environment and place a welcome stress on social relations (World Bank 2000b).

[23]   Convention on the Elimination of All Forms of Discrimination against Women.

Although the comments in Mason and King on women and land are very brief, the phrase 'land rights' occurs in several places, but the pro-customary stance is also there: 'In places, such as SSA, where systems of customary law operate side-by-side with statutory law, special care is needed in the use of statutory changes' '. . . efforts to improve women's land rights in Ghana succeeded because the new incentives under statutory law were consistent with custom' (World Bank 2000b, 15). All signalling, perhaps, that issues about the respective merits of the customary and statutory for women's land access remains unresolved.

Independent Land Policy Advocates: OXFAM GB and the International Institute for Environment and Development (IIED)

The last 20 years has seen a substantial expansion in NGO and other activity in Africa, with the development of a wide range of national and regional African NGOs and European-based organizations also expanding their Africa programmes. OXFAM GB and IIED are two European organizations that have been particularly active with respect to land policy. Both organizations have a position on land tenure reform that is very different in its starting point and objectives from that of the World Bank. A strong hostility to orthodox economic positions and the promotion of registered individually owned freehold land titles is part of their much wider critique of the World Bank's policies throughout the 1980s and 1990s. These organizations have long advocated building on local-level land management, suggesting potential convergence with the new stance by the World Bank's LPD.

OXFAM Great Britain

OXFAM GB runs a specific website on land policy issues[24] and their concern with land issues arises from their commitment to reducing poverty and working for sustainable livelihoods. OXFAM GB's main analysis is of the political processes at play, where it foregrounds the role of international interests in national policy and identifies recent processes common to several African states. National governments set in train land tenure reform 'generally designed to open the door to privatization and greater foreign ownership of land' after consultations that are usually very narrow (Palmer 1998, 2).[25] It also pays attention to the interests of the state in maintaining control over land allocation, and the power and patronage that is built on land relationships: 'Politicians may tolerate bottom-up participatory processes in other areas, but not in matters which require them to relinquish control (directly or indirectly) over land allocation' (Adams personal communication, cited in Palmer 2000, 288). 'In brief, access to land by the poor

[24] http://www.oxfam.org.uk/landrights. This site has details of the relatively large number of publications and conference papers on land tenure issues in Africa that have come out since this paper was written.
[25] Palmer gives Tanzania as an exception.

in many parts of Africa is currently seriously threatened by a combination of privatization and unrestricted market forces; by governments desperately seeking foreign investments including for tourism; and by greed and corruption by the rich and powerful' (Palmer 1998, 1).

OXFAM GB has been heavily involved in supporting NGOs and coalitions in Eastern and Southern Africa for the last ten years; in particular, those NGOs, coalitions and Land Alliances[26] seeking local-level management of land allocation and dispute settlement in order to promote better access to land for ordinary people. Recent documents from OXFAM GB take many cues from Alden-Wily, who emphasizes first, the persistence of customary modes of landholding and dispute settlement, despite the considerable efforts of governments to diminish them, and second, the state's capacity throughout recent reform processes to preserve the link between land relations, power and patronage and its own absolute land ownership (Alden-Wily 2000, forthcoming, cited in Palmer 2000). On the basis of a review of over 60 land laws in Eastern and Southern Africa, she asserts that 'the most radical shift in tenure reform occurring in sub Saharan Africa is that for the first time in 100 years states are being forced to recognize African tenure regimes as legal in their own right and equivalent in the eyes of national law to the freehold leasehold culture' (Alden-Wily forthcoming, cited in Palmer 2000, 271). The persistence of customary modes of landholding and dispute settlement is tantamount to a form of resistance to the state. In her arguments, two important strands are evident. First, there is the idea that statutory procedures can be improved by incorporating some of the principles of customary land-holding systems. The recognition of the customary brings into play new ideas of property and of ownership. Common property can be recognized and new forms of process confirming land ownership – such as verbal contracts – become recognized. Second, there is a firm belief in the ability of local communities to manage their own affairs and the importance in general of letting them do so. The key is community control, when 'the point at which acquisition and disposal of land rights are officially endorsed and regulated is moving closer to the landholder' (Alden-Wily forthcoming, cited in Palmer 2000, 271). She sees the new institutions proposed, or required, for land tenure reform as part of a broader process of democratization and building local-level political and decision-making capacity (Alden-Wiley 2000).

This approach fits in well with OXFAM GB's general support for encouraging participation and building of local capacities. Palmer diagnoses subsidiarity and local devolution as the key objectives in current land reform policy 'meaning that decisions on land management and control should be taken at the lowest

---

[26] Details of current land alliances and networks in Eastern and Southern Africa are to be found on LandWeb, hosted by MWENGO at www.mwengo.org. MWENGO is a reflection and development centre for NGOs in Eastern and Southern Africa. The organization is based in Harare; the Secretariat has been operating since late 1993. The LandWeb is part of a broader project whose main goal is to strengthen the impact of land advocacy by NGOs in Eastern and Southern Africa (ESA). '(This) project was launched in 1999. It was designed in response to the increasing interventions in the area of land by NGOs in most countries of the region' (from www.mwengo.org).

levels possible' (Palmer 2000, 24). He identifies a trend 'towards formal tribunals, independent tribunals with recourse to the ordinary courts, operating at the local level and in some cases operated by community members' (Palmer 2000, 24) and criticizes the role of prominent land lawyers because they adopt centrist top–down solutions. Little of the discussion in OXFAM GB-authored publications examines in detail how the proposed local-level systems might work, including whether the values and processes of customary systems can deliver more equitable land access. There are many warnings that the local level is also the site of power relations. For example, Palmer discusses the danger that NGOs may be inadequate vehicles for equitable land policy, not only because they are sometimes short-lived and often dependent on outside funding, but also because class, ethnicity and other social divisions may be reflected in their memberships. Here we are beginning to see an incipient tension between the customary as the site of resistance to the state, and hence an important discourse around which greater local-level political capacities can be built, and the customary as the site of unequal rural social relations.

International Institute for Environment and Development (IIED): The 1999 DFID Conference

IIED is a UK-based organization undertaking research and lobbying on global environmental and sustainability issues. With a particular emphasis on working with partner organizations and promoting networking, it has also been at the forefront of promoting participatory approaches and is a major resource centre for these. Its main impetus to land work in sub-Saharan Africa comes from its concerns with environmental sustainability, with the growing exclusion of some rural people from the natural resource base and with the proliferating conflicts between different kinds of land user, especially between pastoralists and arable farmers. It has a specific interest in problems of conflict between different land users, especially those with secondary rights (such as pastoralists), in common property resources and how to protect the land claims of small rural producers that are essential to sustainability and to poverty alleviation.

The IIED is an organization with major experience and expertise in land policy issues in Africa and it is not possible to review all its work here.[27] In 1998, it was recruited by DFID to work with the Natural Resources Institute in the UK to organize a conference on land tenure issues in Africa (DFID 1999). DFID has played a major role in land tenure reforms in Eastern and Southern Africa and continues to work extensively with African governments on land policy. The conference brought together many of the main specialists on African land tenure, including African and international legal experts, representatives from international donors and from national and international NGOs and a large number of country experts from a wide spread of Africa's nations. Its papers have been

---

[27] Relevant recent publications include IIED (1999), Toulmin and Pepper (2000), Toulmin et al. (2001).

edited into one of the most up-to-date assessments on current land tenure policy issues in Africa (Toulmin and Quan 2000a).

In their introduction, Toulmin (IIED) and Quan (NRI) distance themselves from the approach taken historically by the World Bank, arguing for a strongly human-centred approach, less driven by economic prescription (Toulmin and Quan 2000b). They rehearse the arguments about the limitations of legislation, reform and registration, paying special attention to the failure to capture second-ary rights, to inequitable outcomes and to the conflict and difficulties of resolu-tion within dispute settlement procedures, points pursued in a number of the other chapters (e.g. Platteau 2000; Lavigne-Delville 2000). The alternative is land tenure reform based on the practices and institutions of customary law, modified so that they reflect the social and political realities of contemporary rural circum-stances. They are against universal solutions and think that the actual forms of reform should differ in different countries. 'A new paradigm is emerging which does not prescribe a specific approach to land reform, based on pluralism and the need for Africans themselves to negotiate their own solutions' (Toulmin and Quan 2000a, 6). Their introduction not only discusses the merits and demerits of customary versus state law, but also steers the discussion in the direction of how to resolve the problems of land tenure within a modified customary law frame-work and what kind of institutional innovations might be needed to do so.

Their justifications for basing reform on customary law are several. Custom-ary law: is able to provide relative security to community members at lower cost than state-run structures, is flexible in that it allows different forms of access, and is more equitable in that it considers the needs of the poor (Toulmin and Quan 2000a, 12). They refer to Sjaastad and Bromley (1997), who argue that custom-ary law, which is neither communal nor ambiguous, is flexible and responding to increasing land scarcity and permitting individualization. Customary law has the merits of being embedded within local social relations and values and could be administered in recognized forms that would meet rural people's need for security of rural people, best guaranteed in the modern world by community social networks and 'the weight of an official stamp' (Toulmin and Quan 2000a, 13). Basing reform on customary law also fits with new global thinking about the need for local people to participate in the management of natural resources and with renewed interest in decentralization. Toulmin and Quan argue that in circumstances where land registration is needed, it should proceed with more respect for customary law; it could be simpler, cheaper and more equitable to register collective rights as opposed to individual rights.

The role given to the state in this new customary law-based framework is relatively limited: to pass enabling legislation, redistribute land if need be and establish the authority of the institutions tasked with managing land. Even so, a modified customary system is not an easy option. It is expensive and long-term. It needs additional measures such as education, support such as credit, extension, inputs, access to land, and so on. Moreover, legal changes to make laws consist-ent with land law are needed. Their bottom–up approach leads them to be relat-ively non-prescriptive about the new institutions required to run these modified customary land tenure systems. They should focus on dispute resolution, but it is very important which institutions are granted the powers to make land decisions. Different implications follow from whether it is the chiefs or an elected local body (e.g. district assembly) that is selected. 'Authority in land whether vested in the chiefs, or in the government officials and political leaders, can in turn, lead directly to private economic benefits for these actors, derived from land accumulation, patronage and land transactions' (Toulmin and Quan 2000b, 6).

Chapters in the book document a number of different experiences of registering customary rights, which have not always ensured protection for the claims of different stakeholders, in particular the poor. The book contains a chapter giving an overview of women's access to land (Hilhorst 2000) and several papers on gender issues were given at the Conference, but no real attempt had been made to subject the policy proposals to a gendered view, despite women being one of the stakeholder categories who have demonstrably lost out in the historical development of land tenure reforms. Later work from IIED on women and land tenure does begin to explore some of the nuances of customary systems for women (Leonard and Toulmin 2000). Leonard and Toulmin argue that women's land access under customary systems is very diverse, and that 'in practice, women do not perceive their rights to land as insecure, as long as their household and community relations remain stable' (Leonard and Toulmin 2000, 4). Women's disadvantages often occurred at divorce or widowhood or because they lacked power in social negotiations. An important theme developed in this account is the issue of women's lack of a voice in rural decision-making. Citing Odgaard (personal communication) with respect to Tanzania,[28] they highlight the enormous difficulties women face in seeking to use the law to claim their rights and identify women's lack of direct participation in village assemblies and similar local institutions as a major stumbling block to greater equity in local resource allocation (Leonard and Toulmin 2000, 14–15). They recommend the strengthening of women's representation in central and local government as integrally linked to more gender equity in land issues.

Both IIED and OXFAM GB, then, emphasize the ways in which recent national land policy has led to important tracts of local resources being alienated by international companies and the close link between national and local politics and landholding. They respond by exploring new forms of ownership supported by local management, devolution, subsidiarity and democratization. In important elements, this response converges with that of the World Bank, especially in the role that the 'modified customary' should play in local-level land management, despite approaching the issue from different positions. For the World Bank, the policy is to encourage these to evolve; for the independent land policy advocates, more democratically accountable management systems are to be introduced to build on what already exists locally. While recognizing that they are constructed, each organization persists in using the term 'customary' to refer to

---

[28] See also Wanitzek (1990), Lawi (2000).

these local-level systems. In no case are the gender implications of these proposals addressed adequately. However, it may be women particularly who have
a great deal to lose from the turn to 'the customary' as a solution to the problems in centralized state-led legal reforms of land tenure. The main constituency
that has addressed these issues are Africa's feminist lawyers and it is to these we
now turn.

African Feminist Legal Discourses

African and Africanist feminist lawyers have long been concerned with drawing attention to women's rights issues within the legal system as a whole and
within different areas of law. Early path-breaking studies (Hay and Wright 1982;
Manuh 1984; see also Armstrong 1987; Armstrong and Stewart 1990) have been
deepened by more specific studies of areas such as family law, inheritance, land
relations and more recently violence against women (Molokomme 1991, 1995,
1996; Cook 1991; the WLSA series: Chuulu et al. 1997; Kidd et al. 1997; Ncube
1997a, 1997b; Temba et al. 1997; Aphane et al., 1998; Letuka et al. 1998). Since
the late 1980s and 1990s, in the context of the series of UN conferences, women
lawyers have become more influential in policy advocacy and demands for legal
reform. During this period, their regional and sub-regional groupings have grown
in strength, and they have been increasingly engaged in advocating law reforms
and the implementation of UN conference outcomes, popularizing laws relevant
to women's rights, and promoting legal literacy and paralegal training for women
(Manuh 1995). In the fight for gender equality, activist feminist lawyers are
oriented towards the international conventions and instruments and a rights
perspective and have a generally positive stance towards the role of the state
and statutory law to deliver rights to women (Butegwa 1994; Cook 1994).

In their approaches to women and land, the most common view is that legally
backed land ownership is critical to rural women's production and economic
efficiency.[29] While some prominent African male lawyers, for example Okoth-
Ogendo (1989) and more recently Shivji (1998), have been at the forefront of the
reappraisal of the ability of customary law to deliver security of land tenure, with
very few exceptions (e.g. Manuh 1994), female lawyers concerned with women
have looked to statutory law to address questions of security for women. They
have mainly explored the ways in which customary law rules currently do not
favour women, and generally argued that both laws and practice discriminate
against women. It is important to understand their critiques of contemporary
African legal systems and the treatment of women by both customary and statutory systems as a basis for this gender difference in approaches to land tenure
policy reform.

One consensus is that legal pluralism has been inimical to women's claims to
land. Knowles, for example, argues that it allows male-dominated society to

---

[29]   A major exception here is Himonga and Munachonga (1991).

resist women's claims by vacillating between the two systems and successfully postponing or neutralizing any reforms that might have been instituted (Knowles 1991, 8). Butegwa also writes that in legally pluralistic states, case law has tended to affirm customary law practices even when they are discriminatory (Butegwa 1991). Another argument has been that the imposition of Western notions of ownership in land relations in Africa had led to much confusion about the character of land tenure, to women's disadvantage (Karanja 1991). Some writers contrast women's social embeddedness in the pre-colonial period with the processes of individualization that accompanied colonial economic and legal change, arguing that the inferiority of their inheritance rights under customary law and practice had less import than it does now. Karanja, for example, argues that in spite of having no inheritance rights, 'women held positions of structural significance, serving as the medium through which individual rights passed to their sons. They enjoyed security of tenure rooted in their structural role as lineage wives . . .' (Karanja 1991, 116). Knowles agrees:

> In theory, customary systems of land tenure and use traditionally provided some recourse for women in need of land for food production. Evidence suggests that this theoretical refuge ran along a continuum from a right to beg for a piece of land from a male relative or acquaintance, to a system where women's rights to land from their native lineages were strong enough to attract them away from their marital residences in patrilocal societies, for the purpose of continuing to cultivate land provided by their natal families. (Knowles 1991, 5)

These positions share McAuslan's analysis of the way African interests in land were extinguished by the colonial state with the support of its judiciary. Safeguards which existed in customary law have been eroded (McAuslan 2000).

The content of customary law, in which women's rights in land are described as derived and secondary and depending on their relations with various men – fathers, brothers, husbands and sons, has also been criticized for playing a part in the erosion of women's interests in land. Either they have no inheritance rights or their inheritance rights are inferior to men's, with some authors pointing out that women themselves might be inherited when their husbands' die (Butegwa 1991; Karanja 1991). 'The whittling away of women's land rights by the changes instituted by these subsequent regimes was a direct result of their disabilities arising from the customary rules of inheritance and the customary division of labour which had resulted in women not being able to acquire land for themselves' (Karanja 1991, 117). Knowles agrees, arguing that as economic and political changes unfold 'at best, women are forced onto the least desirable and productive land and, at worst, their limited rights may be extinguished altogether' (Knowles 1991, 5). She goes on to critique positive attitudes to customary law, arguing that 'many African governments are choosing to make changes at the margin, leaving untouched the customary laws' prohibitions against formal land allocation to women' (Knowles 1991, 11).

Even so, in the writings of African legal feminists, there is clearly some ambivalence to the state and to statutory law. At one end of the spectrum is the view that statutory laws themselves have discriminated against women. Relevant here is the widespread understanding that women's land rights were severely eroded by titling and individualization backed by statutory law in Kenya. 'The process of land reform solidified the role of men as the inextricable link between women and the land and further hardened their land rights into absolute ownership to the exclusion of women' (Karanja 1991, 122). The other position is that while a law may be progressive in its provisions, it is enforcement that is the problem. Butegwa, for example, argues that where statutory law is on the face of it favourable, it is not enforced because of women's lack of awareness and power, resistance from male relations, the fear of sanctions and the lack of political will on the part of government (Butegwa 1991, 57). Furthermore, even where statutory law does in principle govern land relations, customary practices continue to be very important in the determination of land rights. Women's security of tenure thus continues to be threatened by discriminatory customary practices of inheritance, lack of adequate protective legislation and the failure to observe governmental and legal measures intended for the protection of women's land rights. Butegwa calls this the 'inherent limit of law as an instrument for social change' (Butegwa 1991, 55).

In spite of these reservations of feminist lawyers about statutory law, reforming the law is generally seen as offering a better possibility for securing women's rights in land than simply allowing customary law to evolve. Butegwa still prefers statutory law to customary law, arguing that, in the latter, both law and practice are not favourable (Butegwa 1991, 54). Within this broad position, some emphasize changing laws, some emphasize legal training for better implementation, and disagreement exists about which areas of law should be reformed. Karanja (1991), for example, recommends land redistribution, land ceilings, titling and registration. Knowles does not share this positive attitude to titling and registration: she argues that high levels of security can exist without legal title and vice versa. She also notes that titling programmes are male-biased in assuming a nuclear family and a male household head and being generally hostile to secondary interests (Knowles 1991, 11). Butegwa (1991) supports law reform, but argues for an emphasis on inheritance law: 'Where the acquisition of land is mainly through inheritance, giving a woman a contractual capacity and the right to deal in land is irrelevant if she cannot inherit it in the first place' (Butegwa 1991, 57). In contrast, Himonga and Munachonga (1991) stress that it is not women's legal access to land that is the main problem with respect to poverty and their agricultural income, but other structural disabilities. To improve a variety of access problems, they recommend the education of officials and women, special loan facilities for women, more appropriate technologies and the recruitment and placement of more female extension workers (Himonga and Munachonga 1991, 70–1). Butegwa's recommendations also include legal rights education for both men and women, especially men in the local power structures, such as chiefs and dispute-settlement personnel, together with community-level support groups to dissolve male resistance and help women overcome their fears.

Feminist lawyers also differ in the extent to which they recognize that there may be enormous resistance to equitable practices and the fact that it is broader gender inequalities that are at issue. Karanja argues that the poor record of statutory law in promoting gender equity is due to discriminatory law, ignorance of the law, the interplay of customary and statutory law and inequalities in marital relationships that can be addressed by effective legislation (Karanja 1991, 131–2). For Knowles, male resistance is a key issue and law reform must go beyond land rights and tackle broader gender inequalities in society (Knowles 1991, 12–13). Butegwa highlights male resistance in the judiciary and courts where many judges prefer 'to dress personal prejudices and lack of appreciation of the issues in ancient judicial precedents' (Butegwa 1991, 57).

Although both Karanja and Butegwa recognize the difference between formal and substantive rights in their work, the assumption is that women have been unable to enforce their rights out of ignorance, thus down-playing the strength of factors such as inequalities in social relations and institutional and cultural biases which prevent women from succeeding in making claims and sustaining them. An examination of these issues requires a broader framework of analysis. Recent literature available at the national level, in which the doubtful value of the Western jurisprudential framework and the oversimplified approach to legal pluralism are raised, shows signs of the development of such a framework. Karanja (1991) critiques Western notions of ownership and access and the characterization of customary law in the literature, noting that a woman's bundle of rights over land typically does not include any of the hallmarks of Western notions of ownership, i.e. the ability to: loan, rent, sell, dispose of by will, or make permanent improvements. Both Manuh and Manji are at pains to argue that, correctly understood, legal pluralism does not consist of a dichotomy between customary law and statutory law, nor does it imply a hierarchy of norms dominated by statutory law (Manuh 1994; Manji 1998). The latter, moreover, is an invention every bit as much as customary law, in that it also embodies ideological assumptions rooted in the contexts of the colonial reformers (Manuh 1994).

These reflections have begun to dismantle the modernizing discourses that have hitherto dominated the perspectives of legal feminists and by implication these very same discourses are one source of the considerable problems that the formal legal system poses for women. They have not yet, however, led to clear policy recommendations. Manuh has supported Chanock's idea of alternative institutions outside law and state, but her recommendations are very preliminary (Manuh 1994, 224). By and large, the sustained faith in formal law leads many feminist lawyers to underestimate the dynamic power relations that underlie inequity in land relations that ultimately limits the effectiveness of campaigns for women's legal literacy. No doubt some women have been empowered to struggle for their rights because of a growing awareness of legal machinery and of what laws have been passed, but this is not in itself an answer to rural male resistance or to male resistance within legal institutions. However broad or narrow, law reform has to rely on male-dominated institutions to be passed and implemented.

ACHIEVING GENDER JUSTICE IN WOMEN'S ACCESS TO LAND

The (Re-)Turn to the Customary

Recent policy discussions reject land tenure reform based on making a complete
rupture with customary systems and instead stress building on them. The World
Bank wants a flexible system of access, guaranteeing smallholders security and
incentives to invest and now thinks that letting the customary evolve will deliver
land markets and efficient land allocation in a cost-effective and trouble-free
manner. Most of the writers within the Bank's revised thinking say very little
about the anticipated effects on women's land access. Paying scant attention to
the processes by which evolutionary change is occurring, they underplay issues
of equity in the outcome. Customary land law is seen as moving steadily, even if
in a chaotic and problematic way, towards individualized tenure and land markets under its own steam. Oxfam and IIED argue for subsidiarity and the development of local-level management systems for legally backed customary land
tenure practices. Many who hold land under informal systems have no way of
claiming ownership under statutory law, so it is an important first step to recognize and register these entitlements. They have more concern for secondary users
and with the implications of rural power relations, pointing out the link between
the economic gains to traditional leaders and systems that support the idea of
traditional authority. Nevertheless, they still use the terminology of the 'customary'. African feminist lawyers hold a range of views, although for many of them
it is state-backed legal systems that are the key to establishing better access to
resources for women. There is recognition that, in practice, formal legal systems
have often worked to women's disadvantage, but the way forward is to make
the formal system work better. The most prevalent view is that customary
systems enshrine male domination, although some recent commentators are
more positive towards customary law, showing how it has worked to women's
advantage.

   A turn, or re-turn, to the customary raises acutely the question of what we
know about how customary processes actually work. Such a question is an
essential forerunner to the critical issue of the potential of so-called customary
systems to deliver gender justice with respect to land, especially as changing
demands have exposed new ways in which normative principles may be in conflict, bringing individuals into disputes that are difficult to resolve. Although
everyone seems agreed that the customary is historically constructed in form and
content, is flexible and embedded in local social relations, and that conflicting
claims are negotiated on the basis of a series of principles and not on a series of
rules, it is hard not to agree with Okoth-Ogendo that we know very little about
customary land tenure institutions within the modern nation state (Okoth-Ogendo
2000). We now turn to look at a small number of recent studies that have inves-
tigated the actual ways in which land claims have been made, managed and
adjudicated in African rural localities. These show that the customary cannot be
considered in isolation and that its links and interactions with other arenas in

Africa's pluralistic legal systems are critical for women's land claims. Re-examining the debates amongst African feminist lawyers (and some of their international interlocutors), we pose a series of significant questions. What weight does one give to the fact that women and other disadvantaged social groups are able to seize opportunities within systems that discriminate against them to press their claims in deciding whether to change the system or retain it? Does the recognition that statutory interventions, such as titling and registration, may have the effect of rigidifying customary practices and extinguishing some rights under customary law invalidate statutory interventions as a way of proceeding? How different is the recommendation to modify customary systems from the simple 'trust customary law' positions of some mainstream African land special-ists? Is this a call to do nothing about the glaring inequalities in land relations? To comment on these we need to revisit many themes and issues raised in previous sections, but this time more firmly from a gender perspective.

Legal Pluralism and the Customary Reconsidered

Recent local-level studies, especially those undertaken by gender specialists and feminists, have shown that the empirical relation between statutory and custom-ary law is very far from the legal centrist model identified previously. Stewart (1996), for example, argues that the systems are not separate in that, even as they have different bases of legitimacy, they operate in more interconnected ways than is realized. In practice, people, including women, sustain their claims to resources by employing arguments from both the statutory and so-called cus-tomary law. For Stewart, legal pluralism is the consciously constructed dichotomy between statutory and customary. She sees this dichotomy as closely connected to other such dichotomies as male/female, urban/rural, market/personal activity, public/private and modern/tradition employed by powerful people to oppress those with less power. Griffiths, a feminist lawyer writing about local forms of settlement of marriage disputes in a Bakwena village in Botswana, argues that the concepts and objectives from one system seem to slip quite easily to the other and that actors, including law enforcement officers, do not treat the legal ideas in the two systems as hermetically sealed off (Griffiths 1998, 2001). A more appro-priate model of legal pluralism would see them as mutually constitutive.

More generally, recent literature describes as 'forum shopping' situations where individuals are using different courts and other dispute-settlement fora and deploying arguments grounded in either 'customary' or 'modernist' principles, whichever is to their advantage. This conveys a more messy reality in which there are no very rigid boundaries between the plurality of legal fora where different principles of legitimacy and of the basis for claims are brought into play. Recent work in the anthropology of law refers rather to plural legal orders, taking up the term socio-legal to convey both Woodman's idea of sociologists' customary law and to express the ways in which both social and legal are in play in many different legal orders (Wilson 2000). The mingling of social and legal is particularly well brought out by Bosworth, who refers to South Kigezi, in

Uganda, as having a pluralistic legal order (Bosworth 1995). Adapting her account somewhat, there seem to be at least three socio-legal orders in South Kigezi. At the local level there are many informal means of dispute settlement, including kinship mechanisms that use primarily social norms, practices and processes. The formal legal system does not recognize these as legal. This kind of socio-legal order is very important in land claims throughout rural Africa, which leads Okoth-Ogendo, and others, to argue that most adjudication decisions about land operate outside the law.[30] In the Uganda case, not all land claims are through women's husbands. They can also be made through other kin relations, and Bosworth argues that their derived rights were historically very strong claims. However, as lineage members, women had experienced increasing tenure insecurity as senior male lineage members had begun to exercise greater authority over the disposition of lineage lands. This study concurs with many others suggesting that historical transformations have exposed the weaknesses of the customary for ensuring the land access of women as lineage members in situations of land pressure or livelihood insecurity.

Bosworth's second socio-legal order is the formal local-level courts or arbitration fora, whose jurisdiction and scope is determined by the state. These include the Resistance Council courts[31] and the various levels of magistrate's court, and she analyses a series of land-relevant cases brought before them. The court reports give some access to the practices, norms, ideas of evidence, social valuations and so on within this legal arena, and Bosworth stresses that a wide range of social factors is taken into account. Concepts from statutory systems, such as freehold titles, are also in play, but they are only one of a range of resources and only one model of the links between persons that disputants and legal actors call upon. Bosworth gives examples of women in Kabale who have pushed their claims well beyond what is 'customary'. She cites two cases where women had succeeded in getting their names put onto joint titles on land plots with their husbands and had their claims recognized at the local level. In both cases, the women were more educated than the majority of rural women and their husbands were active in the Resistance Councils. A wide range of other persons within a community is involved in dispute settlements, either as witnesses, or as indirect principals. As well as recognizing legal claims to ownership backed by title, women's successful land claims are often based on the fulfilment of social obligations to a range of kin or family members and over long periods of time. The third socio-legal order, not physically present in South Kigezi, but theoretically open to people living there, is the higher formal courts that operate elsewhere in Uganda. These follow statutory law, but may have recourse to a legally constructed notion of customary law, which is far from the actual practices of Kiga people (Bosworth 1995).

---

[30]   This point is also made about Francophone Africa by Lavigne-Deville (2000), who stresses the permanent illegality and insecurity of rural people.
[31]   See Odanga-Mwaka (1998) for an empirical study of Resistance Council courts in Masaka, Uganda.

The South Kigezi material throws light on the arguments about the gendered 'bundle of rights', referred to earlier. It does not seem to be the case that we can generalize that men's interests are primary and women's secondary, although the kinds of interests men and women held were different and these differences form the basis for inequalities, at least in the second half of the twentieth century, if not before. The extent to which women's and men's interests differ and how they differ is very context-specific and cannot be prejudged. Most policy advocates are generalizing on the basis of one particular set of patrilineal practices in their accounts of the secondary nature of women's land claims. Yngstrom, in her study of a land-scarce area in Dodoma, Tanzania, which also has a patrilineal kinship system, shows that in the face of diminishing claims on lineage land, women's main access to land is now through their husbands, and argues that women's claims are not derived or secondary and that this formulation follows a Western legal idea of a hierarchy of rights inappropriate in the African context (Yngstrom 1999). Women did not always fail in land disputes, with significant factors affecting the outcome being the husband's ability to demonstrate land shortage, and the wife's ability to draw on her own lineage men for support. Yngstrom's study encourages a view that variation in the content and strength of women's claims within local-level practices and ideologies more widely in sub-Saharan Africa will markedly affect the potential for these modified local-level systems to deliver gender justice.

In our view, these detailed studies demonstrate that more important than the content of the set of interests, are the processes by which interests and claims are made and secured. The flexibility to respond to new circumstances comes about as individual men and women, young and old, farmer and pastoralist, migrant or autochthon, negotiate over specific parcels of land and over specific kinds of use claim. The factors affecting these struggles and disputes are highly context-specific. The rhetorical recourse by all sides to the contents of long-held practices may or may not be important. The content and direction of the arguments that women make are also highly context-specific, although one recurring powerful set of arguments seems to be that the performance of their social obligations, including those to their husbands, but also to other relatives, builds up claims.[32] A very important limitation on customary systems delivering gender justice lies in these decision-making processes and negotiations and their intersection with rural power relations. Land claims are socially embedded not only in the sense that the network of social relations gives rise to interlinked claims and obligations, but also in the sense that the processes of allocation and adjudication are themselves socially embedded. In part, this is the lesson from Mackenzie's study of a Kikuyu area in Kenya, where in one sense, it was not the statutory that was the problem. Titling could go to women as wives, widows and daughters, but it did not, because local practices and interests intervened (Mackenzie 1993).

---

[32] This point is also made in Kevane and Gray (1999).

Mackenzie suggests that this was not so much because individual men were acting out of economic self-interest, but more because of concerted efforts by male members of the patrilineage to protect the local, kin-based social order. Arguably, however, without the necessity, required by the land reform, to recognize a single claim against land as being ownership, perhaps the customary would have muddled along, with women still able to make their weaker claims. However, once registered titles become an issue, local social relations emerge more clearly as sites of gender power, albeit not ones in which women are simply passive victims, unable to negotiate, bargain and contest sometimes successfully.

The Uganda (S. Kigesi) case study also suggests that letting local-level systems just muddle along will not protect women's land claims as economic change unfolds. Here, women's claims on the land of the patrilineage they had married into were quite strong – for example, one wife was successful in getting the court to overrule her husband selling land given to him by his lineage, which he was required to pass on to her to farm (Bosworth 1995). They had, even so, largely been unable to translate these claims into effective ownership in the land market and husbands had severely curtailed their access to cash income. Three women who had purchased land had done so in their husband's names with potentially significant implications for its disposal without their consent later on.

These studies, then, tend to confirm the critical perspective adopted by some African feminist lawyers with respect to customary practices, whose starting point was that the 'customary', considered as institutions, as social relations and as discourses, are sites where, on the whole, men have more power than women. Rural African societies are, of course, and were, very varied and particularly in the extent of economic and political inequality. Even the most egalitarian societies have been shown to contain significant relations of inequality based in gender and generation. In the past, as today, norms were not universally held, but contested, especially by those whose needs were not met and who lacked voice in decision-making. In those historical periods and regions where there was land abundance and where land tenure was not such an issue, the absence of women's voices may not have affected their access to land. But it is precisely the inequalities in power relations in rural societies, played out in a modern context, that are the mechanism by which women lose claims to land as individualized proprietorship evolves. The flexibility and capacity to change, which are still characteristic of some local level systems, mean that local-level practices are the outcomes of negotiations, but they are negotiations between people with very different quotients of economic and political power. 'In any discussion about land, various interested parties will push claims and interpretations. The ability to make these claims or interpretations stick is a function of local structures of power, influence and personality' (Moore and Vaughan 1994, 211). This implies that the rural customary cannot be left to muddle along without widening the gap between men's and women's land access. It is necessary self-consciously to manage change to produce greater gender justice with respect to resource allocation for rural women. The next section reconsiders the role of the state as a major actor in promoting change.

Managing Change in a Gender-Equitable Manner: The Role of the State,
the Limitations of the Law

Some of the feminist lawyers reviewed earlier brought out some very critical limitations in the use of law to produce gender equity. In the first place, there is a problem of access. Time and again, the point has been made about women's distance from legal processes and their inability to access the courts. This is underlined by how celebrated the cases of the few women who do go to the courts become. While Wambui Otieno and Unity Dow are 'household' names within international and African feminist circles, and are referred to over and over again by academics commenting on women and the law in Africa, it is important to keep in mind their minority status. The work that has gone into promoting legal literacy is important, as is that to strengthen women's access to fora and bodies of law they are more familiar with. But even local-level formal legal fora may have relatively little legitimacy in rural areas, and in many areas women report that they need ways of resolving disputes that are accepted by male relatives and members of the community (Leonard and Toulmin 2000; Odgaad 2000). In arguing for the progressive role of law, then, feminist lawyers need to be more sensitive to the different arenas of struggles for rights and the varied array of forces called forth.

A second set of limitations is that formal legal cultures and institutions are not themselves women-friendly, despite their supposed impartiality and neutrality. Studies of the ways in which statutory law operates in African states, especially those that use case law and records of hearings and case outcomes as their main empirical evidence, have shown very mixed outcomes for women. World-wide, women and feminist lawyers have exposed gender bias in legal cultures and the law, criticizing not just lawmakers and legal practitioners, but many legal concepts. One of the paradoxical features of Africa's legal cultures and law is that some of the gender bias in formal law arises precisely from the construction of 'lawyers' customary law'. In many contemporary African states, lawyers' customary law remains a highly important statutorily defined domain, existing alongside the actual norms, practices and processes in rural communities. When it was created in the colonial era it was precisely many aspects of 'family law' – issues relating to marriage, divorce, children's affiliation and the devolution of property – that were devolved to it. It is these areas of family law that enshrine gender-discriminatory practices in contemporary states. Further bias arises from the ways in which discourses of custom are used within legal cultures and legal institutions. Stewart, especially, has argued that women's claims under modern legal systems in African states are undermined when men argue that their positions are contrary to 'custom'. The language of custom, as she points out, is being used politically in national-level discourses to undermine the legitimacy of women's claims within modern legal frameworks using a rights discourse (Stewart 1996). This leaves feminist lawyers and women litigants little room for manoeuvre. Some of the positions we reviewed earlier suggest a good deal of faith in formal legal concepts and in the power of arguments based on equity and reason to undermine the highly gender-biased legal culture.

A final limitation of the law recalls our discussion of legal pluralism, where we argued that some of the tenets of the formal discourses of law and legality, such as formal equality and individual rights, do not sit easily within customary practices that are embedded in social relations. More than that, those principles, when applied to conflict adjudication or lawmaking, may lead to outcomes ignoring social relations. This is especially important when we consider one of the main ways in which policy advocates are suggesting that modified forms of customary system should form a basis for modern land reform. Codification is being argued for by both the World Bank Land Policy Division and the independent land policy advocates, and the World Bank is currently involved in some pilot codification projects. Lavigne-Delville, writing about attempts to register customary rights in Francophone West Africa, identifies many problems, even where original legal categories are created, derived rights recognized and restrictions placed on the rights to alienate land by the holders of other usage rights (Lavigne-Delville 1999, 17). Land tenure management is removed from its socio-political context and 'becomes an administrative act', in which customary authorities are left with no (or a very limited) role to play. Registering customary practices produces 'a radical transformation of the *ways of managing* land rights and hence the very nature of local landholding systems'. This has implications for 'the whole social structure of local society' (Lavigne-Delville 1999, 17). The point here is that the legal categories of administration and government rest on alienation and decontextualization – the very opposite of the socio-legal principles of indigenous local-level practices. Whether codification can (or under which circumstances it will), protect women's socially embedded land claims is one of the issues in current debates between women's groups in Zimbabwe about codification (Whitehead 2001b).

The State, Democracy and Gender Justice

The array of agents re-appraising the customary is wide-ranging, but one agent that we have paid little attention to is the post-colonial state, which has been balancing many contradictions for decades. In relation to land, different conceptions and practices have developed as carry-overs from the colonial period, although breaks with colonial policy have also occurred. Africa's many states and judiciaries have been actively making land and land tenure policy over these many years, but particularly during the structural adjustment decades. In interpreting its role as creating an enabling environment for foreign investment and in promoting liberalization, how have states considered the land question? Was titling a way of enabling? To what extent is the focus on new forms of land tenure an important part of today's post-SAPs dispensation? The World Bank's attachment to the evolution of local-level systems of tenure and rental is, as we have shown, closely linked to its objectives of deeper and better land markets, and a belief that customary law will deliver, more cheaply, and with less conflict, precisely the individual forms of possession that foreign capital requires.

In this scenario, the language of the customary masks modernization and marketization. It is precisely the recurring discursive power of 'the customary' that is such an important feature of the gender implications of the current policy directions. The idea of the customary carries strong ideological overtones. It is a discourse within what Chanock (1985) has dubbed 'the symbolic capital of tradition'. Claims about the content of 'custom' are rarely reported to have played a part in the local-level negotiations and struggles about changes in resource use going on between men and women.[33] The notion of rural Africa as a 'customary' domain is more often an outsider than an insider perspective. Yet, as we have shown, current land reform debates are dominated by the term, at the same time as there is a good deal of debate and disavowal about its character. Many of our policy advocates prize the consensual and negotiated character of decision-making, a stance, we have argued, that ignores rural power relations. Does part of the attraction of the label lie in idealized versions of its content, as well as the legitimacy it confers?[34]

The term is partly being used because it (often wrongly) implies that rules of land access and so on are long-lived. This is part of a much broader canvas on which practices and values are given legitimacy through their association with culturally specific ways of life of long duration. These more general discourses do not only belong to observers of Africa; they have a very lively currency within the elites of African nation states themselves. The ideas of African/traditional/good versus Western/new/bad have been an important rallying point in many contemporary African states. They are discursive resources of considerable power within many national cultures, particularly associated with bolstering the power of contemporary political elites, part of whose power base lies in so-called traditional offices. African states and their power-holders differ in their links with the institution of chieftaincy, which is a point of change, as well as of continuity, in which the language of the traditional masks what is a contemporary form of political power. To the question, then, of what kind of a political alliance is being made in using the language of the customary, one answer is an alliance with traditional leaders and ideologies. But as with the 'customary' itself, these are contemporary phenomena, part of the array of forces in early twenty-first century African states. The language of chieftaincy and tradition may mask many different kinds of economic and political processes.[35] Many African feminists are alarmed at developments that point to a renewal of chieftaincy and in the activities

---

[33] Carney and Watts (1990) is perhaps an exception here. See also Moore and Vaughan (1994).

[34] See, for example, Platteau, who paints a relatively rosy picture of land access under customary land tenure (Platteau 1996, 75) and Gopal (1999), who blames the harmful effects on women of recent customary practices on the changes brought about by colonial and post-colonial processes and not on the customary itself and argues for looking at the *intentions*, not the actualities of customary norms and practices.

[35] In countries such as Ghana and Cameroon, the retreat of the state under SAPs and political strictures at the national level have coincided with the resurgence of chieftaincy, a process strengthened and signified by the growing phenomenon of urban-based male elite figures becoming chiefs as an expression of their achievements and contributions to their natal villages (Goheen 1996, 163–78).

of elites claiming the legitimacy of tradition in some states. The language of custom has been used oppressively in the politics of gender at national levels in many spheres – from dress, to education, to the use of public space and of course in relation to the operation of the law and legal culture itself (Manuh 1994).

Where does all this leave women? On the one hand, we have some empirical evidence that negative outcomes for women in local-level negotiations and struggles for land are not inevitable. Women are seriously negotiating and making some gains in these processes.[36] The importance of labour for rural production means that women have a serious bargaining chip in their transactions with men and indeed have used it (Okali 1983; Mikell 1989). On the other hand, whether as wives, as sisters or as mothers, case studies show that women still have to fight harder and strategize more skilfully for their access to land. Widowhood, divorce, marriage residence and other life-cycle changes create uncertainties that have to be negotiated carefully. In doing so, women as well as men have recourse to discourses within the customary and to discourses within the modern, whatever the formal or informal arenas of dispute settlement.[37] As Stewart argues, the issues facing women, in terms of law and their rights, is not whether to choose statutory or customary law, but how to maximize their claims under either, or both (Stewart 1996). The question for gender-policy advocates is what stance on the issue of the complex relation between the customary and statutory, as discourses and practices, can best underwrite these claims?

Women in Africa have many reasons to be disillusioned with the state. Many have a history of resisting women's demands and there is a poor record of women's participation in government and in politics at national and local levels. The main holders of national power do not need to use the language of custom to undermine gender justice and women's claims. Recent manoeuvring around Uganda's new land legislation is instructive. Highly effective lobbying and alliance-building strategies by Ugandan women's groups and lawyers resulted in a spousal co-ownership clause being included in the draft land legislation. Despite assurances that this clause would be passed, the final late night parliamentary sittings passed the new land law without these clauses. It remains to be seen if the subsequent bitter recriminations will result in amendments re-instating spousal co-ownership.[38]

Even so, the dangers that we have identified in the turn to the customary suggest that we cannot turn our backs on the state as a source of equity for women in relation to land issues, a point made more generally by Stewart (1996). Rural African women will not find it easier to make claims within a climate of

---

[36] As well as Yngstrom (1999), see Sahelian examples discussed in Leonard and Toulmin (2000), and Vallenga (1985) and Quisumbing et al. (1999), for Ghana.

[37] Manuh recounts how elite women in Ghana seeking to reform family law to get uniformity in inheritance rights for women couched them in terms of 'custom', evoking flexible and fluid versions of customary law that required what was reasonable rather than a fixed set of rules (Manuh 1994). Shipton (1988) suggests some widows benefited from land registration in a Luo area of Kenya.

[38] The story is complicated by the fact that women in the Ugandan parliament were divided and not all of them supported the clause (Mwebaza 1999; Odida 1999).

anti-state discourses. It is true that the many states lack legitimacy in Africa and that women find it difficult to get justice in male-dominated states, but the answer is democratic reform and state accountability, particularly with respect to women's political interests and voices, not a flight into the customary. At a more detailed level, women's land claims need to based on a nuanced and highly sensitive set of policy discourses and policy instruments – ones which reflect the social embeddedness of land claims, the frequent gender inequality in such relations and the rights to livelihood of African women.

The issue of how best to secure rural women's land access depends crucially on democratizing African states, but those processes must engage with issues of gender equity. The main problem is that women have too little political voice at all the decision-making levels that are implied by the land question: in local-level management systems, within the formal law and also within the government and civil society itself. It is here that we should return to the proposals from OXFAM GB and IIED. The political objectives behind their proposals are to strengthen those who have little voice in national decision-making, especially rural farmers. The call for local-level management of land allocation is seen as a major buttress against the processes of land alienation that many national political elites have been facilitating. But there seems to be insufficient interest in making sure that women are amongst the constituency of farmers whose voices are strengthened. Using indigenous institutions is also open to potential abuses of power, and the operation of the 'new or modified' institutions that IIED envisages does not take place in a vacuum, but depends on the way in which local and indeed national power relations feed into the new structures. Moving to community-based management and dispute-settlement systems does not necessarily undermine these power relations. The potential for making new or modified local-level institutions a site of greater gender equity is suggested by a recent study by Odanga-Mwaka. She found that Masaka Resistance Council courts were somewhat more progressive on gender issues than other local legal fora and attributes this firstly, to the stipulation that one-third of the members should be women and secondly to the position adopted on gender issues by the Museveni government (Odanga-Mwaka personal communication).

Toulmin and Quan are aware of the power dimension to rural social relations and its implications for local-level land management. 'The question of who gains access to land and on what terms can only be understood by seeing how control over land is embedded within the broader patterns of social relations' (Toulmin and Quan 2000b, 6). There is a sharp contradiction between this point and the continued use of the term 'customary', which, we have argued, is a discourse that upholds, rather than undermines, social, economic and political inequality. Some of the work calling for new functions for local-level institutions, or new local management systems, carefully avoids using the term 'customary'. Lavigne-Delville says specifically it should not be used, but refers instead to 'local landholding systems and socially determined land use rules' (1999, 2). But at least until mid-2001, this has not been the stance adopted in Toulmin and Quan and on OXFAM GB's land policy website. There seem to us to be too many hostages to fortune in the language of the customary at a national level for it to spearhead democratic reforms and resistance to centralized and elite-serving state power. It certainly will not promote gender justice for women, either in the sphere of land access or more generally. There are simply too many examples of women losing out when modern African men talk of custom. Elsewhere, of course, both IIED and OXFAM GB are aware of the importance of women's land rights. 'Protection of women's and future generations' land rights frequently requires reform of existing inheritance laws, and may in some cases be incompatible with traditional leaders' absolute authority over land' (Quan 1997).[39] The absence of sustained and serious discussion of how new functions for existing local-level institutions, or new local-level land management systems, will ensure that women's land use claims are not systematically undermined is regrettable. It suggests that progressive policy-making on land has its own box of institutions, networks, resources and discourses, while that on gender exists in another. It is high time for informed dialogue between them.

REFERENCES

Alden-Wily, L., 2000. 'Land Tenure Reform and the Balance of Power in Eastern and Southern Africa'. *ODI Natural Resources Perspectives*, 58.

Alden-Wily, L., forthcoming. 'Changing Property Relations of State and People: A Critical Review of Land Reform in Eastern and Southern Africa at the Turn of the Century'. Work in progress.

Armstrong, A., 1987. *Women and Law in Southern Africa*. Harare: Zimbabwe Publishing House.

Armstrong, A. and J. Stewart, 1990. *The Legal Situation of Women in Southern Africa*. Harare: University of Zimbabwe.

Atwood, D.A., 1990. 'Land Registration in Africa: The Impact on Agricultural Production'. *World Development*, 18 (5): 659–71.

Barrows, R. and M. Roth, 1989. 'Land Tenure and Investment in African Agriculture: Theory and Evidence'. Land Tenure Center Paper 136. Madison, WI: University of Wisconsin Press.

Basset, T.J., 1993. 'Introduction: The Land Question and Agricultural Transformation in Sub-Saharan Africa'. In *Land in African Agrarian Systems*, eds T.J. Basset and D.E. Crummey, 3–31. Madison: University of Wisconsin Press.

Basset, T.J. and D.E. Crummey, 1993. *Land in African Agrarian Systems*. Madison: University of Wisconsin Press.

Berry, S., 1989. 'Social Institutions and Access to Resources'. *Africa*, 59 (1): 41–55.

Berry, S., 1992. 'Hegemony on a Shoestring: Indirect Rule and Access to Agricultural Land'. *Africa*, 62 (3): 327–55.

Berry, S., 1993. *No Condition is Permanent: The Social Dynamics of Agrarian Change in Sub-Saharan Africa*. Madison: University of Wisconsin Press.

Berry, S., 1997. 'Tomatoes, Land and Hearsay: Property and History in Asante in the Time of Structural Adjustment'. *World Development*, 25 (25): 1225–1241.

---

[39] See also Quan (2001).

Berry, S., 2000. *Chiefs Know Their Boundaries: Essays on Property Power and the Past in Asante 1896–1996*. Oxford: James Currey.

Blackden, Mark C. and Elizabeth Morris-Hughes, 1993. *Paradigm Postponed: Gender and Economic Adjustment in Sub-Saharan Africa*. Poverty and Human Resources Division, Technical Department, Africa Region. Washington: World Bank.

Blackden, M. and C. Bhanu, 1999. *Gender, Growth and Poverty Reduction: Special Programme for Assistance of Africa, 1998 Status Report in Poverty in Sub-Saharan Africa*. Washington: World Bank.

Bosworth, Joanne L., 1995. 'Land Tenure Systems in sub-Saharan Africa'. DPhil Thesis, Faculty of Social Studies, University of Oxford.

Bruce, J.W., 1986. 'Land Tenure Issues in Project Design and Strategies for Agricultural Development in Sub-Saharan Africa'. Land Tenure Center Paper 128. Madison: University of Wisconsin Press.

Bruce, J.W., 1993. 'Do Indigenous Tenure Systems Constrain Agricultural Development?' In *Land in African Agrarian Systems*, eds T.J. Basset and D.E. Crummey, 35–56. Madison: University of Wisconsin Press.

Bruce, John W., Shem E. Migot-Adholla and Joan Atherton, 1994. 'The Findings and Their Policy Implications: Institutional Adaptation or Replacement'. In *Searching For Land Tenure Security in Africa*, eds John W. Bruce and Shem Migot-Adholla, 251–65. Iowa: Kendall Hunt Publishing Company.

Bruce, J. and S.E. Migot-Adholla, eds, 1994. *Searching for Land Tenure Security in Africa*. Iowa: Kendall Hunt Publishing Company.

Butegwa, Florence, 1991. 'Women's Legal Right of Access to Agricultural Resources in Africa: A Preliminary Inquiry'. *Third World Legal Studies – Special Edition*: 45–58.

Butegwa, Florence, 1994. 'Using the African Charter on Human and Peoples' Rights to Secure Women's Access to Land in Africa'. In *Human Rights of Women: National and International Perspectives*, ed. R.J. Cook, 495–514. Philadelphia: University of Pennsylvania Press.

Carney, Judith, 1988. 'Struggles over Crop Rights within Contract Farming Households on a Gambian Irrigated Rice Project'. *Journal of Peasant Studies*, 15 (3): 334–49.

Carney, J. and Michael Watts, 1990. 'Manufacturing Dissent: Work, Gender and the Politics of Meaning in a Peasant Society'. *Africa*, 60 (2): 207–41.

Chanock, Martin, 1985. *Law, Custom and Social Order*. Cambridge: Cambridge University Press.

Chanock, Martin, 1991a. 'Paradigms, Policies and Property: A Review of the Customary Law of Tenure'. In *Law in Colonial Africa*, eds K. Mann and R. Roberts, 61–84. London: James Currey, Heinemann.

Chanock, Martin, 1991b. 'A Peculiar Sharpness: An Essay on Property in the History of Customary Law in Colonial Africa'. *Journal of African History*, 32 (1): 65–88.

Cheater, A., 1982. 'Formal and Informal Rights to Land in Zimbabwe's Black Freehold Areas: A Case Study from Msengezi'. *Africa*, 52 (3): 77–91.

Cleaver, K. and G. Schreiber, 1993. 'The Population, Agriculture and Environment Nexus in Sub-Saharan Africa'. Technical Dept. African Region. Washington: World Bank.

Cook, Rebecca, 1991. 'Guest Editor's Introduction'. *Third World Legal Studies – Special Edition*: vi–ix.

Cook, Rebecca J., 1994. 'State Accountability Under the Convention on the Elimination of All Forms of Discrimination Against Women'. In *Human Rights of Women: National and International Perspectives*, ed. R.J. Cook, 228–56. Philadelphia: University of Pennsylvania Press.

Davison, Jean, 1988a. '"Who Owns What?" Land Registration and Tension in Gender Relations of Production in Kenya'. In *Agriculture, Women and Land*, ed. Jean Davison, 157–76. Boulder: Westview Press.

Davison, Jean, ed., 1988b. *Agriculture, Women and Land: The African Experience.* Boulder: Westview Press.

Deininger, K., 1998. 'The Evolution of the World Bank's Land Policy'. Mimeo. Washington: World Bank.

Deininger, Klaus and Hans Binswanger, 1999. 'The Evolution of the World Bank's Land Policy: Principles, Experience and Future Challenges'. *The World Bank Research Observer*, 14: 247–76.

DFID, 1999. 'Land Rights and Sustainable Development in Sub-Saharan Africa: Lessons and Ways Forward in Land Tenure Policy'. Report of delegate workshop of land tenure policy in African Nations, Sunningdale, UK, 16–19 February. Mimeo.

Downs, R.E. and S.P. Reyna, eds, 1988. *Land and Society in Contemporary Africa.* Hanover: University Press of England.

EARC, 1955. *East African Royal Commission 1953–1955 Report.* London: HMSO.

Eicher, C.K. and D.C. Baker, 1982. 'Research on Agricultural Development in sub-Saharan Africa: A Critical Survey'. Michigan: Department of Agricultural Economics, Michigan State University.

Falk-Moore, S., 1975. *Law as Process: An Anthropological Approach.* London: Routledge.

Falk-Moore, S., 1998. 'Changing African Land Tenure; Reflections on the Incapacities of the State'. *European Journal of Development Research*, 10 (2): 33–49.

Fallers, Lloyd, A., 1969. *Law Without Precedent: Legal Ideas in Action in the Courts of Colonial Bugosa.* London: University of Chicago Press.

Feder, Gershon and David Feeny, 1991. 'Land Tenure and Property Rights: Theory and Implications for Development Policy'. *The World Bank Economic Review*, 5 (1): 135–53.

Feder, G. and R. Noronha, 1987. 'Land Rights Systems and Agricultural Development in Sub-Saharan Africa'. *Research Observer*, 2 (2): 143–69.

Fleuret, A., 1988. 'Some Consequences of Tenure and Agrarian Reform in Taita, Kenya'. In *Land and Society in Contemporary Africa*, eds R.E. Downs and S.P. Reyna, 136–58. Hanover: University Press of New England.

Fortmann, Louise, Camille Antinori and Nontokozo Nabane, 1997. 'Fruits of their Labors: Gender, Property Rights, and Tree Planting in Two Zimbabwe Villages'. *Rural Sociology*, 62 (3): 295–314.

Gluckman, Max, 1941. 'Economy of the Central Barotse Plain'. Rhode-Livingstone Paper 7. Livingstone, Northern Rhodesia: Rhodes-Livingstone Institute.

Gluckman, Max, 1943. 'Essays on Lozi land and Royal Property'. Rhodes-Livingstone Paper 10. Livingstone, Northern Rhodesia: Rhodes-Livingstone Institute.

Gluckman, Max, 1965. *The Ideas in Barotse Jurisprudence.* London: Yale University Press.

Goheen, M., 1996. *Men Own the Fields and Women Own the Crops: Gender and Power in the Cameroon Grassfields.* Madison: University Press of Wisconsin.

Goody, J., 1980. 'Rice Burning and Green Revolution in Ghana'. *Journal of Development Studies*, 16 (2): 136–55.

Gopal, Gita, 1998. 'Overview'. In *Gender and Law: Eastern Africa Speaks Conference Organised by the World Bank and the Economic Commission for Africa*, eds G. Gopal and M. Salim, 1–22. Washington: World Bank.

Gopal, Gita, 1999. 'Gender-Related Legal Reform and Access to Economic Resources in Eastern Africa'. Washington: World Bank.

Green, J.K., 1987. 'Evaluating the Impact of Consolidation of Holdings, Individualisation of Tenure and Registration of Title: Lessons from Kenya'. Land Tenure Center Paper 12. Madison: University of Wisconsin.

Griffiths, Anne M.O., 1997. *The Shadow of Marriage*. Chicago: University of Chicago Press.

Griffiths, Anne, 1998. 'Reconfiguring Law: An Ethnographic Perspective from Botswana'. *Law and Social Inquiry*, 23 (3): 587–620.

Griffiths, Anne, 2001. 'Gendering Culture: Towards a Plural Perspective of Kwena Women's Rights'. In *Culture and Rights*, eds J. Cowan, M. Dembour and R. Wilson, 102–26. Cambridge: Cambridge University Press.

Hanstad, Tim, 2001. 'Peer Review of World Bank Land Policy and Administration Paper'. Seattle: Rural Development Institute.

Haugerud, A., 1983. 'The Consequences of Land Tenure Reform among Small Holders in the Kenya Highlands'. *Rural Africana*, 15–16: 65–89.

Haugerud, A., 1989. 'Land Tenure and Agrarian Change in Kenya'. *Africa*, 59 (1): 61–90.

Hay, M.J. and M. Wright, eds, 1982. *African Women and the Law*. Boston: Boston University African Studies Center.

Heck, Simon, 1996. 'Sales Contract and Land Tenure Relations in Ankole, Western Uganda'. Boston: African Studies Center, Boston University.

Heyer, Judith and Gavin Williams, no date. 'Oxfam Submission to Tanzanian Land Commission: Agricultural Issues'. Oxfam. Mimeo.

Hilhorst, Thea, 2000. 'Women's Land Rights: Current Developments in Sub Saharan Africa'. In *Evolving Land Rights, Policy and Tenure in Africa*, eds C. Toulmin and J. Quan, 188–96. London: IIED with DFID and NRI.

Hill, Polly, 1972. *Rural Hausa: A Village and a Setting*. Cambridge: Cambridge University Press.

Himonga, C.N. and M.L. Munachonga, 1991. 'Rural Women's Access to Agricultural Land in Settlement Schemes in Zambia: Law, Practice and Socio-Economic Constraints'. *Third World Legal Studies – Special Edition*: 59–74.

IIED, 1999. 'Land Tenure and Resource Access in West Africa: Issues and Opportunities for the Next Twenty-Five Years'. London: International Institute for Environment and Development.

Jacobs, S., 1991. 'Land Resettlement and Gender in Zimbabwe: Some Findings'. *Journal of Modern African Studies*, 29 (3): 523–30.

Karanja, Perpetua Wambui, 1991. 'Women's Land Ownership Rights in Kenya'. *Third World Legal Studies – Special Edition*: 109–36.

Kevane, Michael and Leslie C. Gray, 1999. 'A Woman's Field is Made at Night: Gendered Land Rights and Norms in Burkina Faso'. *Feminist Economics*, 5 (1): 1–26.

Knowles, Jane B., 1991. 'Women's Access to Land in Africa'. *Third World Legal Studies – Special Edition*: 1–14.

Lastarria-Cornhiel, Susana, 1997. 'Impact of Privatisation on Gender and Property Rights in Africa'. *World Development*, 25 (8): 1317–33.

Lavigne-Delville, S., 1999. 'Harmonising Formal Law and Customary Land Rights in French-Speaking West Africa'. Drylands Issue Paper 86. London: IIED.

Lavigne-Delville, S., 2000. 'Harmonising Formal Law and Customary Land Rights in French-Speaking West Africa'. In *Evolving Land Rights, Policy and Tenure*, eds C. Toulmin and J. Quan, 97–122. London: IIED with DFID and NRI.

Lawi, Y.Q., 2000. 'Justice Administration Outside the Ordinary Courts of Law in Mainland Tanzania: The Case of the Ward Tribunals in Babati District'. Mimeo.

Leonard, R. and C. Toulmin, 2000. 'Women and Land Tenure'. Mimeo. IIED Drylands Programme, UK.

Lugard, F.D., 1922. *The Dual Mandate in British Tropical Africa*. London: Blackwoods.

Mackenzie, Fiona, 1990. 'Gender and Land Rights in Murang'a District, Kenya'. *Journal of Peasant Studies*, 17 (4): 609–43.

Mackenzie, Fiona, 1993. '"A Piece of Land Never Shrinks": Reconceptualizing Land Tenure in a Small-Holding District'. In *Land in African Agrarian Systems*, eds T.J. Basset and D.E. Crummey, 194–222. Madison: University of Wisconsin Press.

Mackenzie, F., 1998. *Land Ecology and Resistance in Kenya*. Edinburgh: Edinburgh University Press for IAI.

Mamdami, M., 1996. *Citizen and Subject: Contemporary Africa and the Legacy of Late Colonialism*. New Jersey: Princeton University Press.

Manji, Ambreena, 1998. 'Gender and the Politics of the Land Reform Process in Tanzania'. *The Journal of Modern African Studies*, 36 (4): 645–67.

Manji, Ambreena, 1999. 'Imagining Women's "Legal" World: Towards a Feminist Theory of Legal Pluralism in Africa'. *Social and Legal Studies*, 8 (4): 435–55.

Manuh, T., 1984. 'Law and the Status of Women in Ghana'. Addis Ababa: ECA.

Manuh, T., 1994. *Women's Rights and Traditional Law: A Conflict*. International Third World Legal Studies Association and the Valparaiso University School of Law.

Manuh, T., 1995. *The Women, Law and Development Movement in Africa and the Struggle for Customary Law Reform*. International Third World Legal Studies Association and the Valparaiso University School of Law.

Manuh, T., J. Songsore and F. Mackenzie, no date. 'Gender and Land: the Interface between Legislative Initiatives, Customary Tenure and Land Use Management in Ghana'. mimeo.

McAuslan, Patrick, 1996. 'Making Law Work: Restructuring Land Relations in Africa (3rd Alistair Berkeley Memorial Lecture)'. London: London School of Economics.

McAuslan, Patrick, 2000. 'Only the Name of the Country Changes: The Diaspora of "European" Land Law in Commonwealth Africa'. In *Evolving Land Rights, Policy and Tenure in Africa*, eds C. Toulmin and J. Quan, 75–96. London: IIED with DFID and NRI.

Meek, C.K., 1946. *Land Law and Custom in the Colonies*. London: Oxford University Press.

Migot-Adholla, Shem E., 1999. 'Principles of the World Bank's Land Policy'. Slide Presentation at the DFID workshop on Land Rights and Sustainable Development in Sub-Saharan Africa, Sunningdale, UK.

Migot-Adholla, Shem E. and J. Bruce, 1994. 'Introduction'. In *Searching for Land Tenure Security in Africa*, eds John W. Bruce and Shem E. Migot-Adholla, 1–13. Iowa: Kendall Hunt Publishing Company.

Migot-Adholla, Shem E., P. Hazell, B. Blarel and F. Place, 1991. 'Indigenous Land Rights Systems in Sub-Saharan Africa: A Constraint on Productivity?' *World Bank Economic Review*, 5 (1): 155–75.

Migot-Adholla, Shem E., George Benneh, Frank Place and Steven Atsu, 1994a. 'Land, Security of Tenure and Productivity in Ghana'. In *Searching for Land Tenure Security in Africa*, eds John W. Bruce and Shem E. Migot-Adholla, 97–117. Iowa: Kendall Hunt Publishing Company.

Migot-Adholla, Shem, F. Place and W. Oluoch-Kosura, 1994b. 'Security of Tenure and Land Productivity in Kenya'. In *Searching for Land Security in Africa*, eds John W. Bruce and Shem E. Migot-Adholla, 119–40. Iowa: Kendall Hunt.

Mikell, G., 1989. *Cocoa and Chaos in Ghana*. New York: Paragon House.

Molokomme, A., 1991. 'Children of the Fence: The Maintenance of Extra-Marital Children Under Law and Practice in Botswana'. Research Report 41. Leiden: University of Leiden.

Molokomme, A., 1995. 'Women's Rights to Land and Property in Southern Africa'. Paper presented at the NGO Forum for Women, 4th World Conference, Beijing, China.

Molokomme, A., 1996. 'State Intervention in the Family: A Case Study of the Child Maintenance Law in Botswana'. In *Shifting Circles of Support: Contextualising Kinship and Gender in South Asia and Sub-Saharan Africa*, eds R. Palriwala and C. Risseuw, 270–301. London: Sage.

Moore, H. and M. Vaughan, 1994. *Cutting Down Trees: Gender, Nutrition and Agricultural Change in the Northern Province of Zambia 1980–1990*. London: James Currey.

Moyo, S., forthcoming. 'The Land Question and Land Reform in Southern Africa'. Work in progress.

Mwebaza, Rose, 1999. 'How to Integrate Statutory and Customary Tenure? The Ugandan Case'. Presented to DFID Workshop on Land Rights, Sunningdale, UK, 16–19 February 1999.

O'Rourke, Nancy, 1995. 'Land Rights and Gender Relations in Areas of Rural Africa: A Question of Power and Discourse'. *Social and Legal Studies*, 4 (1): 75–97.

Odanga-Mwaka, B., 1998. 'Widowhood and Property among the Baganda of Uganda: Uncovering the Passive'. DPhil Thesis, Faculty of Law, University of Warwick.

Odgaad, R., 2000. 'The Scramble for Women's Land Rights in Tanzania'. Internet edition www.oxfam.org.uk/landrights.

Odida, I.O., 1999. 'Land Law Reform: Challenges and Opportunities for Securing Women's Land Rights in Uganda'. Paper presented at DFID Workshop on Land Tenure Policy in African Nations, Sunningdale, UK.

Okali, C., 1983. *Cocoa and Kinship in Ghana: The Matrilineal Akan of Ghana*. London: Kegan Paul International for International African Institute.

Okoth-Ogendo, H.W.O., 1989. 'Some Issues of Theory in the Study of Tenure Relations in African Agriculture'. *Africa*, 59 (1): 6–17.

Okoth-Ogendo, H.W.O., 1998. 'Land Policy Reforms in East and Southern Africa: A Comparative Analysis of Drivers, Processes and Outcomes'. Paper for an International Conference on Land Tenure in the Developing World, Cape Town, South Africa.

Okoth-Ogendo, H.W.O., 2000. 'Legislative Approaches to Customary Tenure and Tenure Reform in East Africa'. In *Evolving Land Rights, Policy and Tenure in Africa*, eds C. Toulmin and J. Quan, 123–34. London: IIED with DFID and NRI.

Palmer, R., 1998. 'Oxfam GB's Land Advocacy Work in Tanzania and Uganda: The End of an Era'. Oxfam. Mimeo.

Palmer, R., 2000. 'The Struggles Continue: Evolving Land Policy and Tenure Reforms in Africa – Recent Policy and Implementation Procedures'. In *Evolving Land Rights, Policy and Tenure in Africa*, eds C. Toulmin and J. Quan, 267–88. London: IIED with DFID and NRI.

Phillips, A., 1989. *The Enigma of Colonialism: British Policy in West Africa*. London: James Currey.

Pinckey, Thomas C. and Peter K. Kimuyu, 1994. 'Land Tenure Reform in East Africa: Good, Bad or Unimportant'. *Journal of African Economies*, 3 (1): 1–28.

Platteau, Jean-Phillipe, 1992. 'Land Reform and Structural Adjustment in Sub-Saharan Africa: Controversies and Guidelines'. Rome: Policy Analysis Division, FAO Economic and Social Policy Department.

Platteau, J.-P., 1996. 'The Evolutionary Theory of Land Rights as Applied to Sub-Saharan Africa: A Critical Assessment'. *Development and Change*, 27 (1): 29–86.

Platteau, J.-P., 2000. 'Does Africa Need Land Reform?' In *Evolving Land Rights, Policy and Tenure in Africa*, eds C. Toulmin and J. Quan, 51–76. London: IIED with DFID and NRI.

Quan, J.F., 1997. 'The Importance of Land Tenure to Poverty Eradication and Sustainable Development in Sub-Saharan Africa'. Background Report for the 1997 UK Government White Paper on International Development. London: DFID.

Quan, J., 2000. 'Land Tenure, Economic Growth and Poverty in Sub-Saharan Africa'. In *Evolving Land Rights, Policy and Tenure in Africa*, eds C. Toulmin and J. Quan, 31–50. London: IIED with DFID and NRI.

Quan, J., 2001. 'Review of the World Bank Paper: Land Policy and Administration'. Posted on www.worldbank.org. Washington: World Bank.

Quisumbing, A., R. Agnes, E. Payongayong, J.B. Aidoo and K. Otsuka, 1999. 'Women's Land Rights in the Transition to Individualised Ownership: Implications for the Management of Tree Resources in Western Ghana'. Washington: IFPRI.

Reyna, S.P., 1987. 'The Emergence of Land Concentration in the West African Savannah'. *American Ethnologist*, 13 (3): 523–41.

Rocheleau, D. and D. Edmunds, 1997. 'Men, Women and Trees: Gender, Power and Property in Forest and Agrarian Landscapes'. *World Development*, 25 (8): 1351–71.

Schroeder, Richard A., 1997. '"Re-claiming" Land in the Gambia: Gendered Property Rights and Environmental Intervention'. *Annals of the Association of American Geographers*, 87 (3): 487–508.

Shepherd, A., 1981. 'Agrarian Change in Northern Ghana: Public Investment, Capitalist Farming and Famine'. In *Rural Development in Tropical Africa*, eds J. Heyer, P. Roberts and G. Williams, 68–182. London: Macmillan.

Shipton, Parker, 1988. 'The Kenyan Land Tenure Reform: Misunderstandings in the Public Creation of Private Property'. In *Land and Society in Contemporary Africa*, eds R.E. Downs and S.P. Reyna, 91–135. Hanover: University Press of England.

Shipton, Parker and Mitzi Goheen, 1992. 'Understanding African Land-Holding: Power, Wealth, and Meaning'. *Africa*, 62 (3): 307–25.

Shivji, I., 1998. 'Not Yet Democracy: Reforming Land Tenure in Tanzania'. London, Dar es Salaam: IIED, Faculty of Law, University of Dar es Salaam, HAKIARDHI.

Sjaastad, Espen and Daniel W. Bromley, 1997. 'Indigenous Land Rights in Sub-Saharan Africa: Appropriation, Security and Investment Demand'. *World Development*, 25 (4): 549–62.

Sorrenson, M.P.K., 1967. *Land Reform in the Kikuyu Country: A Study in Government Policy*. Oxford: Oxford University Press.

Stewart, Ann, 1996. 'Should Women Give Up on the State? – The African Experience'. In *Women and the State: International Perspectives*, eds S. Rai and G. Skinner, 23–44. London: Taylor and Francis.

Stewart, J.E., W.E. Ncube, with others, no date. 'Standing at the Crossroads: WLSA and the Rights Dilemma. Which Way Do We Go?' Harare: Women and Law in Southern Africa.

Swynnerton, R.J.M., 1954. *A Plan to Intensify the Development of African Agriculture*. Nairobi: Government Printer.

Toulmin, C. and S. Pepper, 2000. 'Land Reform, North and South'. Drylands Programme Issue Paper 96. London: IIED.

Toulmin, Camilla and Julian Quan, eds, 2000a. *Evolving Land Rights, Policy and Tenure in Africa*. London: IIED with DFID and NRI.

Toulmin, C. and J. Quan, 2000b. 'Evolving Land Rights, Policy and Tenure in Africa – Introduction to'. In *Evolving Land Rights, Policy and Tenure in Africa*, eds C. Toulmin and J. Quan, 1–30. London: IIED with DFID and NRI.

Toulmin, C., P. Lavigne-Delville and S. Traore, eds, 2001. *The Dynamics of Resource Tenure in West Africa*. Oxford: James Currey.

Vallenga, D., 1986. 'Matriliny, Patriliny and Class Formation among Women Cocoa Farmers in Two Rural Areas of Ghana'. In *Women and Class in Africa*, eds C. Robertson and I. Berger, 62–77. New York: Africana Publishing Company.

Wanitzek, Ulrike, 1990. 'Legally Unrepresented Women Petitioners in the Lower Courts of Tanzania: A Case Study of Justice Denied'. *Journal of Legal Pluralism and Unofficial Law*, 30/31: 255–71.

Whitehead, A., 1984. 'Women and Men; Kinship and Property: Some General Issues'. In *Women and Property: Women as Property*, ed. R. Hirschon, 176–92. London: Croom Helm.

Whitehead, A. and M. Lockwood, 1999a. 'Gendering Poverty: A Review of Six World Bank African Poverty Assessments'. *Development and Change*, 30 (3): 525–55.

Whitehead, A., 2001a. 'Trade, Trade Liberalisation and Rural Poverty in Low-Income Africa: A Gendered Account'. Background Paper for the UNCTAD 2001 Least Developed Countres Report. Geneva: UNCTAD.

Whitehead, A., 2001b. 'Policy Discourses on Women's Land Rights in Zimbabwe'. Paper prepared for the UNRISD Project on 'Agrarian Change, Gender and Land Rights'. Geneva: UNRISD.

Williams, Gavin, 1994. 'Modernising Malthus: The World Bank, Population Control and the African Environment'. In *Power of Development*, ed. J. Crush, 158–75. London: Routledge.

WLSA Series

    Aphane, M.-J.D. et al., 1998. *Family in Transition: The Experience of Swaziland*. Swaziland, Manzini: WLSA.

    Chuulu, M.B. et al., 1997. *The Changing Family in Zambia*. Zambia, Lusaka: WLSA.

    Kidd, P.E. et al., 1997. *Botswana Families and Women's Rights in a Changing Environment*. WLSA Botswana, National Institute for Development Research and Documentation, Gaborone.

    Letuka, P. et al., 1998. *Family Belonging for Women in Lesotho*. Lesotho, Morija: WLSA.

    Ncube, W. et al. 1997a. *Continuity and Change: The Family in Zimbabwe*. Zimbabwe, Harare: WLSA.

    Ncube, W. et al., 1997b. *Paradigms of Exclusion: Women's Access to Resources in Zimbabwe*. Zimbabwe, Harare: WLSA.

    Temba E. et al., 1997. *Families in a Changing Environment in Mozambique*. Mozambique: WLSA and Maputo: Centre for African Studies, Euardo Mondlane University.

Wilson, R., 2000. 'Reconciliation and Revenge in Post-Apartheid South Africa; Rethinking Legal Pluralism and Human Rights'. *Current Anthropology*, 41 (1): 75–98.

Woodman, G., 1985. 'Customary Law, State Courts and the Notion of Institutionalisation of Norms in Ghana and Nigeria'. In *People's Law and the State*, eds A. Allot and G.R. Woodman, 143–63. Dordrecht: Foris Publications.

World Bank, 1975. 'Land Reform Policy'. Washington: World Bank Land Policy Division.

World Bank, 1989. 'Sub-Saharan Africa: From Crisis to Sustainable Growth'. Washington: World Bank.

World Bank, 1994. 'Women, Legal Reform and Development in Sub-Saharan Africa'. *Africa Region Findings* Number 20.

World Bank, 2000a. 'World Development Report 2000/01. Attacking Poverty: Approach and Outline'. Edited by R. Kanbur. www.worldbank.org/poverty/.

World Bank, 2000b. 'Engendering Development: The Policy Research Report on Gender and Development'. Edited by A. Mason and E. King. www.worldbank.org/gender/.

World Bank, 2000c. 'Ghana: Country Assistance Strategy'. Washington: World Bank.

World Bank, 2000d. 'Ghana Land Administration Program: Project Concept Development'. Africa Regional Office, Country Department 10. Washington: World Bank.

World Bank, 2001. 'Land Policy and Administration: Lessons Learned and New Challenges for the Bank's Development Agenda'. www.worldbank.org.

Yngstrom, Ingrid, 1999. 'Gender, Land and Development in Tanzania: Rural Dodoma, 1920–1996'. DPhil Thesis, University of Oxford.

Yngstrom, I., 2002. 'Women, Wives and Land Rights in Africa: Situating Gender Beyond the Household in the Debate over Tenure Reform'. *Oxford Development Studies*, 30 (1): 21–40.

4

Piety in the Sky? Gender Policy and Land Reform in South Africa

CHERRYL WALKER

This article examines the disjuncture between high-level commitments to gender equity and practice in South Africa's land reform programme. Weaknesses in implementing the gender policy of the Department of Land Affairs stem largely from limitations within the broader programme, compounded by the inadequate conceptualization and management of the task and an absence of political accountability around women's land rights by the Department and Ministry. The low political priority accorded gender policy is itself a reflection of weak levels of organization among rural women. However, rural women show an interest in strengthening their rights in land and the small number of women whose households have secured land through the programme regard this as a positive achievement.

Keywords: land reform, gender, South Africa

INTRODUCTION

In April 1997, South Africa's Minister of Land Affairs approved a 'Land Reform Gender Policy' document 'aimed at creating an enabling environment for women to access, own, control, use and manage land; as well as access credit for productive use of the land' (Department of Land Affairs 1997a, 2–3). This document committed the Ministry and Department of Land Affairs (DLA) to a wide-ranging set of guiding principles to 'actively promote the principle of gender equity' in land reform; these included mechanisms for ensuring women's full and equal participation in decision-making; communication strategies; gender-sensitive methodologies in project planning; legislative reform; training; collaboration with NGOs and other government structures, and compliance with international commitments, such as the 1995 'Beijing Platform for Action' and the Convention on the Elimination of all Forms of Discrimination Against Women (CEDAW) (which South Africa had re-ratified in 1995).

The approval of the Gender Policy document coincided with the government's formal adoption that same month of its overall framework for land reform, the

I would like to acknowledge UNRISD and especially Shahra Razavi for supporting this work and also the special contribution of Sizani Ngubane and Nomusa Sokhela in the fieldwork. I would also like to thank all those who gave so generously of their time and knowledge in interviews and/or comments on my draft reports.

White Paper on South African Land Policy, which also strongly endorsed gender equity as a key outcome, to be achieved through the targeting of women as beneficiaries (Department of Land Affairs 1998, 17). Yet three and a half years later, DLA officials participating in an internal 'Gender Best Practices' workshop in the KwaZulu Natal provincial office complained that 'gender' was not part of their core business. 'The Department would not walk away from a project where you are not getting cooperation around gender issues', said one participant (Walker 2000a). A Deputy Director in the office described the gender policy as not on the agenda of the provincial Management Committee at all – 'They left it to the Programme Managers how they do it. I don't think there is a common commitment to it' (interview).

The disjuncture between what is said in formal policy documents and the treatment of gender issues in practice lies at the heart of the research project that is reported on here.[1] This article has two main concerns. The first is to examine this disjuncture and why it exists – why the commitment to gender equity has operated mainly at the level of lofty principle, a kind of 'piety in the sky' that has not been translated into vigorous action on the ground. The second concern is to look at how DLA practice has engaged rural women, using as my prism three projects from the first phase of land reform (before 1999) in the province of KwaZulu Natal – Mahlabathini and Ntabeni in the Midlands and The Gorge on the South Coast. As the discussion will show, poor women whose households obtained land through these projects value the relative security of tenure they have gained, the ambiguities of their status within patriarchal relationships and the doubtful economic prospects for their land notwithstanding.

This study recognizes that it is relatively easy to critique the often self-evident weaknesses of land policy formulation and implementation, especially when measured against their ambitious objectives, but harder to craft serious alternatives. Land reform is generally overburdened with unrealistic public expectations of what it should achieve in ushering in the just, productive and tolerant society envisaged by the 1997 *White Paper*. Inflated expectations are certainly evident in the aspirations of many gender activists for land reform to serve as a catalyst for transforming rural gender relations, as well as in the deep disappointment they express at what has been achieved to date. To institute programmes that challenge unequal gender relations is difficult, partly because the subordinate status of rural women is embedded in multi-layered relationships that are not easily reduced to policy prescriptions and managed within bureaucratic budget and project cycles.

---

[1] The research, which was part of the UNRISD project on Agrarian Change, Gender and Land Rights, involved an analysis of primary documents, interviews (a full list of interviews is contained in Walker 2001a), with government officials and land reform experts during 2000, and fieldwork between September 2000 and February 2001. Sizani Ngubane, of AFRA, assisted by Nomusa Sokhela, conducted interviews with land reform beneficiaries on my behalf; their contribution is gratefully acknowledged. This article is a condensed version of the second of two research reports (Walker 2001a). The first report (Walker 2001b) sets out the historical background and context for land reform more fully than is possible here.

In addition, much of the work of shifting gender relations comes after the DLA has 'exited' the project, which is after the land has been transferred to the newly created legal entity that is to hold that land. DLA staff are under heavy pressure from senior management and the Ministry to exit projects as soon as possible after the transfer of land – in large measure, of course, because of the very real political pressure on the government to increase the pace and scope of its land reform programme. This pressure has increased as a result of the crisis unfolding in neighbouring Zimbabwe where, since early 2000, plans to 'fast-track' land redistribution, including through land invasions on white-owned farms, have led to an escalation of political violence and economic meltdown. In her parliamentary budget speech in May 2001 the Minister for Land Affairs highlighted an instruction to senior DLA management 'to drastically reduce the project cycle for land delivery, which at present stands at an unacceptable minimum of nine months' (Minister for Agriculture and Land Affairs 2001, 3). The emphasis on 'delivery' also works against the slower, facilitative processes required to draw women into the programme in more than a token way.

However, while the role of the DLA is circumscribed, this study argues that the weaknesses in its gender strategy stem largely from limitations within the land reform programme itself, compounded by the DLA's inadequate conceptualization of the task and an absence of political accountability by senior managers around women's land rights. The low political priority accorded gender policy is itself a reflection of weak levels of organization among rural women. These problems are unlikely to be addressed in the current phase of land reform (since the national elections of 1999), which emphasizes agricultural productivity and the promotion of a black farming class above land reform as part of a broader, pro-poor development strategy.

The discussion is organized as follows. The first section summarizes the general context for land reform and gives a brief overview of the ANC government's land reform programme since 1994. The DLA's commitment to gender equity at the national level and its failure to turn high-level principles into effective tools for implementation are then examined. The third section looks at the haphazard manner in which national gender policy has been managed in KwaZulu Natal and implemented in three projects within that province. The final section concludes with some observations about the limitations of the land reform programme and how to build on the restricted gains that have been made for women to date.

THE CONTEXT FOR LAND REFORM

The tension between the DLA's commitment to significant social transformation (including in gender relations) and its need to show results in the delivery of land reform (measured generally in crude numeric indicators of hectares transferred and beneficiaries recorded) has operated since 1994. It reflects a deeper ambiguity within the land reform programme, evident in the contrast between the political prominence attached to land issues in the constitutional negotiations of the early

1990s, and the minor role accorded land and agrarian reform in the ANC's macroeconomic strategies since taking office in 1994.

The political and economic pressures for land reform grow out of South Africa's history of colonial dispossession in the eighteenth and nineteenth centuries and the racial pattern of land ownership successive white minority governments enforced after 1910. This saw a mere 13 per cent of the land area of the country reserved for use by the African majority,[2] under increasingly attenuated forms of communal tenure on state-owned land, which was administered on behalf of the state by reconstituted 'traditional' Tribal Authorities. After the apartheid government took power in 1948, a far-reaching programme of spatial control over the black population led to the resettlement of more than 3.5 million people (both urban and rural) in furtherance of white minority rule (Platzky and Walker 1985). Most African relocatees were moved out of what were deemed white areas into resettlement camps within the reserves which, from the late 1950s, were repackaged into ten ethnically based bantustans or 'homelands' for the African population, in a classic strategy of divide and rule. Today some 14 million people (a little under one-third of the population) reside in the former bantustans (Statistics South Africa 1999a and 2000).

For much of the twentieth century, these areas served as labour reserves for the mining and expanding industrial centres of the country. However, as mining declined in importance and industry became less labour-intensive in the second half of the century, so the importance of migrant labour declined and the crisis of poverty in the bantustans deepened. The migrant labour system on which South Africa's economy was historically based was a deeply gendered operation, with government policies targeting men as the migrants and women as the reproducers of the increasingly marginal subsistence economy within the reserves. This led to a marked preponderance of adult women over men in these areas, a feature which persists today (Walker 2001a, 23).

The imprint of the bantustan system appears indelibly etched on South Africa, the legacy of this dysfunctional spatial dispensation undermining present efforts at integrated planning and the redistribution of resources. The suffering caused by these policies was a central theme in the 'master narrative' that drove popular mobilization around land reform in the 1980s and during the constitutional negotiations in the early 1990s (Walker 2000b). Across all sectors of the broad liberation movement the inequity of the 87/13 per cent division of the country between whites and blacks was a symbol of black oppression, its eradication a herald of democracy. At the individual and community level, land remains imbued with cultural meanings that extend beyond its utilitarian value – land as the basis of community and link with previous generations is a potent element in the social

---

[2]   Terminology to describe social groupings in South Africa is always unsatisfactory. I use the term 'African' to refer to the 77 per cent of the population whose ancestry and languages are (primarily) African in origin. I use the term 'black' to refer to all people who were classified as 'non-white' under apartheid, which includes other minority groups, i.e. people of Asian (primarily Indian) descent and so-called 'coloured' ('mixed-race') people as well.

identity of many South Africans, especially but not exclusively in the rural areas. Rural–urban linkages continue to thread town and country together in the economic strategies and consciousness of many people and to feed the urban interest in land reform.

At the same time, severe poverty in the rural areas and high unemployment in the formal economy underpin the rural demand for land. An estimated 70 per cent of the rural population are poor or very poor (May et al. 2000a, 30). In the bantustans, peasant farming has long ceased to be an economic mainstay, but access to land remains critically important in people's daily struggles to cobble together a living from a variety of livelihood strategies. According to May et al. (2000b, 234) agricultural production is the third most important 'livelihood tactic' in rural areas, after wage labour and state pensions. Land has value not only for food and market crops, but also for the non-commoditized resources it offers poor people – grazing, firewood, building and craft materials, medicinal herbs, etc. (see also Ardington and Lund 1996; Shackleton et al. 1999). The symbolic importance of land as a barometer of inequality continues to resonate with policymakers, while politically land reform remains a potential flashpoint, as land invasions in July 2001 at Bredell, on the outskirts of Johannesburg, underscored.[3] Developments in Zimbabwe add another element of volatility.

Nevertheless, despite the multi-faceted importance many South Africans attach to land, land reform has occupied a lowly position as an ANC programme of government. One indication is the DLA's share of the National Budget, which has always been tiny – in 2001 in the region of 0.38 per cent, on a par with the Department of Arts, Culture, Science and Technology and well below the 0.9 per cent allocated to the Department of Trade and Industry and the 1.4 per cent allocated to the Department of Housing (calculated from National Treasury 2001, 9). The main preoccupations of the ANC government, both politically and economically, are urban and industrial – fashioning an investor-friendly macroeconomic strategy, promoting black empowerment strategies in business, addressing the huge backlog in low-cost urban housing, and managing its conflictual alliance with the trade union movement. Throughout the 1990s, government policymakers have tended to regard rural development for those living outside the urban areas as pre-eminently a welfare problem (Walker 2001b, 30–3).

In part, this can be explained by the declining importance of agriculture in the national economy. Agriculture contributes under 4 per cent to South Africa's Gross Domestic Product (Statistics South Africa 2000, 57) and thus plays a much smaller role in the economy of South Africa than in other parts of sub-Saharan Africa, where land tenure reform has been assigned a major economic significance. Alongside this is the political and economic weight of the urban areas, where today some 54 per cent of the population are located (Statistics South Africa 2000, 9). The ANC's focus also reflects a long history of urban bias within

---

[3]   These invasions involved poor and frustrated urban residents seeking peri-urban land on which to build informal houses, but were presented by many media reporters and politicians as a consequence of the failure of land reform policies more generally.

the organization, which was evident even when South Africa was a predominantly rural society (Hart 1996).

At the same time, the radical redistribution programme envisaged by many
ANC supporters in the early 1990s was shackled by the outcome of the constitutional negotiations and the increasingly conservative macro-economic policies
adopted by the ANC in government from 1994. The intense negotiations around
land reform of 1993–4 resulted in a compromise – restitution and redistribution
were endorsed, but within the context of a market-led programme based on
'willing seller/willing buyer' principles and protection for existing property rights.
Within the ANC, there was a steady move away from its 'growth through
redistribution' election manifesto (African National Congress 1994) towards a
host of neo-liberal policy prescriptions for 'redistribution through growth' –
fiscal discipline, public service 'rightsizing', privatization, and the deregulation
of industry and financial controls. These included a dramatic deregulation of
the once heavily protected agricultural sector, to the point where South African
agriculture is now one of the least state-protected agricultural sectors in the
world and struggling to adjust to global market conditions (Van Rooyen 2000).
These policy-shifts came together in the ANC's 'Growth, Employment and
Redistribution' (GEAR) strategy of 1996 and can be explained by a number of
factors, including the external context when the ANC came to power, the internal balance of forces during the political transition, deep ambivalences in its
economic thinking, and the influence of the small but growing black middle class
– between 1991 and 2000 the proportion of the rich classified as black grew from
nine to more than 22 per cent (Walker 2001b, 12–13; see also Marais 1998; Habib
and Padayachee 2000).

The First Phase of Land Reform, 1993–1999

The land reform programme that emerged out of the negotiations and policy
debates of the early 1990s attempted to meld a strong commitment to the goals
of social justice with the principles of market-led land reform. There were three
main components: restitution for those who had lost land rights as a result of
racially discriminatory policies after 1913 (when the Natives Land Act laid the
foundations of the reserve policy);[4] redistribution of land to poor and land-
hungry rural communities, and tenure reform, to strengthen tenure security for
people with insecure rights in land, primarily workers and their families living
on white-owned farms and the people living in the former bantustans.

The DLA's task was mammoth – to meet the very high expectations of rapid
land reform among the newly enfranchised majority, to draft and guide through
an unfamiliar Parliamentary process the legislation to achieve this, and to develop the institutional structures and operating systems to support its work. All
this had to be undertaken within the unsettled context of the political transition,

---

[4]   This programme, initially assigned to a Commission and a Land Claims Court to process, is not
discussed here.

with a very limited budget and a small core of new recruits to government to design the programme. In the early years, the DLA was further handicapped by the isolationism of government departments, often finding itself working at cross-purposes with other departments, especially at the provincial and local level. The complexity of the institutional task was unanticipated by the advocates of land reform – today still politicians, policy-makers and the public grossly under-estimate the multi-dimensional capacity needed for effective implementation.

The redistribution programme was introduced initially as a pilot programme in designated 'Pilot Districts' in each province, while systems and procedures were developed and new provincial offices established. It was aimed at poor black communities with no or insufficient land. Utilizing a state grant package, eligible households could purchase land on the market (generally assisted by the DLA or NGOs) with the balance of the grant (usually very little) available for development of that land. Because of the high cost of farmland relative to the grant, as well as social forces encouraging group mobilization, most projects involved a number of households pooling their grants to buy land jointly. In some cases, strong historical ties held the group together, but often the impetus came more from the exigencies of project design and the aspirations of local leaders than from compelling social or economic considerations.

Thus, in the case of Mahlabathini, the 15 households involved obtained a total grant of R225,000 by pooling their individual household grants of R15,000. The farm cost R90,000, leaving a development budget of R135,000 for very basic infrastructure – an irrigation system and fencing for a four-hectare community garden, three boreholes for domestic water, building materials for pit latrines and some tools and seed (Department of Land Affairs, KwaZulu Natal KNA/4/4/1). At Ntabeni, the land cost R110,000, which almost exhausted the total allocation of R120,000 (R15,000 per eight households). Here community members agreed to make an additional contribution of R3000 per household to project funds, which they raised by selling the only asset they had, cattle (Department of Land Affairs, KwaZulu Natal KNA/4/2/24).

Initially, projects focused primarily on settlement, and the cursory attention to economic development was a frequent complaint of land reform critics, especially in the commercial farming sector. However, over time a range of different 'products' developed under the redistribution umbrella, while DLA began to place more emphasis on smaller projects and ecological sustainability (Levin 2000, 68). In 1999/2000, a departmental 'Quality of Life' study was cautiously positive about some of the achievements. Based on a national sample of 101 projects, it concluded that redistribution was meeting a key objective, to target the poor and the very poor, even if the scale of the programme was very limited (Department of Land Affairs 2000b, v). The study confirmed that residential settlement constituted the major land use (Department of Land Affairs 2000b, iv). However, it also found that 15 per cent of projects reported an income that was 'more than sufficient to lift beneficiaries out of poverty', and that 'land reform beneficiaries enjoy comparatively high levels of services when compared to all African rural households' (Department of Land Affairs 2000b, 138). It concluded on a guardedly optimistic note that 'a properly structured land reform program has considerable potential for productive development and poverty eradication' (Department of Land Affairs 2000b, vii).

Progress in the first few years was extremely slow in all three components of land reform, although redistribution began to pick up noticeably in 1998/9. By December 1999, a total of 667,825 hectares of land had been redistributed (Department of Land Affairs 2000a), while 78,758 beneficiaries were registered on the DLA's redistribution database, covering both completed projects and those still in progress (Walker 2001b, 47). Tentative steps had also been taken to improve the tenure security of occupants on commercial farms through the Land Reform (Labour Tenants) Act of 1996 and the Extension of Security of Tenure Act of 1997. However, by the end of 1999 the redistribution and restitution programmes combined had transferred only 1.13 per cent of agricultural land to black ownership since 1994 (Department of Land Affairs 2000a, 47). Furthermore, arguably the most significant aspect of tenure reform, the Land Rights Bill, which was intended to give statutory protection to people's land rights in the former bantustans, had not been approved by Cabinet (see Claassens 2000). Here the DLA's reluctance to confirm the claims of traditional leaders and tribal authorities to own communal land on behalf of their subjects presented the ANC with awkward political choices, which it was reluctant to address. Since 1994, the ANC has engaged in a complicated political dance with the Inkatha Freedom Party (IFP), the ruling party in KwaZulu Natal, about the place of 'culture' and traditional authorities in rural local government. The IFP's political power base is centred on traditional chiefs (the *amakhosi*); ANC prevarications on how to institutionalize rural democracy have been driven both by its desire to weaken, alternatively co-opt, this power base and by its concern to curtail the extremely high levels of political violence unleashed by IFP and ANC supporters in the province in the mid-1980s. Given that the traditionalism espoused by the IFP and many of its adherents in the Tribal Authorities is deeply patriarchal, the ANC's manoeuvrings around the *amakhosi* have effectively blunted its commitment to gender equity in rural affairs – gender equity is a principle of government more readily endorsed in the urban context (Walker 1994, 2001b).

Women were formally included in the first phase of the redistribution programme, but the official data need to be treated with caution. Thus women accounted for a respectable 47 per cent of the 78,758 beneficiaries listed on the national database in June 2000, but this total includes many joint husband/wife listings and says nothing about actual participation (Walker 2001b, 48). A DLA study in May 1999 found that women were relatively well-represented on project committees – on an average community committee of 12, seven members were likely to be men and five women (Department of Land Affairs 1999a, 13) – but cautioned that the department needed 'to monitor over a period of time whether or not women are retaining their positions' (Department of Land Affairs 1999a, 13–14). The 'Quality of Life' study found that just over 45 per cent of beneficiaries were women, and that, at 31 per cent of the total, 'women headed households are at least proportionally represented in the land reform programme'.

However, it also noted 'that male headed households have access to larger plot sizes on average' and female-headed households were even less likely than male-headed households to use their land for agricultural purposes (Department of Land Affairs 2000b, 26, iii, 52). Unfortunately, limitations in the research design, in particular the reliance on an unproblematized concept of household head, hamper the usefulness of this particular study as a window on gender relations within projects (see Walker 2001b, 50).

Land Reform since 1999

Since mid-1999, when President Thabo Mbeki took office, a new fluidity has entered land reform as a result of significant shifts in the national policy framework – income has been dropped as a criterion of eligibility for land redistribution grants, land reform linked closely to agricultural policy, and a more accommodating stance presented towards traditional leaders. The inauguration of the 'second phase' of land reform took place under Thoko Didiza, who announced a moratorium on existing projects, pending a policy review, after Mbeki appointed her Minister for Agriculture and Land Affairs.[5] Her appointment led to rapid changes in senior management in the DLA, as many appointees of former Minister Hanekom departed, leading (perhaps inevitably) to some accusations and counter-accusations of racism in the department (see Walker 2001b, 56–57). The turnover in senior staff added to the institutional turmoil. Much of 2000 was spent in a difficult process of internal policy formulation between the DLA and the national Department of Agriculture (NDA), which finally resulted in the publication of the 'Land Redistribution for Agricultural Development' (LRAD) policy in November 2000.

LRAD commits to the transfer of 30 per cent of agricultural land from white to black ownership over 15 years and the revamping of the earlier grant system to support 'specifically' agricultural purposes (Ministry for Agriculture and Land Affairs 2000, 1). Grants are awarded to eligible individuals (no longer households, as in the past) along a sliding scale, from a minimum of R20,000 to a maximum of R100,000. The means test has been done away with – now all members of 'formerly disadvantaged' groups (defined to include 'Africans, Coloureds, and Indians') are eligible regardless of income, provided they make an 'own contribution' (payable in either cash or kind) and use the grant for agricultural purposes. The contribution from the grantee increases in proportion to the size of the state grant, from a minimum of R5000 to access the smallest grant of R20,000, to R400,000 (i.e. 80 per cent of the total project cost) for the maximum state grant of R100,000. In setting their targets, the DLA and NDA appear to have dusted off a set of World Bank proposals first made in 1993, which outlined a 'market-assisted' programme to transfer 30 per cent of commercial farm land to black households for productive use (World Bank 1993).

[5] Interestingly, she was formerly an activist in the Women's National Coalition (see below).

However, certain welfare proposals made by the Bank in 1993 – an outright base grant and a 'safety net' programme for families that were too poor to qualify for the small farmer option – have not been pursued.

Some gender activists believe that the shift from household to individual in the new grant system does, in theory, open up possibilities for women to acquire land rights that are independent of family and male control (Centre for Rural Legal Studies et al. 2000, 7). A major concern, however, is that, given the weak economic and social standing of most rural women, only a tiny minority of better-off and better-educated women are likely to benefit from the new opportunities – the R5000 'own contribution' is equivalent to a year's cash wages for many farm workers and represents a substantial amount of money (or labour) for most households, never mind for women as individuals.[6] There are also questions about the attractiveness of farming, even for those potential beneficiaries who can afford the 'own contribution', given the difficulties facing the agricultural sector in the face of international competition and the loss of state support.

The 30 per cent target for land redistribution amounts to some 24.6 million hectares, or an average of 1.64 million hectares a year over 15 years (Walker 2001b, 58). At six times the amount of land transferred in 1998, the most successful year for land redistribution to date, when a total of 273,416 hectares were involved in project approvals and transfer (Department of Land Affairs 2000a, 1), the annual average implies a quite extraordinary escalation in the rate of delivery over the next 15 years. If it is indeed a serious target, then it should imply a dramatic increase in state budgets, staff capacity and general support for land reform across all tiers of government. This commitment is, however, not visible. Rather, while the national budget of the DLA is set to increase over the next three years, the actual allocation to the redistribution and tenure reform programmes shows a budgeted decline from R421.9 million in 2001/2 to R339.5 million in 2003/4. Even more striking, the amount allocated for transfer payments (which covers the actual purchase and servicing of land) declines from R305.8 million in 2001/2 to R195.5 million in 2003/4 (National Treasury 2001, 599, 609). This is substantially below the R360.8 million spent on transfer payments by the redistribution/tenure reform programme in the 1998/9 financial year (National Treasury 2001).

In the meantime, tenure reform has continued to languish, a casualty of the socio-legal complexities and political sensitivities at stake. Only in late 2001 were draft principles finally released for public comment, with draft legislation promised for late 2002. The draft principles argue the case for accommodating traditional leaders as registered owners of communal land, while proposing that provision must also be made for a range of other landowning arrangements (Sibanda Sipho 2001, 10–26). This is in keeping with the views expressed by Didiza in early 2000 that, in disposing of state-owned land in the communal

---

[6]   In 1996 the average annual cash wage for African farm workers in South Africa was R4800 (Statistics South Africa 1996, 11, 14).

areas, the state should build on 'existing local institutions and structures', both to keep costs down and to ensure 'local commitment and popular support' (Minister for Agriculture and Land Affairs 2000, 11). Revealingly, gender equity was not one of the seven 'major principles' that underpin the draft Bill (Sibanda Sipho 2001, 8).

These new policy directions are consistent with the general thrust of ANC policy under GEAR. Driven in part by the policy imperatives of the NDA and its technical advisors for commercial agriculture, but informed also by the aspirations of the black elite, the major task for land reform has been redefined to support black access to land and to commercial agriculture, on the grounds of 'race' and historical deprivation rather than poverty and current need. The emphasis on race and agricultural productivity ensures that the policy commitments of the 1997 *White Paper* to poor, rural women, while not formally disavowed, remain in the background.

DLA'S NATIONAL GENDER POLICY FRAMEWORK

'First-tier' Policy Commitments Not Reflected in 'Second-tier' Policy Documents

Since 1994, the DLA has undoubtedly expressed a consistent commitment to gender equity as a major policy objective at the level of principle. The legal foundations for this come from the unequivocal assertion of non-racialism and non-sexism as founding values in South Africa's new democracy, and the elevation of the 'equality clause' to an overriding constitutional principle in relation to other clauses in the Bill of Rights (Republic of South Africa 1996). During the constitutional negotiations, strenuous lobbying by the Women's National Coalition[7] succeeded in defeating a strong drive by traditional leaders to exempt customary law from the jurisdiction of the equality clause, with potentially important implications for land reform, especially in the former bantustans (Walker 1994). The success of the Coalition reflected an easing of earlier hostility on the part of the national liberation movement towards feminism (before 1990, it had tended to see the fight for women's rights as a Western or bourgeois distraction from the primary struggle), as well as a growing assertiveness among women leaders within the ANC and allied structures. The Fourth World Conference on Women in Beijing in 1995, which was attended by a large contingent of South African women still celebrating the transition to democracy, added respectability to gender equity as an ideal and encouraged the ANC government in its role of champion of human rights.

Thus the 'Core Business Plan' drafted for the Land Reform Pilot Programme in November 1994 stated that 'Overall, the elements of the Programme are intended to enhance the material, political, and social status of women' (Department

---

[7]   The Coalition was launched in 1992, bringing together a wide range of women's organizations across the political spectrum to lobby for women's rights in the constitutional negotiations. See Abrams (2000) for a history.

of Land Affairs 1994, 8), while the 'Draft Land Policy Principles' of 1995 noted: 'It is necessary to ensure that the programme gives priority to facilitating the participation of women' (Department of Land Affairs 1995a, 3). These broad commitments were developed in the 1997 *White Paper*, which also acknowledged that mechanisms to give them effect had 'yet to be adequately formulated' (Department of Land Affairs 1998, 17). The commitment to gender equity at the level of overarching principle has been carried forward into the second phase of land reform. Although earlier versions of the LRAD policy were less forthcoming (for which they were criticized by the NGO sector), the final draft of the LRAD Policy document includes a sub-section on 'Gender and LRAD' which claims that 'LRAD provides an excellent vehicle for redressing gender imbalances in land access and land ownership' and 'will help government meet its international commitments' (Ministry for Agriculture and Land Affairs 2000, 4). It also states that 30 per cent of the land to be transferred to black people through the programme should go to women (Ministry for Agriculture and Land Affairs 2000, 3). At the departmental ceremony to commemorate National Women's Day 2000, senior management signed a Pledge reaffirming their commitment to the Beijing Platform of Action (Department of Land Affairs no date).

These documents are what might be termed 'first-tier' policy documents, operating at a high level of general principle. A measure of the seriousness of such commitments is their treatment in 'second-tier' or middle-level policy documents, such as criteria for project approval and project monitoring, generic briefs for consultants and training materials for staff. These are the documents which begin to operationalize policy, by setting the parameters within which projects will be approved, funds disbursed, consultants appointed, and managers and staff rewarded or penalized for their performance. At this level, the commitment to gender equity is much less forthcoming.

In several key documents, the *White Paper's* intention to direct 'more attention to meeting women's needs and concerns' (Department of Land Affairs 1997b, 17) is missing entirely. Thus, most graphically, the national criteria for project approval developed by Minister Hanekom's team in late 1998 (which reflected many of the lessons learned by then about the problems of large projects and the importance of economic sustainability) employ gender-neutral language in such a way that the undertaking to target women is entirely submerged. In determining whether to approve projects submitted by provincial offices or send them back, the Minister was guided by terms of reference which specified 'landless people', 'unemployed people', 'the group', 'beneficiaries', 'community' and the like – but never 'men' nor 'men and women' nor 'women' as a special target group. (The criteria are set out in Levin 2000, 68–9.) In some second-tier documents, gender policy may be invoked, albeit cursorily, but its operationalization is not actively managed. At Mahlabathini, for instance, a 'Consultant's Brief' identified tenure security for women as an issue of 'specific concern', but the final Development Plan for the project made no proposals in this regard, nor did DLA require the consultants to rectify their oversight (Department of Land Affairs, KwaZulu Natal KNA/4/4/1). In other cases, gender policy may not be mentioned at all. Thus a draft 'Consultants Brief' for the Nkaseni project (also in KwaZulu Natal) did not list the Gender Policy document as one of the 'relevant national and provincial . . . standards and policies' that it directed consultants to utilize (Department of Land Affairs, KwaZulu Natal no date (a), 3).

In training courses, the principle of gender equity has tended to be treated as an add-on rather than a central element of officials' work. For instance, a training course manual developed for DLA staff in the Northern Province in 1999 contains a strong focus on social redress in the overview sections, including references to the Gender Policy document, the national Constitution and 'international instruments', along with statements about the responsibilities of officials to ensure that women 'make up not less than 50 per cent of every decision making structure', disaggregate their data in terms of gender and use 'gender-sensitive participatory methodologies' (Department of Land Affairs 1999b, 5). However, these general prescriptions are not integrated with those sections of the manual that deal with the nitty-gritty of actual steps to be followed in projects. Thus the instructions to DLA officials on the background information they must collect contain no references to disaggregating data by gender; rather, staff are directed to consider only generic 'members' and 'the community' (Department of Land Affairs 1999b, Section 2, 9–10). Furthermore, potential beneficiaries eligible for the land grant are identified simply as 'households', with no acknowledgement of any embedded gender dynamics (Department of Land Affairs 1999b, Section 2, 8).

Institutional and Operational Weaknesses

Part of the problem lies in the way in which responsibility for the gender policy has been managed within the DLA. While senior management agrees that the policy should be 'mainstreamed', day-to-day responsibility for it has been assigned to a Gender Unit, which was established in late 1996 within what was then a distinct Policy Branch of the national DLA (Department of Land Affairs 1997a, 26). The Gender Unit has been handicapped by its weak institutional location and lack of authority. It came into operation as a small sub-directorate, without clear lines of accountability to either policymakers in the national office or implementers in provincial offices. It complains of being marginalized from the general policy process, only drawn in to comment on issues at a relatively advanced stage, when the value of its input is limited. Its staffing complement is relatively junior, without practical experience of land issues and land reform. Communication with other policy-linked sections in the department, such as the Monitoring and Evaluation Directorate and the HIV/AIDS Desk, is unstructured and haphazard (interviews).

The Unit has certainly succeeded in making gender policy more tangible, developing the 'Gender Policy' document of 1997, initiating gender training and commenting on general policy development. However, it has struggled to give content to its prescriptions. A number of DLA officials have reservations about the capacity of the Unit, and the way in which it has gone about its business.

A common criticism is that it has little understanding of the implementation process and has not tried to overcome that handicap by engaging with projects and project staff in the field – it has preferred to work out of the national office, at the level of general principle. One Deputy Director in KwaZulu Natal expressed frustration at the lack of progress in the development of policy since 1997 – 'What are the clear mechanisms? Give them to me and I will implement. We are still at the workshop and T-shirt phase and that's my irritation with it' (interview).

Where there are 'gender-sensitive' guidelines, they tend to be very broad, revealing scant appreciation of the constraints on time and resources facing planners in the field. One Gender Unit document proposes that officials analyze 'all work done in the community and its true value' as well as how the project will 'contribute to the transformation of gender relations and . . . relations between the disadvantaged and the advantaged' (Department of Land Affairs, Gender Unit no date (a), 6). However, the document is silent on how much time should be budgeted for this work in relation to other project requirements and the implications of DLA's limited period of engagement with communities. According to one KwaZulu Natal official, 'Gender . . . always operates at a theoretical level. Nobody has made the shift to how to do this practically' (interview). A senior official in the national office concurred: 'The debate around issues of gender and land reform does not identify the right problem. It is not a policy problem. The focus should be on how to strengthen women in a practical way so that they can make use of the opportunities' (interview).

Conceptual Shortcomings

The failure of the DLA to operationalize its gender policy effectively also reflects weaknesses in the conceptualization of its task. Most gender policy directives operate at the level of general statements and normative prescriptions, which, in the absence of specific operational directions, staff experience as unhelpful, even onerous. 'Gender participatory methodologies?' exclaimed one planner. 'It's Greek!' (interview). The language is abstract and confusing – the task is to change both men and women, yet it is to target women. 'Gender' operates as a fuzzy code word that in everyday parlance has come to mean, in some imprecise way, 'women' – in the words of one male planner, 'Gender issues are about women, women's empowerment' (interview). The slippage can be seen in the Gender Unit's own documents, alongside its careful account of gender as 'the social roles allocated respectively to women and men in particular societies and at particular times'. In the same glossary of terms, 'practical gender needs' get defined solely in relation to women, as 'the needs identified to help women cope better in their existing subordinate positions' (Department of Land Affairs, Gender Unit no date (a), 5).

This is not simply an academic quibble. The slippage between 'gender' and 'women' is implicated in the lack of clarity about how to 'do' gender. Far from making men and women visible, the term 'gender' tends to make both groups indistinct. There are no clearly sexed (and sexual) beings in land reform. Instead, there are 'communities', within which the normative being is male, appended to which there is (from time to time) 'gender', which refers, dimly, to women.

Conceptual fuzziness leading to muddled directives can be seen in the Gender Unit's uncritical adoption of Maxine Molyneux's highly influential distinction between 'strategic' and 'practical' gender interests. Molyneux has herself noted the 'curious' history of her formulation, which was developed in 1985 in an analysis of the women's movement within Nicaragua: '. . . what began as an attempt to render the discussion of interests more sensitive to the complex issues at stake, ended up as an over-simplified model which was sometimes applied in such a schematic way that the usefulness of thinking about women's interests at all was, for some, put in considerable doubt' (Molyneux 1998, 75). In DLA documents, the distinction between strategic and practical gender needs (instead of 'interests') is presented in the abstract as a distinction between good practice and bad. Practical needs are described as relating 'largely to welfare and do not challenge the existing division of labour or the subordinate position of women in society', whereas addressing women's strategic needs 'expedites women's empowerment and facilitates the fundamental social transformation necessary for the establishment of gender equality' (Department of Land Affairs, Gender Unit, no date (a), 5). Thus the DLA's task becomes 'empowering women [in] their position relative to men in a way that will benefit and transform society' rather than seeking 'to increase women's efficiency in their existing roles by making more resources available to them' (Department of Land Affairs 1997a, 3). In adopting this position, DLA has downloaded another theoretical truth from the international literature, that of the distinction between a 'Gender and Development' (GAD) approach and a 'Women in Development' (WID) approach. 'The proposed policy is in line with the GAD approach. It is therefore recommended that the sub-directorate responsible for this policy use 'gender' and not 'women' as its focus' (Department of Land Affairs 1997a).

Yet targeting women as a consequence of 'gender analysis' is not, in itself, the problem. In practical terms, what would a focus on 'gender analysis' in South African land reform lead to, if not the recognition that women are subordinate as a social category and that the DLA should, therefore, address women's weak position around land? Rather, the problem lies in not making the general appeals to gender transformation more specific, nor thinking through when and in what way policy interventions should target women and when they should not, nor recognizing the limited impact of single project interventions on multi-faceted social relationships. As one KwaZulu Natal official pointed out: 'Gender is not only a DLA project. It is a whole social engineering project. DLA's intervention is for a short time. Is there a culture for this? Who supports it?' (interview).

Furthermore, to the extent that the DLA's Gender Policy is carried forward in the field, officials are more likely to follow a 'Women in Development' than a 'Gender and Development' approach. In projects, DLA planners necessarily focus on what, according to the practical/strategic schema, would be classified as practical gender interests for both men and women, such as water supply for irrigation or domestic consumption, fencing, and improved road access to the newly acquired land. Far from being in conflict with the empowerment of women, organizing successfully around a concrete need that women have identified (for instance, prioritizing the supply of domestic over irrigation water) could improve women's capacity to engage in community affairs and enhance their status. The very process of debate about competing 'practical' needs may shift how gender relations are perceived in different communities.

Apart from the danger that an unreflective GAD approach is likely to render the interests of women invisible in the allocation of limited resources, the Gender Unit has not analyzed the specific contribution of land reform to the funda-mental transformation of gender relationships that it presents as the goal. How important is land compared to other resources, such as jobs or education or health services or the reform of discriminatory laws and customs? And given that the function of the DLA is to deliver land and not these other services, what types of land or projects would best empower women? The distinction between strategic and practical interests is not understood politically as requiring an analysis of 'the strategic' in relation to actual possibilities and dynamics on the ground, rather than at a purely 'theoretical' level.

Another issue that has not been conceptualized clearly, or developed in rela-tion to work in the field, is the Gender Unit's advocacy of independent rights in land for women (Department of Land Affairs, Gender Unit no date (c)). It is not always clear whether this call for independent rights refers specifically to indi-vidual rights for women, as distinct from joint rights with their husbands, or to their identification in joint title deeds as full rights holders, along with their husbands, or some combination of both. However, the source of authority for the Gender Unit is Bina Agarwal, whose fourfold case for women's rights in land – welfare, equity, equality and empowerment (Agarwal 1994) – the Unit reproduces in a training document entitled 'Why do Women need Independent Rights in Land (Department of Land Affairs, Gender Unit no date (c)). Cer-tainly, Agarwal comes out strongly in favour of rights that are 'independent of male ownership and control . . . not . . . joint titles with husbands which have several disadvantages for women' (1998, 18–19). Her thesis has been influential among gender activists in South Africa, which she visited in 1997 to deliver the keynote address at a conference on Gender Policy Research on Land Reform and Development. Her point of departure, however, is the position of women in South Asia, where tenure relationships are very different from those in South Africa, with 86 per cent of the land in private ownership in small family farms (Agarwal 2001, 19) and communal systems of tenure insignificant. In endorsing Agarwal's arguments, the Gender Unit did not relate them to South African conditions before passing them on to DLA staff.

This complex issue is revisited below, in the light of the pragmatic preference of most women interviewed in the KwaZulu Natal projects for joint rights in household land, rather than independent rights in individual land. The point here is that DLA's uncritical reliance on external research and international orthodox-ies has hindered critical reflection on South African conditions in its development of its gender policy. 'Theory' is presented in training and policy documents as something static, given, which comes from experts, who tend to be foreign. It does not have a dynamic relationship to actual practice in actual projects. Although the international discourse on gender has been important in legitimizing the struggle for gender equity, the authority accorded international structures and experts is potentially disabling, suggesting there are ready-made solutions to pre-given problems of inequity and subordination. There is little in the DLA's gender policy materials to encourage officials to develop confidence in their own judgement, or to demystify 'gender' and make the task less rather than more intimidating.

Little Political Accountability for Gender Policy

Reinforcing institutional and conceptual weaknesses is the absence of serious political accountability for DLA's gender policy at the highest level. Since 1994 the Minister for Land Affairs and DLA's senior management have treated the goal of gender equity essentially as an undertaking for formal, symbolic occasions, when the broader transformatory goals of liberation are explicitly remembered. It is not a compass for steering the day-to-day decisions that shape land reform in practice.

This is clear in the *laissez-faire* manner in which the policy has been overseen in the KwaZulu Natal provincial office, which is described in the next section – provincial managers have not held their staff accountable for implementing gender policy, nor themselves been held accountable for this omission by the national office. DLA Annual Reports to Parliament do not report on gender targets and few questions get asked the Minister about performance in this regard. The DLA has contributed to the compiling of South Africa's national report to CEDAW, but this is another example of the lofty terrain at which gender policy operates most comfortably – commitments to gender equity are more likely to be reported on to international fora than constituents at home. Outside Parliament, progress for women in land reform has not been subjected to serious scrutiny, apart from questions raised from time to time by gender activists within land-sector NGOs. While the Commission for Gender Equality (CGE) has identified the position of rural women as one of its primary concerns, it has not directed this into effective interventions in government programmes, including land reform, nor does it have any mandate to organize women (see Seidman 2000).[8]

The general measures of success within land reform have been very crude in any case, driven largely by political concerns with showing – or criticizing – progress around land redistribution in terms of the numbers of beneficiaries and hectares involved, rather than engaging a more substantive and nuanced debate

---

[8] The Commission for Gender Equality was established by the Constitution to 'monitor, investigate, research, educate, lobby, advise and report on issues concerning gender equality' (Republic of South Africa 1996, clause 187(2)).

about the broader social and economic objectives of the programme. Where socio-economic concerns have been raised, the public debate has tended to focus in ungendered terms on economic indicators, or on rural security and social stability (particularly from the side of the agricultural unions and business community), or on 'transformation', understood essentially in terms of black advancement.

These dynamics reflect the relative weakness of what may be termed the broad 'women's movement' since 1994, especially in the rural areas, and the very dilute presence of gender concerns in national debates on rural issues. The levels of gender activism around land displayed in the constitutional negotiations of 1993/4 have not been matched since. This was particularly noticeable in the political manoeuvring around the role of traditional leaders in the run-up to the local government elections in late 2000, where there was minimal public input by women's groups on the patriarchal nature of traditional institutions.[9] After 1994, a number of prominent rural women leaders were siphoned off into Parliament, where they have not been as effective in representing rural women as they were in civil society. There is no strong grassroots movement of rural women – the major areas of organization around women's rights have been in the urban areas, especially (and importantly) in relation to violence against women (Walker 2001b).[10]

Land reform is pre-eminently a programme of redress aimed at overturning the huge racial disparities and injustices in the land dispensation, and this, not gender, has shaped the terms of the political debate.

IMPLEMENTATION OF DLA'S GENDER POLICY IN KWAZULU NATAL

The previous sections have analyzed land reform and gender policy at the broad, national level. This section looks at the management of gender policy in the provincial office of the DLA in KwaZulu Natal and extends the analysis by looking at the involvement of women in three land reform projects called Mahlabathini, Ntabeni and The Gorge. All three projects belong to the first phase of land reform, in which the transfer of secure title was the DLA's primary concern. In keeping with the priorities of this phase, the beneficiaries are all poor to very poor landless or tenure-insecure households. Mahlabathini and Ntabeni are both small redistribution projects dating from the earliest days of the pilot programme. In Mahlabathini, a group of 15 former labour tenant households

[9]   The role of tribal authorities had not been finalized either legislatively or politically at the time of these elections. Traditional leaders, with the support of the IFP, refused to accept a proposed non-voting role on District Councils, arguing for full recognition for Tribal Authorities as local government structures. The ANC succeeded in postponing finalization of the matter till after the local elections.

[10]   This compressed set of comments draws on interviews conducted in the first phase of research. See also Hassim (1999).

were given joint title to 112.5 hectares of thornveld from which they had been evicted in 1968. In Ntabeni, a group of eight labour tenant households used the redistribution programme to pre-empt their threatened eviction by a new land-owner and acquire joint title to 151 hectares of the farm on which they were already living. The Gorge project involves the transfer of a state-owned farm, 486 hectares in extent, to a group of some 105 households also already settled on the land. This farm was bought by the state in 1977 for inclusion in the bantustan of KwaZulu but never transferred and was gradually settled by people from different areas, including flood victims from the neighbouring Tribal Authority and people fleeing political violence elsewhere in the district.

It is recognized that caution has to be exercised in generalizing too freely from the provincial to the national picture. Given the huge range of conditions in land reform projects, as well as the different circumstances in each province, one cannot simply extrapolate from this discussion to other projects and provincial offices. However, the issues raised by the KwaZulu Natal material are pertinent nationally. For one thing, the problems of managing the gender policy in KwaZulu Natal relate to the weaknesses already described at the national level, which can be assumed to impact negatively on all provincial offices. For another, KwaZulu Natal is a major site of land reform nationally. It is the most populous province and home to approximately one-quarter of all South Africans classified as 'non-urban' (Statistics South Africa 1999b, 6). It has the third highest level of unemployment among the nine provinces, at 39 per cent (Statistics South Africa 2000, 41), and carries the further burden of being the epi-centre of the HIV/AIDS epidemic ravaging the country. In addition, the *amakhosi* are a particularly strong political constituency. The success or failure of land reform in this one region will thus have a significant impact on the success or failure of the programme nationally, while provincial programmes that successfully target poor rural women will impact positively on national levels of female poverty and landlessness.

Land Reform in KwaZulu Natal from 1995

Even a brief account of land reform in KwaZulu Natal since 1995 illustrates the magnitude of the implementation challenge. President Mandela launched the pilot programme in the Weenen/Estcourt area in March 1995, with a very modest budget of R35 million, of which about one-third was to buy and transfer land (Department of Land Affairs 1995b, 4). The pilot district exemplified the social problems that land reform was intended to address – 'widespread and endemic' poverty, high unemployment, low levels of education (Marcus 1995, 16), and a long history of extreme conflict over land and labour between black peasants and white landowners. The area also has a history of clan-based violence within black communities, fuelled by disputes over their dwindling resources of land (Clegg 1979). Weenen was one of the first districts in the province to experience the official abolition of labour tenancy on white-owned land in the late 1960s, resulting in the eviction of up to 20,000 black people between 1969 and 1972 and their resettlement in rudimentary camps in neighbouring districts of the KwaZulu bantustan (Surplus People Project 1983, 73–4). Research in the pilot district in 1994/5 identified farm workers and labour tenants still living on white-owned land, as well as former evictees in resettlement areas, as potential beneficiaries with the strongest interest in the land reform programme (Marcus 1995, 19). The pilot district is also characterized by a 'deep rural' consciousness, with strongly traditionalist values and well-entrenched views on male authority over women. In the words of the Chairperson of the Mahlabathini Community Trust, 'Women should follow their husbands' (interview).

Confronted with this history, the redistribution programme carried a strong restitution dynamic from the start. Instead of lodging land claims with the less accessible Land Claims Commission, many ex-labour tenants and farm workers chose to work through the pilot district office to regain the land from which they or their forebears had been evicted. For the people of Mahlabathini, the pilot programme represented the opportunity to abandon the 'bad, really bad' conditions in Sahlumbe, the ramshackle, crime-ridden settlement where they had been dumped, and return to land where 'we really feel at home' (interviews). Government officials experienced enormous pressure to return ancestral land to people even when the development prospects for that land were poor, as they were at Mahlabathini (Department of Land Affairs, KwaZulu Natal KNA/4/4/1). One official described the initial process of project identification as driven by intense demand: 'Even in problematic projects, one would struggle to say how it could have been done differently. We addressed the need that was expressed at the time. We could have done better by looking at long-term development plans, but that was not in place . . . and it was not DLA's role at the time' (interview).

The intensity of land issues in the district imbued land reform with an atmosphere of constant crisis, which worked against methodical planning. With limited capacity, DLA staff struggled to keep up with the huge demand, initially for land but thereafter for development on that land as well. The programme's failure to provide even basic services to the early projects led to strong criticism and discontent. In the words of one NGO field worker: 'The problem was, people got their land but nothing was done after that. . . . People were just sitting in isolation' (interview). Nevertheless, observers agree that the pilot programme did help reduce conflict and thus laid a basis on which future development could be built. 'There was so much heat and pressure and hatred', commented another NGO worker. 'It had to be a pressure valve release, there had to be a substantial movement of people' (interview).

Another challenge confronting the DLA was the legacy of a series of ambiguous commitments made by the previous government to various *amakhosi* over land and jurisdiction over the people living on that land. The provincial office attempted to steer a difficult middle course between national DLA policy, which before 1999 was generally unsympathetic to these tribal claims, and local political dynamics, which encouraged them. A 1999 'Ministerial Briefing' noted that 'The demand for additional land in many instances relates to groups caught up in conflict and violence or threats of violence within tribal authority groups'

(Department of Land Affairs, KwaZulu Natal no date (b), 4). The Briefing complained of the 'undefined roles and responsibilities of the various tiers of Government; and lack of clear vision for implementation of the development framework at provincial level':

> For the Provincial Office, the challenge has been to address huge land needs and historically generated expectations from tribal groups in particular, within an undefined provincial framework; while at the same time attempting to shape programmes in line with national policy shifts which are sometimes in conflict with the realities experienced in the Province. (Department of Land Affairs, KwaZulu Natal no date (b), 4)

These dynamics can be seen at The Gorge, where they have delayed the processing of the project and challenged efforts by a DLA official to encourage the participation of women. At the heart of the project lies an ambiguity about the residents' status as beneficiaries of the project in relation to the claims of the neighbouring Tribal Authority. This body regards the land and the people on it as its domain and in 1993 laid a claim with the Advisory Commission on Land Allocation, a body established by the apartheid government to make recommendations on land claims on state-owned land. In one of its many 'legacy' recommendations, this body recommended to the newly appointed Minister of Land Affairs in September 1994 (shortly before its dissolution) that the state should transfer the land to the Tribal Authority. This recommendation Minister Hanekom subsequently approved (Department of Land Affairs, KwaZulu Natal KNA/7/1/3). However, many residents who accept the local *inkosi* as their chief do not want their land to come under his direct control and want to secure individual title, at least to their residential sites: '*Inkosi* was saying the land is his . . . people want title for individuals' (interview). For its part, the provincial DLA has favoured the formation of a Communal Property Association (CPA), to hold the land on behalf of the households registered as project beneficiaries, with Tribal Authority representation on the committee. Minister Didiza finally designated the project in October 2000, but by early 2001 transfer of the land had not yet proceeded as a number of issues were still outstanding, including a decision on the form of ownership. Here an undercurrent of violence, which has seen the murder of several prominent community members in the recent past, adds to the problems – although whether they are associated with the land reform project is not known.[11]

In 1996 new management took over the provincial office and from March 1997 the pilot district became incorporated into its general programme. From an initial staff complement of seven in 1995 (Marcus 1995, 34) – of whom only one was in the field full-time – the provincial DLA expanded rapidly to a total of 75 posts across the regional and several district offices in 1998 (Department of Land Affairs, KwaZulu Natal 1998). This expansion was, however, based largely

---

[11] Two women community leaders were murdered in December 1999, followed by the project Chairman in May 2001.

on contract posts paid out of donor funding, since government policy to reduce the civil service (in line with GEAR) blocked the establishment of permanent posts. Thus instead of developing a relatively stable cadre of officials to deliver land reform, DLA has relied heavily on relatively junior staff on short-term contracts. In early 2001 uncertainty about the continuation of donor funding and the security of contract posts was a serious drain on staff morale.

By 1998, the generic redistribution 'project cycle' had been refined, involving a five-phase process from 'Project Identification and Approval', through 'Pre-planning', 'Designation and Transfer', 'Detailed Planning' and, finally, 'Implementation', the latter envisaged as ultimately the responsibility of provincial and local government, once DLA had transferred to them the 'remaining grants and arrangements for settlement and support' (Department of Land Affairs, KwaZulu Natal 1998, 32). However, the capacity of local government to take over responsibility for land development budgets and service provision, in line with national policy, has been a serious concern (see Walker 2001b, 35–6). This lack of capacity extends to gender policy. Asked to comment on their policy, the Chief Executive Officer of the Uthukela Regional Council answered: 'In all honesty, I think we have passed the buck on that one' (interview).

The problem of poor or non-existent post-transfer support for projects is illustrated by the unravelling of community structures at Ntabeni after DLA formally exited the project in early 2000. DLA has regarded Ntabeni as a success story, because people have shown real interest in developing their land for farming. However, major destabilizing tensions over principles and procedures have since come to the fore, leading to the collapse of the Trust Committee and considerable mistrust and unhappiness in the community (interviews). The dispute centres on whether the arable land should be divided among all eight households equally, since all made an equal contribution to purchase the land, or on the basis of (unequal) historical allocations and current productive use – a decision that was overlooked during the planning stages and is not addressed in the Trust Deed. The Trust Deed is also unhelpful about how the dispute should be managed, highlighting the fragility of the project's legal underpinnings.[12] The DLA official who used to work with this community is reluctant to return, because she has other commitments (interview). The District Council has no staff to deploy in the community (interview) and an NGO that was doing some facilitation work there had to withdraw their field worker when his project funding dried up (Lima 2000).

By October 1998, the provincial office reported a total of 186 land reform projects on its books – 99 redistribution cases, 54 tenure security projects, 27 state land disposal projects and six inherited restitution cases (Department of Land Affairs, KwaZulu Natal 1998).[13] Most projects were still in the preliminary

---

[12]   For a general discussion on the problems of the legal entities set up in land reform communities, see Trench (2000).

[13]   These figures exclude the more than 14,000 land restitution claims lodged with the Regional Land Claims Commissioner by the end of 1998. It should also be noted that figures are not consistently presented in DLA reports.

phase of project identification and pre-planning – land had been transferred and detailed settlement planning completed in only 15 cases (Department of Land Affairs, KwaZulu Natal 1998). By June 2000, a total of 179,027 hectares had been transferred to 8171 beneficiary households (Department of Land Affairs, KwaZulu Natal 2000, 5). This amounted to 4.4 per cent of the area designated as 'farming units' in the province (Statistics South Africa 1999c, 5) – a better record for land transfer than the national figure and a heavy workload for project staff, but a paltry achievement relative to the demand.

Managing Gender Policy

The intense, demand-driven nature of the pilot programme ensured that initially very little attention was paid to gender equity and women's empowerment. Officials worked with already constituted groups and existing power relations between men and women. There were only two measures for women's involvement that the DLA utilized. The first was to include female-headed households on project lists (three out of 15 in the case of Mahlabathini, none in Ntabeni and 26 out of an initial 79 at The Gorge). The second was to ensure that one or two women were appointed to community land reform committees. A female official described the thinking in the pilot district office thus:

> To a large extent it wasn't an issue except . . . there were conscious efforts to ensure women were participating in the discussions and their needs were being met. In the final reports we were trying to see this. But there were no indicators . . . The Pilot Office's relation to DLA was quite removed – if there was policy at the time, it was not clear. So what we were looking at was quite shallow. At times it depended on the facilitator and the facilitator's awareness and how conscious they were about issues and their skills to encourage women to participate, things like that. At the basic level, what was required were so many female beneficiaries and so many on the Committee (interview).

After the DLA had adopted the 1997 *White Paper* and 'Gender Policy' document, this approach did not change. Speaking of her experience in the office since 1998, another provincial planner described office practice as 'basically quite simplistic – trying to see that women participate and are represented on committees'. To get a project through the Provincial Project Approval Committee, 'All you make reference to is the number of women-headed households and women participating. . . . It is not something that is discussed. I think if you did not raise it, it probably would not be raised there' (interview).

The Mahlabathini project highlights the inherent limitations of relying on the addition of a few women to committees to change gender relations. Here two women were chosen for the community committee as a result of DLA's input, but neither were active members. One left to live elsewhere with her daughter, while the other never regarded herself as on the committee for any other reason than to satisfy DLA. It seems she owed her nomination to the fact that her son was already on the Committee. She holds very conservative views on women's place and certainly never considered it her responsibility to champion women's interests – 'I never said a thing on the Committee' (interview). She has since dropped off the Committee, because of her advanced age, and has not been replaced. The Committee is in any case no longer functioning effectively, with the Chairperson assuming a paternalistic style as community leader.

Beyond these efforts to secure formal representation for women, the DLA's gender policy has not been actively managed in KwaZulu Natal. The 'Gender Policy' document does not feature in the induction of new staff. Work towards national gender policy goals is not specified in staff quarterly work plans, which form the basis of performance assessment. The official responsible for The Gorge, who had a strong personal commitment to empowering women, described the process of assessment as involving 'just you and your attitude at the end of the day' – 'Gender appraisal is not in your performance criteria. It's just where you come from' (interview). Very few staff interviewed had been on any specialized gender training courses; most said their general training had been on the job – 'You learn as you go' (interview). While officials knew about the *White Paper*, a number were unaware of the Gender Policy document, copies of which were not readily available in either the provincial or district offices. Those who had seen the document did not consider it particularly helpful. 'I saw it a few years ago', recalled one Project Officer. 'I saw it as normative – there were no real ways how to do anything' (interview). The absence of strong management support means that planners lack guidance and incentives to pursue gender policy object-ives. Said another planner: 'Although there is a policy, the issue has some sensit-ivity. I am not sure really how to approach it' (interview).

Where staff have been active around gender issues, it has generally been as a result of their own initiative. This is demonstrated most clearly by the planner working at The Gorge, who started both a women's group and a youth group outside official hours, with HIV/AIDS education as a primary concern in both. In order to include women on the project committee, she insisted that the com-munity adopt a quota system whereby two women and two youth representat-ives had to be elected. The idea of the quota was her own – her manager, who assisted her to facilitate the elections, noted it as an example of how the integra-tion of the DLA's gender policy into the project cycle is left to individual staff members (interview). Although the planner appreciates the general support she has had from her manager, she has not found support from DLA with specific policy questions. For instance, when registering polygamous households, she could not find a manual to advise her – 'You say: wow, how should I deal with this, and you have to use your own discretion' (interview).

However, although marginal to the mainstream of office activities, organiza-tion to promote gender awareness is sanctioned as a side activity. A number of officials with a particular commitment to the issues have participated in a national Gender Network organized by the Gender Unit. None of the managers interviewed expressed reservations about the legitimacy of the gender policy, although one complained strongly of the absence of clear guidelines that were compatible with work plans (interview). Another admitted that he had not focused on gender awareness in his team, but had assumed that staff would have 'a certain level of understanding', which they would draw on themselves. In explaining his attitude, he referred to the overwhelming pressure he was under 'to focus attention on the movement of projects' and the lack of institutional support he received as a middle manager (interview). In March 2000, the office management approved the establishment of a province-wide Gender Forum, in response to one Deputy Director's concern that gender issues were not receiving sufficient attention. She was promptly given the responsibility for coordinating the Forum. When interviewed in late 2000, she thought that 'possibly' a little more space had opened for gender issues in the office, but was critical of the way that responsibility for the Forum had simply been added to her other commitments (interview).

Women's Involvement in Mahlabathini, Ntabeni and the Gorge

The fact that national policy on women's empowerment and gender equity has not been a major consideration in the implementation of land reform does not mean that land reform has had no effect on women, nor that gender relations in project communities have been left untouched.

In Mahlabathini, although women were largely sidelined in the negotiations, some women took active steps to secure their household interests. One woman told how she took the initiative in the absence of her migrant husband: 'I heard that those who wanted to go back to their farms must go and enlist with Induna Majola. I called on Flominah and her husband said we were wasting our time. Then my husband came back. I told him I had enlisted and had used his name as the household head'. While for the most part the women of Mahlabathini have not openly challenged prevailing norms of female subordination, an all-women group discussion on inheritance and women's rights generated some cautiously dissenting opinions. A couple of women felt that their unmarried daughters should be able to inherit land, even though this was against current norms and practices, 'because situations are not the same and there are no jobs . . . one must not let her kids suffer when there are resources'. There was also tentative interest in the idea of individual land rights for women 'because if you share with your husband you encounter problems'. However, working against this were 'the countryside's rules' (interviews).

Development prospects at Mahlabathini are extremely poor (Department of Land Affairs, KwaZulu Natal KNA/4/4/1). The community is now further from resources such as schools and shops than they were at Sahlumbe and the women regard this as problematic. Yet in comparison to their former situation, where 'there was no firewood, burglary was rife, people randomly shooting one another', the women are positive overall about the benefits of land reform – because it has allowed them to return to land they, along with the men, regard as the land of their forefathers, and because Mahlabathini is a safer environment, offering a more secure base from which to realize their extremely modest expectations of daily life. For them, the indicators of progress are found not in large developmental ambitions, but in basic social and subsistence gains: 'We wanted to plough, keep stock, get firewood and come back to our original land'. 'Here you don't worry about watching your livestock' (interviews).

At Ntabeni, women have been more active in the project process than at Mahlabathini, although also deferring to the overarching authority of men in households and project affairs. Here women benefited in the early stages of the project from the encouragement of a number of external agencies to participate, including AFRA, a land-rights NGO. A number of women spoke also of 'two ladies from Durban who told us we have rights too as women, therefore we must also contribute to the struggle'. When asked if government officials had spoken of gender equality, they recalled the intervention of one who 'asked whether men call us for meetings and they said never, so she told them to call us. After that she told them to let us air our views, and that really occurred'. However, lack of information and access to resources to deal with social problems on an ongoing basis are problems. In the women's discussion group, violence against women was acknowledged as 'sometimes' present, although there was reluctance to discuss it. Women also asked for information about HIV/AIDS, which they claimed was not a problem in their community but worried them as a hazy threat (interviews).

According to project documents, DLA wanted equal numbers of men and women on the Committee, partly to compensate for the fact that no women were listed as Trust members – 'AFRA said that it would be the right thing for the government to have equal numbers of men and women' (interviews). As a result, four men and four women were elected to the Trust Committee. However, what is not provided for in the Trust Deed is an explicit mechanism for ensuring that women will continue to be elected as Trustees in the future (Department of Land Affairs, KwaZulu Natal KNA/4/2/24). The Trust Deed is in any case a highly technical document, written in dense legalese, and thus unhelpful for the conduct of community affairs, as the conflict over household fields has revealed. In a group discussion, the women on the Committee confessed to being uncertain of their role, although they attended meetings conscientiously. They had not thought that being committee members entitled them to take any initiative on issues. Said one: 'Since we were on the Committee, we supported the men'. Fear of ridicule for stepping outside their accustomed roles has played its part: 'We were afraid that we were going to say silly things and be laughed at, which the men used to do' (interviews).

Female participation in community affairs is mediated largely through their marital families. In the dispute that has erupted over fields and the election of a new committee, women have divided along household lines. Yet women recognize their vulnerability in relation to their husbands and, as in Mahlabathini, are interested in exploring ways in which their rights and interests might be better secured. Several women favoured the idea of joint title with their husbands. This appealed to one woman 'because men change': 'He might decide to take a second wife or another woman and leave me but then I will be able to produce my own title deed'. According to her, it would be difficult to have her own land 'so its OK that we share the land but have separate title deeds'. One woman spoke of her interest in individual land 'so that we can recognize gender equity'. On the inheritance rights of girls, the women held a range of views. Concern for the continuity and integrity of the patriarchal household if daughters inherited co-mingled with the desire to boost their daughters' life chances and recognize their contribution to household well-being. One woman thought female inheritance posed a threat to the family when the girl married. Two thought that girls should inherit equally with their brothers, while another thought that girls should only inherit if they did not get married (interviews).

Despite the problems facing the community in 2000/1, the women of Ntabeni also thought land reform had made a positive contribution to their lives. Al-though the promise of making a secure living off their land had not yet been realized, they felt they were much better off having their own land than they were as labour tenants, where 'We were very oppressed'. Their assessment of land reform is thus guardedly positive: 'Our expectations have been met, but we still have a problem with the fields and a tractor' (interviews).

At The Gorge, title had not been transferred at the time of the interviews, so the verdict was still out on land reform – 'Things are not clear, yet, so you can't recommend it', explained one woman. Nevertheless, women have displayed a strong interest in the outcome by attending meetings – the minutes show that they regularly outnumber men at community meetings (Department of Land Affairs, KwaZulu Natal KNA/7/1/3) – and by signing up their households as beneficiaries. However, they have been reluctant to play too active a role pub-licly. One woman reflected that separate meetings for women were important 'because we are free to speak if there are no men' – 'Even we as women gossip if a woman has been vocal at a general meeting' (interview). As in the other pro-jects, the women interviewed were interested in the possibilities of joint land rights with their husbands, while some supported inheritance rights for their daughters. One woman thought that 'the one who is responsible' should inherit, noting that girls were generally more responsible than boys (interviews).

The project is interesting as an example of one official's conscious efforts to insert a 'gender agenda' into the process. Until July 1999, gender issues received little attention. Apart from noting the number of female- and male-headed house-holds, early project records relied on unexamined concepts of household, family and community to describe project dynamics (Department of Land Affairs, KwaZulu Natal KNA/7/1/3). Once a new planner assumed responsibility in mid-1999, this changed. She tells the story of how women insisted on providing their husbands' ID (identity) numbers, even when they listed themselves as bene-ficiaries (interview). One consequence was that Department of Home Affairs' computers kept rejecting the names when authenticating the lists. It took several meetings to persuade the women to use their own numbers. However, at least one still regarded her registration as nominal: 'I am listed as the household head because my husband was not around when registration took place. But as he is my head, I still report everything to him' (interview).

The official's efforts to get women elected to the Project Committee encountered strenuous resistance locally. The DLA was not involved in the process whereby the Tribal Authority chose its representatives – 'We explained we would like to see democratic principles applied but we could not dictate' (interview) – and their contingent included only one woman. In the residents' process, however, the planner insisted on the quota of two women. It took several rounds of general and women-only meetings before 'two women only were nominated and we said that in terms of the agreement they had to be appointed'. The men's response was 'very impatient' (interview). The planner has experienced particular problems with the Tribal Authority, which 'used to talk in a very derogatory way about me, like: that girl from DLA. . . . You could see in their faces that they are thinking: this girl is speaking about land, which is not her business.' Over time she developed strategies to deal with this, but they involved compromises 'all for the sake of the project proceeding' – 'I have resorted to complying in a way. Whenever I experience problems and see a dead end, I rely on male members in my [DLA] team . . .' (interview).

BUILDING ON THE LIMITED GAINS

The previous discussion confirms the disjuncture between principle and practice in the implementation of the DLA's gender policy, highlighting the dense web of constraints that have hampered effective implementation while also suggesting that within specific land reform projects women have made some limited gains. This concluding section looks briefly at some of the limitations and gains and the implications for future policy development and practice.

Limitations

In accounting for the limitations of DLA's gender policy, external constraints have been shown to be significant. These include the relative unimportance of the land reform programme in the ANC's macroeconomic policy and political preoccupations, the prioritization of 'race' as a vector of inequality, the absence of a strong women's movement to raise the political stakes around gender policy, along with the sheer complexity of the issues confronting the DLA and the persistent power of the past. All of these factors have limited the general reach of the programme and blunted its ability to target poor, rural women as a specific category of beneficiaries. However, within this context, internal constraints have played a major part as well. In addition to the conceptual and operational problems with the DLA's gender policy described above, elements in the design of the broader land reform programme have also proved restrictive from a gender point of view – in particular, the project cycle approach and the demand-driven nature of the programme.

Under pressure to improve the throughput of projects, the DLA has, over the years, worked very hard to standardize land redistribution in terms of a project cycle, conceptualized as a series of phases, each with its specific requirements and milestones, through which all projects must pass. In this sequence of steps there is relatively little space for improvization. The approach to land reform has become increasingly technicist rather than transformatory – for many managers and project staff, a series of steps along a route map to a fixed endpoint, which is the transfer of land to people and development budgets to local government.

Clearly, to manage the day-to-day tumble of its work, the DLA requires systems and procedures. However, if gender equity is to be a primary commitment, the preoccupation with technical milestones becomes inhibitory. The process is not amenable to extensive discussions and careful facilitation around issues as complex as the rights of women within land reform projects – this is likely to be an even greater problem in future tenure reform cases on communal land than it already is in redistribution projects. The relative inflexibility of the project cycle also means that issues cannot easily be revisited in the light of new experience and insights once people are settled on the land – for instance, to introduce separate plots for women, or revise the budget allocation, or review the legal framework. Yet, in the words of one official: 'People are not always ready for discussions at the time when they are scheduled or required – it is only once they move on to the land that they realize' (interview). The pressure on DLA to exit as early as possible after land has been transferred, combined with the lack of capacity in other government departments and the NGO sector, also means there is little or no developmental support for land reform projects once DLA has moved on. This puts at risk those limited legal rights and social gains that women may have achieved.

'Social process' work is difficult, time-consuming and also expensive. Requiring consultants to hold separate meetings for men and women, for instance, requires larger budgets; prolonging the process pushes up internal costs and makes staff and managers vulnerable to complaints about project delays and laxity in meeting national targets. Yet, as the case studies make clear, an extended social process is essential if the DLA's gender policy is to serve more than a largely rhetorical function. The process of establishing legal entities can itself not be hurried if DLA wants to ensure a minimum level of understanding among beneficiaries to sustain the new structures once the officials have withdrawn. The challenge is even greater if gender equity is one of the requirements.

This is not to discount the importance of government becoming more efficient in its interventions, but to warn against the speed at which formal requirements are met being elevated to a measure of 'good' land reform. The delivery of land to people who do not have the social and economic resources to manage or develop that land is at best a short-term solution to the pressures on government to 'deliver' land reform. Policy development and public political education have to engage with the intractable trade-offs between prioritizing outcomes and prioritizing process if land reform is to address broader developmental objectives, including gender equity.

The demand-driven approach that has been a cornerstone of the programme since 1994 is another brake on the realization of gender policy goals. Initially, as the KwaZulu Natal pilot programme showed, the popular demand for land reform had a strong element of redress to it and far outstripped the capacity of the programme to respond. The state's programme, however, conceptualized 'demand' essentially in terms of the market – of matching would-be buyers of land with would-be sellers, and not itself intervening in the market to acquire land through expropriation or purchase. This approach has been carried through into the new policy dispensation, albeit with different policy objectives, with the justification again couched in the language of beneficiary preference and control (Ministry for Agriculture and Land Affairs 2000, 9).

Since 1994, land-sector NGOs and analysts have strongly criticized the government's insistence on a demand-driven programme, because it has restricted the potential of land reform by rendering the state reactive to external forces, rather than proactive in acquiring good land for redistribution on a scale that would transform segregated settlement patterns and boost economic opportunities for the poor (see McIntosh et al. 1999, iv). Less attention has been paid to the consequences of a demand-driven programme for gender policy. A strictly demand-driven programme conflicts with the special targeting of women envisaged by the *White Paper* and other high-level policy documents, because it overlooks the way in which power relations and divisions within communities structure how the 'demand' gets articulated and by whom. It commits the state to responding to applications from already constituted groups, in which it is likely that women's role will be a dependent one.

Gains

DLA's most tangible achievements in relation to women's land rights thus far have been at the formal, constitutional level. This is not insignificant – it encourages community debate on the issues, as at The Gorge, and has the potential to create a more positive environment for women within projects, as at Ntabeni. There are interesting parallels with the constitutional gains made by the women's movement at the national level, where in many ways the principle of gender equality is far in advance of social reality, yet creates a space for women to advance claims in other spheres. However, this is also where the limitations of the achievements and conceptualization of gender policy become exposed. Women's presence on land reform committees does not translate automatically into greater influence for women within projects, nor is the longer-term involvement of women in the management of community and household affairs assured.

In this context, the degree of satisfaction women in Mahlabathini and Ntabeni express with the relative gains they have made through land reform, in comparison to what they experienced before and the alternatives, is noteworthy. Clearly, land reform has offered women very little in terms of major developmental gains and new economic opportunities. However, women in these poor communities experience the security of tenure that has been achieved, along with the improved access to very basic resources, such as water, wood and thatching, as positive. Land reform has provided them and their families with a base for modest material advantages compared to their former situations, which augments on-going livelihood strategies. It has also enhanced less tangible but valuable feelings of identity, of belonging – perhaps even, dimly, of citizenship.

Until recently, DLA has based its land reform programme on a model of a relatively homogenous community made up of stable and implicitly egalitarian households. A major consequence has been that women have not gained individual rights in land in the first phase of land reform. Even where they have been listed as independent household heads and as beneficiaries, their access to land has been mediated overwhelmingly through their participation in patriarchal households. As many of the women interviewed in the case studies recognize, this leaves them vulnerable to losing their access to that land if their marriage breaks up. Furthermore, the land rights that women have obtained as listed beneficiaries or members of beneficiary households have not been secured for the next generation of women, because of patriarchal inheritance systems, which favour sons over daughters. While interviews revealed evidence of some support for women inheriting land, including among some men, this is by no means widely sanctioned and project constitutions do not provide for it.

Because of this and because of the conceptualization of gender equity in terms of individual rights, some gender activists have supported the call for independent land rights for women as a major goal (see, for instance, Sunde 1996; Hargreaves and Meer 2000). For this reason, the new LRAD programme is seen to hold out some possibilities for women, even though there are concerns about its class bias and the limitations of a development strategy that is tied so narrowly to agriculture. However, this research suggests that the focus on individual rights for women needs to be tempered by a deeper appreciation of the importance of household membership in poor women's lives – women's rights to household resources should be an important component of policy development and advocacy work as well. It should be clear that had the LRAD policy been in place from the start of the land reform programme, very few, if any, of the women of Mahlabathini, Ntabeni and The Gorge would have accessed land through it as individuals – they are too poor, too isolated, too dependent on male authority. Furthermore, many women beneficiaries endorse DLA's household model. In the communities studied, women have been active in securing household interests. While a minority were interested in the idea of independent rights in land, delinked from that of their husbands or families, few saw this as the solution to their problems. They were more interested in mechanisms for securing, even extending, their rights within their households, including through such mechanisms as joint title and individual copies of title deeds.

Clearly, most women have not had the opportunity to consider individual land rights as an option, and fear the consequences of social disapproval. However, what the women in the case studies are signalling is that they do have strong interests in household and community rights in land in themselves, which should be protected. The relationships within rural households are complex and multi-dimensional – and increasingly vulnerable to dissolution in ways that do not necessarily enhance women's life chances. The impact of HIV/AIDS is set to exacerbate this problem. While the patriarchal household may be a site of oppression for women, it is also a source of identity and support, providing membership in a social network that is often the only effective resource poor women have. The Mahlabathini example, in particular, illustrates the value of household and community bonds and networks for the survival and (relative) well-being of very poor people, which is consistent with the general literature on the 'multiple livelihoods strategies' of the rural poor. Supporting a more gender-equitable reconfiguration of these ties, rather than a politics of withdrawal from patriarchal institutions, seems as important as promoting individual rights for those women for whom that is an option (whether out of choice or circumstance).

Land Reform as a Beginning not an End

Finally, what needs to be remembered is the untidy intersection between government policies and larger processes of social change. An uneven and unpredictable process of social change is underway in rural areas, which is rearranging the contours of gender relationships and creating new spaces from where women's claims for stronger land rights may be advanced. The ebb and flow of women's participation in community affairs in Ntabeni exemplifies this process. It is difficult to work with these dynamics within the timelines of land reform, especially as currently conceived. They cannot be neatly contained within the project cycle, nor contracted out to consultants for managing, nor instructed by Ministers. Nevertheless, they can be encouraged by interventions that promote gender equity as a social ideal and incorporate women into the process of shaping land reform.

Linked to this is the importance of developing a stronger analysis of gender and land reform through research, debate and interaction between government and civil society. There is an important role here for land-sector NGOs and analysts to operationalize their own commitments to 'gender equity' and, in the process, move beyond merely criticizing policy shortcomings at a relatively high level of abstraction. The point is not to refine ever more sophisticated understandings of gender and gender relations as an end in themselves. Rather, it is to develop an analysis that better links theory, policy and practice, to inform a more strategic politics of land reform – one that sees 'piety in the sky' making way for practices that advance the demands of the marginalized for a place on the ground, not as an end of development but as a beginning.

REFERENCES

Abrams, S.K., 2000. 'Fighting for Women's Liberation during the Liberation of South Africa: The Women's National Coalition'. M.Phil. Thesis. Oxford: Faculty of Modern History, Oxford University.

African National Congress, 1994. *The Reconstruction and Development Programme. A Policy Framework.* Johannesburg: African National Congress.

Agarwal, Bina, 1994. *A Field of One's Own. Gender and Land Rights in South Asia.* Cambridge: Cambridge University Press.

Agarwal, Bina, 1998. 'Gender, Property and Land Rights'. Keynote Address at the Conference on Gender Policy Research on Land Reform and Development, Franschoek, November 1977. In *Learning from the Field. Conference* Report, ed. Michelle Friedman and Jackie Sunde, 16–32. Stellenbosch: Centre for Rural Legal Studies.

Agarwal, Bina, 2001. 'Gender and Land Rights Revisited: Exploring New Prospects via the State, Family and Market'. Draft paper prepared for the UNRISD Project on Agrarian Change, Gender and Land Rights. Geneva: United Nations Research Institute for Social Development (UNRISD).

Ardington, Elizabeth and Frances Lund, 1996. 'Questioning Rural Livelihoods'. In *Land, Labour and Livelihoods in Rural South Africa. Volume Two: KwaZulu-Natal and Northern Province*, eds Michael Lipton, Frank Ellis and Merle Lipton, 31–58. Durban: Indicator Press.

Centre for Rural Legal Studies, Land Development Unit (Legal Resources Centre), Programme for Land and Agrarian Studies, Surplus People Project and Trust for Community Outreach and Education, 2000. 'The Integrated Programme of Land Redistribution and Agricultural Development. A Response from Land NGOs'. Submission presented to the Minister of Agriculture and Land Affairs Indaba on the Implementation of the Integrated Programme of Land Redistribution and Agricultural Development, Caesar's Palace, 6–7 November 2000.

Claassens, Aninka, 2000. 'South African Proposals for Tenure Reform: The Draft Land Rights Bill'. In *Evolving Land Rrights, Policy and Ttenure in Africa*, eds Camilla Toulmin and Julian Quan, 247–66. London: DFID/IIED/NRI.

Clegg, J., 1979. 'Ukubuyiswa Isidumbu – "Bringing Back the Body": An Examination into the Ideology of Vengeance in the Msinga and Mpofana Rural Locations (1882–1944)'. Paper presented at the African Studies Seminar, University of the Witwatersrand, 7 May 1979. Johannesburg: University of the Witwatersrand.

Department of Land Affairs, 1994. 'Land Reform Pilot Programme. Core Business Plan'. Document submitted to the Reconstruction and Development Programme, November 1994. Pretoria: Department of Land Affairs.

Department of Land Affairs, 1995a. 'Draft Land Policy Principles to be Discussed at the National Conference on Land Policy'. Kempton Park, 31 August–1 September 1995. Pretoria: Department of Land Affairs.

Department of Land Affairs, 1995b. 'Land Reform Programme'. Launch of the Land Reform Pilot Programme, 26 March 1995. Pietermaritzburg: Department of Land Affairs.

Department of Land Affairs, 1997a. 'Land Reform Gender Policy – A Framework'. Pretoria: Department of Land Affairs.

Department of Land Affairs, 1997b. *Annual Report 01-01-96–31–12–96*. Pretoria: Department of Land Affairs.

Department of Land Affairs, 1998. *White Paper on South African Land Policy*, 2nd edn. Pretoria: Department of Land Affairs.

Department of Land Affairs, 1999a. 'An Assessment of the Participation of the Beneficiary Community in the Land Redistribution Programme'. 25 May 1999, version 3. Pretoria: Directorate: Monitoring and Evaluation, Department of Land Affairs.

Department of Land Affairs, 1999b. *Northern Province Training Course. Land Reform*. Developed by the Department of Land Affairs in collaboration with the Northern Province Department of Agriculture. Pretoria: Department of Land Affairs.

Department of Land Affairs, 2000a. 'Perspectives on the Redistribution Target of 15 per cent'. Internal discussion paper prepared by the Directorate: Redistribution Policy and Systems for the Departmental Strategic Planning Workshop, 20 March 2000. Pretoria: Department of Land Affairs.

Department of Land Affairs, 2000b. 'Monitoring and Evaluating the Quality of Life of Land Reform Beneficiaries: 1998/99'. Report prepared for the Department of Land Affairs, second draft. Pretoria: Department of Land Affairs.

Department of Land Affairs, no date. 'Pledge. Recommitment to the Beijing Platform of Action'. Mimeo distributed at Gender Best Practices Workshop, Hilton, 24–25 October 2000. Pretoria: Department of Land Affairs.

Department of Land Affairs, Gender Unit, no date (a). 'Gender and Development – From WID to GAD'. Mimeo distributed at Gender Best Practices Workshop, Hilton, 24–25 October 2000. Pretoria: Department of Land Affairs.

Department of Land Affairs, Gender Unit, no date (b). 'Proposed Approaches to Integrating Gender into Project Cycles'. Mimeo distributed at Gender Best Practices Workshop, Hilton, 24–25 October 2000. Pretoria: Department of Land Affairs.

Department of Land Affairs, Gender Unit, no date (c). 'Land Rights for Women. Why do Women Want Independent Rights in Land'. Mimeo distributed at Gender Best Practices Workshop, Hilton, 24–25 October 2000. Pretoria: Department of Land Affairs.

Department of Land Affairs, KwaZulu Natal, 1998. 'Land Matters'. Report to the Agriculture Portfolio Committee, October 1998. Pietermaritzburg: Department of Land Affairs.

Department of Land Affairs, KwaZulu Natal, no date (a) [c.1998/99]. 'Labour Tenant Projects. Consultants Brief. The Nkaseni CPA'. Pietermaritzburg: Department of Land Affairs.

Department of Land Affairs, KwaZulu Natal, no date (b) (c.1999). 'Ministerial Briefing on Land Reform in KwaZulu Natal'. Ministerial Briefing Document. Pietermaritzburg: Department of Land Affairs.

Department of Land Affairs, KwaZulu Natal, 2000. 'Land Reform in KwaZulu-Natal'. 20 June 2000. Pietermaritzburg: Department of Land Affairs.

Department of Land Affairs, KwaZulu Natal, File KNA/4/4/1. Mahlabathini case file, Ladysmith District Office. Pietermaritzburg: Department of Land Affairs.

Department of Land Affairs, KwaZulu Natal, File KNA/4/2/24. Ntabeni case file, Ladysmith District Office. Pietermaritzburg: Department of Land Affairs.

Department of Land Affairs, KwaZulu Natal, File KNA/7/1/3. The Gorge case file, Port Shepstone District Office. Pietermaritzburg: Department of Land Affairs.

Habib, Adam and Vishnu Padayachee, 2000. 'Economic Policy and Power Relations in South Africa's Transition to Democracy'. *World Development*, 28 (2): 245–63.

Hargreaves, Samantha and Shamim Meer, 2000. 'Out of the Margins and into the Centre: Gender and Institutional Change'. In *At the Crossroads. Land and Agrarian Reform in South Africa into the 21st Century*, ed. B. Cousins, 264–79. Bellville: Programme for Land and Agrarian Studies (PLAAS), School of Government, University of Western Cape, and Johannesburg: National Land Committee (NLC).

Hart, Gillian, 1996. 'The Agrarian Question and Industrial Development in South Africa: Agro-industrial Linkages through Asian Lenses'. *Journal of Peasant Studies*, 23 (2 and 3): 245–77.

Hassim, Shireen, 1999. 'The Dual Politics of Representation: Women and Electoral Politics in South Africa'. *Politikon*, 26 (2): 201–12.

Levin, Richard, 2000. 'Towards a National Implementation Strategy for Land Redistribution'. In *At the Crossroads. Land and Agrarian Reform in South Africa into the 21st Century*, ed. B. Cousins, 68–74. Bellville: Programme for Land and Agrarian Studies (PLAAS), School of Government, University of Western Cape, and Johannesburg: National Land Committee (NLC).

Lima, 2000. 'Support to Land Reform Projects in Estcourt and Weenen. TNT Funding Agreement 2796/2. Progress Report: January 2000–June 2000'. Interim Report. Pietermaritzburg: Lima Rural Development Foundation.

McIntosh, Alastair, Jan Barnard, Gwendolyn Wellman, Anne Vaughan, Sandy Sejake, Lionel Cliffe, Robin Palmer, 1999. 'Review of the Land Reform Support Programme'. Report for the Department of Land Affairs, the European Union, the Department for International Development, and DANIDA, 30 November 1999. Durban: McIntosh Xaba and Associates.

Marais, Hein, 1998. *South Africa. Limits to Change. The Political Economy of Transformation.* London: Zed Press and Cape Town: University of Cape Town Press.

Marcus, T., 1995. 'KwaZulu-Natal Pilot Land Reform District. An Analysis of Land Availability, Social Demography, Stakeholders and Institutional Arrangements'. Pietermaritzburg: School for Rural Community Development, University of Natal.

May, Julian, Ingrid Woolard and Stephen Klasen, 2000a. 'The Nature and Measurement of Poverty and Inequality'. In *Poverty and Inequality in South Africa: Meeting the Challenge*, ed. Julian May, 19–48. Cape Town: David Philip Publishers.

May, Julian, Chris Rogerson and Ann Vaughan, 2000b. 'Livelihoods and Assets'. In *Poverty and Inequality in South Africa: Meeting the Challenge*, ed. Julian May, 229–56. Cape Town: David Philip Publishers.

Minister for Agriculture and Land Affairs, 2000. 'Policy Statement by the Minister for Agriculture and Land Affairs for Strategic Directions on Land Issues'. Pretoria: Ministry for Agriculture and Land Affairs.

Minister for Agriculture and Land Affairs, 2001. Land Affairs Budget Vote Speech 2001/ 2002 by the Minister for Agriculture and Land Affairs, Thoko Didiza, MP, National Assembly, 15 May 2001. http://land.pwv.gov.za/Docs/landaf-1.htm

Ministry for Agriculture and Land Affairs, 2000. 'Land Redistribution for Agricultural Development: A Sub-Programme of the Land Redistribution Programme'. Final Document, Version 3. Pretoria: Ministry for Agriculture and Land Affairs.

Molyneux, Maxine, 1998. 'Analysing Women's Movements'. In *Feminist Visions of Development*, eds Cecile Jackson and Ruth Pearson, 65–88. London: Routledge.

National Treasury, 2001. 'Budget 2001. National Medium Term Expenditure Estimates'. http://www.finance.gov.za/documents/budget/2001, 5 July 2001.

Platzky, Laurine and Cherryl Walker, 1985. *The Surplus People. Forced Removals in South Africa.* Johannesburg: Ravan Press.

Republic of South Africa, 1996. *The Constitution of the Republic of South Africa,* Act 108 of 1996. Cape Town: National Parliament of South Africa.

Seidman, G., 2000. 'Feminist Interventions: The South African Gender Commission and "Strategic" Challenges to Gender Inequality'. Mimeo. Madison: Sociology Department, University of Wisconsin.

Shackleton, Sheona E., Charlie C. Shackleton and Ben Cousins, 1999. 'The Economic Value of Land and Natural Resources to Rural Livelihoods: Case Studies from South Africa'. In *At the Crossroads. Land and Agrarian Reform in South Africa into the 21st Century*, ed. Ben Cousins, 35–67. Bellville: Programme for Land and Agrarian Studies (PLAAS), School of Government, University of Western Cape, and Johannesburg: National Land Committee (NLC).

Sibanda Sipho, M.D., 2001. 'The Principles Underpinning the Communal Land Rights Bill, 2001'. Paper presented at the National Land Tenure Conference hosted by the Department of Land Affairs, 26–27 November 2001, Durban. Pretoria: Department of Land Affairs.

Statistics South Africa, 1999a. Census Data for Urban and Non-urban Population. From *The People of South Africa. Population Census, 1996*. Pretoria: Statistics South Africa.

Statistics South Africa, 1999b. *The People of South Africa. Population Census, 1996. Census in Brief*. Report No. 03–01–11 (1996). Pretoria: Statistics South Africa.

Statistics South Africa, 1999c. *Agricultural Surveys 1994, 1995 and 1996*. Report No. 11–01–01 (1996). Pretoria: Statistics South Africa.

Statistics South Africa, 2000. *Stats in Brief*. Pretoria: Statistics South Africa.

Sunde, J., 1996. 'Women's Rights in Land: Some Critical Policy Issues'. Paper presented at Department of Land Affairs National Consultative Workshop on Women's Rights in Land, Midrand, 21–22 November 1996. Pretoria: Department of Land Affairs.

Surplus People Project, 1983. *Forced Removals in South Africa. The SPP Reports. Volume 4, Natal*. Cape Town: Surplus People Project and Pietermaritzburg: AFRA.

Trench, Thelma, 2000. 'Towards Communal Property Associations that Work in the Context of Land Reform'. Paper presented at Conference on Security of Tenure and Sustainability Livelihoods in Communal Property Associations, Braamfontein, 4–5 May 2000.

Van Rooyen, J., 2000. 'Producer Support in Cents per Rand by Different Governments'. *The Farmer*, February 2000.

Walker, Cherryl, 1994. 'Women, "Tradition" and Reconstruction'. *Review of African Political Economy*, 61 (21): 347–58.

Walker, Cherryl, 2000a. Research Notes. Department of Land Affairs Best Practices Workshop, Hilton, 24–25 October 2000.

Walker, Cherryl, 2000b. 'Relocating Restitution'. *Transformation*, 44: 1–16.

Walker, Cherryl, 2001a. 'Piety in the Sky? Gender Policy and Land Reform in South Africa'. Paper presented at the UNRISD Conference on Agrarian Change, Gender and Land Rights, Geneva, 6–7 November 2001. Geneva: United Nations Research Institute for Social Development.

Walker, Cherryl, 2001b. 'Agrarian Change, Gender and Land Reform. A South African Case Study'. Social Policy and Development Programme Paper Number 10. Geneva: United Nations Research Institute for Social Development.

Whitehead, Ann and Dzodzi Tsikata, 2001. 'Policy Discourses on Women's Land Rights in sub-Saharan Africa'. Paper presented at the UNRISD Conference on Agrarian Change, Gender and Land Rights, Geneva, 6–7 November 2001. Geneva: United Nations Research Institute for Social Development.

World Bank, 1993. 'Options for Land Reform and Rural Restructuring in South Africa'. Report presented to the Land Redistribution Options Conference, 12–15 October 1993. Johannesburg: Land and Agricultural Policy Centre.

5

Securing Women's Interests within Land Tenure Reforms: Recent Debates in Tanzania

DZODZI TSIKATA

This article is an account of the debates around the recent land tenure reforms in Tanzania. It focuses on the discourses of Government officials, academic researchers and NGO activists on the implications of the reforms for women's interests in land and the most fruitful approaches to the issues of discriminatory customary law rules and male-dominated land management and adjudication institutions at national and village levels. The article argues that from being marginal to the debates, women's interests became one of the most contentious issues, showing up divisions within NGO ranks and generating accusations of State co-optation and class bias. It illustrates the implications of the recent positive reappraisal of African customary laws and local-level land management institutions for a specific national context, that of Tanzania.

Keywords: land reforms, customary law, women, Tanzania

INTRODUCTION[1]

The recent land tenure reform processes in Tanzania and their accompanying debates raised a broad range of questions. These include the focus and direction of national development, the most appropriate models of democracy, the role of different sections of the State in land tenure management, administration and adjudication and the most fruitful approaches to questions of social justice and redistribution. The Tanzanian case is illustrative of how some of the policy discourses around land reform in sub-Saharan Africa have been played out within a specific national context. Particular elements of these discourses, which are discussed in the article by Whitehead and Tsikata (this issue) – the re-evaluation

The research on which this paper is based was part of the UNRISD project on Agrarian Change, Gender and Land Rights.

I am indebted to Professor Marjorie Mbilinyi, Ms Flora Protas, Professor Samuel Wangwe, Yvonne and Tsidi Tsikata, the Tanzania Gender Networking Programme (TGNP) and the Economic and Social Research Foundation (ESRF) for various forms of support with the research for this paper. Many thanks to Yao Graham, Shahra Razavi and Marjorie Mbilinyi for helpful comments on earlier drafts of this article. To Ann Whitehead, my profound gratitude for bringing these issues to my attention in the first place, giving me this opportunity to participate in the debates around them and helping me to work through my ideas.

[1] A glossary of abbreviations used and a list of persons interviewed are included in the Appendix.

of 'customary law' and the role of the State in land tenure, the most effective approaches to the reform of discriminatory laws and the strengths and weaknesses of local-level land management structures – have received an airing.

However, the contours and outcomes of the debate were particular to Tanzania's history of agrarian change and land policies. Different elements of this history – the Colonial Government's policy of favouring plantation export agriculture, its appropriation of the radical title in land, post-Colonial policies such as villagization, and more recently economic liberalization and multi-party rule – provided some of the specificities and concerns which shaped the debates and processes. Also of significance were the processes Tanzania adopted for its land tenure reform and the array of forces they called forth. For example, the President of Tanzania established a Commission of Inquiry into Land Matters[2] chaired by Issa Shivji, a socialist legal expert whose discomfort with the neo-liberal agenda was well known. Shivji then became an influential pillar of NGO advocacy after the Commission's ideas were set aside and was key in shaping the character of the ensuing debates on the land tenure reforms. In addition, the strong presence in the debates of a network of women's rights advocates who tried to steer a course between the State and a more radical civil society agenda gave a particular character to the debates.

This article is an account of the politics and processes of the recent land tenure reforms in Tanzania, which began in 1991 with the appointment of the Presidential Commission on Land Matters and culminated in the passage of two pieces of detailed legislation on land tenure in 1999. It examines the various stages and outcomes of the reforms, the issues which were the subject of debate, the protagonists in these debates and their positions, strategies and alliances. The debates on women's interests within the reforms, particularly the issue of how to address their current and future disadvantages under customary law rules and practices, receive particular attention both for their significance within the Tanzanian debates and in recognition of their wider relevance for evaluating the renewed interest in customary law and local management systems within land policy circles.

The article is structured as follows. It begins with a background discussion of land relations in Tanzania before the reforms, which sets the stage for discussing the reform processes and outcomes in the second section. The debates and the protagonists are then discussed, followed by a discussion of the post-mortems after the passage of the Land Acts. Finally, the implications of the discussion for debates on land tenure reforms in Africa are tackled. The main sources of information for the article are interviews conducted by the author with key NGOs engaged in the land tenure reform debates, academics as well as Government officials. This is supplemented with numerous documents: statements and position

---

[2] This Commission is also referred to in this article as the Presidential Commission, the Commission, the Shivji Commission and the Land Commission for the sake of simplicity and also in keeping with some of the authors cited in the article.

papers of the NGO coalitions and other actors, papers presented by academics at workshops, publications on the subject such as Shivji's prolific work, as well as official documents such as the Land Commission Report, the National Land Policy as well as the Land Acts of 1999.

LAND RELATIONS AND AGRICULTURE IN TANZANIA ON THE EVE OF THE LAND REFORMS

Before the recent reforms (1992–9), processes of agrarian change, population growth and transformation of the wider political economy, which began in the pre-Colonial era but were deepened by Colonial and post-Colonial rule, had reordered land relations in Tanzania, as in many other African countries. These changes were characterized by the growth in land markets, increasing land scarcity, competition and conflict in urban and rural areas and a general dissatisfaction with State-controlled land administration bureaucracies. As we shall see, various social groups had different views of the character and gravity of land tenure problems in Tanzania. One area of agreement, however, was the need to comprehensively address these problems, which had not been tackled in more than three decades after independence.

Questions of agrarian change and land relations have been of widespread concern because 85 per cent of the economically active population are in agriculture, producing food and export crops. Tanzania's agriculture has been described as having a historical export crop bias (Mkandawire 1987; Msambichaka 1987). Even before direct European colonization of the area that became Tanzania, from the 1820s, the expansion of the long-distance spice and ivory trade of Indian merchants based on the island of Zanzibar was an important catalyst for the development of the export orientation of agriculture. Spice plantations were established on Zanzibar for export. The plantations depended on slave labour from the mainland, which was also an important source of ivory and other commodities. The labour and commodity demands of the export trade were experienced in many societies in the hinterland and had an ambiguous impact on the fortunes, political stability and internal differentiation of its kingdoms and lineage-based societies (Giblin 1998). It has been suggested that on the eve of direct European colonization, land relations were undergoing an evolution from a system of collective ownership to one that combined lineage ownership and individual holdings (Giblin 1998). Under German and British rule, these processes were deepened by the actions of State institutions and local office-holders such as chiefs and clan and lineage heads. It has been argued that while clans did not act as corporate bodies in the pre-Colonial period, both local office-holders and their subjects manipulated the idioms of kinship and clan identity in the struggles over land in the Colonial period. One result was that Colonial discourses linked clan with territoriality in unprecedented but quite effective ways. Giblin (1998) thus concludes that while interests in land were structured by use and inheritance, factors such as the structure of political authority and patronage practices were also key.

Colonial agricultural policy was geared towards encouraging foreign corporations and white settlers to enter into large-scale plantation agriculture by supporting them with farm inputs, equipment, labour and land. As a result, large tracts of land were alienated in the service of export crops, especially in places such as the Highlands and urban areas of Tanzania for the benefit of Europeans. Elsewhere, such as in the northeastern Lowlands, the Colonial Government largely kept out of direct land distribution and administration, although here again, large tracts were alienated for forest reserves and plantations. Appointed chiefs were given the task of administering land, but these were under the ultimate power of the Colonial State.

These policies were buttressed by legislation. The German administration passed legislation in 1895 declaring all land as Crown land vested in the German Empire. The British Administration which succeeded it passed the Land Tenure Ordinance No. 3 of 1923, making all land in Tanzania, occupied and unoccupied, public land under the control of the Governor without whose consent no occupation of land was valid. Under the ordinance, the Governor had powers to grant the right of occupancy (known as the granted right of occupancy and defined as the right to occupy and use land for a period of up to 99 years). In 1928, the right of occupancy was redefined to include 'the right of a native community lawfully using or occupying land in accordance with customary law' (p. 7 of the Land Policy Document 1997) thus introducing the deemed right of occupancy. All these had the effect of vesting control over land in the Executive arm of Government. Within the Colonial statutory land regime, a minority held granted rights of occupancy, whilst the majority held their land under the deemed rights of occupancy. There were differences in what these two interests offered their holders. While holders of the deemed rights of occupancy, also referred to as 'customary rights', could go to traditional courts for redress, these processes were subordinate to the Colonial State executive. Even more significantly, Shivji observes that while the relationship between the State and the former was contractual, that between the State and the owners of deemed rights was statutory and administrative (Shivji no date). Okoth-Ogendo has argued that the designation of local land-holding practices as 'deemed rights of occupancy' without any attempt to define their content and character was an example of the contempt for customary tenure. This attitude resulted in the failure of the Colonial legislature and the judicial system to develop customary land law as a serious body of jurisprudence (Okoth-Ogendo 2000, 126). A significant development in this period was the creation and encouragement of individualized freeholds, which were considered a good replacement for customary law rights. Colonial land policy has been described as a form of gender and race apartheid in which Africans were deprived of credit and individualized ownership of land on grounds of custom (Mbilinyi 1997, 341).

An important feature of the Colonial land law regimes in Tanzania and in other African countries was what Okoth-Ogendo has called their 'essentially administrative character' (2000, 127). The Colonial State failed to develop the content of both customary law and the imported English land law, with the result that much of what passed for land law was 'the law of land administration' (Okoth-Ogendo 2000, 127). A complicated set of institutions located within and around the Colonial State was established to administer land tenure. This, together with the State's legislative interventions, strengthened its hand in land matters. As the land bureaucracy grew in power, size and remit, complaints about its inefficiencies, abuse of power and corruption and insensitivity to the problems on the ground grew louder and more insistent (Okoth-Ogendo 2000, 128–9).

The resentments and social tensions generated by these policies propelled the issue of Colonial land policy to the centre of the anti-Colonial struggles in the 1950s (Giblin 1998). In the long term, continuities in policy were critical in shaping Tanzanian agriculture. Mbilinyi notes that, contrary to popular opinion anchored in Colonial myth-making that agriculture in Tanzania was peasant-based, 'half of officially marketed crops were produced on plantation and large estates . . . including some of the most significant export and wage good crops' in the Colonial period and this continues to be the case (Mbilinyi 1997, 332). Furthermore, 20–40 per cent of cultivated land was alienated to settlers by the 1950s in a country where only 5 per cent of the total land surface was being used for agriculture and pasture (Mbilinyi 1997). In both the Colonial and post-Colonial periods, State revenue considerations were powerful incentives for the continuing commodity bias in agriculture.

The post-Colonial State inherited the radical title[3] in land and this was justi-fied in terms of development and nation-building. At independence, freehold titles, which covered less than 1 per cent of land, were converted to leaseholds and then changed to rights of occupancy under Government leaseholds. Also, what is described as a semi-feudal system in the West Lake Region was abolished (National Land Forum 1997; Shivji no date). These policies were justified as an attempt to prevent the creation of a landless class and in keeping with the prin-ciple that land could be secured with use. For the next two decades, individual-ization, titling and registration (ITR) as occurred in Kenya were not on the cards (Shivji 1998a, Kapinga 1998). However, the ITR approach was only part of the larger modernization paradigm that dominated development discourse and prac-tice in Africa in the early post-Colonial period and while Tanzania did not em-brace this particular element of the paradigm, other areas of agricultural and land tenure policy reflected its influence.

Following the Arusha Declaration in 1967 and the adoption of the policy of Ujamaa, which was also known as African Socialism, the Tanzanian State be-came extensively involved in the productive and social sectors of the economy. The period saw the establishment of a vast array of State enterprises and the

---

[3] Okoth-Ogendo defines the radical title as 'the final or ultimate root from which all other land rights recognised by the juridical system of a given polity are derived' (2000, 124). Simply put, the radical title is the highest interest in land and is equated with ownership of the land. Section 4 (1) of the new Land Act of 1999 declares that all land in Tanzania 'shall continue to be public land and remain vested in the President as trustee for and on behalf of all citizens in Tanzania'. This continues the tradition of the President of Tanzania as the holder of the radical title.

expansion of Government support for education, health and other social services. In the sphere of politics, the one-party State was consolidated and hitherto autonomous civil society organizations absorbed into the ruling Chama cha Mapinduzi (CCM). Rural development was organized in two main ways: large-scale ranching and agriculture under para-statals, and small-scale agriculture under villagization. Villagization involved the resettlement of over nine million peasants in villages. Implemented largely without consultation with, and the consent of, the resettled, and without regard for the pre-existing systems of land tenure, resettlement was implicitly justified in terms of the State's ownership of land (Ngware et al. 1997). Within the Ujamaa paradigm, while customary law rules governed everyday transactions and inheritance, there was an overarching influence of State structures and practices. This led to complaints of abuses of the rights of rural and peri-urban land users, particularly groups such as pastoralists and socially disadvantaged groups within many communities such as women and the youth (Shivji no date; Ngware 1997). For the majority of Tanzanians who lived in villages, the rules that governed land relations under customary land tenure and under villagization policies did not quite deliver security of tenure.

Both small and large-scale African producers benefited somewhat from these policy and legislative reforms in terms of access to land and inputs. However, this did not go far enough and even the Ujamaa policies did not reverse the distribution patterns established in the Colonial period. While some local producers did expand their holdings and improve their productivity, they had to rely more intensively on family and household labour and earnings from non-farm occupations. Eventually, the continuities in policy affected food production. By the 1970s, Tanzania was spending one-fifth of its export earnings on food imports such as maize, rice and wheat (Msambichaka 1987). In any case, the attempts at redistribution were ended by Structural Adjustment policies that favoured large-scale export agriculture and the use of market instruments for economic policy (Mbilinyi 1997). This resulted in the reversal of Ujamaa and created conditions for renewed interest in the burgeoning land markets and related problems of land scarcity and disputes.

Land Relations and Women's Interests

State policy had implications for land relations and created various forms of differentiation. The most obvious were the differences between foreign large farmers and trans-national corporations on the one hand and local farmers on the other hand. There was also growing differentiation among local farmers, between a small group of large-scale peasants and the majority poor and middle-level peasants. This was manifested in various ways. For example, while the small-scale farmers produced some crops for the market, they were more involved in domestic food crops sold in unofficial markets. The opposite was true for large-scale farmers, a situation reinforced by differences in access to productive resources, including land. This differentiation was complicated by social groups structured through the intersection of class, gender, inter-generational differences and kinship. These were manifested by changes in the fortunes of men in relation to women within lineages, young people in relation to their elders and household heads in relation to household members. As Mbilinyi (1997) argues, access to capital, land, livestock and labour depended on the class relations of a household, gender relations within it and clan and lineage relations.

The relations of production, consumption and distribution within the peasant household were framed and affected by relations with players outside the household. Important among them were the TNCs, whose large tracts of land and superior access to foreign markets created stresses in land availability; the World Bank, whose macro-economic policies form part of the framework in which intra-household relations are structured; and the State, whose institutions and policies govern these interactions (Mbilinyi 1997). This viewpoint is demonstrated in some of the anthropological work on women's interests in land, which have argued that women did have some significant interests under customary land tenure that have been eroded by Colonial and post-Colonial processes and policies such as agrarian change and the codification of customary law. Also, they have suggested that women have contested and resisted this erosion of their interests in various ways[4] (interviews with MM, BK, 2001; Mbilinyi 1988, 1991; Odgaard 1997, 1999).

One of the responses to changes in the political economy of Colonial Tanzania was the largely male but also some female labour out-migration. The scale and patterns of out-migration were problematic for rural agriculture, especially because of the resulting labour deficit in rural areas. However, in some cases, wages were reinvested in agriculture to beneficial effects. As well, it resulted in changes in the gender division of labour, which affected the social relations of gender more broadly and had contradictory implications for women. Some women were able to benefit from the opportunities created by the possibility of rural urban mobility and more generally, there were new possibilities for renegotiating gender relations and accessing productive resources such as land through the manipulation of Colonial discourses, institutional ideologies and their labour power. On the other hand, a number of processes such as the codification of traditional laws by the Colonial State were not helpful for women as they had the effect of rigidifying what were seen as more fluid and negotiated relations. While various factors affected the outcomes of these processes and their implications for women's interests in land and other resources, it has been the judgement of commentators that, overall, these changes were mostly detrimental to women, although not in a simple linear fashion (Mbilinyi 1997; Odgaard 1997).

Anthropological studies have been especially useful in providing evidence for these viewpoints. Three examples will suffice. Odgaard's research in Iringa and Mbarali Districts among the Hehe and Sangu found that historically both male

---

[4]   This tradition has also tended to justify its focus on women's interests in land in economic terms, usually on grounds of their predominant role in agricultural production, but also less usually in terms of the importance of land for other economic activities.

and female children were entitled to a share of their father's property. Inheritance was predicated on responsibility for children, the old and the sick. Sons and brothers inherited larger portions of a deceased person's land because they were expected to shoulder the bulk of such responsibilities. Odgaard reports that women's inheritance rights were now increasingly being disputed by their brothers. Marital residence, which was patrilocal, did not favour women because their share of property was often left in the care of brothers to be reclaimed by women in case of divorce or widowhood. The growing incidence of divorce, single parenthood and male labour migration and the increase in avenues of formal education meant that more women had to take responsibility for family members in the countryside. As a result, many fathers were supporting daughters' claims, thus underlining the argument that inheritance goes with responsibility for the welfare of the living (Odgaard 1999).

In the case of the patrilineal Pare of the Kilimanjaro Region, studies found that although men mostly controlled land, women had both use and control rights over small plots around the homesteads. A father gave such land to his daughter on her marriage. She could allocate such land to another person when she was not using it, but could only pass it on to her own daughters. Because these plots were around the homestead – a location that was favoured for coffee growing that was predominantly male-controlled – women came to lose their interests in such land. In addition, pressures on such land created by population changes and the advent of cash crops resulted in the lapse of this customary practice (BK, personal interview 2001; Omari and Shaidi 1992; Lusugga and Hidaya 1996). Similarly, research among the patrilineal Nyakyusa in Rungwe District in the Mbeya Region found that women's rights had been determined throughout their lives by their status – as girls, as married women and as widows – and therefore, their rights and obligations were to different communities (natal and marital) at various stages in their lives. These were different from the more established and abiding rights that men had as members of one community. Processes such as the growing individualization of land rights and land shortages had resulted in the increasing concentration of land in male hands. Daughters were no longer able to inherit land and women's access to land was now largely through marriage (Odgaard 1997).

In the post-Colonial period, under the rules of villagization, the designation of all adults as village members entitled to land irrespective of gender and marital status had revolutionary implications which were stymied, however, by a competing principle of the homestead as the basis for land distribution. In various villages, these principles were implemented in ways that had different outcomes. According to Mbilinyi, while women in some cases found themselves with multiple labour responsibilities, they were also very active participants in collective farming and consumer cooperatives, which allowed them some freedoms and community-sanctioned powers (Mbilinyi 1997).

A common conclusion of the anthropological studies was that, in spite of these processes of erosion, there were some practices that reduced women's land tenure insecurities. As well, women themselves made efforts to safeguard their rights by recourse to favourable traditional practices, and less commonly, by recourse to legal processes. One such traditional practice is the institution of female husband, by which widows safeguard their interests in their husband's land by marrying a woman who then provides labour and also children, who are born in the name of the deceased husband. In some communities, parents distributed land to daughters and sons in their lifetime as a social security device. Village authorities were also reported to be supportive of claims of daughters when male relations challenged them directly or in legal processes. Once these cases got to the courts, however, customary law rules both of the codified and court determined varieties, were asserted to the detriment of women (Mbilinyi 1999). This general picture is punctuated by a number of court cases affirming women's interests under customary law, the most famous of these being Epharahim v. Holaria Pastory.[5]

Feminist lawyers, in making the case for law reform, have argued that customary law rules discriminate against women – as daughters, wives, widows or divorcees – in terms of access to, control and inheritance of land. Also, the ambivalence of State courts in the adjudication of women's claims has proved detrimental to their interests (Gender Land Task Force 1998; Rwebangira et al. no date). Shivji's contribution to these discussions has been to point out that women's land issues were less about access and more about control and ownership because the evidence showed that, as the 'real producers/labourers', women in Tanzania had access to land (Shivji 1998a, 84).[6] In relation to ownership, neither men nor women, or even communities owned land because it was vested in the State. The rights available to them were of occupancy, in other words control, which on the face of it both men and women could have. However, control was mostly in male hands because of poverty and patriarchal practices within families, communities and the society at large (Shivji 1998a, 86). Also, men as clan and family elders and village leaders were in sole charge of decisions about allocating and disposing of land. In addition, rules of inheritance and divorce practices discriminated against women. These various accounts point to differences in approach or emphasis among anthropologists, feminist lawyers and radical lawyers writing about women's land interests and how to secure them. As we shall see, these differences came to be reflected within the debates on the land reforms.

The Immediate Context of Land Reforms in Tanzania

The push for land reforms in Tanzania came from various quarters. Developments such as the continuing export crop bias, the growing demand for land

---

[5] *Epharahim* v. *Holaria Pastory and Another*, Unreported Primary Court (Civil Appeal) No. 70 of 1989.
[6] But see Koda (1997), who disputed this, arguing that access to land was not a problem only in parts of Tanzania with very poor basic infrastructure and low population density. In other parts of Tanzania, there was evidence that women and youth had difficulty with access to land (interview with BK 2001).

from the large-scale mining and tourist industries, the competition and conflicts between farmers and pastoralists, between locals and foreigners and between locals and Government conservation agencies had contributed to problems such as land scarcity, tenure insecurities and land degradation. These had culminated in accusations of widespread abuses against State agencies and demands for land reforms across Tanzania in order to safeguard the interests of locals. The push for land reform also came from other quarters. The World Bank, for example, saw land reforms as an important component of the process of creating an enabling environment for foreign direct investment (see Whitehead and Tsikata, in this issue, for a discussion of the World Bank's positions).

On the eve of the land reforms, the Tanzanian State and political economy were in transition from State socialism to a thoroughgoing liberalization under strong pressure from donors and the international financial institutions. The transition began in the late 1970s and gathered pace with the departure of Nyerere from the presidency in 1985 following the adoption of an IMF/World Bank-approved Economic Recovery Plan under President Ali Hassan Mwinyi (Gibbon 1995). By 1995, some important changes had taken place in the economy, one of the most significant for land relations being the dramatic growth of the mining industry, which resulted in coffee being replaced by gold as the 'single most important cash crop' (Gibbon 1995, 9; Chachage 1995). More recently, the growth of the tourist industry also raised concerns about land.

The economic reforms were accompanied by political reforms, which included the adoption of a multi-party system of governance, the loosening of ties between the State and the ruling CCM with the express support of ex-President Nyerere and the substantive abandonment of socialism as the ruling party's ideology. This political transition created more space for the expansion of the NGO sector and its strong entry into policy advocacy. It also brought longstanding simmering conflicts around race, religion and that between the Tanzanian mainland and Zanzibar increasingly into the open (Gibbon 1995; Kiondo 1995). The putting down by force of protests in Zanzibar over election results in January 2001 is an example of the more open appearance of these conflicts. Under the leadership of President Benjamin Mkapa, successor to Mwinyi, the economic liberalization and political transformation of the Tanzanian State has been firmed, the death of Nyerere symbolizing the end of the era of African socialism in Tanzania.

Thus the appointment of Shivji, a well-known critic of liberalization policies, as Chairman of the Presidential Commission of Inquiry into Land Affairs in 1991 may have been an indication that the post-Nyerere transition to liberalization, though far gone, had not run its course at the time. It may also have been a response to the strength of feeling within the country about the impacts of liberalization and the activities of foreigners on access to land. However, events subsequent to the Shivji Commission showed that the paradigm shift from African socialism to liberalization had finally taken place within the Tanzanian State. The next section discusses these developments as they unfolded.

THE RECENT LAND REFORM PROCESSES: 1992–1999

Official Processes: From the Lands Commission to the 1999 Land Acts

The Land Commission. In January 1991, the Presidential Commission of Inquiry into Land Affairs (hereafter known as the Shivji Commission and the Lands Commission) began its work. For 18 months, the Commission visited most of the districts of mainland Tanzania, interviewing people about problems of land tenure. Around the same time, the Ministry of Lands, Housing and Urban Development (MLHUD) also established a committee with a less ambitious brief to review land tenure using different methods of data collection, such as workshops, seminars and desk research.[7] In November 1992, the Report of the Shivji Commission was submitted to the Government of Tanzania (The United Republic of Tanzania 1994).

Of the four underlying principles guiding the Commission's work, the most significant for women's land interests was 'the modernization of tradition as opposed to the imposing of modernization on tradition' (Kapinga 1998).[8] The Commission made recommendations in three broad areas: policy and questions of law; administration and adjudication of disputes; and gender equity. On questions of policy and law, the Commission recommended that the shape of a new land tenure system be stated in Tanzania's Constitution to give it legitimacy and protection from political and administrative excesses. Another recommendation was that the radical or ownership title over all lands no longer be vested in the President of the Republic as head of the executive. Instead, national lands should be vested in the Board of Land Commissioners within a National Lands Commission, while village land is vested in Village Assemblies.[9] These holders of the radical title would also be constitutional bodies (Shivji 1998a, 49; Kapinga 1998).[10]

The Commission recommended making village lands inalienable to outsiders of all categories and placing limits on the size of allocations (of a maximum of three acres and a customary lease not exceeding ten years, but renewable) to persons from outside the village interested in small-scale investment of benefit to themselves and the village.[11] Other Commission recommendations were the

---

[7] Chachage argues that the Ministry's committee 'was not interested in the restructuring of the system, but in its streamlining so that responsibilities could be clearly defined and delegated. Its stated main concern was how to protect small holders from land grabbers, while at the same time responding to interests of the investors' (1996, 5).

[8] The other three were the democratization of land tenure control and administration; the idea that rules of tenure should facilitate 'accumulation from below' and the underlying principle of 'security and safety of land rights first' (Kapinga 1998, quoting from the Shivji Commission Report Vol. 1, p. 131).

[9] A Village Assembly is composed of all adult members of a village (18 years and above), while the Village Council is composed of 25 elected representatives of the village.

[10] Shivji argued later that this was the chosen alternative to individualization of land tenure and the vesting of the radical title in individuals (Shivji no date; interview with IS 2001).

[11] The Commission also recommended a ceiling of 200 acres on land ownership in the village. This amount was considered sufficient for medium-size ranching and mechanized agriculture. The village commons, e.g. water catchment areas, sacred sites, pasturelands, were also to be declared inalienable and under the direct supervision of the Village Assemblies.

simplification of the registration process for village land and the mandatory inclusion of the name of a spouse or spouses on the Certificate of Title to Village Land – what Shivji was later to call a village-based titling system (interview with IS 2001).

For the governance and adjudication of land disputes, the Commission recommended the establishment of the National Land Commission to be headed by a Board of Land Commissioners, whose members will be nominated by the President and confirmed through public hearings. At least two of these were to be members of Village Assemblies.

In relation to Village Assemblies (VAs), the Commission recommended the establishment of a quorum and a mandatory minimum percentage of women. VAs were to elect a Council of Elders with fixed, though renewable, terms. This Council, which was to have both civil and criminal jurisdiction, would settle disputes involving village land. Appeals from the Council decisions would go to the Circuit Land Court sitting at the location of the land in dispute, with an advisory panel of three elders whose views the judge was not bound to take, but not without justification.[12]

The Lands Commission stated in its Report (The United Republic of Tanzania 1994) that it had received both 'direct and indirect' information about gender inequalities in access to and control over land. However, it concluded that inheritance was the most serious of the issues facing women with regard to land (The United Republic of Tanzania 1994, 249). Of the three major bodies of law governing inheritance and succession in mainland Tanzania – statutory law, Islamic law and customary law – the most egalitarian on questions of inheritance was statutory law. However, the Commission found that it was rarely applied in mainland Tanzania, where customary law rules were the most used. Among a wide range of patrilineal communities,[13] an important customary principle was the protection of clan land from alienation by outsiders. This had formed the basis for discrimination against women as daughters, wives, divorcees and widows (The United Republic of Tanzania 1994, 251).[14] Though Islamic law provided that a share of a deceased person's property be inherited by females, they tend not to be provided for in practice.

The Commission discussed four possible approaches to the problem of succession. These were the (a) hard law, (b) soft law, (c) evolutionary and (d) customary law approaches. The hard law approach involved the passage of a uniform law on succession for everyone and the abolition of personal laws.[15] The soft law approach continued the application of personal law but subject to certain

[12]   This recommendation, according to Shivji, was to ensure that judges and magistrates would understand the values and notions about justice and equity informing land relations within communities.
[13]   The Commission noted that 20 per cent of rural communities practised matrilineal inheritance. However, the discussion focused on patrilineal communities.
[14]   The Commission cited the provisions regarding intestate succession in patrilineal communities in the codified customary law, the Local Customary Law (Declaration) (No. 4) Order, 1963 as an example of such discrimination.
[15]   Personal laws are the 'customary laws' of a person's natal group regarding matters of marriage and divorce, child custody and maintenance, succession and inheritance.

principles embodied in statute.[16] In the evolutionary option, personal laws would continue to apply, but gender inequalities in other laws in other spheres of life would be addressed in the hope that changes in other areas of law would eventually affect succession. The customary law option involved letting the customary law continue to operate in the hopes that it would evolve through the struggles of people themselves rather than through legislative intervention.

The Commission took the position that the hard law and soft law approaches were not helpful or feasible because they (a) would not satisfy all communities; (b) would be difficult to enforce and more likely to be breached than observed; and (c) raised questions of the rights to cultural diversity and expression.[17] The Commission described the evolutionary and customary law approaches as the most feasible, but stated a preference for the evolutionary option on the grounds that change processes needed to be nudged in a positive direction and that without such interventions, change could be extremely slow (The United Republic of Tanzania 1994, 256).[18] These recommendations were to become the subject of a vociferous national debate involving the Government, academics and NGOs. The debates were sparked off by the Government's draft National Land Policy document that was judged to have rejected some of the fundamental recommendations of the Lands Commission.

The Land Policy Document. In January 1995, the Government organized a National Workshop at Arusha to discuss its draft National Land Policy Document. In the intervening period between the submission of the Lands Commission Report and the Arusha meeting, the Government, with the financial support of the World Bank,[19] commissioned several local and foreign experts to investigate aspects of land tenure (Chachage 1996; interview with FKM 2001). Chachage (1996) has argued that these studies formed the basis of the Draft National Land Policy because of Government dissatisfaction with some of the recommendations of the Shivji Commission.

In the Draft National Land Policy document, the Government of Tanzania laid out the justification for and objectives of the policy, identified the problems it wanted to address and made policy statements about them. It also stated that

---

[16] For example, TWLA lobbied to have the Constitution amended to include sex as one of the outlawed bases of discrimination. This was achieved in 2000 and TWLA believed that this strengthened the basis to struggle against discriminatory provisions in other laws (Tanzania Women Lawyers Association 2000).

[17] The Commission recommended close study of the successes and failures of succession laws, stating that imposing legislative change in personal laws has never been easy. And yet, elsewhere, the Commission suggests that legislation, while it may not have immediate effect, encourages certain trajectories (The United Republic of Tanzania 1994, 254).

[18] Interestingly, the Law Reform Commission of Tanzania has recommended a unified Law on Succession, to the Government. That law is yet to be tabled before Parliament. In doing this, the Law Reform Commission is following practice in Zambia, Kenya, Uganda and Ghana. It has been suggested that the reason for the delay in tabling the new law is because of fears of disturbing the sensitivities of a particular religious grouping (interview with JW 2001).

[19] The World Bank also supported the Ministry for Women's Affairs' efforts to intervene in the land tenure debates through a PRA study.

the Government's response to the Shivji Commission was incorporated into the Policy. The document affirmed the retention with modifications of the four central tenets of land tenure in Tanzania. The first two were (a) land is publicly owned and vested in the President of the Republic and (b) the rights of occupancy under both statutory and customary law would be the only recognized interests in land. The third and fourth were that land speculation would be controlled and land rights would be based mainly on use and occupation.

The customary and statutory rights of occupancy were to be equal in law and provision was made for the registration of land titles. There was a provision to restrict the access of foreigners to customary land as well as policy statements about the protection of land from speculation. In addition, there were recommendations regarding registration of land titles in general, as well as specific provisions regarding the protection of village land holdings. Regarding conflicts between statutory and customary law, the policy stated that customary law was not automatically extinguished in planning areas and that due process must be followed to extinguish such rights.

Most important for our purposes were those provisions regarding women's interests in land. They included a statement that women had inferior land rights relative to men and that their access was indirect and insecure. It was also stated that the traditional provisions which protected women's land use rights had been eroded and that village councils had used customs which discriminated against women to allocate land to heads of households who were usually men (Land Policy 1997, section 4.2.5, 12). It was therefore provided that women would be entitled to acquire land in their own right through purchase and through allocations. However, it was stipulated that the inheritance of clan land would continue to be governed by custom and tradition, provided it was not contrary to the Constitution and principles of natural justice.

Some anthropologists criticized the National Land Policy of 1995 for disregarding the fact that in many communities, women did have strong claims to land. Furthermore, the Policy's recommendation that traditions or customary law and practice be observed with regard to family land ignored the fact that some important traditions of women's access to and control of land were not widely known. This was because traditions of male control had become the dominant discourse on land rights in spite of the more complex character of realities on the ground (BK interview 2001). These arguments are in line with the 'invention of tradition' literature which has drawn attention to the constructed, dynamic and contested character of customary law (see Whitehead and Tsikata, this issue, for a fuller discussion of the (mis)uses of customary law in the land tenure debates).

After the National Land Policy was adopted with minor modifications of the draft (Ministry of Lands and Human Settlements Development 1997), the Government of Tanzania hired a British land expert, Professor Patrick McAuslan[20] to draw up new legislation on land in 1999. This Draft Legislation was debated and

---

[20]   He was described as a legal consultant of the Overseas Development Administration, now known as Department for International Development (DFID).

passed in Parliament into law in 1999. The Lands Acts 1999 were made up of two pieces of legislation: first, the Village Land Act (The United Republic of Tanzania 1999a), which governed lands within villages; and second, the Land Act, which covered all other land in mainland Tanzania (The United Republic of Tanzania 1999b). In keeping with the National Land Policy, all lands were to continue as public land vested in the President of the Republic as trustee for and on behalf of all citizens. Use and occupation of land would continue to be through granted and customary rights of occupancy, the two types of occupancy to have the same status at law, i.e. one would not be considered superior to the other. Land under the Acts was classified into three categories – general, reserved and village land. Village land was put under the jurisdiction of the Village Council, reserved lands under a number of statutory bodies and general land directly under the Commissioner for Lands at the Ministry of Land and Human Settlements. All three categories of land, however, were under the ultimate administration of the Commissioner for Lands who in turn was responsible to the Minister. The Commissioner also had the power to allocate both general land and reserved lands, with the advice of a Land Allocations Committee. Thus the administration, management and allocation of land were retained under the control of the central Government.

In the case of village land, certificates would be issued to village councils to confirm their management powers over village land. Members of the community would be issued certificates of customary right of occupancy, not automatically, but through a process of adjudication and titling. The Acts had special provisions dealing with women's participation on Village Land Councils and the National Advisory Board.

Commentators have argued that although the Government had justified the land tenure reforms in terms of addressing local land conflicts, they were actually to facilitate the land access of foreign investors and prosperous Tanzanians and were carried out under pressure and guidance from donors and the International Financial Institutions (IFIs).[21] This view of the National Land Policy was supported by the observation that the Land Policy prohibited shifting agriculture and nomadism (Kapinga 1998). It was sentiments such as these that contributed to the explosion of debates and advocacy around the land tenure reforms in Tanzania.

Challenging Liberalization, State Control and Gender Inequalities:
The Land Forum and the Gender and Land Task Force

The National Land Forum,[22] a coalition of NGOs and concerned individuals, was the outcome of a two-day meeting held in Dar es Salaam in May 1997 to

---

[21] Shivji (no date), Juma (1996), The Declaration of the National Land Forum (1998), Manji (1998), Kapinga (1998), Mbilinyi (1999). To support this point, Kapinga quotes President Mkapa's statement that some of the aims of the land policy would be to make land rights more permanent, recognizable and legal so that land becomes an asset capable of being deployed to satisfy the borrowing conditionalities of commercial banks, for investment and share-holding (interview with President Mkapa quoted in Kapinga 1998, 4–8).
[22] Ulingo wa Kutetea Haki za Ardhi (UHAI) in Swahili.

debate the proposed Land Bill. Organized by HAKIARDHI,[23] the meeting, attended by NGOs, media institutions and concerned individuals, heard papers and debated various aspects of the Bill. The Forum then elected a coordinating committee, the National Land Committee (NLC), made up of a number of NGO representatives, to steer its affairs. It also issued a Declaration on the Land Bill supporting the major recommendations of the Shivji Commission; the Declaration is discussed in more detail below (Land Coalition 1998). The Forum then organized a number of workshops in the period leading to the passage of the Land Acts.

Once the draft Land Bill became public knowledge, women's and gender equality advocacy groups began to mobilize to ensure that the Bill reflected their concerns (Meena 2000). The Tanzania Women Lawyers Association (TWLA) organized a consultative workshop in March 1997 to discuss strategy to secure a gender-sensitive land law, which would address the issues of marginalized groups of women, men and youth. The meeting, which was attended by a broad range of civil society actors and Government representatives, formed a coalition to be coordinated by TWLA. The coalition established a seven-member committee, the Gender Land Task Force (GLTF) to champion the interests of disadvantaged groups, women and youth in particular. Three members of the GLTF, TWLA, the Tanzania Media Women's Association (TMWA) and the Tanzania Gender Networking Programme (TGNP), were already members of the National Land Forum and its steering committee, the National Land Committee. For a while, the NLC and GLTF processes ran in parallel streams.

In 1998, the GLTF entered into alliance with the National Land Forum in order to ensure that both gender and 'progressive'[24] issues within the Land Bills were addressed and to establish a stronger coalition. The merger, known as the Land Coalition, which was assumed to be the sum total of the two coalitions, soon had to face the fact that there were serious differences within it. The issues that were to prove divisive were who should control the radical title in land? How should discriminatory customary law rules be reformed and what powers should be given to State and village-level land management and adjudication institutions? There were also tensions around the allocation of donor funding, with the result that individual organizations within the coalition began to organize independently and pursue their separate agendas in the period leading up to the passage of the Land Acts by Parliament (Tanzania Gender Networking Programme 2000).

Taking Shivji and Women's Advocates to Task: Gender Perspectives on
Official and NGO Processes

This section reviews an important article discussing how the Shivji Commission and gender and land advocates tackled the issues of women's interests during the

---

[23]   Also known as the Land Rights Research and Resources Institute (LARRI).
[24]   It is interesting that the concerns of the Land Forum were referred to as progressive issues and distinguished from gender issues (see, for example, Tanzania Gender Networking Programme 2000).

reforms. In this article, Manji (1998) responds to Shivji's defence of the Presidential Commission's approach to women's interests in land under the reforms and his analysis of women and land issues. Also, the article critiques the work of women's and gender equality advocates in the land reform processes. While some of the critique has been overtaken by events because the article was written a few years before the final push for the land reforms in 1999, many of its insights remain important for understanding how issues of women's interests were addressed by different players.

The gender and land debates, as well as NGO activism on women's interests within the reforms, have been dated from the 1995 Arusha Conference on the National Land Policy. The Tanzania Gender Networking Programme (TGNP) for example, which had barely been established at the time Shivji Commission begun its work, dates its involvement in the land issue from when it was invited to participate in the Arusha meeting (interview with AM and MJ 2001). Thus the observation that women's groups and women's rights advocates did not focus either on rural or urban land issues in the period before 1995 (Manji 1998) is correct.

It was also in 1995 that the Land Commission's Report began to receive criticism from women's advocates that it had not seriously engaged with gender issues. As one respondent said during the interviews in 2001, 'While women may have participated in the Land Commission's hearings, the type of questions it posed meant that women could not articulate their issues' (BK personal interview 2001). Shivji himself quotes the co-chair of the Land Tenure Study Group (LTG), Professor Anna Tibaijuka, as criticizing the Commission for arguing for the maintenance of the *status quo* in relation to gender relations in the midst of extremely radical proposals about land tenure reforms (Shivji 1998a, 83).

In its Report (1994), the Commission defended its approach on three grounds: (a) its terms of reference did not require it to focus on gender issues; (b) women's land issues were mainly succession issues and therefore outside the purview of land law reform; and (c) women would in any case benefit from the reforms being proposed in the Lands Commission Report, for example, the proposal to include the names of both spouses in the customary land certificates (The Land Commission 1994, 249).

These arguments were challenged by Manji (1998), who argued that it was a particularly narrow interpretation of the Commission's brief to put gender issues outside its areas of concern and that the convention of dividing the relevant legal provisions into succession and land laws as though they were discrete was quite artificial. Furthermore, women's land issues were not confined to succession matters, but included problems of access, control and the impacts of land grabbing (Manji 1998, 652).

Both TWLA and the Government of Tanzania appeared to share the view of the Presidential Commission that succession was the main problem area for women's land rights. For example, in 1997, when TWLA executive members met President Mkapa to discuss women's situation in Tanzania, of the seven demands they made of the Government, inheritance and succession were second.

The issue of women's land access was not raised at all (Tanzania Women Lawyers Association 2000). The Government for its part directed the Shivji Commission to tackle the issue of female succession, and not access to land in general (The United Republic of Tanzania 1994, 250).

Manji's more general critique of the Land Commission Report's approach was that it did not make proposals based on the evidence it had heard, but attempted to demonstrate that its recommendations would have a positive impact on gender relations, without explaining how or why. For example, the Commission believed that some of its recommendations would address many of the injustices women experienced in relation to land. These included vesting the radical title in the Village Assembly and the recording of names of spouses on land certificates. Another such recommendation was that land could not be disposed of if the Council of elders had reason to believe that the spouse and children of the disposer would be impoverished or if a spouse's agreement is not sought. While the latter two recommendations could be seen to be in the interests of women, the beneficial impacts on women of the radical title recommendation which was a central plank of the Commission's approach to issues of equity were less clear cut. Indeed, the Commission admitted that it was on less firm ground in relation to this issue. While it argued that vesting the radical title to village land in the Village Assembly should theoretically undermine the concept of clan land, the Commission also accepted that this would not necessarily happen because clan lands had co-existed with public lands in Tanzania all this while. Also, the impact of the public land concept on clan land was not very clear. However, the Commission argued that 'vesting of lands in the village assembly, on the other hand, is much closer to home. Village assembly is a body in which both men and women participate. The impact of this on gender relations so far as land is concerned remains to be seen' (The United Republic of Tanzania 1994, 249). Not surprisingly, many women's advocates did not see the value of this proposal for women.[25]

Manji had noted that gender equality issues were almost totally absent from the mainstream of the debates around land reforms. This was before the most intense period of advocacy around the land reforms and therefore did not anticipate some of the developments. Initially, issues of women's land interests did not receive much attention from officials and civil society advocates. However, they came to acquire national status, complete with a dedicated coalition by the time the Land Acts were passed. Women's rights advocates succeeded in positioning their issues in a way that made them worthy of attention. That Shivji wrote a chapter on gender and land in his review of the land reform process (Shivji 1998a) and subsequently made extensive criticisms of the gender and land lobby's

---

[25]   TMWA reports that there was division within the gender and land coalition around the radical title, with some persons expressing concern that some men might take advantage of this to sell their land if they felt that they had the sole right over it (interview with JM 2001). Whether or not these concerns are reasonable is not the point. That they were expressed showed that the Land Commission had to do more than simply argue that women might benefit from having the radical title vested in the Village Assembly.

positions and strategies after the Land Acts were passed (Shivji 1998b) is another sign that the issues became important in the national space.

In addition to the critique of the Land Commission, Manji also tackles the policy proposals and politics of the gender and land advocates. Some of her critique needs qualification. While it is true that the GLTF's critique of the Land Bills was not written with the same level of sophistication and detail as the Land Forum's Declaration, the GLTF position paper did raise important questions. For example, one of the issues which engages Manji's attention, women's access to the judicial process, was also raised by the GLTF in relation to the draft laws' provision declaring discriminatory customary law rules null and void. This issue also came up in interviews (Gender Land Task Force 1998; interview with TS 2001). While it might not have discussed the pros and cons of the different approaches to customary law as the Shivji Commission did, the GLTF statement made clear that it did not support either an evolutionary or customary law approach, with reasons to support its position.

Manji's comments about the conduct of the land debate by feminist groups in Tanzania also raised a number of issues. She criticized them for their failure to see the importance of the land reform debates because of their preoccupation with employment and due to their technocratic and legalistic approach to the issue when it came to their attention. Because of their late entry, she argued, they were not able to set the agenda for the debate on women's land rights, but came to react to reports and draft legislation. The class composition of the dominant women's groups limited their capacity to engage with an issue that concerned rural women most and also created a conflict of interest because they stood to benefit from liberalization in ways that rural women could not (Manji 1998; see also Shivji 1998a, 1998b). While some of these points are uncontroversial, as formulated together, they raise questions. The most difficult of these is the notion that the class interests of women's advocacy groups and Western feminist and foreign aid agenda drive their work. This issue will be discussed at greater length in the penultimate section of this article.

The critique of the reactive, technocratic and legalistic approach to the land reform issues taken by the GLTF is fairer. The GLTF's position paper on the land reforms could be described as technocratic and narrowly focused on the text of the proposed Land Acts. As Manji argues, the idea that the problems of the Land Acts could be fixed by the addition and subtraction of a few paragraphs of legislation was at best optimistic. Moreover, the GLTF paper failed to engage with some of the existing historical and anthropological work on women's interests in land in Tanzania (see, for example, Mbilinyi 1988; Omari and Shaidi 1992; Lusugga and Hidaya 1996; Odgaard 1997, 1999; Mtengeti-Migiro 1990). Some consideration of this literature would have been very beneficial to the position paper. This is not to argue that the literature is without problems. For example, there has been a tendency in some of the literature to overstate the strength of women's position in pre-Colonial land relations, particularly the significance of their social embeddedness for the potency of their claims to land. This does not pay sufficient attention to the question of how it was that these strong claims came to be set aside so successfully (see Whitehead and Tsikata, this issue, for a discussion on contestations of the implications of social embeddedness). However, in leaving the task of drawing up its positions to the women lawyers alone (all the authors of the GLTF position paper were TWLA members), the GLTF probably did deprive itself of the opportunity to make a fuller and stronger statement about women's land rights. This may also have been a factor shaping the GLTF's positions on customary law, as well its less than full engagement with, and silence on, some of the other issues raised by the Land Forum, a situation which contributed to the fragility of the civil society alliance. The Land Forum for its part also did not take the trouble to engage fully with gender issues.

On the other hand, reactive and legalistic documents do have their value, particularly when one is trying to influence the chapter and verse of a piece of Legislation.[26] Moreover, the GLTF's work did not end with the position paper. Sections of the task force, especially the groups involved in community mobilization and media work did give a political slant to the campaign (TGNP 2000). In the next section, some of the issues of convergence and divergence among the different parties – the Presidential Commission, the Government, the Land Forum and the Gender and Land Taskforce – will be discussed.

THE STRUGGLE OVER THE DRAFT LAND BILLS: THE DEBATES AND THE PLAYERS

The Government versus Shivji and the National Land Forum

Essentially, the Government's view of the Land Commission was that it was one of a series of activities it had initiated to deal with land tenure reform. Also, that the differences between the Government and the Commission were minor matters of detail.[27] This position is in clear contrast with Shivji's contention that in spite of a similarity in terminology and recommendations, the National Land Policy and the Acts were totally opposite in spirit to the Commission's Report. The Policy and Acts, according to Shivji, demonstrated the State's distrust of ordinary people and their elected representatives. More specifically, he charged that the documents were steeped in the values, assumptions, biases and traditions of the modernization and developmentalist paradigms. They signalled a reversal of the Commission's perspectives on 'justice, community participation and the development of a more legitimate Tanzanian common law' (Shivji no date, 20).

There certainly were important differences between the Government and the Presidential Commission. Among other things, they disagreed about the nature of the problems of land tenure. While the National Land Policy suggested that

---

[26] The Land Forum also commissioned and/or benefited from such documents (see Maoulidi no date; Wily 1998).
[27] Interview with FKM, Ministry of Lands and Human Settlements, 2001.

the land tenure system was fundamentally sound (Ministry of Lands and Human Settlements Development 1997, 9), Shivji (1996, 1998a, 1998b) argued that it was fundamentally flawed (see also Heyer and Williams no date; Ngware 1997; Rugumamu 1997; and Kapinga 1998, who shared Shivji's position). Thus the National Land Policy sought to modify the existing system of land tenure while retaining its central tenets, whereas the Shivji Commission sought to make fundamental changes such as divesting the executive of the radical title. The Government suggested that the radical title needed to remain with the Government to enable critical decisions of national import on land to be made without too much trouble. Shivji for his part argued for a separation between having the radical title and the ability to acquire land for national and public purposes (Shivji no date). Related to this, the Commission sought to expand the notion of customary law being used in the courts to include customs recognized by communities and neighbourhoods, to turn the repugnancy clause[28] on its head and redefine the role of the *wazee* (the elders) within the land adjudication system.

Finally, there were some differences in approach to land tenure reform. For example, McAuslan was quoted as arguing that a more detailed new land law, in which legal rules replaced administrative and political action based on goodwill and common-sense, was more revolutionary than the Commission's proposals (cited in Shivji no date, 23).[29] Shivji argued in response that many of the abuses in land tenure were committed not by local people but by well-informed officials. He also argued that the proposed certificates of customary occupancy would not be much different from processing a granted right of occupancy. Such an approach, which was an attempt to smuggle individualization, large-scale titling and registration through the back door, was not feasible in the light of past experiences. The Government disputed this characterization, arguing that the titling being proposed was discretionary with regard to customary land rights and only mandatory with regard to statutory rights in land. However, all landholders were being encouraged to register their titles in order to enjoy the advantages (interview with FKM 2001).

Shivji found strong support for his views in the National Land Forum, which he was instrumental in establishing. The key issues identified by the participants in its inception workshop in 1997 as constituting the basis of a national debate in land were similar to those points of contention between the Land Commission and the Government.[30] The Forum demanded a national debate on land and

---

[28]   The repugnancy clause is an omnibus provision within Colonial jurisprudence, which subjects all customary law provisions to European notions of equity, justice, morality and good conscience.

[29]   Not surprisingly, the position that detailed legislation is preferable to shorter legislation with unclear procedures was shared by the Government.

[30]   The nine issues for debate identified by the Declaration are in the areas of the radical title or the ownership and control of land, the classification of land into general, village and reserved land, the authority of land administrators under the Bill and accountability institutions. Others were the acquisition of land by foreigners, the grabbing of village land, adjudication, titling and registration, gender equality and land rights and the dispute settlement machinery (National Land Forum 1997).

issued a Declaration. The Declaration's first criticism of the Land Bill was the undemocratic approach to its drafting and preparation.[31] The Declaration argued that the Bill had taken away the rights of the majority of land users to participate in decision-making with regard to land and endangered their security of tenure by facilitating the ability of foreigners and wealthy and powerful nationals to acquire land belonging to the poor. The Bill also sought to perpetuate the discrimination and inequality of vulnerable groups such as women, pastoralists, hunters and gatherers, youth and the small and poor peasantry, as well as instituting complicated bureaucratic processes for administering land (National Land Forum 1997).

The Declaration also had recommendations for addressing issues such as the radical title and the village adjudication structures. As many of the recommendations were similar to those of the Presidential Commission, they will not be repeated in detail. The Declaration, however, was weak on the implications of the reforms for women's interests in land. It simply contended that the Bill's claims to promote gender equality were not realized in its provisions. Beyond this, no specific recommendations were made to promote gender equality.

The Gender and Land Debates: The Gender and Land Taskforce, Shivji and the Government

The gender and land debates were contained in the GLTF's position paper, Shivji's writings and the study commissioned by the Ministry of Community Development, Women's Affairs and Children. The GLTF's paper outlining its positions on the land reforms was presented by one of its authors during a meeting on the Land Bill organized by the National Land Forum in 1998. It was one of only two presentations made at this forum, which was chaired by the chair of the National Land Committee. The GLTF's recommendations focused on four issues: customary law, titling and registration, representation and youth (Gender and Land Task Force 1998).

On customary law, the group felt that the declaration in the Land Bills that customary land law would continue to be the law governing land rights in Tanzania was unconstitutional and against women's rights. This is because the rules of customary law in 80 per cent of Tanzania either excluded women from inheriting lineage/clan land or did not allow them to pass on such land to their children. Also, it would contradict the presumption of joint property under the Law of Marriage Act 1971. In relation to the proviso that unconstitutional customary law rules would be declared null and void, the GLTF raised the difficulties of enforcement arising from the expensive and time-consuming nature of litigation. The GLTF therefore recommended three possible courses of action. The first involved acknowledging the contribution of labour to the development of land by giving spouses joint occupancy rights in land belonging to either of

---

[31] Many commentators have made this critique of the land reforms. See, for example, Mbilinyi (1999, no date).

them, making the sale of such land by one without the other's consent an offence which would render the transaction void. Another was the abolition of customary law and the institution of statutory law to guide land relations,[32] the third being the strict separation of land between clan and family land so that customary law would govern the former, leaving family land and the rest of land under statute (Gender and Land Task Force 1998).

With these proposals, the GLTF showed more concern about joint occupation, ownership and registration of spouses than about the wider question of titling and registration as an approach to security of tenure. Similarly, the GLTF was more interested in the poor representation of women and youth in proposed land management and adjudication structures of the Land Bills than the question of which institutions would best deliver justice to village communities, including women members. It was only during the discussions that followed the GLTF position paper that the implications of these and other ongoing controversies, such as the radical title, the liberalization of land markets, the separation of powers between the executive, legislature and judiciary in the administration and management of land and the problems of immigrants and pastoralists for women were raised. This gave ammunition to the accusations of class bias against the GLTF.

The GTLF's recommendations about customary law did not appear to have been debated during the workshop, although they were at variance with those stated in the National Land Forum's Declaration. It became clear as time went on that there were differences within the Land Coalition. In addition to differences about how to respond to discriminatory customary law rules, some members of the GLTF also did not share the dominant position within the Coalition about the radical title (Tanzania Gender Network Programme 2000). By the time the Land Acts were passed, these differences within the Land Coalition had become quite sharp.

The Ministry of Community Development, Women's Affairs and Children's study of five Regions in mainland Tanzania,[33] which it commissioned jointly with the World Bank to collect views of communities on the gender dimensions of land tenure issues and the extent to which the national land policy and proposed Land Bills had addressed them, gave TWLA another opportunity to express its views.[34] While the study questioned the Shivji Commission's claim to have engaged in widespread consultations, it shared the Commission's main findings and conclusions about customary law rules and the representation of women on village structures. For example, the study agreed with the Commission that the effect of registration of co-ownership by spouses would render

---

[32]   In interview, TWLA says its demand was the amendment of customary law practices to remove the discriminatory provisions (interview with JM, chairperson of TWLA, 2001).

[33]   The communities Kilimanjaro, Kagera, Arusha, Mbeya and Lindi were chosen for their contrasts in relation to traditional practices as well as descent and inheritance systems, the extent of land pressure and shortages arising from plantation agriculture, reserved and alienated land and mining.

[34]   A founding member of TWLA, Magdalena Rwebangira, led the study team, which was dominated by lawyers.

changes in inheritance laws unnecessary. Also, in so far as the Village Land Bill outlawed discriminatory customary practices, it could be argued that inheritance laws had now been somewhat modified by the Bills (Rwebangira et al. no date).

The study found that in all the study areas, women lacked direct access, user rights and control over land. For many women in both patrilineal and matrilineal areas, access to land was indirect and came through husbands, fathers, sons or administrators.[35] In a few districts (e.g. Rungwe and Mbeya), male and female youth were given small pieces of land to farm for themselves, with girls usually receiving smaller pieces than boys (Rwebangira et al. no date, 3). In many cases, not only did married women not control land, but they also did not control the livestock and farm produce and did not make the decisions about what to grow and when. Even women's much mentioned control of food produce was limited to that for home consumption. Examples were cited of matrimonial conflicts in Kilimanjaro arising from recent male involvement in the dairy business, traditionally women's work, but now proving to be more lucrative than the male-dominated coffee-growing business. In all communities, women lost their investment in matrimonial land on divorce. As well, widows could access land only through their children, or if they were themselves inherited, or if they returned to their natal family land, where in many cases they could not inherit unless there were no brothers or their male offspring. Even where women inherited some land, their right to sell off or bequeath such property/inheritance had been the subject of fierce contestation because of fears that land would be lost to the clan. In some patrilineal communities, women are not allowed to settle on their father's land with their children (Rwebangira no date).

The particular problems of female-headed households were also examined. The study found that households headed by divorcees, widows and single women were generally excluded from accessing land unless inheritance rules allowed it. Village governments were in principle disposed to allocate land to them, but much of the good land was under customary law and so they were disadvantaged from the start. Purchasing land was a possibility rarely exercised because of the lack of resources.

In relation to clan, village and district decision-making and adjudication structures, the study found that women's representation tended to be below the prescribed minimum number, which itself did not give equality of representation.[36] The study also found that women were unhappy with the composition of dispute settlement institutions for reasons of corruption, under-representation of women and bias against them arising from prejudices and ideologies which cast them as less reliable protectors of clan land than men (Rwebangira et al. no date, 7).

---

[35] According to the Lands Commission, 80 per cent of rural communities are patrilineal and 20 per cent matrilineal (The United Republic of Tanzania 1994, 249).

[36] For example, the study notes that although village councils have been in operation since 1975, it was only in 1992 that they were required to have at least eight women out of their membership of 25. The same kinds of proportions are prescribed for Ward Tribunals.

The study found that women tended to be enthusiastic about titling because it offered them the possibility of co-ownership of family property. Men were concerned that it could be used to levy new taxes and lead to the dissipation of clan land through women bequeathing such land to their children. There was also a preference for statutory courts, not because they were considered free of corruption but because they could hand down binding decisions, as opposed to the decisions of traditional courts. The main finding of the study was that there was a demand for giving full land rights to women, including the ability to bequeath land to descendants, and that education to promote women's rights in land was an absolute necessity. These findings, which go against the grain of the Shivji Commission recommendations and the feminist anthropology literature (e.g. Mbilinyi 1999), are significant because they suggest strongly that the differences between the Land Forum and Gender Land Taskforce were wider than their differences over women's interests. This might have accounted for the appearance that their differences could not be reconciled.

Out of the findings of the Rwebangira et al. study, three main demands were generated. These were: the joint ownership of land by spouses; equal representation of women and men, including the youth, in decision-making and adjudication bodies; and a sensitization and education campaign before and after the passage of the new laws. As well, it was recommended that laws promoting discrimination under inheritance rules on all land, no matter its status, should be repealed.

THE POST-MORTEMS: REAL GAINS FOR WOMEN OR CO-OPTATION OF GENDER EQUALITY DISCOURSES?

With the passage of the Land Acts, civil society groups involved in advocacy around the issues of reform began to draw up a balance sheet. There were those who felt that they had substantially achieved their aims (TWLA, WAT) and others such as HAKIARDHI who had no cause to celebrate (Shivji 1998b). The TGNP's balance sheet approach to the outcome of the land reform struggles captured by its view that there were 'achievements and gaps' (TGNP 2000) straddles the divide between these two opposite camps (see also interview with AM and MJ 2001).

TWLA lists among the positive provisions in the Acts the equal representation of women on various committees, the outlawing of discrimination against women, children and persons with disabilities in holding, acquiring, transmitting and dealing with land and the rendering null and void of discriminatory customary law rules. Other gains were the rights of women to acquire and register land in their own names; the recognition of the interest of a spouse whose name was not on the title deed; and the gender neutral language of the Acts (Tanzania Women Lawyers Association 2000).

The TGNP shared the position of TWLA and WAT that they were successful in making some important changes to the Land Act. Like TWLA, it cited the provision that women can own land in their own capacity and also through their families[37] and equal representation of men and women on all land adjudication bodies[38] as significant achievements. In addition to the above, the Ministry of Land also listed as a positive development for women the fact that in the case of dispositions (e.g. mortgage, leases or sale) of matrimonial land, the consent of a spouse(s) was required. The spouse(s) had first priority in the event of a person surrendering land to the village; if there is more than one wife, the first had priority (interview with FKM 2001). Beyond these, the TGNP mentioned the provision that no investors were allowed to own land and the special provisions to protect pastoralists as achievements. Unlike TWLA, however, the TGNP considered the Act's provisions on customary law to be unsatisfactory,[39] a position shared by the Law and Human Rights Centre (LHRC), a group which participated in both the Land Forum and the Gender and Land Task Force. The LHRC argued that the conditional acceptance of customary law did not go far enough because it placed the onus on people who found particular provisions discriminatory to challenge them (interview with JW 2001). The LHRC, HAKIARDHI and the TGNP all agreed that the retention of the radical title by the President was a grave setback for the coalition and presented dangers for the implementation of the advances women's rights advocates secured on paper, something disputed by WAT and TWLA.

The claims and counterclaims about the achievements and setbacks of the various coalitions are worth a more detailed consideration. Even the more acrimonious exchanges highlight clear differences of approach both to alliance building and to the substantive issues. For example, Shivji asserts that women's groups were used by the State to divide civil society ranks because their demands were more easily met and did not threaten the free market paradigm and the promotion of foreign investors over local communities. In the interviews, some participants in the GLTF also expressed discomfort about a sense of co-optation and manipulation by Government (see interviews with TMWA, MM 2001). However, members of the coalition felt that the demands being made by the Land Forum regarding the land reform process and citizens' participation and the radical title were unrealistic, considering the Government's record of concessions. Therefore it was considered more productive to ensure women had a fair deal in whatever was on the table and that whatever gains were made could be built upon in future struggles (interviews with TWLA and TMWA 2001). Things were not helped by the fact that both the Land Forum and the Commission, whose positions were similar on many of the important issues being debated, were closely linked with Shivji, whose views women's advocates were very critical of (interviews with MM, AM and MJ, TS and BK 2001).[40]

---

[37]   Section 3(2) and 3(3) of the Land Acts 1999.
[38]   Section 60 (2).
[39]   Section 20 (2).
[40]   Shivji himself admits that there was a lot of opposition to gender equality issues on the Commission, but argues that the single female commissioner was not the most vocal on gender issues (Shivji 1998; interview with IS 2001).

The GLTF did cooperate with the Ministry of Lands and Human Settlements. An advertisement put out by the Ministry to publicize and defend the Land Acts praised the GLTF for inviting the Government to participate in discussions and supplying Government with its resolutions and asserted that the GLTF demands were taken into account in the legislative process.[41] The Ministry's praise of the GLTF does not fully account for the contestation within the GLTF itself, nor the intense lobbying and other forms of advocacy it took the GLTF to achieve the gains women's groups were celebrating. The interviews revealed that there were differences in attitude to the Government as well as tensions about the way different members of the coalition had conducted the campaign (interviews with TGNP, TMWA 2001). For example, TWLA's role in the Ministry of Community Development, Women's Affairs and Children study, attempts by the Ministry's officials to participate in the GLTF and the fact that a GLTF member organization was led by a Member of Parliament of the Ruling Party were mentioned as complicating factors in the GLTF's campaign (interview with AM and MJ 2001).

The politics within Parliament itself around the customary law clause in the Land Act Bill have also been hinted at. It appeared that, at different points in time, the provisions outlawing discriminatory customary law provisions were in danger of being thrown out. It took very intense lobbying by the Prime Minister and some members of Parliament to retain them in the form in which they finally appeared in the Acts (interview with TS 2001).[42]

Some of Shivji's criticisms of the GLTF are depressing in their familiarity. Women's groups (with the exception of a few) were cast as middle class, uninformed, easily co-opted and pandering to class and foreign interests, allowing their aid dependency to determine their agenda (Shivji 1998b; see also Manji 1998). These arguments, which have been the staple of criticisms of women's rights advocates all over Africa for decades, ignore the fact that the majority of civil society advocacy groups in Africa share these characteristics (i.e. of middle-class leadership, aid dependency and being influenced by 'Western' ideas and concepts). Groups such as HAKIARDHI, TGNP and TWLA are similar in this regard, but have taken different positions in the land debates. To pursue the class and aid dependency points to their logical conclusion would be to disqualify much of the academic writing and civil society advocacy in Africa today.[43]

---

[41]   Ministry of Lands and Human Settlements Development Advert, *The Guardian*, 30 January 2001. The cooperation between the Government and the GLTF was also mentioned during the interview with the Ministry of Lands official (interview with FKM 2001).

[42]   Unfortunately, not enough information was gathered during the Tanzanian interviews about the currents in Parliament.

[43]   And yet, the coalition in which Shivji worked also received resources from foreign donors. The National Land Forum's Declaration on land rights carries an Oxfam copyright, no less! Also, Shivji's publication on the subject in 1998 was funded by SAREC, NORAD and DANIDA through the International Institute for Environment and Development, IIED.

Shivji was also very critical of the GLTF's desire for legislative reforms. As he argued in acerbic tones:

> Legislation to outlaw gender inequality in the laws of succession might be a short cut and pleasing to advocacy groups who would have something to show to their sponsors and feminist lobbies in Western capitals. But experience shows that this would not necessarily benefit the large majority of women in the village. What is more, it is obviously contrary to a democratic bottom up approach. (Shivji 1998a, 89)

The above quotation raises a substantial question about the pros and cons of a legislative approach to women's interests, which is discussed briefly in the last section of this article.

In relation to women's representation in village decision-making bodies, Shivji argued that the Acts had not advanced the cause of women by providing that they participate in village land councils and the national advisory board, largely because these bodies had very little power. Secondly, he argued that equality with men was necessary but not sufficient to create equitable access to land, if the majority of both men and women were deprived of their security of tenure and were faced with the threat of landlessness (Shivji 1998b, 8). Without male land rights, who would women be enforcing their rights against, Shivji asked rhetorically (Shivji 1998b). Other commentators agree. For example, Mbilinyi's research in villages in and around the Ngorongoro Conservation Area and Serengeti National Park found that livelihoods had been eroded by the loss of vast tracts of village lands to wildlife conservation programmes and private investors in hunting and tourist companies and ambiguous Government policies towards the rights of locals. Elsewhere, the establishment of mines and plantations had resulted in land scarcity with locals becoming casual labourers. The scale of dispossession in these areas had endangered more vulnerable rights in land. In such situations, where communities have found themselves dispossessed and impoverished by processes which have attacked their cultural identity, it was logical for them to reassert tradition in discourses about land, thus worsening the situation of women on whose unpaid labour many smallholder economies depend (Mbilinyi 1999; see also Chachage 1996; Rogers et al. 1996, for similar analysis). One of the conclusions of such work has been that no discussion of women's land issues can ignore the broader land issues facing whole communities.

One key recommendation that the GLTF did not succeed in getting the Government to adopt was that customary law be abolished or severely circumscribed. The GTLF recommendation is neither new nor uncontroversial, even among women's rights advocates. For example, Lussuga and Hidaya have argued that, as a recommendation, it ignores the resilience of customary law to change (1996, 11). Mbilinyi has also argued that while the decision to apply customary law and practice to village land was a case of the Government supporting discriminatory laws, the recommendation to completely abolish customary law and leave the land to market forces was not in the interests of local communities and their members (Mbilinyi no date, 3).

As we have already indicated, the Land Commission, and presumably the Land Forum, did not share the GLTF attitude to customary law. Shivji argued that it was erroneous to see the issue in terms of customary law being anti-women and statutory law being pro-women and that it was more about how to make progress within the customary land tenure system, rather than abolishing or replacing it. This was especially since individualization and titling had not necessarily worked in favour of women (interview with IS 2001). As Shivji notes:

> The Commission neither rejected wholly nor accepted uncritically the law or legal methodology to effect a radical reform of the tenurial system, but was minded to reform the statist top-down institutional structures so as to create space for the forces, conceptions and perspectives from the bottom to assert their interests. (Shivji no date, 27)

He defends this approach as arising directly from interviews with the people[44] about their problems. This he contrasted with demands for statutory interventions, which in his view were top–down, undemocratic and, with the benefit of experience, futile. Interestingly, this was a point on which Shivji and the Government were in agreement.

The insistence on democratic processes is within the evolutionary approach to customary law, with which many gender equality advocates do not have patience (see Whitehead and Tsikata, this issue, for a discussion of the evolutionary approach in land tenure debates). The lawyer-led women's land coalition was very clear about the importance of statutory law interventions to address women's issues within the land reforms. In one interview, it was argued that customary law would take too long to evolve. Therefore an opportunity to pass progressive laws had to be supported and seen as a basis for advocacy (interview with AM and MJ 2001).

IMPLICATIONS OF THE TANZANIAN CASE FOR LAND TENURE REFORMS IN AFRICA: DEBATES ON TITLING, CUSTOMARY LAW AND WOMEN'S RIGHTS

The Tanzanian debates have raised questions that have also arisen within other African land reform contexts, but with Tanzanian specificities. These include issues of economic liberalization, land grabbing by foreigners and wealthy nationals, the increasing dispossession of large sections of smallholder farmers and pastoralist communities and problems of over-centralized and weak administrative structures. As we have seen, many of the national commentators have charged that the land reforms were to protect foreign investors at the expense of local communities.

---

[44] But see Manji's (1998) comments on Shivji's use of the people as though they were a homogenous group with the same interests in land issues. Shivji's answer was that the fears being expressed to the Commission by both men and women were with regard to foreigners coming to grab land and not rich peasants (interview with IS 2001).

A feature of the Tanzanian case was that while the new Land Acts made explicit provisions to address some of the concerns of women and land advocates, they fell short of their demands for the reform of customary law. And yet, some leading women's advocates spoke in terms of a victory for women. The discussions around customary law raised the question of the most fruitful approach to the reform of discriminatory customary practices. Also they raised the issue of the breadth and depth of approaches to women's interests in land, i.e. whether to focus solely on gender equality or take also into account more general issues which could undermine women's gains. The implication here was that the law reforms had to be judged by multiple criteria, that is women's interests were best served by simultaneously addressing broader local and community interests as well as gender discrimination. Within such an approach, commentators have suggested that the Land Acts have been a setback for local communities in spite of what women have gained. As Mbilinyi notes, 'the irony is that whereas women's rights to land e.g. as wives seem to be protected under the new Village Land Law, their rights as members of communities are at risk given the liberalization principles and the administrative structure established' (Mbilinyi 1999, 5). Not all women's advocates shared this dim view of liberalization. Some of the most influential groups in the GTLF supported the liberalization in land markets, land titling and registration as creating opportunities for women to purchase land on their own account and have it registered in their own name to be inherited by their descendants.

None of the protagonists in the land law reform debates made a total condemnation of legislation as the way to change discriminatory customary laws and practices. However, it was considered by some as unhelpful in relation to matters of personal law and custom, and by implication, also to women's interests in land. While there was general agreement that legislation to change social practice was difficult to implement, and women's advocates were recommending intensive public education to address this, they were also optimistic about the value of legislative intervention. The real question, in our view, is whether implementation and other difficulties have rendered statutory law, whatever its purpose and character, totally pointless. Or, to put it another way, is there any purpose to be served by legislation? If there is, what precisely can be legislated and what cannot be and why? The lessons learnt from the reform of Succession Laws across Africa would most certainly provide valuable insights into this issue, but it would be doubtful if the message would be an invalidation of all forms of statutory intervention.

Legislative approaches have raised issues, some of which came up in the Tanzanian debates. One of these is the issue of State efficiency, corruption and accountability. Proponents of wholesale privatization of State-owned enterprises and services used this argument to demand the State's withdrawal from the provision of social services. It is this same logic that lies behind the demand that the State withdraws from land ownership, management and adjudication and statutory law interventions to address discrimination in access to and control over land. Until we do away with the State, it continues to be an important instrument of change, for good or bad. Having its force behind a policy or piece of legislation does greatly influence the direction of social change.

If customary law can be codified and applied by the courts, then legislation, which tries to reform discriminatory customary practices, has its uses. The danger of such a law being breached and made redundant raises important issues about how to improve the efficacy and the quality of implementation of laws. The position that resistance to legislation can be addressed through public education is at best hopeful, stemming as it does from a certain belief that discriminatory rules, decisions and practices arise from ignorance. The Ministry of Community Development, Women's Affairs and Children's research, for example, suggests that there are struggles over power and resources behind the seemingly commonsensical ideologies about safeguarding clan land, which do not arise from ignorance or lack of awareness.

The Commission's arguments that Village Assemblies applying customary law was more democratic than State control and statutory law deserve comment. For many women, neither the State nor the Village Assembly may be the highest expression of democratic principles. While a Village Assembly may be 'closer to home', in the words of the Shivji Commission, its existence may be a necessary but not sufficient condition for women's interests in land to be guaranteed. The Village Assembly may be more democratic and representative, but it may also have a stronger interest in protecting customary practices, such as the ones that discriminate against women. If customary practices need to be changed with care, then surely women need all the help they can get to achieve this and statutory law may be one of a number of measures that are needed, even granting all its limitations and what is required to make it work. The Legal and Human Rights Centre, for example, has argued that since elements of customary law are codified, they can be amended through the same processes, i.e. legislation (interview with JW 2001).

The Shivji Commission also criticized statutory law options on grounds of democratic principle and rights. The Commission is on weak ground here, as there are competing democratic principles and rights in question. The right to one's cultural practices is being pitched against the right not to have one's livelihood threatened by discriminatory practices in the name of culture and tradition. The right to participate in decision-making on all issues that affect one's life, i.e. the bottom–up approach is pitched here against the right to have democracy in substance as well as in form. Which of these prevail at any time is more a result of the balance of forces than high principle. To ask women to wait until customary practices have themselves evolved through contest within their societies is to deny them a level playing field, and that is discriminatory. Furthermore, it has been suggested that there is nothing like pure evolution (interview with BK 2001). Evolution is influenced by many factors. Its trajectories, therefore, cannot be determined beforehand unless there is some conscious intervention to influence its directions. There is no process of change, whether democratic or not, that is easy or welcome or likely to please all persons, especially those who stand to lose their privileges. Can persons engaged in practices judged as undemocratic and discriminatory in turn plead democracy and rights as justification? The Lands Commission itself had proposed legislative changes. It would seem, then, that the question that is posed for any statutory intervention, whether it is to divest the State of the radical title or reform discriminatory customary law rules, is how to bring statutory law closer to ordinary people and how to encourage its implementation in a democratic and equitable manner.

APPENDIX

List of Abbreviations Used

BAWATA	Baraza la Wananake la Taifa
CCM	Chama cha Mapinduzi
DANIDA	Danish Development Agency
DFID	Department for International Development (UK)
ESRF	Economic and Social Research Foundation
GLTF	Gender Land Task Force
HAKIARDHI/LARRI	Land Rights Research and Resources Institute
IFIs	International Financial Institutions e.g. World Bank and International Monetary Fund and Regional Institutions such as the African Development Bank
IIED	International Institute for Environment and Development (UK)
ITR	Individualization, titling and registration
JET	Journalists Environmental Association of Tanzania
LHRC	Law and Human Rights Research Centre
LTG	Land Tenure Study Group
MCDWAC	Ministry of Community Development, Women's Affairs and Children.
MLHUD	Ministry of Lands, Human Settlements Development
MP	Member of Parliament
NLP	National Land Policy
NGOs	Non-Governmental Organizations
NOCHU	National Organization for Children, Welfare and Human Relief
NORAD	Norwegian Development Agency
PRA	Participatory Rural Assessment
SADC	Southern African Development Community
SAREC	Swedish International Aid Agency
TAHEA	Tanzania Home Economics Association
TMWA	Tanzanian Media Women's Association
TWLA	Tanzania Women Lawyers Association
TGNP	Tanzania Gender Networking Programme
UHAI	Ulingo wa Kutetea Haki za Ardhi or the National Land Forum

VA   Village Assembly
VLA   Village Land Act
WAT   Women Advancement Trust
WLAC   Women's Legal Aid Centre

Persons Interviewed (between 29/1/2001 and 3/2/2001)

1. Dr. Bertha Koda, Institute of Development Studies, University of Dar es Salaam (BK)
2. Prof. Marjorie Mbilinyi, University of Dar es Salaam (MM)
3. Jessie S. Mnguto, Chair woman of TWLA (JM)
   Aggripina Mosha, programme officer and Miranda Johnson, assistant programme officer, TGNP (AM & MJ)
4. Fidelis Kashumba Mutahyamilwa, Land Development Service, Legal Department, Ministry of Lands and Human Settlements (FKM)
5. Prof. Issa Shivji (IS)
6. Madam Tabitha Siwale, WAT (TS)
7. John Wallace, LHRC (JW)
8. Pius Nambra Wanzala, TMWA (PNW)

REFERENCES

Chachage, C.S.L., 1995. 'The Meek Shall Inherit the Earth but not the Mining Rights: The Mining Industry and Accumulation in Tanzania'. In *Liberalised Development in Tanzania*, ed. P. Gibbon, 37–108. Uppsala: Nordiska Afrikainstitutet.

Chachage, C.S.L., 1996. 'The Land Policy Paper and the Tenure in National Parks, Game and Forest Reserves'. Paper presented at a Workshop on the National Land Policy, British Council Conference Hall, Dar es Salaam, LARRI-HAKIARDHI.

Gender Land Task Force (GLTF), 1998. 'Comments on the Status of the Land Bill with a Gender Perspective'. Prepared by T. Silaa, R. Kerefu and N. Mazora (all of TWLA) and presented at the Land Forum, 20 June 1998, Russian Cultural Centre.

Gibbon, P., 1995. 'Mechanisation of Production and Privatisation of Development in Post-Ujamaa Tanzania: An Introduction'. In *Liberalised Development in Tanzania*, ed. P. Gibbon, 37–108. Uppsala: Nordiska Afrikainstitutet.

Giblin, J., 1998. 'Land Tenure, Traditions of Thought about Land and Their Environmental Implications in Tanzania'. *Tanzania Zamani*, 4 (1 and 2): 1–56.

Heyer, J. and G. Williams, no date. OXFAM Submission to Tanzanian Land Commission: Agricultural Issues.

Juma, I.H., 1996. 'The Policy Paper in the Context of Existing Land Law and Practice'. Paper presented at a Workshop on the National Land Policy, British Council Conference Hall, Dar es Salaam, LARRI-HAKIARDHI.

Kapinga, W., 1998. 'Some Reflections on the Land Commission Report and the National Land Policy'. Paper presented at a National Land Committee Seminar on the Media and Land Issues, Silver Sands Hotel, Dar es Salaam.

Kiondo, A.S.Z., 1995. 'When the State Withdraws: Local Development, Politics and Liberalisation in Tanzania'. In *Liberalised Development in Tanzania*, ed. P. Gibbon, 37–108. Uppsala: Nordiska Afrikainstitutet.

Koda, B., 1997. 'The Development of Entrepreneurship in Tanzania: A Gender Perspective'. In *Gender and Agrarian Change in Tanzania*, eds S. Ngware, R. Odgaard, R. Shayo and F. Wilson, 29–45. Dar es Salaam: DUP Ltd.

Land Coalition, 1998. *The Campaign on the Land Bill*. Press release.

Lusugga, K. and K. Hidaya, 1996. 'The Relationship Between Gender, Access to Land and Poverty in Tanzania: Cases from the Bukoba Area of Tanzania'. Paper prepared for the First REPOA Research Workshop, Dar es Salaam, 16–18 April.

Manji, A., 1998. 'Gender and the Politics of the Land Reform Processes in Tanzania'. *The Journal of Modern African Studies*, 36 (4): 645–67.

Maoulidi, S., no date *A Review of the Land Act 1998 Bill*.

Mbilinyi, M., 1988. 'Agribusiness and Women Peasants in Tanzania'. *Development and Change*, 19 (4): 549–84.

Mbilinyi, M., 1991. *The Big Slavery*. Dar es Salaam: Dar es Salaam University Press.

Mbilinyi, M., 1997. 'Beyond Oppression and Crisis: A Gendered Analysis of Agrarian Structure and Change'. In *Engendering African Social Sciences*, eds A. Imam, A. Mama and F. Sow, 317–64. Dakar: CODESRIA.

Mbilinyi, M., 1999. 'Land Rights for Whom? Issues of Community, Class and Gender'. Presentation at Forum on Land Rights for Whom, Organised by the University Consultancy Bureau and FEB Foundation, Dar es Salaam.

Mbilinyi, M., no date. *The Land Issue*.

Meena, R., 2000. *The National Machinery for the Advancement of Women in Tanzania*. Accra: Third World Network-Africa.

Ministry of Lands and Human Settlements Development, 1997. *National Land Policy*. Second edition. Dar es Salaam: Government of Tanzania.

Ministry of Lands and Human Settlements Development, 2001. *Land Reforms in Tanzania: Development and Implementation of the National Land Policy of 1995*. Advertiser's Announcement, *The Guardian*, 30 January.

Mkandawire, T., 1987. 'The State and Agriculture in Africa: Introductory Remarks'. In *The State and Agriculture in Africa*, eds T. Mkandawire and N. Bourenane, 1–25. London: CODESRIA Book Series.

Msambichaka, L., 1987. 'State Policies and Food Production in Tanzania'. In *The State and Agriculture in Africa*, eds T. Mkandawire and N. Bourenane, 117–43. London: CODESRIA Book Series.

Mtengeti-Migiro, R., 1990. 'The Division of Matrimonial Property in Tanzania'. *Journal of Modern African Studies*, 28 (3): 521–26.

National Land Forum, 1997. Azimio La Uhai. Declaration of NGOs and Interested Persons on Land Issued by the National Land Forum, A Coalition of NGOs and Interested Persons. Dar es Salaam, 1997.

National Land Forum, 1998. 'Report of the National Land Forum', the Russian Cultural Centre, Dar es Salaam, 28 June 1998.

Ngware, S., 1997. 'The Agrarian Question in Tanzania, Historical Legacies and Contemporary Challenges'. In *Gender and Agrarian Change in Tanzania*, eds S. Ngware, R. Odgaard, R. Shayo and F. Wilson, 13–28. Dar es Salaam: DUP Ltd.

Ngware, S., R. Odgaard, R. Shayo and F. Wilson, eds, 1997. *Gender and Agrarian Change in Tanzania*. Dar es Salaam: DUP Ltd.

Odgaard, R., 1997. 'The Gender Dimensions of Nyakyusa Rural–Rural Migration in Mbeya Region'. In *Gender and Agrarian Change in Tanzania*, eds S. Ngware, R. Odgaard, R. Shayo and F. Wilson, 46–70. Dar es Salaam: DUP Ltd.

Odgaard, R., 1999. 'The Scramble for Women's Land Rights in Tanzania, Researching Development'. *Quarterly Newsletter from the Centre for Development Research*, Copenhagen.

Okoth-Ogendo, H., 2000. 'Legislative Approaches to Customary Tenure and Tenure Reform in East Africa'. *In Evolving Land Rights, Policy and Tenure in Africa*, eds C. Toulmin and J. Quan, 123–34. London: DFID/IIED/NRI.

Omari, C. and L. Shaidi, 1992. *Women's Access to Land among the Pare People of Northern Tanzania.* Research Report. Nairobi: IDRC.

Rogers, P.J., D. Brockington, H. Kiwasila and K. Homewood, 1996. 'Environmental Awareness and Conflict Genesis: People Versus Parks in Mkomazi Game Reserve, Tanzania'. Paper presented at Livelihoods from Resource Flows Conference, Sweden.

Rugumamu, W., 1997. 'Resource Management and Agrarian Change in Semi-Arid Tanzania: A Gender and Ethnic Perspective'. In *Gender and Agrarian Change in Tanzania*, eds S. Ngware, R. Odgaard, R. Shayo and F. Wilson, 79–100. Dar es Salaam: DUP Ltd.

Rwebangira, M., F. Temu, K. Mutakyamirwa, J. Baghadella and J. Magingo, no date. *Participatory Rural Appraisal on Women's Access, Use and Control of Land.* A Report for the Ministry of Community Development, Women Affairs and Children and the World Bank.

Shivji, I., no date. *Contradictory Perspectives on Rights and Justice in the Context of Land Tenure Reform in Tanzania.*

Shivji, I., 1996. 'Grounding the Debate on Land: The National Land Policy and its Implications'. Paper presented at a Workshop on the National Land Policy, British Council Conference Hall, Dar es Salaam, LARRI-HAKIARDHI.

Shivji, I., 1998a. *Not Yet Democracy: Reforming Land Tenure in Tanzania.* London: IIED, HAKIARDHI, and the Faculty of Law, University of Dar es Salaam.

Shivji, I., 1998b. 'Contradictory Perspectives on Rights and Justice in the Context of Land Tenure Reform in Tanzania'. *Tanzania Zamani*, 4 (1 and 2): 1–56.

Tanzania Women Lawyers Association (TWLA), 2000. '10th Anniversary, 1990–2000, Justice and Peace'. *TWLA Special Bulletin.*

Tanzania Gender Networking Programme (TGNP), 2000. *NGOs Implementation of the Beijing Platform for Action: Where Are We?* Special Newsletter on Beijing +5.

The United Republic of Tanzania, 1994. 'Report of the Presidential Commission of Inquiry into Land Matters'. Vol. 1, *Land Policy and Land Tenure Structure.* Ministry of Lands, Housing and Urban Development, in cooperation with the Scandinavian Institute of African Studies, Uppsala, Sweden.

The United Republic of Tanzania, 1999a. *The Village Land Act, 1999.* Dar es Salaam: Government Printer.

The United Republic of Tanzania, 1999b. *The Land Act, 1999.* Dar es Salaam: Government Printer.

Wily, L., 1998. 'A Look at the Land Act 1998 Bill'. Unpublished comments.

6

Gender and Land Rights Revisited: Exploring New Prospects via the State, Family and Market

BINA AGARWAL

The question of women's land rights has a relatively young history in India. This paper briefly traces that history before examining why gendering the land question remains critical, and what the new possibilities are for enhancing women's land access. Potentially, women can obtain land through the State, the family and the market. The paper explores the prospects and constraints linked to each, arguing that access through the family and the market deserve particular attention, since most arable land in India is privatized. On market access, the paper makes several departures from existing discussions by focusing on the advantages, especially for poor women, of working in groups to lease in or purchase land; using government credit for land rather than merely for micro-enterprises; and collectively managing purchased or leased in land, the collectivity being constituted with other women, rather than with family members. Such group functioning is shown to have several advantages over individual or family-based farming. This approach could also help revive land reform, community cooperation and joint farming in a radically new form, one centred on poor women.

Keywords: women's land rights, inheritance, land reform, land market access, group farming, India

INTRODUCTION

In recent years there has been a resurgence of interest in land reform and the agrarian question, among both academics and policymakers.[1] However, on the question of land rights for *women*, two features are striking. On the one hand, the question remains peripheral to the mainstream academic debate,[2] despite

The author is grateful to Janet Seiz, Patricia Uberoi, S.M. Agarwal, Deniz Kandiyoti, Shahra Razavi and the journal's anonymous referees for their comments on an earlier draft; and to Ruth Hall for sharing her draft note on her field work in Andhra Pradesh.

[1] See among others, Agarwal (1994), Banerjee (2000), Besley and Burgess (2000), Byres (1991), Cousins (1997), de Janvry and Sadoulet (1989), Deere and Leon (2001), Deninger (1999), El-Ghonemy (1990), Government of India (1989, 2000), Herring (1999), IFAD (2001a), Kandiyoti (2001), Lipton and Lipton (1995), Reidinger (1995), Sobhan (1993) and Swinnen (1997).

[2] Among the few within the mainstream who touch on it is Herring (1999).

growth in feminist writings on the subject.[3] On the other hand, in contrast to the agrarian reform debates of the 1950s and 1960s when the gender question was largely ignored, today there is noteworthy, albeit limited, recognition of its importance among grassroots groups and policymakers. This paper begins by briefly tracing the history of this shift in the Indian context and the issue of women's voiced and unvoiced needs, as a prelude to examining why gendering the land question remains critical, and what the new experiments and prospects are for enhancing women's land access.

More generally, the paper revisits the issue of gender and land rights in India and outlines the possibilities and constraints to land access through the State, the family and the market. In particular, it examines the new institutional forms of cultivation being tried out by some NGOs, especially through collective investment and farming by groups of women.

In developing this argument the gendered path of agrarian transition in India is also briefly described, and the reasons why independent land rights continue to be important for women's welfare, efficiency and empowerment are reiterated. The male bias in land transfers from the State, and possible reasons for the bias are then traced, followed by a section focusing on land transfers from the family and constraints thereof. The penultimate section examines the possibilities of obtaining land from the market and analyses some of the forms in which women are practising group cultivation. The last section contains concluding comments.

HOW HAS THE QUESTION BEEN RAISED?

A Brief History

The question of women's land rights in India, and more generally in South Asia, has a relatively young history. In the mid-1980s, when I first began writing on this issue,[4] there was very little policy and grassroots focus on it, and even less academic work (with a few notable exceptions).[5] At best, the question had surfaced in scattered ways, both in research[6] and direct intervention. Among the best-known grassroots interventions were two peasant movements: the Bodhgaya movement in Bihar, catalysed by the Chatra Yuva Sangharsh Vahini in 1978, and the Shetkari Sangathana's movement for farmer's rights launched in Maharashtra in 1980. In both instances, the question of women's claims to land was raised, with some success in transferring land to women (Agarwal 1994).[7]

Alongside, and articulated more quietly, were occasional grassroots demands by women, including the 1979 demand by a group of poor peasant women in

---

[3]　See, for example, Agarwal (1988, 1994, 1995, 1998, 2002a); Deere and Leon (2001); Meer (1997); Davidson (1988); Hirschon (1984) and Kandiyoti (2001).

[4]　See, for example, Agarwal (1988), also presented at several conferences during 1986–7.

[5]　Of course, discussions on women's legal rights in property go further back, especially to the early twentieth century, but the debate then was confined largely to inheritance laws, and land was subsumed under property in general.

[6]　For example, Sharma (1980).

[7]　See also Manimala (1993) and Omvedt (1990).

West Bengal to their women *panchayat* representatives: 'Please go and ask the *sarkar* [government] why when it distributes land we don't get a title? Are we not peasants? If my husband throws me out, what is my security?'[8] Such demands were subsequently included in the recommendations (placed before the Indian Planning Commission) of a 1980 pre-plan symposium organized by eight women's groups in Delhi.

Meanwhile, the 1979 FAO report of the World Conference on Agrarian Reform and Rural Development (WCAARD) held in Rome recommended that gender discriminatory laws in respect to 'rights in inheritance, ownership and control of property' be repealed and measures adopted to ensure women's equitable access to land and other productive resources (FAO 1979). These recommendations (in diluted form) were adopted in the country review follow-up to WCARRD by the Indian Ministry of Agriculture and Rural Development (CWDS 1985, 89–94). This also led to a policy statement in the Sixth Five Year Plan (1980–5) that the Government would 'endeavour' to give joint titles to spouses when distributing agricultural land and home sites. Subsequent Plan documents, as outlined later, have had a chequered history, with either passing or no reference to the issue, until the Ninth Plan which (through my involvement) provided detailed recommendations. Alongside, the *National Perspective Plan for Women: 1988–2000 AD*, drawn up at the initiative of the Indian Ministry of Human Resource Development, made several substantive recommendations for closing the gender gap in access to land (Government of India 1988). And the Report of a national seminar on land reform, held by the Planning Commission in 1989, at which I presented the case for women's land rights, incorporated most of my recommendations on this count (Government of India 1989).

But all this did not amount to a sustained or widespread focus on the question of women and land. As traced in Agarwal (1994), several factors constrained this: first there was (and still is) an ambiguity among groups and individuals who have otherwise been strong advocates of redistributive land reform, namely Marxist political parties and left-wing non-party organizations, most of whom see class issues as primary and gender concerns as divisive and distracting. At the same time, most gender-progressive groups, including women's organizations, not only had quite divergent concerns and approaches, but they focused on issues other than land. [The Deccan Development Society (DDS) in Andhra Pradesh – whose work is discussed later – was a rare exception.] Among urban groups, violence against women was the main unifying issue, and women's economic situation took secondary place. Moreover, barring some notable exceptions, those concerned with women's economic position, including rural-based groups, were preoccupied with wage employment, non-land related income-generating schemes, and micro-credit for small enterprises, as *the* means

---

[8] Personal communication, Vina Mazumdar, Center for Women's Development Studies, Delhi, 1992.

of improving women's economic welfare.[9] They paid little attention to land and property access, and took inadequate account of the stage of India's agrarian transition, wherein agriculture was still the main source of livelihood, but in much greater degree for women than men. And working on land without rights in it meant a high vulnerability to poverty. This broader picture, which warranted prioritizing land access for women, even while other employment avenues and micro-credit schemes were worth pursuing as supplementary measures, was somehow missed. Also, while inheritance laws were made more gender equal in a few states, most amendments did not touch agricultural land and, except in Maharashtra, appear not to have been pushed by civil society (Agarwal 1995, 2002a).

Indeed, some left-oriented women's organizations I spoke with in the mid-1980s even felt that advocating individual property rights for women went against their understanding of a socialist society. Yet, to my knowledge, they did not raise similar objections to redistributive land reform or peasant struggles through which (typically male) heads of landless households gained rights in land. Another factor that appears to have influenced South Asia's left-wing (including women's) groups are Engels' writings, which emphasized women's entry into the labour force as a necessary condition for their emancipation.[10] Such groups too gave centrality to women's employment, but the necessary accompaniments emphasized by Engels, namely the abolition of private property in male hands and the socialization of housework and childcare, remained largely neglected.

Yet there was clearly an unfulfilled need for a gender perspective on the land question, not just academically but in policy and grassroots action, as indicated, for example, by the catalytic effect of *A Field of One's Own* (Agarwal 1994). Some illustrative examples of governmental and grassroots responses in South Asia and beyond are given below.

Within the central government, for instance, the book prepared the ground for the incorporation of fairly radical recommendations in the Ninth Five Year Plan.[11] It also led the Ministry of Rural Areas and Employment in November 1997 to set up a three-member Committee for Gender Equality in Land Devolution in Tenurial Laws,[12] to reform the rules governing the inheritance of agricultural land. Since agriculture is a State subject, changes in tenurial laws are undertaken by State legislators. The Committee's Report (Agarwal et al. 1998) recommended full gender equality in the devolution rules and outlined in detail the changes needed. Most state governments have yet to respond to the

---

[9]   Among individuals, notable exceptions include Chetna Gala and Manimala (active in the Bodhgaya movement); Gail Omvedt (who, along with Gala, played a lead role in the Shetkari Sangathan's Mahila Agadi); Madhu Kishwar, who filed a petition in India's Supreme Court challenging the denial of land rights to Ho tribal women in Bihar (Kishwar 1987) and P.V. Satheesh and Rukmani Rao of the DDS, who began promoting land acquisition and collective farming by women.

[10]   Engels had a similar influence in the former Socialist countries (Molyneux 1981).

[11]   See the section 'Land Transfers and the State' for details.

[12]   The Committee was constituted under my chairpersonship, the other two members being law professors Lotika Sarkar and the late B. Sivaramayya.

recommendations, but I understand that one state, Uttar Pradesh (UP), has gone some way toward reform by seeking to amend the UP Land Reform Act of 1950, by bringing the widow on a par with sons in the inheritance of agricultural land.

In another state – Madhya Pradesh – the Government's *Policy on Women* drafted in 1995 drew from the book to bring in the land question as a central issue, and recommended that land distributed by the Government would, in future, be in women's names, with preference given to groups of poor rural women. Also, unmarried adult daughters, who until then had been ignored in land distributed under resettlement schemes, would be placed on a par with adult sons (Government of Madhya Pradesh 1996). Some of these recommendations have since been implemented, although mainly in terms of giving women joint titles with husbands.[13]

Grassroots responses have similarly taken different forms: workshops, action plans and, most importantly, pilot projects. Some workshops have been conducted by NGOs themselves, others by me at their request. Either way, they reveal an emerging need and have led to plans for concrete action. For instance, a Bangladesh workshop that I conducted in 2000, under the aegis of the Association for Land Reform and Development (ALRD), aimed at evolving strategies for promoting gender equality in land rights. Attended by about 30 (mostly male) NGO representatives as well as academics, the participants' action plan included advocacy for gender equality in inheritance law and practice on a secular and uniform basis for all communities; promoting legal literacy; registering women's inheritance shares; and changing gendered attitudes (ALRD 2000). ALRD is a network of 220 NGOs that has undertaken land reform advocacy for empowering the landless since inception, but its interest in gender is recent. At a similar workshop I conducted in June 2002, the participating NGOs from rural Gujarat enthusiastically outlined plans to enhance women's land access within their respective concerns, be it livelihood enhancement, women's empowerment or watershed development. The issue has also been carried forward by NGOs in other Indian states, such as in Delhi and UP by Action India (Bharti 2000; Roy Chowdhury 2001), as well as in Nepal,[14] and outside South Asia.[15]

These emerging initiatives highlight a slow but encouraging recognition by policymakers and many grassroots groups (who had hitherto focused on land in an ungendered way) of the need to enhance women's land rights, for both livelihood security and gender justice.[16] In this context, the pioneering but under-recognized efforts of a few grassroots groups, such as the Deccan Development

---

[13] Personal communication, the Chief Minister of Madhya Pradesh, August 2001.

[14] Here elements within international agencies such as ICIMOD and UNDP have also become active, and an UNDP event I spoke at included Parliamentarians.

[15] For instance, I was privileged to be invited to facilitate a 1997 conference in South Africa, attended by NGOs and officials from the Department of Land Affairs from across the country (see Friedman and Sunde 1998 for the conference report).

[16] Alongside, and independently of, discussions on the land question, there have been some noteworthy proposals by gender-aware individuals in India to reform gender-unequal inheritance laws (see, for example, Working Group on Women's Rights 1996; also Agarwal 2002a, 2002b).

Society, which began work on this aspect around 1989–90, also provide the much needed ground experience from which other NGOs can learn (for details, see the penultimate section).

Women's Voices and Unvoiced Needs

What about women's own voices? Are rural women themselves demanding land rights? Yes, in many cases, especially since the mid-1970s,[17] but there are also examples where women have not identified this as a priority. The question is: does the absence of a widespread demand indicate the absence of a need? Some feminist academics have disquietingly argued that women's land rights do not deserve policy attention, since rural women themselves are not demanding this. One UK-based South Asian academic, for instance, commented at the 1997 UNRISD workshop on women, poverty and well-being, held at the Center for Development Studies, Kerala, that: '[Land rights] is not the issue that people are raising most. So I am not sure it is something that is shared by grassroots women.'[18] Likewise, another UK-based scholar, Cecile Jackson, noted at the same workshop: 'I have also worked in Zimbabwe, where I was surprised at how few women expressed a demand for land and were in fact much more interested in employment . . .'.[19] This line of argument is disquieting because it assumes that voiced demand (or its lack) is a sufficient indicator of needs and preferences, and an adequate basis for social policy.

This echoes a growing populist emphasis in some quarters on identifying priorities for the poor solely or largely on the basis of their expressed wants, assuming as unimportant that which goes unmentioned. Documents such as the World Bank's three volume *Voices of the Poor* (Narayan et al. 2000a, 2000b, 2002), although written with a different objective, can also lend themselves to this use.

This is not to deny the critical importance of asking the deprived their priorities. But it is equally critical to recognize that the deprived may have incomplete information about all options, and thus fail to mention those that seem out-of-reach. Or they might shape what they reveal about their priorities according to how an interview is conducted. Or they might adapt their preferences and felt needs to what they see as attainable.[20]

Take the issue of adapted needs and preferences. Sen (1984, 309) gives a striking example from a 1945 survey conducted a year after the Great Bengal

---

[17] See, for example, the many quotations in Agarwal (1994), Hall (1999) and Bharti (2000); see also Narayan et al. (2000).

[18] UNRISD's transcripts of the seminar. The participant did not say which geographic context she had in mind. But even in Bangladesh (her region of research focus), major NGOs such as ALRD, Nijera Kori, and the Bangladesh Rural Advancement Committee are now seeking to enhance women's land rights; and my field visits to some of Nijera Kori's fieldsites in Noakhali revealed immense land hunger.

[19] UNRISD's transcripts.

[20] See also Nussbaum's (2000) excellent discussion on adapted preferences, and Sunstein (1993) on how people's preferences are shaped by existing endowments.

Famine. The survey found that only 2.5 per cent of the widows compared with 48.5 per cent of widowers reported themselves 'ill' or in 'indifferent' health, even though the former were widely recognized to be the more deprived. As he notes, 'The deprived people tend to come to terms with their deprivation because of the sheer necessity of survival, and they may, as a result, lack the courage to demand any radical change, and may even adjust their desires and expectations to what they unambitiously see as feasible.' (Sen 2000, 63).[21] I would add that this could happen not only if the deprived adapt their needs and preferences (as Sen and some others rightly emphasize), but equally if the deprived adapt what they reveal of their needs and preferences according to who asks the question and how, and what the respondent thinks the researcher wants to hear. As I have argued at length elsewhere, drawing on a variety of evidence, women may not reveal their real preferences overtly, but may do so through their covert actions (Agarwal 1994, 1997).

That women under deprivation often limit their stated needs was also strikingly revealed during my November 1997 visit to a land occupation and resettlement site in the Cramond area near Pietermaritzburg, South Africa. I went there at the invitation of the Association for Rural Advancement (AFRA, an NGO working with rural communities to redress the country's legacy of an unjust land dispensation), accompanied by Suzani Ngubane, a committed woman activist from AFRA with long years of grassroots experience. At the site, occupied by a large number of families, mostly women and children had carved out small plots for vegetable and poultry farming, while most men were away in other jobs. During my discussion with a group of 25–30 women, I asked: in whose names will these plots be registered? They said, their husbands, after which their oldest sons would inherit the land, under the customary practice of primogeniture. My further query – wouldn't it be better if the land was in your names or in joint titles, since you are the ones farming it – was greeted with silence. I repeated the question. This caused a buzz. Finally, one of the younger women answered: 'We are taking so long in answering because no one had ever asked us this before! It seems like a dream that we might have land of our own.' I asked: what advantages might that give you? She and some others said that this would reduce their risk of being evicted by their sons; enhance their freedom to take independent decisions on land use without waiting for migrant husbands; enable them to obtain production credit; give them greater control over the farm's income for home use; allow them to offer security to daughters (and daughters' children) abandoned by husbands; and so on. Their only fears were male resistance to joint titles and administrative bottlenecks. They felt, however, that AFRA should help them, now that 'you have opened our eyes to the possibility'.

---

[21] Lest it be misread, I'd like to clearly distinguish between Sen's argument here (with which I agree) that the deprived may adapt their preferences according to what appears feasible, and another argument by Sen elsewhere (which I have disputed) that the deprived may suffer from a form of false consciousness and may thus become complicit in their own oppression (Sen 1990; Agarwal 1997).

These women had not considered having land in their own names as an option, since even AFRA had not discussed this possibility with them. The women's response also surprised Suzani, who subsequently took up women's land claims on a pilot basis in some other AFRA fieldsites and found that men's resistance was neither that strong, nor insurmountable. In January 1998, two months after my visit, she emailed me:

> At the end of the year I convened a provincial women's workshop and shared the knowledge I gained both from your presentation at AFRA and the presentation you did at the Cape Town conference. Women are very excited. There is a community just near Pietermaritzburg which has just got a huge piece of land. This means that your ideas came at the right time for this community, because together with the community I am looking at how the titling could include women's names – it seems like it is not going to be a problem. I have introduced the subject to the men and they are taking it in a good spirit although they have questions like: what is going to happen now to the male heirs? . . . But . . . they are [not] trying to resist the initiative. We are planning to help the community to build a women's movement which is going to see to it that these ideas are implemented.

Indeed, Suzani has since sought to make women's land claims integral to AFRA's approach. In February 1998, she wrote:

> I am pushing for the issue of joint titles to be put on top of AFRA's agenda. . . . We are having a week long annual [meeting for] strategic planning. It is going to be one of the hot issues. I have introduced it to another restitution community and it is taken seriously, but men are asking questions like: 'are we saying that African culture should do away with the system it has been using, which is that of a male heir?' Women are able to argue that one, because according to our culture . . . that heir provided for the deceased man's family. This is not happening any more – the heir collects whatever he inherits and takes it to his own family, forgetting the family of the deceased. I am sure we are going to win this one.

This example strikingly illustrates that rural women's failure to raise the land demand did not imply its lack of importance to them. More generally, identifying priorities for women's enhancement based purely on their expressed need could prove unduly self-limiting, and even misleading, in some contexts.

THE CONTINUED IMPORTANCE OF LAND RIGHTS FOR WOMEN

The issue of women's land rights is not only important today, it is likely to become increasingly so over time. In particular, India's agrarian transition has been slow, uneven and highly gendered. There are also serious gender inequalities in intra-household allocations from resources controlled by men, and a notable potential for production inefficiencies with gender unequal land distribution.

A Gendered Agrarian Transition

Agrarian transitions, among other things, typically involve a shift of labour from agriculture to non-agriculture. But there need be no uniformity by gender. In India, the percentage of all rural workers in agriculture declined from 84 in 1972–3 to 76 in 1999–2000. However, this decline was due largely to male workers moving to non-agriculture, while women remained substantially in agriculture; indeed their dependence has increased in recent years, and the gender gap is growing. Today, 53 per cent of all male workers, 75 per cent of all female workers, and 85 per cent of all *rural* female workers, are in agriculture. And, for women, this percentage has declined less than four points since 1972–3 (Government of India 2001).

Although the absorption of both sexes in the non-farm sector has slowed down since 1987–8, for women the slowing down has been dramatic: the compound growth rate of female non-agricultural employment fell from 5.2 per cent over 1978–88 to 0.2 per cent during 1988–94 (Chadha 1999). Over this latter period, while 29 per cent of rural male additions to the labour force in the over-14 age group were absorbed into non-agriculture, less than 1 per cent of the additional female workers were so absorbed (Government of India 1990, 1996a). Women's low absorption has been compounded by the general stagnation of rural non-farm employment in the post-reform period.

Moreover, the non-farm sector is very heterogeneous, containing both high return/high wage activities and low return/low wage ones. These variations are apparent both regionally and by gender. A 1997 countrywide survey by the National Commission on Self-Employed Women and Women in the Informal Sector (*Shramshakti* 1988), and micro-studies of women workers in individual occupations,[22] suggest that women are largely concentrated in the low-and-insecure-earnings end of the non-farm sector. Women's domestic work burden, lower mobility, lesser education and fewer investable assets limit not only their entry into non-agriculture in relation to men, but also their range of non-farm options. Today, even though male workers still constitute some 60 per cent of the total agricultural workforce, this percentage has declined and that of female workers has increased in recent years.

All said, we appear to be observing early signs of a feminization of agriculture. Several Southeast Asian countries underwent a somewhat similar process in the early 1970s. In Malaysia, for instance, as more men moved to non-agriculture, women began to undertake traditional male tasks such as land preparation (Stivens et al. 1994).[23] But, subsequently, while women in Malaysia and some other parts of Southeast Asia were largely absorbed into non-farm jobs, in India and many other parts of Asia they remain largely confined to

---

[22]   See, for example, Singh and Kelles-Vitanen (1987).
[23]   Also noted among some tribal communities in India (Fernandes and Menon 1987).

agriculture.[24] Indeed, existing figures provide little justification for the sweeping arguments some scholars have used to set aside the land question, for instance that 'everywhere that you look in the world, land is becoming less and less important as the critical resource for employment' (The earlier-quoted South Asian Scholar, transcripts of the 1997 UNRISD workshop).[25]

Moreover, a large percentage of India's rural households are *de facto* female-headed, due to widowhood, marital breakdown or male outmigration, estimates ranging from 20 per cent (Buvinic and Youssef 1978) to 35 per cent (Government of India 1988). And we can expect female-headed households to increase in number. Marriages are less stable today, kinship support systems less reliable, and rural to urban migrants are still largely men.

At the same time, the nature of agricultural work that women do is to a greater extent than for men casual in nature. And while casualization has grown for both sexes, the increase since 1987–8 has been more for women. Moreover, the rise in real agricultural wage rates for both sexes and the decline in the gender wage gap, apparent between the mid-1970s and mid-1980s, has not been sustained into the 1990s. Compared with men, women still have lower real wage rates in most states, and lower average real wage earnings in both agriculture and non-agriculture in all states (Unni 1996).

In other words, we can expect a growing gender divergence in dependence on agriculture. As more men shift to non-farm livelihoods, an increasing number of households will become dependent on women bearing the larger burden of farm management. But women in agriculture operate as disadvantaged workers, whether as casual labourers or as self-employed workers. Unlike self-employed men, self-employed rural women are mostly unwaged workers on male-owned family farms. They seldom own or control the land they cultivate.

This, in turn, has implications for welfare and efficiency, apart from equality and empowerment (as elaborated in Agarwal (1994) and briefly outlined and updated here).

Welfare

The negative relationship between the risk of rural poverty and land access is well established.[26] Land can provide both direct and indirect benefits. Direct

[24] Although today in Malaysia and the Republic of Korea less than 15 per cent of total female workers are in agriculture and related occupations, the percentages are substantial elsewhere: 75 per cent in India, 77 per cent in Bangladesh, 66 per cent in Pakistan, 93 per cent in Nepal, and between 40 and 50 per cent in Indonesia and Thailand (see Government of India 2001, for India; Acharya 2000, for Nepal; and ILO 2000, for the other countries).

[25] Of course, there have been shifts over time, but for many regions these have been marginal and gender-unequal. Hence, for both sexes but especially for women, agriculture remains a critical source of employment in large parts of the developing world. Moreover, leaving agriculture for better prospects is quite different from being pushed out by poverty and landlessness.

[26] See especially Ali et al. (1981), Lipton (1985), Besley and Burgess (1998) and IFAD (2001a, 2001b).

advantages can stem from growing crops or fodder or trees. Indirect advantages can take various forms: owned land can serve as collateral for credit or as a mortgageable or saleable asset during a crisis. Land (whether owned or controlled) increases the probability of finding supplementary wage employment, enhances bargaining power with employers, pushes up aggregate real wage rates, and is an important asset base for rural non-farm enterprises (Agarwal 1994). But land access by men alone cannot be assumed to benefit women and children equitably. The significant body of evidence that has emerged over the last 25 years or so shows systematic gender inequalities in access to basic necessities within households.[27] There are also notable gender differences in income-spending patterns (Dwyer and Bruce 1988). Women and children's risk of poverty can thus depend crucially on women's direct access to income and resources, and not just access mediated through husbands or male relatives. In addition, owning land would enhance women's self-confidence and ability to demand their due in government programmes, such as for health care and education.

The links with poverty apart, there is growing evidence of links between assets in women's hands and child welfare. In urban Brazil, the effect on child survival probabilities was found to be almost twenty times greater for unearned income (from rent, physical and financial assets, etc.) that accrued to the mother, compared with that which accrued to the father (Thomas 1990); and assets owned by the mother had a bigger positive impact on the anthropometric outcomes of daughters relative to sons, while the same was not true for fathers (Thomas 1994, cited in Strauss and Beegle 1996). Kumar (1978) found that among marginal farmer households in Kerala, the mother's cultivation of a home garden (the output of which she controlled) had a consistently high positive effect on child nutrition. Moreover, children in rural India are found more likely to attend school and receive medical care if the mother has assets (Strauss and Beegle 1996).[28] In other words, secure land rights for rural women today could enhance their children's, especially daughters', prospects for education and non-farm employment in the future.

For widows and the elderly, owning land could improve welfare not just directly, but also by enhancing their entitlement to family welfare (Caldwell et al. 1988). Relatives, including sons, often do not provide the expected economic security. Many widows and the elderly thus end up living on their own, and in poverty.[29] As some argue, if they had property children would look after them better (Caldwell et al. 1988).

It needs emphasis that access to land is important, even where it cannot serve as the sole basis of livelihood. Indeed, a large proportion of rural households do not own enough land for all family members to subsist on that basis alone. *But even a small plot can be a critical element in a diversified livelihood system and can*

[27]   Reviewed in Agarwal (1994).
[28]   See also Quisumbing and Maluccio (2000) for Bangladesh.
[29]   See, for example Chen (1998), and Panda (1997).

significantly reduce the risk of poverty and food insecurity. Some land is usually necessary even for viable rural non-farm activity. It expands the range of non-farm
options, and increases the potential for non-farm earnings several fold: small
farmer households are found to earn many times more from rural off-farm self-
employment than landless labour households (Chadha 1993). Hence, for ensuring rural women's entry into the higher-earning segments of the non-farm sector,
an initial strengthening of their land rights might prove essential in many
regions.

Efficiency

As agriculture gets feminized, an increasing number of women will be faced
with the prime responsibility for farming, but without rights to the land they
cultivate. Production inefficiency associated with tenure insecurity continues to
be one of the important rationales for land reform. But the rationale has not been
extended to cover family members. In fact, in many contexts, enhancing women's
land rights could increase overall production. While systematic evidence on all
the aspects noted below is not available for India, evidence from other regions
provides pointers and underlines the need for similar studies in India.

First, there is an incentive effect, namely the effect of secure rights in land and
control over its produce on the farmer's motivation to put in greater effort and
investment in the land. This important effect, extensively emphasized in land
reform literature, especially under tenancy reform, has received little attention in
relation to family members. This is presumably because the latter are assumed to
put in their best effort, even if the land is owned by the male household head,
due to family loyalty and/or because the benefits would be distributed equitably.
Recent evidence from Africa, however, suggests that disincentives can exist equally
within the family. In Kenya, for instance, in a context where men and women
cultivated both separate and joint plots, the introduction of weeding technology
in maize production raised yields on women's plots by 56 per cent where women
controlled the output, and only by 15 per cent on the men's plots where women
also weeded but men got the proceeds (Elson 1995).

Second, if land access is through titles, it would enhance women's ability to
raise production by improving their access to credit, as well as their independent
access to cash flows for reinvestment.[30]

Third, evidence suggests that women might use resources more efficiently
than men in given contexts. This has been noted not only for credit (as in the
Grameen Bank experience in Bangladesh), but also land. For example, a study in
Burkina Faso found that because of women's choice of cropping patterns, women's
plots produced much higher values of output per hectare than their husbands'
plots (Udry et al. 1995). And although women had lower yields for given
crops, Udry et al. attribute this to women's lesser access to inputs, which were

---

[30]   For links between land titles and credit access, see, for example, Feder et al. (1986).

concentrated on the men's plots. The study estimated that output could be increased by 10–20 per cent, if factors of production (such as manure and fertilizers) were reallocated from men's plots to women's plots in the same household. While some other studies caution against simple policy prescriptions based on Udry et al.'s single crop results which, they argue, would be tempered if account were taken of the social complexity of households and the livelihood system as a whole (see, for example, Whitehead 2001), for our purposes the important point is the need to be alert to the neglected links between allocative efficiency and the gender distribution of land and inputs (see also, Quisumbing 1996). Other efficiency links arise from differential access to extension services – improving women's access could enhance productivity: in Kenya, maize yields were found to be almost 7 per cent more on female-managed farms than on male-managed ones, when they had the same access to extension (Dey 1992). Systematic research on the efficiency implications of more gender-equal access to land, production inputs and technical information is also warranted in the Indian context. More generally, existing findings underline the importance of linking land transfers to women with infrastructural support.

Fourth, including women as farm managers would make for a more talented and better-informed pool than one consisting solely of men. In many South Asian communities, for example, women are often better informed than men are about traditional crop varieties (Acharya and Bennett 1981). A more diverse system of cultivation could also result from gender differences in crop preferences, as found in the Burkina Faso study (Udry et al. 1995), and among women's farming groups in Andhra Pradesh (India).[31]

Fifth, possessing land (especially titles) empowers women and places them in a stronger position to demand their due in government schemes, and in infrastructure and services. It also helps them be more assertive with agencies that provide inputs and extension information.[32]

Some oppose women inheriting land on the grounds that it will reduce output by reducing farm size and increasing fragmentation. However, as elaborated in Agarwal (1994) and Banerjee (2000), evidence from South Asia gives no reason to fear an adverse size effect: the negative relationship between size and productivity is found to still hold after the green revolution. And fragmentation can arise equally with male inheritance. Moreover, land leasing arrangements help consolidate cultivation units, even where the ownership units are fragmented. There has also been a spurt in farmer-initiated consolidation in India in the post-green-revolution period (Ray 1996). Probably due both to this and to government consolidation efforts, the number of fragments per holding at the all-India level has declined from 5.7 in 1960–1 to 2.7 in 1991–2 (Government of India 1997a, 17). In addition, as discussed in the penultimate section, the unit of

---

[31] Author's field visits to DDS sites in 1998.
[32] See the penultimate section; see also Herring (1999) for links between land ownership and participation in local institutions.

ownership need not define the unit of cultivation, if collective investment and cultivation is undertaken by groups of women.

These potential efficiency implications are important not just in some aggregate sense for increasing agricultural productivity, but especially for improving the food security of women's own households.

Equality and Empowerment

While the welfare and efficiency arguments are concerned with women having some land in absolute terms, the empowerment and equality arguments are concerned with women's position *relative* to men, and particularly with women's ability to challenge unequal gender relations within and outside the home.

The equality issue can of course be argued in various ways, but here its link with empowerment needs emphasis. The parameters of empowerment are complex and multi-dimensional. As outlined in Agarwal (1994), land rights can make a notable difference to women's bargaining power within the home and community, enhance their confidence and sense of self-worth, enable them to negotiate better deals in the wage labour market, increase the respect they command within the community, facilitate their participation in village decision-making bodies, and so on. Empowerment in one or more of these forms has emerged wherever social movements or NGOs have helped women gain access to land. Consider too, women's own perceptions: in the Bodhgaya movement in Bihar, when women received land in two villages, they graphically contrasted their earlier voicelessness to their situation now, 'now that we have the land we have the strength to speak and walk' (Manimala 1983). Similarly, after purchasing land with the help of DDS, poor *dalit* women in Andhra Pradesh could say:

> Now even the government is following us. Not because they love women [but because] they know that loans for land are safer with women. Having land in women's name has made an enormous difference – learning to take on land means taking on more power and wisdom. Once we got land, our eyes opened. (Narsamma, Kalbaman village, cited in Hall 1999)

What then are the prospects for enhancing women's land access?

LAND TRANSFERS FROM THE STATE

Potentially, there are three main sources of arable land: the State, the family and the market. Consider first, State transfers. The State distributes land in various ways: as part of traditional land reform measures, typically taking away land from those owning more than a specified ceiling and endowing the landless with the ceiling surplus land; in resettlement schemes as compensation for land lost due to displacement, say, by a large dam; and as a poverty alleviation measure. All three forms of distribution are, however, gender biased. Typically, the Government allots land to male household heads. In addition, adult sons often get special consideration, but adult daughters seldom do.

Land Reform

For a start, the land reform programmes of all political parties in India have been strongly male biased. As noted, the male household head is the typical recipient. In addition, in fixing ceilings, and often also in land distribution, virtually all states give adult sons special consideration. Typically, a family is defined as constituted of a cultivator, a spouse and minor children. An adult son is usually counted as a separate unit. This means that households with adult sons can hold additional land, or each adult son can hold land in his own right. By contrast, unmarried adult daughters get totally excluded in most states, since they are not counted as members of their natal families, and being unmarried have no marital families from which to claim. Only Kerala counts both unmarried adult sons and daughters as separate units, likely due to the state's matrilineal tradition.

Underlying the ceiling specifications is the understanding that those recognized either as part of the family unit or separate (as with adult sons) will be maintained by the land allowed within the ceiling. Here we have a curious situation where the subsistence needs of unmarried adult daughters are ignored in many states, even while the legal age of marriage for girls is 18. Moreover, giving adult sons additional land while ignoring adult daughters assumes that only men take responsibility for family provisioning.

These male biases would have been less surprising in the 1950s and 1960s, when the gender question was somewhat dormant, than in the 1970s, when it had entered the public domain. The 1970s brought some State recognition of women's claims, but only on paper. For instance, West Bengal's *Operation Barga* programme, an important land reform initiative undertaken in the late-1970s for the registration of tenants, essentially registered men. Although an exception was made, in principle, for single women households (those divorced, deserted etc., and without adults sons), few, even among them, received land in practice. A village in Midnapur district studied by Gupta (1993) is indicative: 98 per cent of the 107 *khas* holdings distributed there went to men. In nine out of the ten female-headed households, the land went to the women's sons; and only eight of the 18 single women received land. None of the married women received joint titles. It is notable that in its 1991 election manifesto, the CPI (M), under whose aegis *Operation Barga* was undertaken, was the only political party that had promised to ensure women's equal rights in landed property. The promise remains unfulfilled.

Resettlement Schemes

Privileged male entitlement also characterizes land allotment in resettlement schemes. Consider four major projects: Sardar Sarovar Project (across Gujarat, Madhya Pradesh and Maharashtra); the Tehri Project (Uttarakhand); the Upper Krishna Project (Karnataka); and the Upper Iravati Project (Orissa). In each of these, the resettlement packages for landed families are male biased. In male-headed households, all land transfers are to men alone. In five of the six states (the exception being Karnataka), there is no provision for widows. Another five of the six have special provisions for adult sons, but only two have such provisions for adult unmarried daughters, in one of which the daughter has to be above 35 years in age (Agarwal 2002b).

As some of the tribals displaced by the Sardar Sarovar Project asked me during my field visit there in 1992: 'What about those of us who have only adult daughters?' Also, in the scheme, a widow (with an adult son) is counted not as a household head but as a dependent, and is therefore not entitled to land or house ownership (Bhatia 1998).

Poverty-alleviation Programmes

These have had a mixed history. The first five Plans paid little attention to women's land claims. In India's Sixth Five Year Plan (1980–5), however, a separate chapter on 'Women and Development' mentioned that the Government would give joint titles to spouses in the distribution of land and home sites. But this directive was not reiterated in the Seventh Plan (1985–90). The Eighth Five Year Plan (1992–7) took up the thread again, but in a limited way. It recognized that sons and daughters should get equal shares in parental property; and directed state governments to give 40 per cent of ceiling surplus land to women alone, and the rest jointly to both spouses.

The Ninth Plan (1997–2002), however, made a distinct departure. During its formulation, as a member of the steering committee on poverty-alleviation, I was able to negotiate that 'ensuring women's effective command over land will be one of the new priorities of the Ninth Plan'. An entire section on 'Gender and Land Rights' was included, incorporating part of my justification on why land is important for poor women and many of my recommendations, including distributing titles mainly to women; the promotion of collective rights and group farming among women's groups; and providing women farmers with information, inputs, credit and marketing support. It also emphasizes the need to collect gender-disaggregated data on land ownership and use, in the Agricultural Censuses and National Sample Surveys. Another section recommends amending the tenurial laws to ensure equality of inheritance in agricultural land.[33] This Plan is also somewhat unusual in the importance it gives to land reforms in general as a significant part of the poverty reduction strategy. However, as the Plan's term draws to a close, the gap between stated policy and its implementation remains wide.

Regionally, some states, such as Andhra Pradesh and Madhya Pradesh, have taken small steps to improve women's land access. For instance, the former gives subsidized loans for land purchase to poor women and the latter has been promoting joint titles. Most other states, however, have made little such progress.

---

[33] Government of India (2000: sections 2.1.130 to 2.1.134, 2.1.81 and 2.1.90).

Factors Underlying the Gender Bias

What underlies the gender bias in public land distribution? To begin with, in classic land reform terms, the claimant is the one who tills the land. As Thorner (1956, 79) elaborated: 'We may begin [land reform] . . . by putting forward one fundamental principle: lands and the fruits thereof are to belong to those who do the tilling, the tillers being defined as those who plough, harrow, sow, weed, and harvest.'

While this definition works fairly well if applied to the household, it is less applicable to individuals, given the gender division of labour. Women would get excluded as they typically do not plough (indeed, are socially barred from doing so). But clearly the definition alone cannot explain women's exclusion, since if applied literally it would also exclude many men, as most male farmers neither sow nor weed. I believe at least four other factors underlie the gender bias.

One, men are perceived as the breadwinners and women as the dependents. The male household head is thus seen as the legitimate claimant. Even under *Operation Barga*, the claims of poor widows who were leasing out their land and could thus lose control over it, were set aside with the argument: '[T]he number of such widows left alone without any adult male relatives looking after them cannot be very large' (Dasgupta 1984, A90). This view unquestioningly endorses women's dependency on male relatives, and assumes that the latter will look after them well. Evidence, quoted earlier, on the situation of widows without their own assets, indicates otherwise.

The second factor is the social perception about women's lesser capabilities and their appropriate roles. Here, patrilineal biases have permeated even matrilineal communities. For instance, in Meghalaya, when I asked officials why even in this traditionally matrilineal society they did not allot plots to women, I was told: 'Women cannot come to our office to fill out papers.' Yet in nearby streets there were numerous women traders selling their wares.

The third factor is the assumption of the household as a unitary entity in mainstream economic theory, most public policy, as well as the popular imagination. The unitary household model assumes that family members pool all resources and incomes, and share common interests and preferences (Samuelson 1956), or an altruistic head ensures equitable allocations of goods and tasks (Becker 1981). In recent years, virtually every assumption of this model has been challenged effectively on the basis of empirical evidence, including assumptions of shared preferences and interests, pooled incomes and altruism as the guiding principle of intra-household allocations.[34] Gender, in particular, is noted to be an important signifier of differences in interests and preferences, incomes are not necessarily pooled and self-interest resides as much within the home as in the marketplace, with bargaining power affecting the allocation of who gets what and who does what. Among other things, therefore, the household's property status and associated well-being cannot be taken as automatically defining the

[34]   On the problems associated with the unitary household model see, for example, Haddad et al. (1997), Doss (1996), Hart (1993), Agarwal (1994, 1997), Seiz (2000) and Sen (1990).

property status and well-being of all household members, irrespective of gender or age. Nevertheless, the hold of the unitary household model remains ideologically strong.

The fourth factor is the notion of the household as a space of harmony ('the heart of a heartless world') that property considerations would shatter. In 1989, for instance, following my invited presentation on gender and land, at a Planning Commission seminar on land reform attended by two Cabinet ministers, the then Minister of Agriculture exclaimed: 'Are you suggesting that women should be given rights in land? What do women want? To break up the family?' Ironically, what this statement effectively implied was that family stability rests on gender inequity, which women, once they have property, may be unwilling to tolerate.

•

Bias apart, there is little public land left for distribution. A stricter implementation of ceilings could increase the amount, but not dramatically. According to mid-1996 figures (Government of India 1996b), the area declared surplus (above the ceiling) to date, for all-India, came to only 3 million ha or 1.6 per cent of arable land, and just 0.2 per cent of arable land was still available for distribution. In addition, there is some limited common land – about 13 per cent of India's arable land. Even in West Bengal, which had the largest area declared surplus to date, total ceiling surplus land came to only 8.7 per cent of the state's arable land, and today almost none is left for distribution.

Of course, despite the limited arable land in government hands, it is essential to eliminate gender bias in its distribution, since State policy can influence social norms and attitudes toward women's claims in private land. A related issue is whether women should receive titles jointly with husbands or individually.

Joint or Individual Titles?

The emphasis thus far has been on joint titles, and less on individual titles. The Eighth Five Year Plan, as noted, recommended that 60 per cent of all land distributed to the landless should be as joint titles.

While having some land is better than having none at all, joint titles with husbands also present problems for women. For instance, women often find it difficult to gain control over the produce, or to bequeath the land as they want, or to claim their shares in case of marital conflict. As some Bihari rural women told me: 'For retaining the land we would be tied to the man, even if he beat us'. Wives may also have different land use priorities from husbands, which they would be less in a position to exercise with joint titles. Most of all, joint titles constrain women from exploring alternative farming arrangements collectively with other women.

Individual titles, in contrast, can provide more flexibility. At the same time, individual women often lack enough investable funds, and with small holdings individual investment in capital equipment can prove uneconomical. For instance, although the Bodhgaya movement in Bihar enabled many women to receive an acre each in their own names, several of them had to mortgage their holdings later because they lacked funds for profitable cultivation. To bypass this problem, a possible solution could be to encourage collective investment and cultivation, as discussed in the penultimate section.

Consider now the possibilities of women getting land through their families.

LAND FROM THE FAMILY

In India today, about 86 per cent of arable land is private,[35] and 89 per cent of rural households own some (Government of India 1995), even though most hold very small plots. These figures belie the popular perception that access to privatized land is important to only a small percentage of rural women. Even by the most conservative assessment, about 78 per cent of rural households own some land.[36] Hence a very large percentage of rural women have a stake in family land, access to which is mainly through inheritance (and limitedly through the market).

How do women fare in terms of land inheritance? Unfortunately, no large-scale rural surveys collect gender-disaggregated data on land ownership and use. But gleaning from numerous village studies, and a 1991 survey on widows by development sociologist Marty Chen, it is clear that few women inherit land; even fewer effectively control any. In Chen's sample of rural widows across seven states, only 13 per cent of the 470 women with land-owning fathers inherited any land as daughters (the figure being 18 per cent for South India and 8 per cent for North India: Agarwal 1998). This means that 87 per cent of the surveyed women did not receive their due as daughters. Among widows, of the 280 whose deceased husbands owned land, 51 per cent inherited some, but this still means that almost half the widows with claims did not inherit anything. And of those that did, typically their shares were not entered formally in the village land records. Other studies show that where the land is so recorded, the widow's name is invariably entered jointly with adult sons, who effectively control the land.[37] The popular perception is that the widow's share is for her maintenance and not for her direct control. Widows without sons rarely inherit. Moreover, widows constitute only about 11 per cent of rural women, 75 per cent of whom are over 50 years old, many of them too old to work the land effectively. Recognizing widows' rights alone is thus inadequate for women to

---

[35] Computed from the latest available land use statistics. See Agarwal (1994, 24, note 52) for the method of calculation.

[36] The figure of 89 per cent includes households owning agricultural land as well as those owning only homestead land (Government of India 1995). There is no direct information on households owning only agricultural land. An indirect indicator is that 21.8 per cent of rural households cultivated no land in 1992 (Government of India 1997b, 17), but this includes both households owning no agricultural land and those leasing out all such land. The actual percentage owning no agricultural land would thus be under 21.8 per cent; conversely, those owning some would be at least 78.2 per cent.

[37] Nandwana and Nandwana (1998), Agarwal (1998).

reap the efficiency or welfare benefits that would accrue if they also inherited as daughters.

What obstructs women from realizing their claims in family land? The obstacles are partly legal and in large part social and administrative.

Unequal Laws[38]

Legally, although women enjoy much greater inheritance rights today than they did, say, at the turn of the century, substantial inequalities remain. To begin with, the inheritance laws of both Hindus and Muslims treat agricultural land differently from other property. For instance, the Hindu Succession Act (HSA) of 1956 exempted tenancy rights in agricultural land from its purview. Women's inheritance rights in tenancy land thus depend on state-level tenurial laws. In the southern, western and eastern states, since the tenurial laws are silent on devolution it can be presumed that for Hindus the HSA will also apply to tenancy land. In most north-western states, however, tenurial laws do specify an order of devolution, and one that strongly favours male agnatic heirs, with women coming very low in the order of heirs, as was the case under centuries-old customs. Moreover, in Uttar Pradesh (UP) and Delhi, the definition of tenants in the land reform laws is so broad as to include under that category interests arising from *all* agricultural land. Hence in these two states, of which UP contains one-sixth of India's population, women's inheritance rights in most agricultural land stand severely curtailed.

A second source of inequality in Hindu law lies in the continued recognition in the HSA of *Mitakshara* joint family property in which sons but not daughters have rights by birth. Again, while three of the southern states (Andhra Pradesh, Tamil Nadu, Karnataka) and Maharashtra have amended this by including daughters as coparceners, and Kerala has abolished joint family property altogether, all other states remain highly unequal (Agarwal 1995).

Likewise, the Muslim Personal Law (Shariat) Application Act of 1937, which still defines Muslim inheritance rules in India, excluded all agricultural land (both tenanted and owned) from its purview. Subsequently, some of the southern states extended the Act's provisions to also cover agricultural land. In other regions, however, the treatment of agricultural land, unlike other property, continues to devolve variously on customs, tenurial laws, or other pre-existing laws. Such laws and customs give very low priority to Muslim women's property rights in most of Northwest India. In addition there is the inherent inequality of daughters being allowed only half the share of sons under Islamic law.

The regional contrast is striking in both Hindu and Muslim law. If we map Hindu law, for instance, gender inequality increases as we move from south India northwards. In the four southern states, women can inherit agricultural land, whether owned or under tenancy, and with amendments in the HSA

---

[38] For details, see Agarwal (1994, 1995).

daughters have shares on a par with sons in joint family property, including land. In the north-western states, however, women are still seriously disadvantaged in relation both to agricultural land and joint family property. Middle India comes in-between. Women's legal rights under Muslim law show a similar contrast between Northwest India and the rest of the country.

Unequal laws, however, cannot explain the enormity of women's *de facto* disinheritance. Rather, among the critical factors underlying both unequal laws and the vast gap between law and practice are social and administrative biases.

Social and Administrative Bias[39]

To begin with, there is the gap between legal rights and actual ownership. In most communities which were traditionally patrilineal (i.e. where inheritance was through the male line), there is strong male resistance to endowing daughters with land. Quite apart from the reluctance to admit more contenders to the most valuable form of rural property, resistance also arises if traditional marriage systems forbid marriages within the village and with close kin, as is the case among upper-caste Hindus of northern India. Here social taboos against parents seeking any help from married daughters during economic crises also largely persist. Under these conditions, endowing a daughter with land is seen by the natal family as bringing little reciprocal benefit, and any land inherited by her as lost to the family. Daughters face the greatest opposition to their claims among such communities. Opposition is somewhat less in South and Northeast India where, even among Hindus, in-village and close-kin marriages are allowed,[40] and parents can seek economic support from married daughters during crises.

Many women also forego their shares in parental land in favour of brothers. In the absence of an effective state social security system, brothers are seen as an important source of security, especially in case of marital break-up. Cultural constructions of gender, including how a 'good sister' should behave, also discourage women from asserting their rights, as does the emphasis on female seclusion in many areas.

Where women do not 'voluntarily' forgo their claims, male relatives have been known to file court cases, forge wills or resort to threats and even physical violence. In eastern India, most of the witch murders among tribal groups in recent decades are found to be of widows who typically have customary claims (mostly usufruct rights) to land.

These constraints are compounded by the unhelpful approach of many government functionaries who typically share the prevalent social biases and often obstruct the implementation of laws in women's favour. The bias is especially prevalent in the recording of daughters' inheritance shares by the *patwari* (the village land records official) in northern India.

---

[39] For a detailed discussion and mapping across five South Asian countries, see Agarwal (1994).
[40] Among Muslims, such marriages are allowed everywhere in principle, although geographically variable in practice (Agarwal 1994).

The Gap between Ownership and Control

The gap between legal rights and ownership is matched by that between owner-ship and effective control. Marriages in distant villages make direct cultivation by women difficult. This is compounded in many areas by social restrictions on women's mobility and public interaction. In particular, the ideology of female seclusion (which operates in complex ways and is more widespread than the practice of veiling) restricts women's contact with men by gendering behaviour and public and private space. Indeed, in many north Indian villages, women are expected to avoid spaces where men congregate, such as the market place. This territorial gendering of space reduces women's mobility and participation in activities outside the home (especially in the market place), and disadvantages her in seeking information on new technologies and practices, purchasing inputs and selling the product. Purdah practice is strongest in Northwest India and virtually absent in the South and Northeast. Of course, the cultural construction of gen-der, which defines appropriate female behaviour and roles, is not confined to the north; it also restricts women in southern India. But the strong purdah ideology in the Northwest circumscribes women in particular ways.

Other difficulties facing women farmers include their limited control over cash and credit for purchasing inputs, gender biases in extension services, ritual taboos against women ploughing and demands of advance cash payments by tractor or bullock owners for ploughing women's fields. (No such demand is usually made of male farmers, who, even if they are small owners, are assumed to be creditworthy.) Taboos against ploughing increase women's dependence on male help, and can reduce yields if timely help is not forthcoming.

However, the factors that constrain women in either claiming or cultivating land are not uniformly strong. South India has the least obstacles. Here legal rights are relatively more equal, in-village and close-kin marriage are allowed, there is virtually no purdah and female labour force participation is medium to high. Northwest India is the area of most difficulty on all these fronts. Northeast and central India come in-between (Agarwal 1994). It would thus be opportune for both grassroots and Government interventions to make a beginning in south-ern India, by systematically recording women's inheritance shares, supporting women's farming efforts through infrastructural provisioning, and overall improving women's prospects for gaining land rights. This would also have an important demonstration effect in other regions.

LAND THROUGH THE MARKET AND GROUP CULTIVATION

The third source of land is through the market. There has been much discussion recently of market-negotiated land reform. For instance, it is a central compon-ent in South Africa's land reform programme.

In India, purchasing agricultural land is a limited option, since little is usually available for sale. An all-India study of land sales among a sample of land-owning households in the early 1970s found that only 1.75 per cent had sold any during the survey year (Rosenzweig and Wolpin 1985). Another study in Uttar Pradesh found that over a 30-year period (1950s to the 1980s), only 4.1 per cent of owned agricultural land had been sold (Shankar 1990). Apart from restricted land markets, which affect both sexes, women also face more financial constraints.

Hence market purchase is not an option that can compensate women for the inequalities in inheritance or Government transfers. But it can supplement those means. To do so effectively, however, will require tackling the constraints to land purchase and cultivation that women face. For instance, market access could improve if women dealt with land markets not as individuals but as a group, pooling their resources and their negotiating power. Financial support would also help. Leasing arrangements are another important way of obtaining land through the market, but here again a group approach would work better in overcoming resource constraints.

Equally, women seeking to invest in land and cultivate individual plots face resource constraints for buying inputs, and scale diseconomies if they invest in capital equipment on small plots. Individual women landowners also face considerable pressure from male relatives who want to control the land themselves (Agarwal 1994). In addition, there remains the question of who would inherit the land from the women. If women end up bequeathing it to sons, the land would revert to male hands in the next generation.

There are, however, institutional solutions to these problems if we abandon the long-standing assumption in public policy that farms should be cultivated (or owned) only on a family basis. Today, the assumption of family-based farming underlines all forms of land distribution to the landless. The alternative could be various forms of collective investment and cultivation by women, wherein units of investment and cultivation would be larger than the unit of ownership.

Indeed, the advantages of a group approach are well brought out by the experience of several NGOs in South Asia, who have helped landless women use subsidized credit to lease in or purchase land in groups, and cultivate it jointly. Among the most prominent of these NGOs, with sustained experience on this count, is the Deccan Development Society in Andhra Pradesh. It is therefore useful to examine its experience in detail.

The Deccan Development Society (DDS)

The DDS, which works in Medak district – a drought-prone tract of Andhra Pradesh (AP) – has enabled women belonging to poor families to lease in or purchase land through a variety of government schemes.[41]

Established in 1983, DDS initially worked only with male farmers until (says P.V. Satheesh, founder member and Director, DDS) the village women challenged DDS, asking: 'Why don't you work with women?' Subsequently, DDS set up

---

[41]   The discussion below is based on Satheesh (1997a, 1997b, 2001); Hall (1999); Menon (1996); DDS (1994–5); my field visits to DDS in 1998 and conversations with several women's *sangams* and key women informants; and my discussions with P.V. Satheesh and Rukmini Rao over 1998–2002. I also give individual attributions when using quotations or specific information from a key person.

both men's and women's groups (*sangams*), initially as credit and thrift groups. As problems of corruption and cooperation undermined the men's groups, DDS shifted almost entirely to all-women *sangams* (like the Grameen Bank in Bangladesh, which also began with men's savings groups and then moved almost entirely to women's groups). In addition, taking serious note of women's perceptions that what they needed was land for subsistence farming, DDS began to focus more centrally on improving women's land access. Today, DDS is working in 75 villages. Its essential focus is on poor, low-caste women. The central plank of its approach is to ensure food security in an environmentally friendly fashion, through organic farming, multiple cropping and wasteland development. The institutional basis is collective farming.

Land leasing. With the help of DDS, poor women, organized into groups, lease in and cultivate land collectively. Initiated in 1989, the programme now involves 629 women cultivating 623 acres across 52 villages. Initially, they leased on a sharecropping basis but are now moving to cash rents. Some 25 per cent of the rent is paid by *sangam* members themselves and the rest through interest-free loans from DDS, which they repay over time.[42] Very poor women can substitute their labour for cash, or borrow individually from DDS. Today, most lease groups consist of 5–15 women, but in the past many had 30–40 and one even had 60 women leasing 40 acres. Sometimes women lease land from two or three landlords.[43]

Women collectively undertake all tasks, except ploughing. For this operation the *sangams* hire the services of a bullock-owner. I understand from P.V. Satheesh that the groups are financially viable. After paying the rent and other costs, as well as DDS's loan (in instalments) and keeping aside grain for seed, the remaining harvest is shared equally among the lease group members.

In some instances, high-caste landlords wanting to lease out their land have themselves approached women's *sangams*, confident that the women's group, unlike individual leasers, would not default, and that DDS would provide backup support for inputs, etc. Where possible, women seek a lease of at least 3–5 years. Typically, after a lease ends the group negotiates a new one, but sometimes the members reconfigure into new groups.

DDS also successfully lobbied the state government to allow women's groups to use the loan money available via the Government's poverty alleviation scheme, DWACRA (Development of Women and Children in Rural Areas), for leasing-in land, rather than for conventional uses such as tailoring, milch cattle, handicrafts, etc. Women's Committees examine the lease proposals put forward by the women's groups, assess the land's quality, keep records of each woman's work input, and ensure equitable distribution of wages and produce. Fifteen women's groups have used the revolving fund provided under this scheme to collectively lease in and cultivate land. In 1995, each woman participant received enough cereal and pulses to feed the whole family for a month, in addition to harvest wages.

---

[42]   DDS has a rotating fund for this purpose, to which the *sangams* can apply.
[43]   Personal communication from P.V. Satheesh, August 2001.

Land purchase. Since 1994, DDS is also supporting land purchase by groups of women, taking advantage of a scheme initiated by the Scheduled Caste Development Corporation (SCDC) of AP. The SCDC provides financial support to landless scheduled caste women to buy agricultural land. Half the money is given as a subsidized loan repayable within 20 years and the rest as a grant. Catalysed by DDS, women form a group and apply for the loan after identifying the land they want to buy. Land records are scrutinized to ensure that the title is litigation-free, and an endorsement is obtained from the *patwari* and the Mandal Revenue officer that the women applicants are indeed landless. The purchased land is then divided among the group members. Each woman is registered as a plot owner. Today, 24 women's groups in 14 villages are cultivating 474 acres of purchased land, each woman owning about one acre but cultivating it jointly.

Usually, leasing serves as a precursor to purchase. This enables women to judge the land's quality and potential productivity, and also gives them experience in functioning as a group. In some cases, good harvests have enabled women to accumulate enough funds for buying additional land.

Both on leased-in and purchased land, DDS encourages women to practise organic farming and intercropping (the simultaneous cultivation of several crops). They grow a combination of millets, pulses, green vegetables and oil-producing plants. Some grow up to 24 crop varieties a year. This reduces the risk of total crop failure, provides a balanced diet, etc. Some women also use innovative cropping patterns for 'crop fencing', by planting crops on field boundaries that cattle won't eat.

Purchasing vs leasing. How does land leasing compare with land purchase? According to Ratnamma (Humnapur village, cited in Hall 1999), it is useful to lease the land before purchase, for several reasons:

> We get to understand the land, its quality, which crops to grow on it. We learn whether we want to buy, which land to buy, how much to buy. We make a more knowledgeable purchase. Also, we can see if there will be problems in the group or if the group will work well together.

As a lease group, the women thus learn to tackle any problematic group dynamics before taking the important step of purchase. Working first as a lease group also builds trust and solidarity among members. In addition, lease groups are better able to tackle free riding. As Satheesh (personal communication to author, 1998), put it:

> Leasing is not a lifetime commitment. When groups form they eliminate the slow workers. In land purchase, those entitled remain entitled. Also in lease, since they invest they make rules of the game straightaway. If they renege they are warned and if they continue defaulting, they are thrown out of the group.

According to DDS, only 5 per cent of the lease groups have failed thus far.

At the same time, leasing also has disadvantages. If the crop fails the landlord not the tenant receives the state's compensation, as happened to the women's *sangam* in Indoor village when they lost their pigeonpea crop (Hall 1999). Also, compared with purchased land, women feel less secure, and less motivated to invest in the land. According to Chilkamma (Krishnapur village, cited in Hall 1999), women had been leasing land for 10–12 years, but still had no security. With purchase, 'even with less than an acre, we can invest in inputs, put in our labour, do whatever we want . . . this is a great feeling'.

However, finding land to purchase is difficult, since the land market is under-developed and the desirable plots have often been bought by others. Some groups also face problems repaying the SCDC loan. And, in certain conditions, groups working with purchased land are more vulnerable to splitting up, as discussed below.

Prioritizing single women. An important aspect of DDS' approach is to reach the especially disadvantaged. In this spirit they have prioritized single women (the widowed, deserted and, occasionally, the unmarried) for their support in acquiring land. In Pastapur village, for instance, the single women's *sangam* has 12 deserted women with children and no economic support from husbands or parents (although some parents give moral support). They were agricultural labourers or construction workers earlier. Under the SCDC land purchase scheme, the women collectively bought 11 acres and registered equal amounts in each woman's name in 1995. But they cultivated the whole plot collectively. DDS served as an intermediary between the women and the SCDC. In some villages, women have supplemented the SCDC loan with loans from money-lenders, adult children and even errant husbands.[44]

However, single women's *sangams* have been a bone of contention in some villages. Villagers argue that these will encourage women to become single and break up families. In Metlakunta village, Hall (1999) reports, some men also argued: 'you are giving land to women from other villages and denying land to women from this village' (although 9 out of the 10 single women were originally from Metlakunta and had returned to it due to marital break-up). In this village, the conflict led DDS to withdraw entirely for a while, and return only after the villagers agreed to run their *sangams* on their own for some months, and to allow priority to the single women.

Alternative public distribution system. Another type of institutional arrangement catalysed by DDS is to have women jointly oversee the cultivation of under-cultivated or fallow land held by private owners. They have also set up a Community Grain Fund (CGF) in the process.[45] Most of the land is ceiling surplus land distributed by the Government to landless men. The land was of very poor quality and remained mostly uncultivated, while the families depended heavily

---

[44] Hall (1999), and my conversations with P.V. Satheesh in 1998.
[45] For details, see Menon (1996), Satheesh (2001).

on a public distribution system (PDS) which was woefully inadequate for providing food security. Supported by the Ministry of Rural Development, DDS initiated this programme to bring fallow land under cultivation, by extending loans to the owners. Each participating farmer can enter two acres, and get Rs. 2600 in instalments over three years. In return, over five years, the farmer gives for the CGF a specified amount of the grain he harvests. Committees of women manage the whole programme, identifying the land to be used, ensuring that the farmers use the loans for cultivation, supervising the operations, ensuring the use of organic manure and mixed cropping, and collecting the harvest share for the CGF. Each village under this scheme typically has a committee of five women, and each woman personally oversees about 20 acres. The women's committee identifies the poor and ranks them from the most needy to the less than poor. The poorest are eligible for the most grain. The grain is sold (to offset costs) but at a low price. The CGF thus serves as an alternative PDS.

In the first phase, the project started in 32 villages. This has now increased to 43, covering about 3200 acres and some 2200 marginal and small farmers (Satheesh, personal communication, 2001). Apart from bringing a substantial area of marginal fallow land under cultivation, the scheme has increased employment, and helped produce an extra 800,000 kg of sorghum in the first phase villages, thus providing nearly 3 million extra meals. The fodder obtained has also helped sustain 6000 cattle (Satheesh 2001). The programme's benefits extend well beyond the *sangams*: up to 70 per cent of PDS entitlements have gone to non-*sangam* members.

Benefits and problems of group cultivation. Women report substantial benefits from collective cultivation, as well as some problems. On the positive side, while working together they have learnt to survey and measure land, hire tractors or bullocks, travel to distant towns to meet government officials, obtain inputs and market the produce. Many women also find it useful to have the flexibility in labour input that collective cultivation allows. In addition, they can pool their differential skills to best effect, and share the cost of tractor or bullock hire.

Based on her experience, Chinanarsamma (Pastapur village, cited in Hall 1999) provides some insightful arguments in favour of collective farming:

> Women can share the profit and the responsibility. In individual cultivation, different women have different levels of agricultural knowledge and resources for inputs. [So] in collective cultivation they may make unequal contributions. Those with less can compensate the others through taking a reduced share of the harvest, or by repaying them in instalments. Different levels of contribution are fine, because the women all know what each other's resources are. Knowledge of each other's family needs also leads to tolerance of women not appearing for work in the fields – to some extent. The levels of sharing are agreed on and fixed before the season: each woman should get an equal share unless her contribution falls below that of the other women. There are no disputes about shares: all the women are

involved in dividing the crop, so none can be accused of taking more than her fair share.

Many other women share this perception: 'Collective cultivation is better; both the labour and the produce is shared. It builds a better feeling.'

At the same time, the *sangams* have to be vigilant about several potential problems. One is to ensure that each group member puts in the expected labour. Especially during peak seasons, when wage labour demand is high, absenteeism can occur and negatively affect productivity. The *sangams* impose penalties for default (as agreed by the group collectively), and also call defaulters to account in their weekly meetings. These meetings are a crucial monitoring mechanism. The fact that women are all from the same village, know each other and are co-dependent in other ways, also creates peer pressure against default. The penalty varies by circumstance. Reproduced below is an excerpt from my interview with a Krishnapur village *sangam*:

Q: How do you deal with differences in work effort?
A: We supervise and see if anyone is slackening intentionally or due to compulsion. For example, if it is an old woman we sometimes take care of her labour share. If a woman is ill she can send other family members to substitute. If a young woman does not turn up, she has to send two persons the next day or give two person's wages. This rule is followed strictly, especially if she goes to work on another farmer's field or on her own land.

Q: Have you had to penalize women often?
A: Not really. In general people work hard, and we were able to increase the leased in amount to 40 acres from four landlords. This is in four different patches. Weeding and harvesting is done collectively. Our *sangam* also does not maintain caste divides. We have women from all castes, including the *dalits*.

Nevertheless, groups do occasionally split over work-shirking, especially where the land is purchased. This happened in Humnapur village, although, interestingly, the women later reconstituted new groups, which were smaller and more cohesive, and restarted collective cultivation. Even those who chose to remain separate worked out labour-sharing arrangements for weeding, harvesting etc. on each other's land (Hall 1999). Similarly, when a *sangam* split in Pastapur village, the women continued with labour-sharing arrangements (personal communication, Satheesh 2001). In other words, having worked together demonstrates the advantages of collective farming and builds a habit of cooperation.[46] In some cases, their prior experience of labour exchange also strengthens cooperation.

A second type of problem can arise from a conflict of priorities, especially in peak seasons, if *sangam* women also own some family land. In practice, however, the women I spoke with felt this was not a major problem. Chilkamma

---

[46]   See Seabright (1997), on how cooperation can be 'habit forming'.

(Krinshnapur village), for instance, told me: 'We all know that the [*sangam*] land will yield well, men too know this. Also the number of days that anyone has to put in on the communal land is not excessive, since the whole *sangam* works together. After that women can work on their family's land. So there is no serious conflict.' This may also be because most *sangam* women belong to families owning very small unirrigated plots, or none.

A third type of problem can stem from a breach of trust by a group member. Within the single women's *sangam* in Pastapur village, for instance, Hall (1999) reports that 'bitter quarrels' ensued because at the end of their first season of cultivating together, the woman leader who had been entrusted with a portion of the produce to repay an instalment of the group's loan from DDS, failed to do so. Finally, the *sangam* sought DDS's intervention to get the woman to repay. The same happened with another woman leader the following year. It is notable, though, that the women are still cultivating collectively, because they feel that until the loan is repaid 'in spite of our conflicts, it is better for us to work collectively than separately', 'then we will re-evaluate'. This was women's preferred option, since the collective loan was a joint responsibility and could only be repaid by everyone through collective cultivation.

A fourth type of difficulty that *sangams* face is motivating people to stay together when individual cultivation becomes more profitable. In Krishnapur village (see Hall 1999), for instance, 13 women bought 13 acres, which they cultivated collectively till they got lift irrigation wells in 1995. There were four or five women per well, on receiving which they decided to divide the land and cultivate individually, while sharing the wells. They also began to grow crops for sale, rather than only for subsistence. They justified the move to individual cultivation saying that it was simpler to work separately, since water-sharing involved greater responsibility. They felt they risked losing water if women did not cooperate when electricity was available. But clearly an important factor was also that an assured supply of irrigation water reduced cultivation risk and enhanced the prospects of profit, while in dryland farming group cultivation was especially important for risk sharing.

Potentially, groups cultivating purchased land would be more prone to such splitting, since women have an exit option here which lease groups do not. In practice, though, cases like Krishnapur's are uncommon even among purchase groups. Almost all the others continue cultivating collectively.

Some of these problems also decline as trust builds. If needed, the groups reconstitute into new, more workable units, after evicting defaulters, as noted in Humnapur and Pastapur villages. In other cases, as in Krishnapur, although jointness in cultivation has broken down, there is still jointness in investments such as irrigation wells; and those sharing the wells are now veering toward other forms of cooperation. Moreover, there are additional positive externalities of group functioning, which are both economic and social in nature, as discussed below.

Effect on gender relations. Collective functioning improves gender relations. In the beginning, the men resented women setting up the *sangams* and holding weekly meetings (usually held at night). Sateesh (cited by Hall 1999) provides insights on how this resentment was overcome:

> The empowerment of *sangams* was gradual, and 'almost subversive'. The precursor to the *sangams* was the tradition of women getting together in chit-funds which were never formalized. Therefore, *sangams* were seen as the formalization of these structures. Men were irritated that women were staying out at meetings late into the night. Some asked their wives to stop going, but the women would go to recalcitrant husbands and convince them that there was no harm. The men were curious at first; they would come and sit in *sangam* meetings, would talk, even interfere sometimes. . . . Women used the presence of DDS to say to men that this needed to be the space for women to talk to each other . . . [Men's] interventions dwindled as they got bored, and also some men silenced others. The men gradually stopped coming. . . . Anyway, [they] knew that they would benefit indirectly, through their wives. . . .

After several years of working in *sangams*, the women report a decline in social ills, such as male drunkenness, domestic violence, bonded labour and caste indignities, and an increase in their self confidence, and the respect they now receive within the village.

In economic terms, two indirect benefits are especially notable. One, they are now able to bargain for higher wages when they need supplementary work and, two, many now exercise greater control over household income. For instance, Narsamma (Kalbaman village) reported to Hall (1999) that the daily wage-rate for casual labour had increased in the village due to *sangam* formation. For weeding (a peak labour operation) women bargained for and received two and a half times the previous daily wage-rate. They were able to exert this leverage over employers because they worked as a group and had other options, such as reverting to working on their *sangam*'s 16 acres, and also taking up wage work on a DDS wasteland development project. 'So we had a choice . . . We could refuse all jobs [which would pay] less than Rs. 10 a day.' Other *sangams* I spoke with also reported an increase in their bargaining power in the rural labour market.

Again, within the household, women now exercise greater control over earnings. For instance, Chilkamma (Krishnapur village) told Hall that about half the women now control the produce and income from their land. This is an improvement, even though for the remaining half spouses continue to control the produce and any cash generated. In this village, among the *sangam* households, the husbands work on their wives' land since none have their own.

Women identify the gains from several years of *sangam* activity in various ways:

> Initially the men said: If women go to meetings, what should we men do – wash the dishes? We said, men and women should work equally . . . Are we the only persons born to work? Earlier we ate half a *roti*, now we eat one. (Sharifabi to author, 1998)

It is [now] better. If a man beats his wife she will now ask: why are you beating me? Earlier she would not confront him. Also other women challenge him: why are you beating her? Earlier we would have left the family alone . . . There is also less drunkenness. (Chilkamma to author, Krishnapur village, 1998)

Our husbands used to drink and beat us. Now the buffaloes are ours, the land is ours and they are working too. Nobody is taking advantage of us women. (Ratnamma, Algole village, cited in Hall 1999)

Now [with land] we have the courage and confidence to come out and deal with people and property by ourselves. (Chilkamma, Krishnapur village, cited in Hall 1999)

They [the high caste people] used to call us with the caste name which was very derogatory. They would also call us in the singular form. Now they put the motherly (respectful) suffix and give us equal seats. . . . It is only because we have an organization that they [the landlords] won't touch us – that they are scared to cross us. (Ratnamma, Algole village, cited in Hall 1999)

The fact that we sit down and talk together has made the men listen. The younger generation is [no longer] an obstructive force. They used to make a noise during our meetings to disrupt it, but don't anymore. (Narsamma, Kalbaman village, cited in Hall 1999)

For single women too, the *sangams* have brought some obvious gains:

Initially, when we came together, 10 of us went to meetings and our families would say: why are you going to meetings at night? But we found that during the course of these meetings, we became a kind of mutual support group. If any woman fell ill or had a problem, the others would try and help. So it became a habit to meet, and we were not afraid of family disapproval. Gradually the family realized the importance of our meetings to us and fell silent. (Women to author, 1998)

There have also been improvements in well-being. In Algone village, the women reported to me that bonded labour had now disappeared, health care was better and their diet was more varied due to multiple cropping. Similarly, the single women of Pastapur reported to Hall (1999) that: '. . . now we are self-sufficient. [We are] able to get food and clothing'. 'Previously we had nothing and had to say yes to everything; now we have status because we have the land'. Their children are being educated. And although the community disapproves, these women are willing to help other deserted women to form a *sangam*. Many of the *sangam* women are now also active in other village activities. Moreover, Hall notes that in Metlakunta village some husbands returned to their wives after the latter purchased land, and most women said that spouses were now more willing to listen to them. Also, '*sangam* woman' is a special designation of respect in the village; and according to some women (corroborated by DDS senior staff) they are given priority over individual men by local government officials.

In general, Satheesh (cited in Hall 1999) notes:

The first sense of empowerment came to women and men in the community when the women started leasing in land. Men, and especially powerful men in the villages, had the perception that women were useless, as agricultural labourers they could only work under supervision. This perception was slightly internalized by the women. The land leases completely debunked this view.

When women acquire land, there is a win-win situation for everybody. The landlords who are not cultivating get money. Women improve the land and get produce.

However, one question remains contentious where the land is purchased: will the land remain with the women? Here the link with inheritance is critical. The women, when asked to whom they would bequeath the land, gave various answers to Hall and myself. Most wanted to endow their sons, if they had any. Only sonless women were usually open to endowing daughters. Some worried: 'If we give our land to our daughters, what will society say?' However, others responded: 'But what has society done for us? We must make some provision for our daughters' security'. A few want to leave their land to all the children but feel the plot is too small to be divided. Some remain undecided.[47]

Other NGOs

DDS' efforts have been pioneering in many different ways and provide a significant learning experience. The approach of joint leasing or joint purchase of land and collective cultivation could be tried out by NGOs in other states as well, on the basis of other Government schemes. For instance, since 1995–6, loans can be obtained by the poor for land purchase through the central Government's Integrated Rural Development Programme directed to alleviate poverty (Government of India 1996c).

Also, some other Indian NGOs have been encouraging land leasing by women, although on a smaller scale. Michael Tharakan (1997, and personal communication) describes a village in Kerala's Kunner district, where three women's groups are leasing-in land from farmers in the off-season for vegetable cultivation. In Bangladesh, the Bangladesh Rural Advancement Committee (BRAC), an NGO which provides credit and technical support to poor rural men and women, also helps women to lease and cultivate land collectively. In a number of cases they have been able to do so successfully despite opposition from orthodox villagers (Chen 1983).

However, apart from land lease and purchase, it is worthwhile experimenting with two other types of institutional arrangements, one that involves less collective functioning than joint farming, and the other which involves much more.

---

[47] Interviews by me in 1998 and Ruth Hall in 1999.

Under the first category come cases where women who own individual holdings (whether obtained through inheritance, purchase or Government transfer)
cultivate individually, but invest in capital equipment jointly with other women.
There are also examples of the Government funding groups of farmers, including sometimes groups of women farmers, to invest jointly in irrigation wells.[48]
Krishnapur village in the DDS area is also illustrative: here, as noted, although
women stopped cultivating jointly they continued sharing the irrigation wells.
Group investment, however, does not solve other problems facing individual
women, such as family pressure to relinquish their land, or the issue of inheritance.

These problems could be solved, however, through another type of collective
functioning, namely, if poor rural women, as a group, held usufruct rights over
land distributed by the Government, but not the right to dispose of the land.
The daughters-in-law and daughters of such households who are resident in the
village would share these use rights. Daughters leaving the village on marriage
would lose such rights, but could establish them in their marital village, if a
similar arrangement were operating there. Also they could re-establish their rights
in their parental village by rejoining the production efforts should they need to
return on desertion or widowhood. In other words, land access would be linked
formally with residence and working on the land (see also Agarwal 1994). I
recently learnt that an NGO in Gujarat has initiated a pilot project, a short while
ago, very much along these lines.

Also, several women elected to *panchayats* in Madhya Pradesh, whom I met in
1995 and asked about their perceptions of the advantages and disadvantages of
individual titles, joint titles with husbands and group rights (as in this last alternative), strongly supported the idea of group rights for women.

•

The institutional arrangements I have described have four important ingredients.
Three of these – the presence of a gender-progressive NGO, a group approach
and a focus on landless women – are found in many cases of poor women's
economic betterment in India. But the fourth ingredient is rarer, namely their
focus on land, linked with collective cultivation, in contrast to the typical and
usually less viable or sustainable income-generating activities promoted under
many Government and NGO programmes.

Also, functioning in groups helps resolve many of the difficulties women face
in obtaining and cultivating land individually. It provides ways by which women
can access land without depending only on inheritance, namely through the
market or through the community – access that women operating as individuals
rarely have. And where linked with joint investment and collective management, these arrangements can overcome any problems of small size and fragmentation. In fact, if collective farming were attempted by women even on the
land they inherit, it could undercut the oft-stated resistance to women's claims

---

[48]   This was done, for example, in Bihar, after the Bodhgaya struggle.

on the grounds that it will increase fragmentation and so reduce output. Indeed, given that some 72 per cent of land-owning households today own under one hectare (Government of India 1995, 22), it also appears important to examine men's prospects of undertaking collective investment/management on their hold-ings. It is notable that some of the landless beneficiaries of West Bengal's *Opera-tion Barga* are now pooling their land and cultivating it collectively (Patnaik 2001). For women, a collective approach can also help them mobilize funds for capital investment, take advantage of economies of scale, and cooperate in labour sharing and product marketing. If, in addition, women have group rights in the land (as in the last type of arrangement), this would strengthen women's ability to withstand pressure from male relatives and retain control over the land; and it would by-pass the problem of inheritance, since the women's group would have use rights but not rights of alienation. It would also bypass the problem of outside-village marriages, since women's rights would be established only by residence.

Linking Micro-Credit to Land

Given the continued importance of land in rural livelihoods, it is important to reconsider the large-scale push being given by international aid agencies, most rural-development NGOs and the Government, to micro-credit for poor women, essentially for non-land-related activities. Undeniably, poor rural women often need credit. But what could be its best use? Often women take loans not for their own enterprises but for their sons or husbands, and the poorest of the poor usually get excluded (IFAD 2001b). Many women also face problems in retain-ing control over their loans (Goetz and Sengupta 1996), and the impact of micro-credit on female poverty remains uncertain. Most importantly, the privileging of this one form of support over all other livelihood options could prove counter-productive. As many NGOs are now arguing, a standardized spread of one type of scheme, namely micro-credit, is proving diversionary, and can exacerbate gender inequalities in major assets such as land. The title of the ALRD Bangla-desh workshop (mentioned earlier) was telling: 'Land for men, only micro-credit for women?' However, one way forward, in contexts where women are depend-ent on agriculture, is to provide credit to women's groups for jointly leasing in or purchasing land, as done by DDS. But this would require a new orientation for the current micro-credit programmes. It would also need greater flexibility in terms of group size, according to the needs of viable farming.

Infrastructural Support

Finally, critically linked to the success of women's farming efforts, whether as individuals or groups, is infrastructural support. There are significant gender and class inequalities associated with access to credit, labour, other production inputs (including hired equipment), and information on new agricultural technologies. Poor women cultivating marginal plots are the most disadvantaged in this regard.

The cultural constructions of gender roles and behaviour also reduce women's ability to function effectively in factor and product markets, as well as more generally in the market place.

Here a systematic effort is needed to remove prevailing biases in the delivery mechanisms of Government infrastructure. A greater female presence in agricultural input and information delivery systems (women extension agents are often recommended for the latter) would no doubt help, but it appears equally necessary to reorient male functionaries toward recognizing the importance of assisting women farmers. Non-governmental initiatives would also be important here. Certainly in the delivery of credit to poor women, organizations such as the Grameen Bank in Bangladesh and the Self Employed Women's Association in India, have been markedly more successful than Government agencies. NGOs could similarly supplement Government efforts in providing technical information, production inputs and marketing facilities to groups of women farmers. More generally, a systematic promotion of women's cooperatives for production inputs and marketing could prove fruitful.

IN CONCLUSION

Within the re-emerging debate on the land question, it appears imperative that the issue of women's access to land is given critical attention. A growing body of evidence indicates that this is likely to have positive effects on women's and their family's welfare, agricultural productivity, poverty reduction and women's empowerment. And while all channels for women's economic empowerment, including non-farm employment and various self-employment enterprises need pursuing, these latter channels alone cannot realistically help more than a small percentage of women, especially in countries such as India, where 85 per cent of rural women workers are still dependent on agriculture (and hence on land) as their main source of livelihood.

Potentially, women can obtain land through the State, the family and the market. This paper has explored the prospects and constraints to women's access to land from all three sources. But while it is important to make public land distribution more gender equal, access through the family and the market deserve particular attention, given that most arable land in India is privatized.

In relation to market access, this paper makes a number of departures from existing discussions by focusing on the new prospects that could open up (especially for poor women) through: (a) women working in groups rather than as individuals or as members of families, to lease in or purchase land; (b) the use of Government credit for land access rather than just for micro-enterprises; and (c) collective investment in and cultivation of purchased or leased-in land, the collectivity being constituted with other women rather than with family members. As noted, such group functioning offers many advantages to women, over individual or family-based farming. And the advantages could also extend to women inheriting small plots, should they seek to invest in them collectively with other women.

In itself, the idea of people cooperating in farming ventures is not new; several elements in the institutional arrangements described here were part of traditional agrarian institutions. But the traditional arrangements focused on households. For instance, in the reciprocal labour-sharing arrangements that were customary in agriculture, the terms of reciprocity were typically established between households, to support family-based farming. Similarly, in the 1950s and early 1960s, when land reform and cooperative farming were the buzzwords of rural development, the focus was on households and on male heads as representatives of households. At that time, not only was gender ignored, socio-economic inequalities between households also received inadequate attention. As a result, cooperatives often (albeit not uniformly) tended to be large-farmer dominated. Today, we need to recognize not only that households can be arenas of gender-based conflict of interests, but also that communities are spaces that are often both class/caste differentiated and highly gendered. This impinges on the kind of institutional forms that would be effective. In the forms discussed here, factors such as class and gender are centrally recognized, in that the groups described are constituted of women from poor rural households. Often the groups are also of the scheduled castes or tribes. This approach could open a window of opportunity to revive land reform, community cooperation and joint farming in a radically new form, by centring them on poor women.

Of course, the collective approach, in whatever form, cannot be assumed to work successfully everywhere, nor should it be pushed as a formula, but it does need to be a significant part of a potential package of approaches. And within the package there could be various levels of collectivity: while full collective ownership and management could work in some contexts, more limited joint investment could work well elsewhere.

Finally, both for improving the implementation of women's inheritance claims and for trying out some of the alternative arrangements for land management, the southern and western states of India could be starting points, since in these states both laws and the social context are relatively more favourable to women. Success in these contexts could have a notable demonstration effect in other geographic regions as well.

REFERENCES

Acharya, A., 2000. *Labour Market Developments and Poverty: With Focus on Economic Opportunities for Women.* Kathmandu: Tanka Prasad Acharya Foundation/FES.

Acharya, M. and L. Bennett, 1981. *An Aggregate Analysis and Summary of Village Studies, The Status of Women in Nepal*, II, Part 9. Kathmandu: CEDA, Tribhuvan University.

Agarwal, B., 1988. 'Who Sows? Who Reaps? Women and Land Rights in India'. *The Journal of Peasant Studies*, 15 (4): 532–81.

Agarwal, B., 1994. *A Field of One's Own: Gender and Land Rights in South Asia.* Cambridge: Cambridge University Press.

Agarwal, B., 1995. 'Women's Legal Rights in Agricultural Land in India'. *Economic and Political Weekly*, 30 (12): A39–56.

Agarwal, B., 1997. '"Bargaining" and Gender Relations: Within and Beyond the Household', *Feminist Economics*, 3 (1): 1–50.

Agarwal, B., 1998. 'Widows versus Daughters or Widows as Daughters: Property, Land and Economic Security in Rural India'. *Modern Asian Studies*, 1 (1): 1–48.

Agarwal, B., 2002a. 'Bargaining and Legal Change'. Working Paper No. 165, Institute of Development Studies, Sussex.

Agarwal, B., 2002b. '"The Family" in Public Policy: Fallacious Assumptions and Gender Implications'. In *Facets of the Indian Economy. The NCAER Lectures*, ed. Rakesh Mohan, 301–48. Delhi: Oxford University Press.

Agarwal, B., B. Sivaramayya and L. Sarkar, 1998. *Report of the Committee on Gender Equality in Land Devolution in Tenurial Laws*. Report submitted to the Department of Rural Development, Government of India, February.

Ali, I., B.M. Desai, R. Radhakrishna and V.S. Vyas, 1981. 'Indian Agriculture at 2000: Strategies for Equality'. *Economic and Political Weekly*, 16 (10–12): 409–24.

ALRD, 2000. *Gender, Land Rights, Livelihoods and Laws: ALRD Workshop Report*. Report of a workshop entitled: 'Land for Men, Only Microcredit for Women?', 18–19 February, Association for Land Reform and Development, Dhaka.

Banerjee, A.V., 2000. 'Land Reforms: Prospects and Strategies'. Mimeo. Massachusetts: Department of Economics, Massachusetts Institute of Technology.

Becker, G.S., 1981. *A Treatise on the Family*. Cambridge, MA: Harvard University Press.

Besley, T. and R. Burgess, 2000. 'Land Reform, Poverty Reduction and Growth: Evidence from India'. *Quarterly Journal of Economics*, 115 (2): 389–430.

Bharti, 2000. 'Women and Land Rights: Report of Regional Workshops, 1999–2000'. Saharanpur, India: UP Land Reforms and Labour Rights Campaign Committee, VIKALP, New Cambridge School.

Bhatia, B. 1998, 'Widows, Land Rights and Resettlement in the Narmada Valley'. In *Widows in India: Social Neglect and Public Action*, ed. M. Chen, 257–60. New Delhi: Sage.

Buvinic, M. and N.H. Youssef, 1978. 'Women-Headed Households: The Ignored Factor in Development Planning'. Report submitted to AID/WID, International Centre for Research on Women, Washington, DC.

Byres, T.J., 1991. 'The Agrarian Question and Differing Forms of Capitalist Agrarian Transition: An Essay with Reference to Asia'. In *Rural Transformation in Asia*, eds J. Breman and S. Mundle, 3–76. Delhi: Oxford University Press.

Caldwell, J.C., P.H. Reddy and P. Caldwell, 1988. *The Causes of Demographic Change: Experimental Research in South India*. Wisconsin: The University of Wisconsin Press.

Chadha, G.K., 1993. 'Non-farm Sector in India's Rural Economy: Policy, Performance and Growth Prospects'. VRF Series No. 220. Tokyo: Institute of Developing Economies.

Chadha, G.K., 1999. 'Non-farm Employment in Rural Areas: How Well Can Female Workers Compete?' In *Gender and Employment in India*, eds T.S. Papola and A.N. Sharma, 139–77. Delhi: Vikas Publishing House.

Chen, M.A., 1983. *A Quiet Revolution: Women in Transition in Rural Bangladesh*. Cambridge: Schenkman.

Chen, M.A., ed., 1998. *Widows in India: Social Neglect and Public Action*. New Delhi: Sage.

Cousins, B., 1997. 'How Do Rights become Real? Formal and Informal Institutions in South Africa's Land Reform'. *IDS Bulletin*, 28 (4): 59–68.

CWDS, 1985. 'Rural Women's Claim to Priority: Selected Documents from International and National Archives 1975–1985'. Mimeo. New Delhi: Center for Women's Development Studies.

Dasgupta, B., 1984. 'Sharecropping in West Bengal: From Independence to Operation Barga'. *Economic and Political Weekly*, 19 (26): A85–96.

Davidson, J., ed., 1988. *Agriculture, Women and Land: The African Experience*. Boulder, CO: Westview Press.

DDS, 1994–5, *Deccan Development Society Report 1994–95*. 1–11–242/1, Street 5, Flat 101, Kishan Residency, Begumpet, Hyderabad – 500 016, India.

De Janvry, A. and E. Sadoulet, 1989. 'A Study in Resistance to Institutional Change: The Lost Game of Latin American Land Reform'. *World Development*, 17 (9): 1397–409.

Deere, C.D. and M. Leon, 2001. *Empowering Women: Land and Property Rights in Latin America*. Pennsylvania: University of Pittsburg Press.

Deninger, K., 1999. 'Making Negotiated Land Reform Work: Initial Experience from Colombia, Brazil and South Africa'. *World Development*, 27 (4): 651–72.

Dey, J., 1992. 'Gender Asymmetries in Intra-Household Resource Allocation in Sub-Saharan Africa: Some Policy Implications for Land and Labour Productivity'. Paper presented at IFPRI workshop on Intra-Household Resource Allocation, International Food Policy Research Institute, Washington, DC.

Doss, C.R., 1996. 'Testing Among Models of Intrahousehold Resource Allocation'. *World Development*, 24 (10): 1597–609.

Dwyer, D. and J. Bruce, eds, 1989. *A Home Divided: Women and Income Control in the Third World*. Stanford: Stanford University Press.

El-Ghonemy, M.R., 1990. *The Political Economy of Rural Poverty: The Case for Land Reform*. London: Routledge.

Elson, D., 1995. 'Gender Awareness in Modelling Structural Adjustment'. *World Development*, 23 (11): 1851–68.

FAO, 1979. *Report of the World Conference on Agrarian Reform and Rural Development (WCARRD)*. Rome: Food and Agricultural Organization.

Feder, G., T. Onchan and T. Raparla, 1986. 'Land Ownership, Security and Access to Credit in Rural Thailand'. Discussion Paper ARU-53. Washington, DC: World Bank.

Fernandes, W. and G. Menon, 1987. *Tribal Women and Forest Economy: Deforestation, Exploitation and Status Change*. Delhi: Indian Social Institute.

Friedman, M. and J. Sunde, 1998. *Learning from the Field: A Conference on Gender Policy Research on Land Reform and Development*. Stellenbosch: Center for Rural Legal Studies.

Goetz, A.M. and R. Sengupta, 1996. 'Who Takes the Credit? Gender, Power, and Control Over Loan Use in Rural Credit Programs in Bangladesh'. *World Development*, 24 (1): 5–63.

Government of India, 1988. *National Perspective Plan for Women*. New Delhi: Department of Women and Child Development, Ministry of Human Resource Development.

Government of India, 1989. *Proceedings and Papers of the Seminar on Land Reforms – Retrospect and Prospect*. New Delhi: Planning Commission.

Government of India, 1990. *Sarvekshana*, September, S188–9.

Government of India, 1995. *Report on Some Aspects of Household Ownership Holdings, 48th Round, 1992*. National Sample Survey (NSS) Report No. 399. New Delhi: Department of Statistics.

Government of India, 1996a. *Key Results on Employment and Unemployment, Fifth Quinquennial Survey*. NSS 50th Round (July 1993–June 1994). NSS Report No. 406. New Delhi: Department of Statistics.

Government of India, 1996b. 'Quarterly Progress Report (Cumulative) on Implementation of Land Ceiling Laws for the Quarter ending Sept. 1996 (2nd Quarter)'. Mimeo. New Delhi: Planning Commission.

Government of India, 1996c. 'Draft Report of Steering Group on Poverty Alleviation and Area Development in Rural India for the Ninth Five Year Plan'. New Delhi: Planning Commission, November.

Government of India, 1997a. *Livestock and Agricultural Implements in Household Operational Holdings, 1991–92.* Land and Livestock Holdings Survey, NSS Forty-Eighth Round, NSS Report No. 408. New Delhi: Department of Statistics.

Government of India, 1997b. *Some Aspects of Operational Holdings, 48th Round, 1992.* Land and Livestock Holdings Survey, NSS Report No. 407. New Delhi: Department of Statistics.

Government of India, 2000. *Ninth Five Year Plan: 1997–2002.* New Delhi: Planning Commission.

Government of India, 2001. *Employment and Unemployment Situation in India, Part I.* NSS 55th Round 1999–2000, Report No. 458. New Delhi: Department of Statistics.

Government of Madhya Pradesh, 1996. *The Madhya Pradesh Policy for Women.* Bhopal: Department of Women and Child Welfare, Government of Madhya Pradesh.

Gupta, J., 1993. 'Land, Dowry, Labour: Women in the Changing Economy of Midnapur'. *Social Scientist*, 21 (9–11): 74–90.

Haddad, L., J. Hoddinott and H. Alderman, eds, 1997. *Intrahousehold Resource Allocation in Developing Countries: Methods, Models and Policy.* Baltimore, MD: John Hopkins Press.

Hall, R., 1999. 'Alternative Means by which Women have acquired Land: An Indian Case Study'. Draft mimeo. Delhi: Institute of Economic Growth and Stellenbosch: Center for Rural Legal Studies.

Hart, G., 1993. 'Gender and Household Dynamics: Recent Theories and Their Implications'. In *Critical Issues in Asian Development*, ed. M.G. Quibria, 39–74. Bangkok: Asian Development Bank, and New York: Oxford University Press.

Herring, R., 1999. 'Political Conditions for Agrarian Reform and Poverty Alleviation'. Paper presented at the DFID Conference on 2001 World Development Report on Poverty, Birmingham, UK, 16–17 August 1999.

Hirschon, R., 1984. *Women and Property, Women as Property.* London: Croom Helm.

IFAD, 2001a. *Report: The Challenge of Ending Poverty.* Rome: International Fund for Agricultural Development (IFAD).

IFAD, 2001b. *Assessment of Rural Poverty in Asia and the Pacific Region.* Rome: IFAD.

ILO, 2000. *Yearbook of Labour Statistics.* Geneva: International Labour Organization.

Kandiyoti, D., 2001. 'Agrarian Reform, Gender and Land Rights in Uzbekistan'. Paper prepared for the UNRISD Project on Agrarian Change, Gender and Land Rights, UNRISD, Geneva.

Kishwar, M., 1987. 'Toiling Without Rights: Ho Women of Singhbhum'. *Economic and Political Weekly*, 22 (3): 95–101; 22 (4): 149–55; 22 (5): 194–200.

Kumar, S.K., 1978. 'Role of the Household Economy in Child Nutrition at Low Incomes'. Occasional Paper No. 95, Department of Agricultural Economics, Cornell University.

Lipton, M., 1985. 'Land Assets and Rural Poverty'. Staff Working Paper No. 744. Washington, DC: World Bank.

Lipton, M. and M. Lipton, 1995. *Land, Labour and Livelihood in Rural South Africa.* Durban: Indicative Press.

Manimala, 1983. 'Zameen Kenkar? Jote Onkar! Women's Participation in the Bodhgaya Land Struggle'. *Manushi*, 14: 2–16.

Meer, S., ed., 1997. *Women, Land and Authority: Perspectives from South Africa.* Claremont: David Philip and Oxford: Oxfam.

Menon, G., 1996. 'Re-negotiating Gender: Enabling Women to Claim their Right to Land Resources'. Paper presented at the NGO Forum of the UN Conference on Human Settlements – Habitat II, Istanbul, June.

Molyneux, M., 1981. 'Socialist Societies Old and New: Progress Towards Women's Emancipation'. *Feminist Review*, 8: 1–34.

Nandwana, R. and S. Nandwana, 1998. 'Land Rights of Widows'. In *Widows in Rural India*, ed. M. Chen, 228–40. New Delhi: Sage.

Narayan, D., R. Chambers, M.K. Shah and P. Petesch, 2000a. *Voices of the Poor*. Vol. I: *Can Anyone Hear Us?* Delhi: Oxford University Press and Washington, DC: World Bank.

Narayan, D., R. Chambers, M.K. Shah and P. Petesch, 2000b. *Voices of the Poor*. Vol. II: *Crying Out for Change*. Delhi: Oxford University Press and Washington, DC: World Bank.

Narayan, D., R. Chambers, M.K. Shah and P. Petesch, 2002. *Voices of the Poor*. Vol. III: *From Many Lands*. Delhi: Oxford University Press and Washington, DC: World Bank.

Nussbaum, M.C., 2000. *Women and Human Development: The Capabilities Approach*. Cambridge: Cambridge University Press.

Omvedt, G., 1990. 'Women, Zilla Parishads and Panchayat Raj: Chandwad to Vitner'. *Economic and Political Weekly*, 25 (31): 1687–90.

Panda, P.P., 1997. 'Living Arrangements of the Elderly in Rural Orissa'. Working Paper No. 277. Thiruvananthapuram, Kerala: Center for Development Studies.

Patnaik, U., 2001. 'Global Capitalism and its Impact on the Agrarian Transition in Developing Countries'. Paper prepared for the UNRISD project on Agrarian Change, Gender and Land Rights, Geneva.

Quisumbing, A., 1996. 'Male–Female Differences in Agricultural Productivity: Methodological Issues and Empirical Evidence'. *World Development*, 24 (10): 1579–95.

Quisumbing, A.R. and J.A. Maluccio, 2000. 'Intrahousehold Allocation and Gender Relations: New Empirical Evidence'. Discussion paper 84. Washington, DC: International Food Policy Research Institute.

Ray, S.K., 1996. 'Land System and its Reforms in India'. *Indian Journal of Agricultural Economics*, 51 (1–2): 218–37.

Reidinger, J.M., 1995. *Agrarian Reform in the Philippines: Democratic Transitions and Redistributive Reforms*. Stanford: Stanford University Press.

Rosenzweig, M.R. and K.I. Wolpin, 1985. 'Specific Experience, Household Structure, and Intergenerational Transfers: Farm Family Land and Labour Arrangements in Developing Countries'. *Quarterly Journal of Economics*, Supplement, 100: 961–87.

Roy Chowdhury, B., 2001. 'Women and their Land Rights'. New Delhi: Vikalp, Saharanpur and Action India.

Samuelson, P.A., 1956. 'Social Indifference Curves'. *Quarterly Journal of Economics*, 70 (1): 1–22.

Satheesh, P.V., 1997a. 'History in the Making: Women Design and Manage an Alternative Public Distribution System'. *Forests, Trees and People*, Newsletter No. 34, September.

Satheesh, P.V., 1997b. 'A Background Note on the Alternative Public Distribution System and the Current Controversy'. Mimeo, 18 September. Hyderabad: DDS.

Satheesh, P.V., 2001. 'An Agenda for a Sustainable Community Managed PDS'. Mimeo, August. Hyderabad: DDS.

Seabright, P., 1997. 'Is Cooperation Habit-Forming?' In *The Environment and Emerging Development Issues*, eds P. Dasgupta and K.-G. Maler, 283–307. Oxford: Clarendon Press.

Seiz, J., 2000. 'Game Theory and Bargaining Models'. *Elgar Companion to Feminist Economics*, 379–90. Cheltenham Elgar.

Sen, A.K., 1984. *Resources, Values and Development*. Oxford: Clarendon Press.

Sen, A.K., 1990. 'Gender and Cooperative Conflicts'. In *Persistent Inequalities: Women and World Development*, 123–49. New York: Oxford University Press.

Sen, A.K., 2000. *Development as Freedom*. Delhi: Oxford University Press.

Shankar, K., 1990. *Land Transfers: A Case Study*. Delhi: Gian Publishing House.

Sharma, U., 1980. *Women, Work and Property in North-West India*. London: Tavistock.

Shramshakti, 1988. *Report of the National Commission on Self-Employed Women and Women in the Informal Sector*. New Delhi: Government of India.

Singh, A.M. and A. Kelles-Vitanen, eds, 1987. *Invisible Hands: Women in Home-based Production*. Delhi: Sage.

Sobhan, R., 1993. *Agrarian Reform and Social Transformation: Preconditions for Development*. London: Zed Books.

Stivens M., C. Ng, K.S. Jomo and J. Bee, eds, 1994. *Malay Peasant Women and the Land*. London: Zed Books.

Strauss, J. and K. Beegle, 1996. 'Intrahousehold Allocations: A Review of Theories, Empirical Evidence and Policy Issues'. MSU International Development Working Paper No. 62. East Lansing, MI: Department of Agricultural Economics, Michigan State University.

Sunstein, C.R., 1993. *The Partial Constitution*. Cambridge, MA: Harvard University Press.

Swinnen, J.F.M, ed., 1997. *Political Economy of Agrarian Reform in Central and Eastern Europe*. Aldershot: Ashgate.

Tharakan, M., 1997. 'Towards a Humane Community: Local Efforts and Economic Liberalisation'. In *History and Society: Essays in Honour of Professor S. Kadhirvel*, ed. K.A. Manikumar, 249–64. Madras (published privately).

Thomas, D., 1990. 'Intra-household Resource Allocation: An Inferential Approach'. *Journal of Human Resources*, 25 (4): 635–63.

Thomas, D., 1994. 'Like Father Like Son, or, Like Mother Like Daughter: Parental Education and Child Health'. *Journal of Human Resources*, 29 (4): 950–88.

Thorner, D., 1956. *The Agrarian Prospect in India*. Five Lectures on Land Reform delivered in 1955 at the Delhi School of Economics, University of Delhi. Delhi: University Press. 2nd edition published by Allied Publishers, Bombay, 1976.

Udry, C., J. Hoddinott, H. Alderman and L. Haddad, 1995. 'Gender Differentials in Farm Productivity: Implications for Household Efficiency and Agricultural Policy'. *Food Policy*, 20 (5): 407–23.

Unni, J., 1996. 'Women Workers in Agriculture: Some Recent Trends'. Paper presented at the IEG-ISLE Seminar on 'Gender and Employment in India: Trends, Patterns and Policy Implications', Institute of Economic Growth, Delhi, December.

Whitehead, A., 2001. 'Trade, Trade Liberalisation and Rural Poverty in Low-Income Africa: A Gendered Account'. Background Paper for the UNCTAD 2001 Least Developed Countries Report.

Working Group on Women's Rights, 1996. 'Reversing the Option: Civil Codes and Personal Laws'. *Economic and Political Weekly*, 31 (21): 1180–3.

7

The Cry for Land: Agrarian Reform, Gender and Land Rights in Uzbekistan

DENIZ KANDIYOTI

Agrarian reform in Uzbekistan has been informed by contradictory objectives and priorities. Legislation has oscillated between measures to increase private access to land, in line with populist pressures and the structural reform agenda of international agencies, and counter-measures to tighten and restrict such access in response to the Government imperative of retaining control over the production and export earnings of cotton. Drawing on fieldwork carried out in the provinces of Andijan and Khorezm in 2000–1, this article analyses the role of gendered divisions of labour in the maintenance of a commercial cotton sector alongside a smallholder economy that has become the mainstay of rural livelihoods since the post-Soviet collapse of public sector employment and wages. It also discusses the outcomes of different types of farm restructuring and highlights the gender differentiated outcomes of a reform process that forces a growing number of women out of the recorded labour force into casual, unremunerated and informal work.

Keywords: post-Soviet reforms, Uzbekistan, farm restructuring, gender

INTRODUCTION

Agrarian reforms in countries undergoing post-socialist transitions have involved remarkably diverse processes. These have ranged from the reconstitution of private land ownership rights in Eastern Europe to various types of enterprise restructuring in the former Soviet Union (FSU). The Central Asian republics that are more heavily reliant on agriculture and primary extraction have exhibited configurations of transition to the market that have differed from those of the European republics of the former Soviet Union (Lerman 1998). Central Asian governments have themselves introduced different types of land reform legislation with varying degrees of State monopoly over agricultural land and central controls over production decisions (Spoor 1995).

In contrast to the rich and growing literature on gender and agrarian change in the global South (Davidson 1988; Agarwal 1994; Deere and Leon 2001; Razavi

This paper is based on research undertaken as part of the UNRISD project on Agrarian Change, Gender and Land Rights.

My thanks are due to Nadira Azimova for her assistance with fieldwork, to UNDP, Tashkent for administrative support and to Shahra Razavi for close readings and incisive comments on this and earlier texts.

2002), the ways in which these changing property and production regimes impact upon gender relations and are, in turn, shaped by them is a topic that has barely begun to be addressed in so-called transition economies (see Bridger 1987, for a notable exception).

In this article, I argue that gender analysis illuminates our understanding of agrarian transformation in Uzbekistan on at least two levels. First, it is possible to demonstrate that gendered divisions of labour are centrally implicated in the reproduction of a rural economy based on the operations of an export-oriented commercial cotton sector that relies on an unremunerated or underpaid workforce which is, in turn, dependent on entitlements to land for self-subsistence. Second, current pathways of farm restructuring and the loss of employment opportunities and social welfare entitlements in the Uzbek countryside are eroding well-being and security in gender-differentiated ways. While the thrust of the first point is mainly analytic, the second calls forth more activist concerns with issues of equity and rights.

Gender analysis must, however, necessarily be set in the specific context of the political economy of Uzbekistan. Uzbekistan was absorbed into the Soviet Union as a primary commodity producer, consolidating a pattern evident since the Tsarist conquest of Central Asia.[1] This has led many commentators to remark on the deleterious social, political and ecological consequences of the mono-crop cotton economy (Carley 1989; Rumer 1989; Gleason 1991, 1997; Spoor 1993; Pomfret 1995; Fierman 1997; Thurman 1999).[2] The large rural labour surplus of Uzbekistan, the low levels of rural wages and labour mobility compared to the rest of the Soviet Union, were already widely documented (Lubin 1984; Craumer 1992, 1995). After the break-up of the Soviet Union, the agricultural sector has acted as a 'shock absorber' providing livelihoods for an ever-greater number of people, putting further pressure on a limited resource base.[3] However, the initial decline in GDP experienced across the countries of the FSU was less steep in Uzbekistan due to the fact that the country produces a major export crop that could find alternative export markets. State elites retain a continuing interest in maintaining cotton deliveries and controlling export revenues. The first part of this article discusses the dilemmas posed by this particular constellation of influences and their impact on the pace and content of agrarian

---

[1] Agriculture accounts for 30 per cent of GDP, 60 per cent of foreign exchange receipts and about 40 per cent of employment. Uzbekistan ranks as the world's fourth largest producer of cotton, its exports account for 16 per cent of global trade in cotton and cotton alone accounts for nearly 50 per cent of export earnings.

[2] I have argued elsewhere (Kandiyoti 2002) that this particular mode of incorporation into the Soviet system has meant that discussions of Central Asia have mainly been informed by variants of dependency and post-colonial theory.

[3] Between 1989 and 1994, employment in agriculture grew at an annual compound rate of 4.6 per cent, while agricultural output declined by 3.8 per cent (Khan 1996). It must be noted here that only 10 per cent of the territory of Uzbekistan is habitable land and that the rural population, over 60 per cent of the total, is concentrated on 4.5 million hectares of irrigated arable land in oases and along rivers. The amount of arable land per rural resident (0.37 ha) is low compared to other FSU republics (2 ha per person in Ukraine and 0.75 in densely populated Moldova).

reform. The second part introduces enterprise-level case studies to illustrate how different paths of farm restructuring both draw upon and transform existing gender divisions of labour. The closing sections explore the implications of changing rural livelihood portfolios and marital rights for women's entitlements and rights.

THE DILEMMAS OF AGRARIAN REFORM

In the immediate aftermath of independence in 1991, the Government of Uzbekistan was faced with two immediate crises. First, Uzbekistan was cut off from the budgetary grant it received from the USSR and the Government was forced to find new sources of revenue. Extraction of surplus from agriculture by driving a wedge between the procurement price and the export price of cotton was a readily available alternative. Agriculture was squeezed through a system of low output prices and high input prices. Prices for cotton and wheat are subject to a mandatory system of production quotas and state orders,[4] complemented by rationing of inputs, water and equipment and financed with 'centralized credits' by Government-controlled banks. Prices are set as a result of negotiations between the producers and Government-controlled product processing associations, which are monopsonistic buyers. These are below world market prices.[5] Producers also have to contend with late payment for their deliveries, which further erodes their returns due to high inflation. Input prices, on the other hand, have been subject to large increases while direct subsidies to producers have been sharply reduced (*de facto* subsidies now consisting of free use of the irrigation system and debt relief and rescheduling). As a result, the terms of trade for agriculture deteriorated drastically. By 1994, the procurement price for cotton in real terms was a fraction of what it was in 1990.[6] Although agriculture accounts

[4]   Wheat is subject to a two-tiered pricing system; 25 per cent at the State order price and 25 per cent at a higher administered price, the 'negotiated' price. In fact, this amounts to 50 per cent, since the additional negotiated price is, in practice, mandatory. The State order for cotton is 30 per cent of planned production. Producers who meet production targets, in principle, have the right to sell the residual 70 per cent to the State marketing board for a higher price. However, producers who do not meet their production targets do not have the right to sell any cotton at the higher price. For this reason, actual State procurement is much higher than the formal State order, since ambitious production targets are frequently not met. However, the Government of Uzbekistan has signed a letter of intent with the IMF (dated 31 January 2002) indicating that dispositions concerning State procurement of wheat and cotton will be amended by May and August 2002, respectively. It also sets the procurement prices for the 2002 cotton crop at the world market level. Since these represent major steps, it will be interesting to monitor the speed of their full implementation.

[5]   By way of comparison, Chinese farmers received the full international price at the farm gate, US$1590 per ton in 1998, in contrast to US$775 per ton received by Uzbek producers. With prices at 60–65 per cent of international levels and the condition that foreign exchange must be surrendered at the official rate, cotton producers in Uzbekistan are clearly disadvantaged (World Bank 1999). In 2000, the price gap between State purchasing boards and world market prices for cotton and wheat was 70 per cent and 60 per cent, respectively.

[6]   The fall in world cotton prices was not felt until 1995 and overall revenues only declined since 1997 due to both declining crop yields and China's entry into the world market as a major cotton exporter, which further depressed prices.

for about 25 per cent of GDP, it receives less than 7 per cent of total investment (IMF 1998).

The break-up of the Soviet Union also meant that the trading links with other republics were disrupted, leading to a shortfall in grain and shortages of flour in many parts of the country. The response of the Government was to expand the acreage of land devoted to wheat production substantially[7] and to increase the size of private plots that the population is entitled to. With production of an estimated 3.7 million tons of wheat in 1998 – six times the level of 1991 – Uzbekistan has largely achieved the goal of drastically reducing grain imports. According to World Bank estimates, household plots comprise about 3 million holdings encompassing 10 per cent of arable land (World Bank 1999), a substantial enlargement of the acreage devoted to private use. This measure was also, in part, a palliative for the fact that public employers were chronically in arrears with wages and households were becoming increasingly reliant on self-provisioning and the sale of their private produce for survival.

The decline in cotton revenues, resulting from a fall in international cotton prices since 1995, as well as a decline in cotton production itself of about 20 per cent since 1991 (World Bank 1999), had negative consequences for foreign currency earnings, deepening the crisis in public finance and aggravating the tensions between Tashkent and the provinces. The accommodations between the Tashkent-based elite that retains control over cotton deliveries and exports, the major source of hard currency, and the provincial and district governors who have to fulfil the cotton procurement quotas set by the State started coming under new sources of strain. The latter were increasingly deprived of their share of cotton export revenue to consolidate Central Governments' monopoly over all exports. The Government has drastically reduced the latitude of collective enterprises in decision-making regarding sowing policies.[8] Ilkhamov (2000) suggests that the economic resource base of local elites is shrinking as they have less and less discretion over the export-oriented cotton economy. This binds them more tightly into informal networks and patron–client relationships that share out the net aggregate revenue generated in the domestic peasant economy. It is therefore in their interest to shift resources from the official register to the much less accountable petty commodity economy. This leads to a process of concealed erosion of the basis of the export economy and creates grounds for conflict between central and regional elites. This conflict sometimes erupts into the public arena

---

[7]   Government objectives to pursue wheat self-sufficiency had a major impact on cropping patterns since independence. Between 1990 and 1996, there was a reduction in the areas sown to cotton (from 44 to 35 per cent) and forage (from 25 to 13 per cent), while the share of arable land allocated to cereals increased (from 24 to 41 per cent). However, the drop in forage crops caused a decline in animal husbandry and a critical shortage of feed and the substitution of cereal for cotton lowered the returns from agriculture (land used for cotton produces 1.2–3.0 times more added value per hectare than land sown to wheat) (Trushin 1998).
[8]   Compulsory quotas for the distribution of crop acreages have been adopted by governmental decree and passed down to the provincial, district and farm levels (Decree of the Cabinet of Ministers, No. 317, 24 June 1997).

with the not infrequent dismissal of governors charged with corruption and inefficiency.[9]

What further complicates the range of pressures under which the Government has to operate is the fact that international agencies are also involved in setting the agrarian reform agenda, insisting on privatization and structural reform. The establishment of secure and tradable property rights and the removal of barriers to farmers' incentives by eliminating the massive price distortions for cotton and wheat are central to these prescriptions (Herman 1999).

These varied pressures are manifest in the vagaries of the agrarian reform process itself. Land reform legislation reflects a bundle of contradictory priorities and objectives, oscillating between increasing private access to land, in line with populist pressures and the structural reform agenda of international donors, on the one hand, and counter-measures to tighten and restrict private access to land in response to the imperative of retaining control over the production of cotton, on the other.

An examination of changing legislation between 1990 and 1998 suggests that after an initial spate of measures to expand households' access to private hold-ings,[10] the emphasis shifted to distinguishing between a smallholder sector with few prospects of graduation to commercial farming, using small plots mainly as a social safety net, and providing more restricted access to a commercial sector of independent farms that are tied into the State procurement system through their leaseholds and contracts.[11]

Despite the gradual nature of the changes in land tenure patterns, the share of the individual sector (household plots and peasant farms) in agricultural

---

[9] Parallels with previous conflicts between Moscow and republican elites in Uzbekistan necessarily come to mind. The latter responded to increasingly unrealistic Plan targets by defrauding the Central Government through an elaborate system of bribe-taking and padding reports in an episode known as the 'cotton scandal' (also referred to as the 'Uzbek affair'). Moscow allegedly paid more than one billion roubles in 1978–1983 for cotton that was never produced, based on an inflation of cotton output by as much as 4.5 million tons. This led to a purge of Uzbek officials that provoked an upsurge of nationalist feeling. People were less concerned about corruption, especially if it had the effect of diverting funds into Uzbekistan, and more about the persecution of Uzbek cadres (Pomfret 1995). Karimov issued a decree on 25 December 1991 pardoning most of those convicted in the 'cotton scandal'.

[10] New legislation in the immediate aftermath of independence allocated more private land to households for their own use. According to one estimate, the amount of land for personal plots increased from 110,000 ha before independence to 630,000 ha in 1994 (362,840 ha of which was crop land). However, legal norms are subject to local availability. In high population density areas, new families may not receive an allocation or their plots may be well below the legally allowed norm.

[11] The law passed in April 1998 introduced new criteria that are designed to tighten access to the status of independent farmer and to make a distinction between owners of smallholdings (now called '*dekhan*' (peasant) farmers) and independent farmers (now called just *farmers*). The main intent of the April 1998 Law appears to be the introduction of a distinction between a small-holding sector subject to a size 'ceiling', on which the State makes no demands aside from land tax, and a 'commercial' sector which has more latitude for expansion in terms of acquiring land and non-family labourers, but is tied into the State procurement through a system of contracts. The leasehold contracts (*shartname*) stipulate the size of acreage to be allocated to specified crops and what proportion of the crop is subject to State deliveries. This represents an attempt to pass on the risks of production to independ-ent farmers, whilst maintaining the State procurement system of certain strategic crops such as cotton and wheat.

production has increased substantially (from 28 per cent in 1990 to 41 per cent in 1994 and 53 per cent in 1997). The production of meat and milk has shifted almost entirely to the household sector.[12] The apparent dynamism of this sector should not, however, make us lose sight of the rigidity of what Ilkhamov (1998) has described as a three-tiered rural economy. This structure consists of collective enterprises (now restructured into Joint Stock Companies, JSCs, called *shirkat*), still occupying the major part of irrigated, arable land,[13] a thin layer of independent farms (called 'farmers' under the 1998 Law), and a mass of collective farm employees who cultivate smallholdings (or '*dekhan* farmers' under the 1998 Law) in addition to their work on *shirkat* plots.

Current land tenure arrangements give rural households access to different types of plots. The first type is the *household plot* on which the house is built and also contains a small garden plot (or *agarot*).[14] The second type of plot is the *tamorka* or private subsidiary plot to which all citizens were entitled with expanded rights since *perestroika*.[15] The acreage allocated to households was expanded more than twice compared to 1989. The legal size of private plots was increased from 0.06 ha to 0.25 ha, and eventually 0.35 ha of irrigated land and 0.5 ha of non-irrigated land. These are usually allocated from the land reserves of collective farms and based on transactions between the collective and the household head. The actual size of the plot and its distance from the house depend on local conditions of availability.

---

[12]   This was in part related to an acute shortage of feed crops that has worsened with the conversion of land planted with barley and lucerne to wheat (the aggregate feed available in 1997 was about one-third of 1991).

[13]   *Shirkat* lands are cultivated through the *pudrat* system, whereby families are allocated a particular acreage of land (depending on their labour resources) under contract to produce a specified quantity of crops. The standard size of 1 ha gave rise to the term *hektardji* to denote these labourers. The term 'family leasehold' is a misnomer here, in the sense that the *pudratchi* are, in fact, contract labourers. Although a lease agreement is transacted, this is largely a formality since land is allocated based on an annual production plan where decisions on sowing have already been taken and written into the *pudrat* contracts. Some members of family leaseholds are registered with the *shirkat* and have a right to a salary (*ish hakki*) and social benefits even though, in fact, the entire family contributes to production. In practice, even the registered members of the *pudrat* do not receive a cash wage but are paid in kind for their year round work in the fields. Only harvesting wages are paid in cash.

[14]   Household plots are held in perpetuity and are inheritable, even though strictly speaking only the house is private property. Women do not normally have claims on either house or plot since post-marital residence is virilocal and the dwelling is considered as the property of the husband's family. In cases where there is more than one son, it is usually the youngest who is expected to cohabit with parents and inherit the house.

[15]   Kitching (1998) argues that in the case of post-Soviet Russia the expansion of 'private plot' production has been an important cause of the current crisis of large farm (collective) production. He argues, furthermore, that smallholders have no wish to expand their enterprises and certainly not without the help and subsidies they receive from the collective sector in the form of inputs or transportation. This is clearly not applicable to the case of Uzbekistan where (a) unlike Russia, there is a significant rural labour surplus and household holdings are not large enough to absorb this excess labour, (b) the collective sector is mainly involved in the production of a non-food crop destined to different markets than the food crops produced on private plots, (c) the 'symbiotic' relationship between the large farm sector and smallholders also works to the advantage of the former through the deployment of an underpaid or casual female workforce in cotton operations.

Former *sovkhozes* and *kolkhozes* (now restructured as *shirkats*) still continue to occupy the bulk of irrigated land and account for almost half of the value of all crops, mostly producing cotton and wheat. Members of collective farms are organized into family brigades and allocated a specific acreage to farm on a contract basis. The shift from work brigades to family leaseholds (*oila pudrati* or *arenda* in Russian) was the product of the Union-wide reforms adopted during the *perestroika* period.[16] This also gives them the possibility of growing additional crops on leased land after the wheat harvest and benefiting from membership in the collective for securing inputs for their household and *tamorka* plots.

Finally, as explained above, the Land Law includes provisions to create independent farms that have the status of separate juridical entities, the right to open their own bank accounts and to hold leases of up to 50 years. Initially, such farms were formed as leaseholds that remained tied to collective farms.[17] These types of farms increased significantly between 1991 and 1995, but they still accounted for only 6 per cent of total arable land and have recorded a decline since 1995 in certain provinces (TACIS 1996). With the 1998 Law, access to the status of independent farmer is being restricted further. The applicants who want to become private farmers now have to meet more stringent criteria and pass a formal examination to receive a farmer's certificate. In the provinces of Khorezm and Andijan, the acreage cultivated by independent farmers represented 2 per cent and 4 per cent of total agricultural land according to 1999 figures.

In practice, decisions concerning land allocation still reside with enterprise managers (except, as shall be seen later, in cases where collectives have been dismantled altogether) who have to adjudicate among different categories of claimants such as rank and file *shirkat* workers pressing their statutory rights to personal subsidiary plots and aspiring independent farmers who may apply for leases of up to 50 years.

This process of allocation is taking place in a context where the importance of land in sustaining livelihoods has increased significantly. Whereas informal incomes deriving from private cultivation and trading activities existed under the Soviet system as additional incomes (Grossman 1989), Humphrey (1998) notes that they have now moved to centre stage as the arena where new survival strategies are enacted in the post-Soviet republics. Uzbekistan now presents the spectacle of a country where schoolteachers, local administrators, doctors and agricultural workers are all vying with each other to get a toehold in agricultural land as a result of the collapse of public sector wages and of retrenchment in the

---

[16] This system was modelled on the Chinese household responsibility system. However, it did not grant farmers the decision-taking freedom that was a key element in China's agrarian success in the 1980s (Pomfret 2000).

[17] The decree of 18 March 1997 separated independent farms from collective enterprises by granting them independent juridical status, the right to hold their own bank accounts and to enter into transactions with buyers of crops and suppliers of inputs in their own right. This was due to the fact that as collectives got into deeper financial problems, they started to be in chronic arrears of payments to farmers who could not get the money for the crops they produced. This resulted in a spectacular rate of failure and bankruptcy (TACIS 1996).

services and rural industries. Rural households have responded by adopting a mixed portfolio of activities, allocated along age and gender lines combining salaries and wages (in cash or in kind), self-provisioning and sale or barter of produce from personal plots or animals, income from trading and other informal activities, and benefits and entitlements (such as pensions and maternity benefit) (Kandiyoti 1998).

The simultaneous attempt by enterprise managers to provide smallholders with a subsistence base whilst developing and diversifying leasehold markets in land represents a precarious balancing act. The presence of different categories of claimants within the same territory sets up a zero sum game among them. Thus, land leased to independent farmers on a long-term basis can only be compensated for by reducing allocations made to households by collective enterprises (or by altogether refraining from allocating land to new families). The alternative would represent an out and out loss of the collectives' own productive capability. In the shake-out accompanying this process, the weakest players, namely collective farm workers who rely on their small plots, are likely to be the losers. These dilemmas, which were freely acknowledged by the farm managers interviewed, are being played out in various ways in the context of different types of restructured farming enterprises. The gendered outcomes of these processes are analysed by means of case studies below.

PATHWAYS OF FARM RESTRUCTURING: LEASEHOLDERS, FARMERS AND CASUAL WORKERS

> If women didn't work here, the land would go to rack and ruin. (Head of village council, Andijan, 2000)

The most common path of enterprise restructuring in Uzbekistan is the transformation of former *kolkhoz* and *sovkhoz* into joint-stock companies (JSCs) or *shirkats*. Under this model, the assets of the enterprise are evaluated and the total share value (or some portion of it) is distributed to collective farm members on the basis of salary, length of service and other assessments of labour input. The organization of production remains essentially unchanged and continues to rely on the *pudrat* or family contract system. However, a new system of management making each production unit a separate accounting unit responsible for losses and profits has been introduced. This pathway will be illustrated by means of two case studies: the Ok Bugday *shirkat* in Khorezm and Eski Kishlak *shirkat* in Andijan.[18]

A pattern that is less common is the complete liquidation of former collective enterprises and the reallocation of the land to independent farmers. In this case, what is at stake is not the distribution of shares but of actual land parcels. This requires additional decisions concerning which individuals will exercise legal

---

[18]   The names of the enterprises are pseudonyms adopted to protect the anonymity of respondents.

rights over which land parcels.[19] The Yengi Kishlak Farmers' Association in Khorezm, which represents one of the early examples of this pathway, will be used as a case study to illustrate this pathway.

Leaseholds and Private Plots: Women's Burdens in Ok Bugday

Ok Bugday became a joint-stock company in 1999.[20] This collective owns 2740 ha of cultivable land, about 60 per cent of which is allocated to growing cotton, followed by rice (15 per cent), sugar beet (11 per cent) and wheat (7 per cent), the remainder being sown to feed crops and vegetables. This land is cultivated by 1800 family *pudrats*.[21] Although this system was in place since 1985, the shift to the *shirkat* brought about two further changes; the distribution of shares to members of the collective and the redefinition of family leaseholds as separate accounting units.

A long-serving woman brigade chief who worked in that capacity for over 20 years, acknowledged that the transition from work brigades to family contracts and now to *shirkat* have represented a progressive retrenchment of labour. In the process of turning into an association of shareholders, the *kolkhoz* had to shed a further 425 brigade members who are now unemployed (almost 20 per cent of the total workforce of 2250). Of these, 65 per cent are women. The effect of retrenchment is the casualization of agricultural labour; fewer workers are officially 'on the books', thereby losing their social benefits. This is a process that is acknowledged to disproportionately affect women.

In terms of the organization of production itself, however, the shift to *shirkat* status does not appear to have introduced significant changes. The procurement

---

[19]   There is a programme of 'sanation' (*sanatzia*) of agricultural enterprises, which entered its second round in 1999–2000. 'Sanation' consists of a two-year pre-bankruptcy process, which aims to re-establish the creditworthiness and economic viability of an enterprise. The main instruments are external management, debt restructuring, sale of unnecessary assets and stocks, strengthening financial controls, laying off surplus workforce and cleaning inter-farm irrigation and drainage structures. After the sanation period, enterprises that are able to improve their performance are being restructured into *shirkats*, while those showing no sign of improvement are liquidated and transformed into Associations of Private and Dehkan Farmers. As of January 2001, a total of 213 enterprises nationwide were under sanation and 74 enterprises had been restructured into Associations of Private and Dehkan Farmers. Both the scope of this programme and the number of liquidated collective enterprises is likely to grow.

[20]   All those who have worked for the *kolkhoz* for more than two years (including pensioners) were eligible to receive shares. The criteria for the size of shares were based on length of service and salary level. A total of 3500 shares were distributed; of these 800 were given to pensioners, 270 to technicians, tractor drivers and other technical personnel and the rest allocated to current workers in family brigades. The *paychik* (shareholders) have the right to pass on these shares to their heirs. The benefits accruing from shareholding are, at present, hypothetical rather than substantive since the enterprise is in arrears of debt payments to various input providers and unable to pay their members regular wages, let alone dividends. Shareholding also brings with it the possibility of having to shoulder the debts of the collective if it were to go into liquidation. Women are entitled to shares but their years of service and the fact they are mainly unskilled workers means they receive *de facto* fewer shares.

[21]   The size of land allocated to each family depends upon the crops for which there are different norms. These are 5 ha for wheat, 1.1 ha for rice and 1.7 ha for cotton. The labour power available to households is also taken into account.

quotas for each crop are still allocated to different brigades, which divide the land among family *pudrats*.[22] A significant departure from the past is that brigades are no longer the unit responsible for production. They only work on common maintenance tasks, like cleaning and repairing water canals. The responsibility for meeting production targets rests with each family *pudrat*, which now constitutes a separate accounting unit.[23] This internal accounting system should, in principle, increase pressures on those who do not fulfil the terms of their contracts and are in debt. In practice, however, the farm manager acknowledges that many are chronically indebted to the *shirkat*:

> When a member of the shirkat approaches me saying 'I need 40 kg of rice and 20 l of oil for my son's wedding' what am I supposed to do? How can I refuse him? We need to be able to look each other in the face. I have to be able to say *selam-in aleykom* (good day in Arabic) to them. A lot of the debt comes from such ceremonies.

This statement goes to the heart of the social contract between the *kolhozdji* (workers in collectives) and their management. The ties that still bind workers to the collectives consist of a mixture of lack of alternatives, on the one hand, and forms of paternalistic protection, on the other, which are coming under increasing strain as the resources of collective enterprises dry up. Apart from keeping their workbooks registered in the *shirkat* for the purposes of pensions and social benefits, there are a number of incentives that members of the collective receive. They have access to cotton stalks (*xozapaya*) of the harvested fields as cooking fuel and animal fodder, they use *shirkat* land to graze their private animals,[24] they have the right to sell cotton oil from any excess production of cotton or sugar from their sugar beet. Family brigades are also given the possibility of planting crops, such as carrots, beans or other fast-growing crops, for their own use on *shirkat* land, on a leasehold or sharecropping basis after the wheat harvest. Most

---

[22]   There are currently 20 cotton brigades, five rice brigades, two wheat brigades, two sugar beet brigades and two animal fodder brigades. The delivery contract for cotton the previous year, for instance, was 4600 tons. This was divided among the 20 cotton brigades, which comprise 957 family leaseholders. The yields expected from each family leasehold are set according to production norms for the different crops.

[23]   Every leaseholder enters into a contract with the *shirkat*, which is transacted yearly, specifying the acreage of land they lease and how much they will produce and receive in payment. They are provided with a notebook and chequebook where they record all the expenses they have incurred for inputs. At the end of the year, when they settle accounts, the costs of inputs that are owed to the *shirkat* and the salary costs of the technical services provided are deducted from the amount owed to the leaseholder according to contract stipulations. In the case of a leaseholder who has produced 6 tons of cotton fetching approximately 300,000 sums, about half will go towards expenditures covered by the *shirkat* as advances for inputs and about 40,000 sums will be deducted towards the salary costs of the *shirkat* administrative staff (book keepers, water services and agronomists). The net return will be of around 70,000 sums which constitutes about 25 per cent of the sum appearing on the contract.

[24]   A number of governmental decrees introducing punitive measures (including surveillance by mounted militia) have been introduced since 1994 to prevent crop damage due to grazing. This appears to have had little effect, since enterprise managers tend to turn a blind eye to this infraction.

importantly, the access of households to private subsidiary plots is mediated by membership in the collective enterprise.

These mutual accommodations have led some observers to argue that the cotton export-sector is dependent upon a stagnating smallholder economy on which it draws for its manpower needs, while the latter is parasitic upon the hidden benefits referred to above (Ilkhamov 2000). A much less noted feature of this mutual dependency, however, is that it is based on a gendered division of labour that produces an intensification of women's agricultural labour on both household plots and family brigades.

The women of Ok Bugday divide their time between work on their family leaseholds and their private household plots. On the latter, the high cost of inputs such as machines, fertilizer and pesticides leads them to substitute their own labour and less costly inputs wherever possible.[25] Reciprocal harvesting arrangements and labour exchanges without cash payments among neighbours and kin are common and widespread. These patterns were quite clearly illustrated in the cases of Sanem, Munavvar and Ziver, who are registered leaseholders with Ok Bugday.[26]

Sanem, who is 50 years old and the mother of seven children, is the head of her family leasehold. This is not unusual for a woman of her age, who has to coordinate an almost exclusively female workforce of daughters-in-law and daughters. The male members of her household have alternative employment, putting her in a more advantageous economic position. Sanem leases 5 ha of cotton land, which she cultivates with her two daughters-in-law. Work for cotton starts in January with the leeching of the fields.[27] This process was completed for her around mid-March. The ploughing was done by a tractor they hired from the *shirkat*, but the sowing, which took place in early April this year, was done by

---

[25] Until recently, not only was there a tendency to divert inputs from the collective enterprise to private plots, but an implicit expectation that the collective would 'help' with private plot cultivation by facilitating access to machinery or providing fertilizer and pesticides. Nowadays, *pudratchi* often complain that the inputs they receive fall short of what is necessary for their *shirkat* work, let alone their private plots. They feel bitter at being held responsible for the yields they achieve on *shirkat* land with fewer and overpriced inputs. This does not mean that attempts at diverting resources have ceased but that they take place in a context of more restricted opportunities, which are further aggravated by increased commodification. For instance, a lucrative market for tractor hire has put tractors out of the reach of many smallholders. In the past, they were better able to transact informal arrangements with tractor drivers in collective enterprises.

[26] Women may become heads of their *pudrat* for a variety of reasons (their husbands may be engaged in alternative work, they may be widows or they may arrive at this arrangement by other routes). Generally, older women who are able to command a workforce of children and daughters-in-law are more commonly found in this position, although there are no statistics to back this observation. My observations lead me to conclude, however, that the gender of the official lessee is irrelevant to the labour process itself and the ways in which production tasks are shared. Adult men are not involved in the manual operations of weeding, thinning and picking cotton. The operations in which they are involved (such as ploughing and irrigation and maintenance works) require a much smaller workforce. The exception to this rule is in livestock *pudrats*, where direct male involvement is much higher.

[27] In Khorezm, because of the high level of soil salinity, cultivation is impossible before the fields are leeched up to three times between January and April.

the women manually, 'because we are more careful with the seeds'. By June the cotton had flowered and in August it was ready for picking.[28] Sanem rents a combine for the main harvest of her 5 ha of cotton land, which points to the relative affluence of her household. Most leaseholders harvest manually.[29] All the work on the household plot, where they grow vegetables, and on the *tamorka*, which is planted to rice, is also done manually.

Sanem says about their private (*tamorka*) plot, 12 sotka (0.12 ha) of paddy; 'this plot is for our own benefit'. Like other workers on family leaseholds, she sees her work in cotton as an obligation that brings little profit. The *tamorka* plot is cultivated very intensively; double cropping of wheat and rice is not unusual. Sanem rented a tractor for ploughing, but did everything else by hand. The rice was planted in mid-May. Three women (herself and two daughters-in-law) did the job with the help of a few relatives. Weeding, pest control (for which Sanem uses ash, rather than chemical insecticides), fertilizing and harvesting were all done by the women.

Munevvar, who is 48 years old and the mother of five children, is also the head of a family leasehold of 4.5 ha of cotton. She works with her daughter-in-law and her two daughters. She acknowledges that more machines were used during the cotton harvest previously, but claims that handpicked cotton is cleaner and better. She claims to have picked as much as 3 tons of cotton per week with her two daughters and her daughter-in-law. She relies on her family only, except during peak harvest time, when women from other brigades (for instance, those in the rice brigades who are free at that time) come and pick for them at piece-work rates. Women also frequently enter into labour exchanges and reciprocal harvesting arrangements, which lower the costs of production, especially on their *tamorka* plots. Munavvar also has a *tamorka* of 12 sotka, where she has been planting rice for four or five years because it is more profitable. She gets a double crop by planting rice before and after growing wheat. Again, all the work except for ploughing is carried out manually by women.

---

[28] There are several cotton-picking periods, as bolls mature at different times. The first harvest, which starts at the bottom of the bush, is the first 'sort', which fetches the highest price. There are four 'sorts' between the end of August and November, with both the quantity and quality getting lower. Eighty per cent of the cotton is picked during September and is of the best quality.

[29] In his speech to the Tenth Session of the Oliy Majlis, President Karimov acknowledged the decline in levels of mechanization, in particular in the use of combine harvesters for the cotton harvest. Whereas in 1992–3 combines harvested up to 40 per cent of the crop, in 1996 this went down to 6 per cent and only 4 per cent in 1997. In many places, and in Ferghana especially, practically the whole crop is picked manually. Although local authorities blame this on the shortage of machines or their bad state of repair and maintenance, there is evidence that machines may be lying idle: of 1480 units of machinery in Dzhizak, only 542 were utilized; in Syrdarya of 1453 machines, only 867 worked (Karimov 1997). Many enterprise managers argue that not only is there enough surplus labour, but that many households rely on harvesting wages as their only source of cash. Others point out that the machines are so old and in such a bad state of repair that they make the cotton 'dirty' and lower its quality, hence a preference for 'clean' manually picked cotton. A manager in an area of labour shortage, who had purchased a new American harvester, felt that machine harvested cotton was just as clean because of the quality of his machine.

Ziver, who is 38 years old, does not yet have daughters-in-law but relies on her school age children. She echoes Sanem and Munavvar on the question of their self-sufficiency in labour: 'We have enough labour power to do our own work. I have four children, two are still in school but the others have finished. They all help. We do everything by hand on our *tamorka.*'

Clearly, women's labour plays a crucial role both in the *shirkat* and small-holder economy. The 'feminization' of collective work, especially in the cotton fields, is not new. While the administrative/managerial cadres of collectives as well as the skilled jobs (such as tractor and harvester operators and irrigation engineers) are occupied by men, the bulk of the manual work is done by women. This involves the operations of *jagona* (weeding), *chikanka* (thinning cotton bolls) and picking. This work has become more onerous since the introduction of polythene covers as protection from late frosts. This does not only lengthen the growing season, but also necessitates back breaking work, since hoes can no longer be used for weeding and thinning. Women report weeding with spoons (*loshka*), bent over low, under the glare of plastic sheeting. Apart from harvest-ing wages, which are paid weekly and in cash, women only receive payment in kind for their work in the cotton fields.[30] Women's contribution to private plot production depends on a wide range of factors such as the availability of irriga-tion, the type of crops grown and the age and gender composition of their households.[31] The extent to which women's unremunerated labour and non-monetized exchanges between female kin and neighbours contribute to keeping both the cotton economy and the smallholder sector afloat is a question that deserves further detailed scrutiny.[32] However, the accommodations described in the case of Ok Bugday may become inoperative under conditions where the crop mix permits the fuller development of competitive leasehold markets and where access to land for *shirkat* workers is further curtailed. This is what we see in the case of Eski Kishlak in Andijan.

[30] In 1997, I calculated the cash equivalent of the in-kind payment made to a *hektardji* (someone who takes care of 1 ha of cotton year round) as follows: 15 litres of oil at 140 sums per litre (2100 sums), 30 kg of rice at 80 sums per kg (2400 sums), 70 kg of flour at 40 sum per kg (2800 sums), making a total of 7300 sums. If calculated as a yearly wage, this would fall below the then official minimum wage of 750 sums per month. However, the work is seasonal and there is a break during the winter months. The cotton harvest, which is paid extra in cash, provided her with a 2-week supply of oil plus some extra cash at 4 sums per kg of cotton.
[31] For instance, in the semi-arid province of Kashkadarya, private plot production remains limited to poor quality wheat and forage crops and men predominate in the livestock economy, which is the mainstay of rural livelihoods. In Andijan, by contrast, rice is the main household cash crop and absorbs all available labourers in a context of high unemployment and underemployment. Women have to allocate their labour between *shirkat* and household plots, whereas unemployed men tend to work on private plots.
[32] Similar arguments have been made elsewhere, suggesting that women's subsistence production in agriculture subsidizes the non-agricultural workforce. However, such assertions need to be carefully qualified in different contexts. For instance, Hart (1994) refutes this notion in the Malaysian case, since the State itself provides generous subsidies to rice producers in the form of inputs and price supports. What lends such a contention greater credence in the case of Uzbekistan is that agriculture is being squeezed and women's unremunerated labour is central to this process. Moreover, women's labour is deployed both in the subsistence and export sectors.

The Rise of the Mardigor:[33] *Land Hunger in Eski Kishlak*

Eski Kishlak *sovkhoz*, in Andijan province, was transformed into a closed joint stock company (JSC) in 1999. The process of distribution of shares, the organization of production through contracts with family leaseholders and the chequebook system for accounting follow the principles described in relation to the Ok Bugday *shirkat* above, with minor differences.[34] However, there have been significant changes in cropping patterns in Eski Kishlak. The drive for self-sufficiency in grain since independence has meant that part of the acreage previously allocated to feed crops and cotton is now planted to wheat. Until five years ago, there was relatively little wheat cultivation in Eski Kishlak. In 1997, *shirkat* land was allocated to the following crops: cotton (1429 ha), wheat (429 ha), rice (10 ha) orchards (8 ha) and other crops (90 ha).[35] By 2000, this balance had changed in favour of wheat (1050 ha), with more than a doubling of acreage in the space of three years.

These shifts in cropping patterns have had a more profound impact on land tenure and labour deployment than farm restructuring *per se*. Unlike cotton, wheat makes it possible to plant other crops after the harvest in June. Those who can afford it have started leasing land from the *shirkat* at competitive prices to grow rice after the wheat harvest. There has also been a shift from *devzire* (the local variety) to *ak shali* (white rice), which has much higher yields (almost double) and fetches a similar price. Whereas previously local *devzire* rice was planted in early spring, now a second crop of white rice is planted after the wheat harvest in July. This crop is ready for harvest in September. The fact that the rice harvest coincides with the cotton-picking season does not appear to create labour bottlenecks because of the high number of unemployed (*bekarjilar*). In 1997, there were already some signs that unemployed women were coming together in teams of casual labourers (*mardigor*), offering their services mainly on paddy fields. Although most people still harvest their own rice, those who have larger plots and all independent farmers increasingly employ *mardigors*.

The visible increase in the supply of casual agricultural labour in Eski Kishlak is the result both of growing unemployment and of changing cropping patterns that have produced a substantial increase in labour intensive operations. There is a gendered division of labour among casual workers; teams of men equipped with scythes (*orakchi*) work at the rice harvest, whereas teams of women work at weeding. In 2000, men received 6 kg of rice per sotka harvested (amounting to a minimum of 1500 sums per day), whereas women received a daily wage of about

---

[33]   Local term for casual wage labourer (from Persian).
[34]   Here the holders of chequebooks are the brigade chiefs who act as intermediaries between family leaseholders and *shirkat* management. There is considerable confusion over the use of these chequebooks and a great deal of bitterness on the part of leaseholders, who complain that the *shirkat* fails to provide them with timely inputs of fertilizer and technical support and yet holds them responsible for their yields.
[35]   These data were obtained from earlier fieldwork in 1997–8 (see Kandiyoti 1999a, Rural Domestic Economy and Female Labour Supply in Uzbekistan: Assessing the Feasibility of Gender-targeted Micro-credit Schemes, Final Report, DFID, ESCOR Unit, Grant no. R6978).

700 sums, amounting to less than half.[36] To the extent that both avenues for alternative earnings and access to additional plots have been decreasing, new pressures are at work to find additional earnings in casual work in agriculture.

The case of Mavluda, who is the head of a team of ten women *mardigor*, is indicative of these pressures. Her husband, who is employed by the poultry factory in Eski Kishlak, received 15 sotka of land as his wage (*ish hakki*). However, the poultry factory only provides land to those who accept to grow corn as chicken feed for the factory or to provide the corn in exchange for the land. Some years ago, they had not been able to obtain any land, since they had no money to purchase corn. Mavluda's earnings as a casual worker made it possible to make the purchase and secure the plot where they now grow rice. Mavluda had already lost her own job as a cleaner in a school and has since taken up casual agricultural work on a regular basis. This provides her and her team with some earnings almost year round.[37] The best-paid work is in rice operations, although it is now men who have taken over the more lucrative harvesting operations.[38]

Other members of Mavluda's team also report using their wages from casual work to raise money for other activities. Rahima, who is 17 years old, has been working as a *mardigor* for two years. She trained as a dressmaker and uses her earnings from casual agricultural work to finance a more lucrative activity, namely sewing school uniforms for children. She is under great pressure to bring in additional earnings and describes the situation of her family as follows:

> We are twelve in our house. My father is a *hektardji* and leases 2.5 ha of cotton land from the *shirkat*. My mother is a pensioner. My older brother also works in a cotton brigade with his wife. They have two children. My other older brother also works in the *shirkat*. His wife is on maternity leave now. They also have two children. I have another older brother who is single like me. We all work together on the family leasehold. We have 20 *sotka* around our house but no private plot (*tamorka*). We don't qualify for more plots unless my brothers get separate houses, but they can't do it. We put in a petition asking for separate house plots three years ago, but we didn't get them. Nowadays it is very difficult to get a plot and so many families like us are staying together because they can't separate.

Many *mardigor* live in households where labour resources far outstrip their access to land and where opportunities for alternative earnings are severely limited. They have either lost their existing jobs or failed to find a job after leaving school. In Eski Kishlak, there is a recognized category of unemployed and landless

---

[36] This means, in effect, that a family leaseholder has an interest in letting the women of his household get on with the cotton harvest for the *shirkat* while he hires himself out as an *orakchi* at higher rates of pay.

[37] In March they plant cotton, in April and May they work at *jagona* (weeding) in cotton fields, in June they work on paddy fields, in July they have the onion harvest and from August to November they pick cotton.

[38] The same team of women *mardigor*, which was smaller at the time, reported working at the rice harvest in 1997.

people (*yersizler ve ishsizler*) whose number is estimated at about one third of the population. However, this is a process of 'hidden' landlessness. What typically happens is that newly married couples who apply for a separate house plot (*chek*) and want to register as a separate household unit, thereby meeting the legal requirement for receiving an additional private subsidiary plot, are denied the possibility of doing so. As a result, multiple family households continue to live together with only one *tamorka* to share among them. Since they technically constitute a single household unit, they are not considered as landless. However, the supply of household labour is far greater than their access to productive resources or to paid employment.

This situation is undoubtedly aggravated by the fact that Eski Kishlak is situated in the province of Andijan, which has the highest population density (of 513.7 people per square km as compared to the national average of 54.2) in the country. The fertile Ferghana valley, an ancient centre of sedentary farming in a semi-arid zone, has long been recognized as a demographic time bomb and noted for its high rates of unemployment and underemployment.[39] However, this is not the only phenomenon at work. A process of incipient commodification through the operations of a leasehold market in land is polarizing access to land, squeezing out weaker claimants. Before the expansion of wheat cultivation in Eski Kishlak and the change in cropping patterns referred to above, the amount of common land that could be redistributed for personal use was relatively limited, since the cotton crop cycle does not permit replanting after harvest. Household land resources consisted of house plots, *tamorka* land and, less frequently, leased non-irrigated land. With the increased acreage of wheat, the quantity of common land that can be reallocated to household use has, in fact, increased. *Shirkat* workers who receive no remuneration (except for a limited quantity of foodstuffs) feel they are entitled to a share of that land and express bitterness about being fobbed off with tiny parcels of bad quality land.

These sentiments were expressed by Oyashkhon, who is the leader of a team of four family leaseholds working on 5 ha of cotton land. She and the other four members on her team had not been paid their wages, although they performed all the manual operations on the cotton crop.[40] Hers was a tale of broken promises and unfair dealings. She resented the fact that she was held responsible for the cotton yields when, in fact, the *shirkat* failed to provide the amount of irrigation and fertilizer that was necessary. She also felt indignant at the fact that she

---

[39] One of the policy responses during the Soviet period was the reclamation of desert and steppe land with 'virgin lands' projects. These were capital-intensive projects requiring massive investment in irrigation, farming equipment and social infrastructure. The new collectives attracted migrants, mainly from parts of the valley experiencing acute land shortages. These tended to be younger families that paternal households and local enterprises were unable to accommodate. Out-migration from the valley to 'desert' *oblasts* even further afield (such as Djizzak and Surhandarya) was not uncommon. The current fiscal crisis has hit such enterprises particularly hard. Lack of water means that self-subsistence and petty trade from household plots is not a livelihood option here. As a result, there is evidence that many families have started to leave and are going back to their villages of origin in the Ferghana Valley.

[40] Instead, they each received 1 kg of butter, 2 kg rice, 5 kg of pasta and 100 kg of wheat.

was only given a bad quality 10 sotka plot after the wheat harvest, on which she could only grow sunflowers and sweet corn, while the good land was 'sold' to those who could afford to pay. 'I have approached the manager several times', she said, 'but he tries to evade me'.

To better grasp the sense of grievance expressed by *shirkat* workers, we must remind ourselves of the terms of the social contract between collective farm managers and their workforce during the Soviet period. Work on cotton plots has long been regarded as a form of *corvee* labour, which hardly paid a living wage, even less so since the financial collapse of the collective farming sector. However, *kolkhoz* workers were given various forms of usufruct rights to common land and to personal plots in compensation for their collective labour obligations. There was also an expectation of receiving some assistance with inputs such as tractors and fertilizer for the cultivation of personal plots. Access to formal benefits was complemented by more informal mechanisms of paternalistic responsibility *vis-à-vis* workers, such as helping them to defray the costs of life cycle ceremonies or assisting those stricken by personal tragedy (as we saw above, in the case of Ok Bugday).

These accommodations are being tested to breaking point in Eski Kishlak. Land leased to independent farmers and tenants on a short- or longer-term basis reduces the pool out of which allocations can be made to households. This has meant that the claims of *shirkat* workers to additional plots are marginalized in favour of those who have the means to pay. The fact that this is taking place in a context of contraction of alternative, non-farm employment, which might have created avenues for diversification, fuels intense land hunger and a consequent sense of betrayal. Nonetheless, *shirkat* employees, such as Oyashon, strive to retain some of their prerogatives and to exert pressure on the management to honour what they see as their implicit normative obligations. This fallback position is denied to members of bankrupt collective enterprises that are in the process of being dismantled under the terms of the 'sanation' programme mentioned earlier. Some of the consequences of the liquidation of collective enterprises are illustrated below.

Liquidating the Collective: Reluctant Farmers at Yengi Kishlak

A volatile and uncertain future seems to await the members of enterprises that have moved to outright liquidation. This is apparent in the case of Yengi Kishlak Farmers' Association (*farmer birlashmasi*) in Khorezm. When the Yengi Kishlak kolkhoz was declared bankrupt in 1999, a Liquidation Committee was set up by the *hokimiyat* (district governorate). This Committee sold all the assets of the collective to pay off its debts and the remainder was taken over by those former members of the collective who became the new independent farmers.[41] The land

---

[41] These debts were owed to the providers of various inputs, such as MTPs (machine-tractor parks), the State petroleum company and agrochemical firms and amounted roughly to 50,000 sums per hectare in debt arrears for each farmer with five years to repay the debt.

of the collective was made available to prospective farmers by advertisement and applications were sought from members of the former collective. An examination was organized by a committee of 14 experts, headed by the deputy governor of the province (in line with the provisions of the 1998 Land Law), as a result of which 53 new farms were created. There are now a total of 65 farms including 12 that had been formed prior to the break-up of the collective; one is a livestock farm, 11 are fruit farms on orchard land and 56 are mixed cotton and grain (rice and wheat) farms.

The existing demarcations of land lots were kept intact and land parcels were allocated to prospective farmers by lottery to avoid disagreements over size and quality. The parcels range from a maximum of 97.7 ha to 1 ha. Moreover, the enterprises designated as 'farms' are not homogenous entities. They range from single household operations (as in the case of 11 households that cultivate orchards) to groups of family leaseholders cultivating the same parcel. On larger tracts of cotton and rice fields, there may be anything up to 15 or more former family leaseholders (*oila pudratchisi*), an important point to which we shall return.[42]

Whereas previously independent farmers were allocated land by applying to the collective farm and seeking approval of its General Meeting, these new farmers had their allocations directly ratified by the Land Registry. In principle, they have leases ranging between a minimum of 10 and a maximum of 50 years.[43] Each year a new contract is transacted between these farmers and the district branches of Government-controlled product processing associations. They have state orders (*Goszakaz*) for different crops and have to deliver 50 per cent of their wheat and rice and 100 per cent of the cotton. They may receive credit at a discretionary rate of 15 per cent and have a tax holiday for two years.

Some of the tensions inherent in this process of 'farmerization' may be best understood with reference to concrete cases. Munavvar Hodjaeva is the only new woman farmer in Yengi Kishlak Farmers'Association. She is an attractive 37-year-old mother of two children, who is an agronomist by training. She studied at the Tashkent Agrarian Institute, where she specialized as an entomologist. She

[42] Before the break-up of the collective, *kolkhoz* land was cultivated by 550 family leaseholds (*oila pudrati*). The management entered into contracts with the various buyers and providers of inputs on behalf of the whole enterprise. Now that each farmer transacts his/her own contract directly with input providers and with the buyers of crops, they also receive their production advances directly from the buyers, in accordance to the terms of their contracts. However, the former family leaseholders are still working on the same land. The new farmers have to draw up yearly work contracts with them (*mihnat shartnamesi*) undertaking to pay a monthly salary for their work (*ish hakki*) depending on the acreage that they cultivate. In principle, the farmers have the legal right not to renew these contracts, but the prospect of evicting fellow members of the collective who have cultivated the same family leaseholds for long years must present thorny problems. There is some anecdotal evidence about people 'changing places' to be with their relatives and of new farmers inviting members of their wider kin group to work on their farms. However, it is too early yet to draw any inferences from such information.

[43] However, some respondents reported shorter leases. If after two years the farms fail to keep to the terms of their contract, their leases may be revoked and the land reallocated, pointing to a probationary period in this instance.

used to work for the collective as an agronomist and received a salary of 6000 sums per month. However, she lost her job when the collective was liquidated and applied to become a farmer. She was allocated 26 ha of land on which six families worked as leaseholders: 13 ha of this land is planted to cotton and 12.5 ha to rice.

At first sight, the appearance of a relatively young woman among the ranks of the new independent farmers seemed unexpected. In those instances where rural women are found in decision-making roles, there is often a bias towards older, post-menopausal women with married children and daughters-in-law. However, this apparent anomaly disappeared upon closer scrutiny of the profiles of those who were selected as farmers out of the total pool of applicants at Yengi Kishlak.

Sixty-two per cent of the new farmers are members of the technical/administrative cadres of the former collective, with only 38 per cent rank and file *kolkhoz* workers whose primary occupation is agriculture.[44] In keeping with this profile, 32 per cent of the farmers have University-level education, 29 per cent technical/vocational education and 38 per cent only middle school education. This amounts to a high proportion of farmers (61 per cent) with tertiary level schooling.

My initial interpretation of the technocratic discourse implicit in the 1998 Land Law (with its insistence on formal examinations to issue farmers' certificates) was that it represented an attempt to underscore the meritocratic basis of the decisions taken, presenting them as devoid of favouritism or preferential treatment. The data from Yengi Kishlak suggests that more pressing concerns may also be at work. The redeployment of former technical cadres made redundant by the break-up of the collective clearly constitutes a top priority. It must be recognized that these cadres possess 'social capital' accrued from their experience with collective farming; their ability to enter into transactions with input providers and marketing boards in their own right is higher than that of rank and file members of the collective. It is as a member of this stratum, as a trained agronomist, that Munavvar Hodjaeva found herself among the ranks of the new farmers. Needless to say, this type of recruitment has a built-in gender bias. Very few women occupy administrative and technical positions in collective enterprises. Women are concentrated either in unskilled agricultural work or in social sector jobs in health and education.[45]

---

[44] Their occupational breakdown is as follows: Teacher, 6 (9 per cent); Agronomist, 4 (6 per cent); Book-keeper, 13 (20 per cent); Engineer/mechanic, 9 (14 per cent); Water engineer/technician, 3 (5 per cent); Construction technician, 1 (1.5 per cent); Veterinary, 1 (1.5 per cent); Legal expert, 2 (3 per cent), Librarian, 1 (1.5 per cent); *Kolkhoz* worker, 25 (38.5 per cent); this makes a total of 65.

[45] The management of farms (as distinct from agricultural work) is seen as an unambiguously masculine role. This is clearly illustrated by the case of Mahbuba Albaeva, a widow who started her own enterprise in December 1997. She was trained as an agronomist and was formerly a brigade leader on the Amir Timur *kolkhoz* in Andijan, where she worked for 20 years. She was also a union (*profkom*) representative and the deputy head of the *selsovyet*, which means that she was well integrated into the circle of local administrators in her district. Although Mahbuba is the head of the farm, she hires the services of a male manager (*ish yurutudju*) whose job is to find fertilizer, draw up the contracts with crop marketing boards and hire mechanics when necessary.

It would be highly pertinent to compare the profiles of independent farmers who applied for land allocations on an individual, voluntary basis with the 'new' farmers of liquidated enterprises. Although no systematic data exist on this subject, it is possible to infer that the 'early' farmers were individuals in a position to initiate and carry through the complicated bureaucratic steps involved in receiving an allocation. This required, among other things, adequate knowledge of the application procedures and good relations with district authorities who have the final say. Not surprisingly, members of collective farms who are in higher administrative echelons are best placed to clear the necessary hurdles. Paradoxically, the fact that many aspiring farmers were still in employment as managerial or technical cadres may inadvertently have increased the number of 'registered' women farmers. Since only 'full-time' farmers are legally entitled to receive land, men holding administrative posts resorted to registering their wives as the titular head of their farming enterprise. Therefore, the number of registered women farmers provides a very imperfect guide to women's land entitlements and offers little insight into the actual mechanisms that lead women to become the titular heads of farms.

Leaving farming altogether is an option that is unavailable to the majority of technical cadres in Yengi Kishlak in a context of deepening unemployment. The farming option, on the other hand, brings with it new problems and dilemmas that are well illustrated by the case of Munavvar Hodjaeva.

The 26 ha of land Munavvar was allocated already had six family leaseholders working on it. They each cultivate the same mix of crops, 2.5 ha of cotton and 2 ha of paddy, with one family also raising silkworm. All the families, including her own, retain their *tamorka* plots, which are planted with wheat and vegetables on a double-cropping basis. These 'sitting tenants' now have to be incorporated into Munavvar's farm as workers. She signed work contracts (*mihnat shartnamesi*) with six individuals who are the heads of their family leaseholds. Only those individuals are entitled to receive a salary (*ish hakki*), although she acknowledges that they actually work as entire families, with at least three or four people contributing to production. At the peak of harvest, they may also employ occasional labourers, who only get daily wages. Asked whether she had any difficulty keeping up with these payments, she acknowledged she had encountered serious problems. Although she had received her first tranche of advances for cotton and for silkworm, the money had not been sufficient. She had to use her own resources by selling her animals and the produce of her *tamorka*. She was aware of the precariousness of her situation, but could not entertain the possibility of depriving the family leaseholders, who were after all her neighbours and colleagues, of their plots by substituting them with rented machinery and casual labour. Asked what she would like to do if she had a choice, she unhesitatingly replied that she wanted her former job back.

Similar sentiments were echoed by other 'new' farmers. One of them exclaimed: 'We sold 88,000 sums worth of animals. You see, we were dreaming of a plot of 4–5 hectares. Instead we drew a plot of 37 ha. What misfortune!'.

Although it may seem surprising that anyone should bemoan receiving a large parcel of land, the conditions under which these allocations were made make this reaction quite understandable. Although the land now 'belongs' to individual farmers on long leases, the conditions under which production decisions are made have not changed. The farmers are still tied into the unprofitable procurement system. Aside from meeting the terms of their delivery contracts, they now have the additional burden of having to pay their own workforce and remaining solvent all at once. This means, in effect, that both the social costs of production and the risks involved have been passed on to them. In a relatively short period many may face the dilemma of having to evict most of their workforce or face bankruptcy. Setting up as farmers has meant, in many cases, having to dig into private household reserves by selling animals or using *tamorka* crops to capitalize their enterprise. Since they do not have the option of diversifying into more profitable crops, they can only attempt to cut their costs.

Writing in the very different context of reconstitution of private landownership rights in Eastern Europe, Verdery (forthcoming) argues that land in Transylvania is being devalued and turned into a negative asset through privatization by covertly assigning risks and obligations to new owners. She argues that decollectivization is about making land a carrier of liabilities, giving people land rights to produce owners who will take on the debts for the costs of machinery, inputs, irrigation and repairs and eventually liability to tax. In Uzbekistan, where the rights of ownership are, in fact, reduced to leaseholding under binding contractual obligations that leave little room for manoeuvre, the new farmers are faced with unacceptable liabilities. While those who have become reluctant farmers struggle with their current predicament, former family leaseholders are likely to be marginalized in the process of liquidating collective enterprises. This will further intensify the search for alternative sources of livelihood.

In summary, different patterns of restructuring can be seen to produce different outcomes for women. In Ok Bugday, there is an intensification of women's allocation of labour time to different plots (family leaseholds, house and *tamorka* plots). The decline of mechanization, changes in the production of cotton[46] and the high cost of inputs mean that manual labour and non-monetary exchanges are substituted on both leaseholds and household plots. The same applies to women in Eski Kishlak. However, higher population pressure and the polarization of access to land means that there is now a growing pool of casual agricultural labourers, with women concentrated in the lower wage operations. In Yengi Kishlak, the liquidation of the collective farm and the creation of independent farms has a clear bias in favour of the technical/administrative cadres of the former enterprise. This, by and large, excludes women who are very weakly represented among these cadres. While women in the collective sector are mainly unskilled workers, women in skilled professions are found in non-agricultural occupations. It is to the fortunes of these occupations that we turn our attention next.

---

[46] The most relevant in terms of increasing women's workloads is the use of polythene sheeting as protection for cotton seedlings.

JUGGLING LIVELIHOODS: DIVERSIFICATION OR INVOLUTION?

Social infrastructure, especially in health and education, was relatively well developed in Soviet Uzbekistan. Rural industries – often directly related to the collective farm sector – also existed in many localities. Non-agricultural occupations in teaching, health services and rural industries represented a significant alternative avenue for gainful employment for women in rural Uzbekistan. These sectors were major casualties of the post-Soviet recession. Many rural industrial enterprises have either closed down altogether or continue to operate with a reduced workforce that receives irregular wages or payments in kind. However threadbare the safety net afforded by these enterprises, women consider it a privilege to remain 'on the books', since it gives them access to benefits. Enterprises endeavour to maintain this safety net by refraining from outright dismissal, resorting instead to putting workers on extended unpaid leave or maternity leave.

Women workers at the towel factory in Eski Kishlak and the poultry factory in Yengi Kishlak conceded that, although shift work increased their work burden considerably, since they were also expected to work on household plots and family leaseholds, the right to maternity benefits which are paid in cash (in an otherwise de-monetized economy) provided a powerful incentive to stay on.[47] However, 'informalization' is now built into the structure of employment in formal enterprises. Women getting paid in kind (such as receiving towels, eggs or chickens) means that wages have to go through the medium of informal trade or interaction with wholesalers to take the form of cash. Thus any distinction that may have existed between salaried employment and the second economy has now dissolved. It may be argued, nonetheless, that women affiliated to an enterprise strengthen their fallback position when they enter the informal labour market, since they have recourse to benefits and claims to factory land that are denied to those who no longer have a registered job.[48] This combination of a registered job, with very low or nominal wages but with pension rights, and more lucrative informal occupations is one way of maximizing options within the current context of constraints. Household livelihood portfolios may be constructed around achieving optimal combinations of occupations carrying benefits with more lucrative informal pursuits. Thus, as we saw in the case of Mavluda above, a woman *mardigor* may opt to use her earning in casual agricultural work to finance production on a household plot that her husband is entitled to by virtue of being a factory worker. Or a woman rice trader may decide to keep her teaching job on a part-time basis to retain her pension rights, although it is trading that actually provides her with a livelihood.

---

[47] There is a certain irony to this, since women's likelihood of receiving actual cash incomes increases when they are on benefit than actually at work. This does not mean that maternity and child benefit is always paid on time and being put on maternity leave is sometimes a euphemism for being laid off. However, the young women interviewed reported receiving the benefits on time.

[48] Employment in Uzbekistan continues to be tied to the workbook system (*mihnat daftachasi*) inherited from the Soviet period. For further details, see Kandiyoti (1999b).

However, labour retrenchment in social services, industry and collective enterprises has caused numerous women to fall through the safety net altogether. Under these circumstances, the only avenues for income-generation are found in precarious forms of self-employment in informal trade and services. The trajectory of Rosa, a 51-year-old, divorced Korean woman with a single daughter, illustrates the increasing precariousness of these livelihoods. She went from being a trained book-keeper working for the *sovkhoz* to being employed at a poultry factory where she lost her job and finally took up catering out of her home, taking orders for cakes and bakery items for special occasions and selling pickled vegetables and Korean salads. Her daughter also works from home as a dressmaker.

Although Rosa feels that she and her daughter have an established clientele, the problem with the type of work they engage in is that many women possess similar skills. There has been a veritable explosion of women offering dressmaking or catering services for relatively meagre returns. The market for their services is relatively limited, since there is an oversupply of such services and a shortage of cash. This is also the case for the preparation of food, which draws on an even more abundant skill than sewing. Especially in the winter months, when there is neither agricultural work, nor any cash salaries coming in, peddling ready-cooked food in local markets is resorted to by many women. Men previously working in construction brigades or technical jobs with skills such as carpentry, brick-laying or motor maintenance are better able to secure lucrative forms of self-employment. In the case of women, the competitive niches they occupy, already oversupplied by armies of unemployed, seldom constitute a viable avenue of diversification into non-farm self-employment, but instead increase the already existing pressures on these limited avenues of income generation. Whereas some skilled men may achieve more sustainable forms of self-employment, women's attempts to reduce poverty have involutionary properties that do not offer good long-term prospects.[49]

The more lucrative trading operations that women engage in, whether as middle women, wholesalers of agricultural produce, clothing or domestic appliances, require courage, wit and resourcefulness. The most profitable types of activity involve forms of cross-border trade that are not without a certain amount of risk, since women have to negotiate border crossings and bazaar permits.[50] Moreover, this type of option is mainly open to women who have both the perceived justification (being widowed with children, having an unemployed husband) or the moral authority (relatively advanced age) to be allowed a higher

---

[49] Hart (1994) makes a distinction between diversification for accumulation and diversification for survival. Women's informal activities in rural Uzbekistan, with few exceptions, generally fall into the latter category. Ellis (1998) also draws attention to gender-based constraints to diversification.

[50] Women rice traders reported crossing the border to Osh or Jalalabad to sell their produce and suggested that differences in exchange rates accounted for most of their profit. However, access to such markets has become severely restricted since Afghanistan became a war zone. The implications of this conflict for rural livelihoods in Uzbekistan certainly deserve separate attention.

degree of mobility. There are signs, however, that younger women are under increasing pressure to conform to ideals of full-time domesticity and many would settle for less than ideal circumstances in marital unions that afford them fewer rights than previously.

A POST-SOVIET CONJUGAL CONTRACT?

Intra-household gender relations are highly variable and culturally embedded. In the case of the former Soviet Union, several paradoxes of Soviet policies, especially among non-European nationalities, have been noted. Despite the uniformity of the economic and legal changes imposed on Soviet rural life, especially the rigid limits set on productive property allowed to each household, the organization of the domestic domain remained highly specific to different localities and reflective of local conceptions of kinship (Humphrey 1983). This was also the case in Uzbekistan, despite the fact that the emancipation of women was a major item of Soviet ideology and practice in Central Asia (Massell 1964; Lubin 1981; Alimova 1991, 1998; Tokhtahodjaeva 1995; Kemp 1998). Whilst the norm of small, egalitarian families was being promoted by Soviet modernizers, ethnographers of Central Asia (such as Snesarev 1974; Poliakov 1992) were documenting the persistence of large, patriarchal families, the marriage of underage girls, and the payment of brideprice (*kalym*).

Family structure and the domestic cycle in rural Uzbekistan present significant similarities to patterns in the Middle East, South and East Asia where post-marital residence is virilocal, descent is traced through the patriline and son preference is a widespread norm. Although the Soviet system effectively restricted possibilities for accumulation and transmission of property, customary law that recognizes the marital domicile as the property of men continued to prevail. Widowed women with older children could be found as heads of their own households. However, divorced women and young widows are expected to return to their parental home and cannot lay claims to their marital residence.

However, despite similarities with patterns in the wider Muslim world and parts of South and East Asia, there are some distinctive features of rural women's employment in Uzbekistan that have been noted earlier. These have to do, on the one hand, with women's high literacy rates, due to an effective system of universal education and, on the other, a developed rural social infrastructure, providing women with a significant source of salaried jobs and opportunities for non-farm employment. These avenues for rural livelihoods are effectively being closed off, leaving their place to increasing 'informalization' and casual employment.

It is possible to detect a parallel erosion of the Soviet marital contract in favour of more fluid domestic arrangements. Under the Soviet system, the marriage ceremony had a dual structure; the religious ceremony of *nikoh* officiated at home or in a familiar setting and official civic registration of the marriage with the ZAGs (the registry office), usually followed by a visit to the local Lenin monument. Official registration gives women the legal means of pressing their rights to alimony in cases of divorce (*aliment*) and to child benefit. Nowadays, the expense of registration has increased substantially. Many couples only choose to register their marriage after their first child is born. Filing for an official divorce has become so prohibitively expensive that many separated couples dispense with this formality altogether. If they want to remarry, they simply resort to *nikoh*. This makes an accurate estimate of the actual incidence of polygyny in Uzbekistan virtually impossible. A man who only has one 'official' wife may take another spouse by *nikoh*. The children of these unions are recognized, however, and the mother receives her child benefit.

This state of affairs was confirmed by all the divorcees interviewed. For instance, Matluba, the owner of a private shop who separated in 1996, dispensed with an official divorce altogether. Her husband simply divorced her by *talaq* (pronouncing the formula 'I divorce thee'). He remarried by *nikoh* and has other children. If she had money to spare, she would invest in buying a separate house for herself and her young son rather than go through the expense of an official divorce. Although she currently co-habits with her parents, there will be no place for her when her single brothers marry and claim new living units for their families. This patrilineal bias makes Matluba feel so vulnerable that she entertains the possibility of remarriage as a second wife, despite her relative success in running her small business.

Although many justify *nikoh* and polygyny with recourse to Islamic custom, women admit upon further probing that they are deterred from having any dealings with bureaucracy because of the costs involved. This exposes them to greater vulnerability, since they have no recourse to the law. On the other hand, their apparent indifference to this state of affairs also suggests a lack of confidence in the use of official and bureaucratic channels to press their rights.[51]

During the Soviet period, women's interests were represented at the local level through the Women's Committees. Women had, in principle, access to a public forum to make complaints about domestic violence, drunkenness or neglect. Women's Committees still exist within *mahalla* (neighbourhood) committees, whose duties have now been enlarged to include the distribution of targeted welfare to the poorest (*nachar yordimi*).[52] There is some evidence that they are still used by women as a possible resource in cases of conflict, but this is taking place against a background of hardening attitudes regarding women's work and mobility.

Women's work was laden with positive value and made the object of persistent propaganda in Soviet Central Asia. Propaganda aside, mobility through education was not an unrealistic prospect and many women from rural backgrounds were recruited into a variety of professions. Nowadays, not only is education an

---

[51] Recourse to kin and to local mechanisms of mediation and settlement are probably used to greater effect, although a detailed study of how these mechanisms actually operate would be needed to draw any further inferences.

[52] The Government of Uzbekistan has since 1994 opted to target assistance to low-income families by devolving the distribution of assistance to local community groups, the neighbourhood or *mahalla*. For an assessment of this system, see Coudouel and Marnie (1999).

expensive commodity but the equation between obtaining a diploma and making a good living has been totally disrupted in a context where a flagging public sector remains the principal employer. This is compounded for women by a new emphasis on 'traditional' Uzbek values that are being promoted and valorized as an item of post-Soviet nation-building. It would be too simplistic to attribute growing social conservatism to a tide of Islamic feeling in a context where the Women's Committee of Uzbekistan, which reflects governmental positions, staged a nation-wide competition in 1998 to identify the 'Best Daughter-in-Law'. This contest, which was beamed to the nation on television day after day, highlighted the qualities of docility, maternal caring and competent housekeeping as the ideals of Uzbek womanhood. The 'Year of the Family' that followed reinforced the same message.

The decline in women's opportunities for gainful employment is accompanied by an 'informalization' of the marriage contract.[53] The official registration of marriage and divorce are seen as costly obligations that can easily be dispensed with in favour of *nikoh* and *talaq*. Although there have been no legal changes sanctioning polygamy or unilateral divorce, these may become widespread in practice as more and more people resort to them. The male bias inherent in Uzbek kinship practices, which may have been somewhat attenuated under the Soviet system through the provision of free universal education and the sanctioning of female employment, may assert itself in new and more self-consciously ideologized ways. Although the effects of these shifts in mood and ideology may appear intangible, they do modify the social rules of access to non-domestic arenas and the legitimacy of women's economic pursuits.

These changes are taking place in the absence of women's movements or civic platforms where women's interests may be articulated. The structure of Women's Committees at all levels of governance (from province to *mahalla* level) put in place during the Soviet period is still operational and serves mainly as a conduit for the transmission and implementation of governmental policy priorities. These policies, which during the Soviet period took the form of 'protection' of women's rights as working mothers (through protective legislation and generous benefits), are now continuing to target women primarily as reproducers of the new nation. The most active campaigns have focused on maternal health and family planning programmes (with special emphasis on birth spacing) as a means of producing a 'healthy generation'. There are few local NGOs with a specific interest in women's employment or income generation.[54] The reach of these projects remains limited and many initiatives have an urban bias.

---

[53]   It is not being suggested that there is a direct link between the two. Rather, we are witnessing the effects of a complex set of mutually reinforcing influences. The loss of jobs deepens poverty, which, in turn, produces a reluctance to resort to bureaucracies whose employees tend to introduce 'informal' charges to complement their own meagre incomes. This is taking place in a context where censure for polygyny is not as severe as it was during the Soviet period, since it can be justified with recourse to Islam.

[54]   Such as the Business Women's Association, which has served as the conduit for a number of gender-targeted micro-credit schemes.

CONCLUSION

The pace of agrarian reform in Uzbekistan has been slow compared to both its neighbours in Central Asia and to other countries undergoing market transitions in the FSU. The continued reliance on cotton as the major export crop and the stake the State retains in the maintenance of existing export revenues has made a shift away from the institutional structures of the former command economy a halting and difficult process.

Changing agrarian reform measures between 1990 and 1998 reflect different and somewhat incompatible priorities. An initial spate of legislation intended to expand households' access to private holdings was superseded by directives that distinguish between a smallholder (*dekhan*) sector with few prospects of graduation to commercial farming and a commercial sector of independent farms that, alongside restructured collective enterprises, are tied into the state procurement system through their contracts (*shartname*).

However, an exclusive focus on legal rights, reflected in changing codes, does very little to elucidate processes of transformation in social entitlements and access to land in rural Uzbekistan. As Hann reminds us, the focus on formal legal codes 'must be broadened to include the institutional and cultural contexts in which such codes operate' (1998, 7). When we conceptualize property in terms of the distribution of social entitlements, it is possible to detect a strongly gendered pattern of growing disadvantage among rural producers.

An understanding of changing entitlements must necessarily take account of the type of social contract represented by the Soviet collective farming system. In line with the more general principle of 'labour decommodification' operative in Soviet labour markets (Standing 1996), wages of collective workers were always low, but compensated for by a bundle of social benefits channelled through membership in enterprises, including access to a plot for household use. These formal benefits were complemented by more informal mechanisms of paternalistic responsibility *vis-à-vis* workers, such as helping them to defray the costs of life-cycle ceremonies or assisting those stricken by disease or personal tragedy.

The crisis in public finance that followed the break-up of the Soviet Union had important repercussions on the agricultural sector. Heavily indebted collective enterprises were no longer able to pay their workers' wages. As a result, reliance on household and subsidiary plots for self-subsistence and on off-farm and non-farm informal activities increased. Rural Uzbekistan underwent a dual process of *demonetization* and *reagrarianization*. The simultaneous objectives of the maintenance of cotton revenues and the provision of a basic level of self-subsistence for workers acted to consolidate the division between a stagnating smallholder sector and the export sector, the two being mutually dependent upon one another.

However, a thorough understanding of the actual workings of this mutual dependency must pass through gender analysis. An examination of labour allocation to family leaseholds, on which cotton production is based, reveals a clear preponderance of women. All the manual operations involved in the production of cotton are carried out by women, assisted by children. Although only one member of a leaseholding unit holds a contract that carries payment rights (*ish hakki*), all the female members of households, regardless of whether they also have other occupations, are expected to contribute. Divisions of labour on small-holdings (*tamorka*) vary in function of the livelihood portfolio of the household and the nature of the crops cultivated. However, as a general rule smallholders strive to economize on inputs and to substitute their own labour for machines and resort to reciprocal harvesting arrangements with neighbours and kin in order to make their plots go further, again increasing the demands on women's labour time. Under conditions of growing inequality in access to land and high levels of labour retrenchment in non-farm occupations, a growing number of men and women are also looking for casual agricultural work as *mardigor*. There are significant wage disparities between male and female *mardigor*.

In contrast to the marked feminization of labour in the family leasehold and smallholder sectors, the management of independent farms is recognized as a masculine pursuit. Not only are the numbers of registered women farmers small, but even fewer among those registered are actual managers of their enterprises, as opposed to being titular heads acting as a proxy for husbands or sons. Women farmers who act as managers, although they continue to be at a disadvantage in the exclusively male networks of input providers and crop buyers, tend to have a track record of administrative/technical responsibility in the collective farming sector.

Non-agricultural occupations in health, education and rural industry were major casualties of the post-Soviet recession. However threadbare the safety net afforded by employment in these sectors, women endeavour to stay 'on the books' even when they stop receiving cash wages. The most vulnerable are women who have fallen through the safety net altogether and have lost their entitlements to either land or benefits. The shift from brigade work to family contracts and, more recently, to shareholding *shirkats* have represented a progressive retrenchment of the agricultural labour force. The majority of those who have lost their registered jobs are, by the admission of all enterprise managers interviewed, women. This does not mean, however, that they are any less involved in agricultural production. They continue to work on land either as unpaid family labourers whose access to a plot is mediated through membership in a *shirkat* household or as casual labourers earning piece-wage rates mainly during the cotton harvest. Heads of Dekhan and Farmers' Associations suggested that alternative provision for women working in the *dekhan* sector is now legally available through contributory pension schemes. However, the notion that the resource-strapped smallholder sector will find the means to invest in the social security of its members is extremely far fetched. It is more likely that an increasing number of women will find themselves deprived of social benefits at a point in time when their claims to productive resources as members of collective enterprises are being rapidly eroded.

Under these circumstances, the only avenues for income-generation are found in precarious forms of self-employment in informal trade and services. There are increasing pressures on these occupational niches, however, since they are sought after by different categories of women for different reasons; those who are engaged in agriculture but experience seasonal unemployment during the winter months, those engaged in non-farm activities but unable to receive a living wage and finally those who have lost all other possibilities of gainful employment.

The cry for land among rural women in Uzbekistan is clamorous.[55] However, this is the product of a very specific conjuncture. It corresponds to a point in time when labour retrenchment in rural enterprises and growing inequalities in access to land are not attenuated by significant mechanisms of rural out-migration, receipts of migrant remittances and diversification into non-farm activities or viable forms of self-employment. Women are experiencing significant job losses in both the agricultural sector and in non-farm occupations against a background of mounting demands on their labour time in family leaseholds and on smallholdings as unpaid family labourers or as casual wage-workers. Prospects for expanding their access to land look dim in a context where access continues to be mediated through membership in enterprises, from which they are increasingly being excluded, or through leasehold markets and the independent farming path which also marginalizes them. Furthermore, land is not a commodity that can be purchased, sold or mortgaged and the rules of access continue to consist of a mixture of administrative fiat and market mechanisms that can be highly unpredictable in terms of security of tenure.

As we saw in the case of the reluctant farmers of Yengi Kishlak, land may become a carrier of liabilities which most farmers, including women, would wish to avoid. Hence an unambiguous preference by most women for their former, non-agricultural occupations.

Women's current hunger for land must therefore be understood in the context of both a wish to reinstate the terms of their former social contract with collective enterprises and their despair in the face of the apparent lack of any other alternatives. While the former is already a lost cause, the latter is a hostage to future developments. The revitalization of rural non-farm employment through new investment in industry and services and the adequate capitalization and diversification of their informal income-generation activities would offer many women more realistic short-term solutions to their current predicament. It is more difficult, however, to envisage how landless or poor rural women's organized interests might be represented in a context where neither civil society

---

[55] This was especially evident in Andijan, where all those interviewed, with the exception of a divorced caterer with a single daughter, vocally complained of not having access to sufficient land. However, this emphasis on land is shorthand for a more complex reality. Access to land under the Soviet system was organized through membership in enterprises. For instance, wage-work in factory was a route of access to a household plot. The loss of jobs is, in this context, equivalent to losses of entitlement to land as well as benefits. Among those in non-agricultural occupations, the utter hopelessness of getting their former jobs back reinforced their resolve to retain some access to land. Among agricultural workers the inability of former collective enterprises to honour their obligations to the workforce found expression in anger at being denied access to what was rightfully theirs. Under these circumstances, land becomes both a lifeline and focus for a more generalized narrative of 'loss'.

organizations, such as NGOs or professional associations, nor political parties or social movements have any significant presence. Their problems in finding a public voice may prove even more intractable than the economic hardships occasioned by post-Soviet recession and market transition.

REFERENCES

Agarwal, B., 1994. *A Field of One's Own*. Cambridge: Cambridge University Press.

Alimova, D., 1991. *Zhenski Vapros V Crednii Azii*, Tashkent.

Alimova, D., 1998. 'A Historian's Vision of *Khudjum*'. *Central Asian Survey*, 17 (1): 147–55.

Bridger, S., 1987. *Women in the Soviet Countryside*. Cambridge: Cambridge University Press.

Carley, P.M., 1989. 'The Price of the Plan: Perceptions of Cotton and Health in Uzbekistan and Turkmenistan'. *Central Asian Survey*, 8 (4): 1–38.

Coudouel, A. and S. Marnie, 1999. 'The Mahalla System of Allocating Social Assistance in Uzbekistan'. In *Central Asia 2010: Prospects for Human Development*, 182–90. New York: UNDP.

Craumer, P., 1992. 'Agricultural Change, Labor Supply and Rural Out-Migration in Soviet Central Asia'. In *Geographic Perspectives on Soviet Central Asia*, ed. R.A. Lewis, 132–80. New York: Routledge.

Craumer, P., 1995. *Rural and Agricultural Development in Uzbekistan*. London: The Royal Institute of International Affairs.

Davidson, J., ed., 1988. *Agriculture, Women and Land: The African Experience*. Boulder, CO: Westview Press.

Deere, C.D. and M. Leon, 2001. *Empowering Women: Land and Property Rights in Latin America*. Pittsburgh, PA: University of Pittsburgh Press.

Ellis, F., 1998. 'Household Strategies and Rural Livelihood Diversification'. *The Journal of Development Studies*, 35 (1): 1–38.

Fierman, W., 1997. 'Political Development in Uzbekistan: Democratisation?'. In *Conflict, Cleavage and Change in Central Asia and the Caucasus*, eds K. Dawisha and B. Parrott, 360–408. Cambridge: Cambridge University Press.

Gleason, G., 1991 'The Political Economy of Dependency under Socialism: The Asian Republics in the USSR'. *Studies in Comparative Communism*, 24 (4): 335–53.

Gleason, G., 1997. *The Central Asian States: Discovering Independence*. Boulder, CO: Westview Press.

Grossman, G., 1989. 'Informal Personal Incomes and Outlays in the Soviet Urban Population'. In *The Informal Economy*, eds A. Portes, M. Castells and L.A. Benton, 150–70. Baltimore, MA: The Johns Hopkins University Press.

Hann, C.M., ed., 1998. *Property Relations: Reviewing the Anthropological Tradition*. Cambridge: Cambridge University Press.

Hart, G., 1994. 'The Dynamics of Diversification in an Asian Rice Region'. In *Development or Deterioration? Work in Rural Asia*, eds B. Koppel, J. Hawkins and W. James, 47–71. Boulder, CO: Lynne Rienner.

Herman, M., 1999. 'Sustainable Agricultural Reform – the Case of Uzbekistan'. In *Central Asia 2010: Prospects for Human Development*, 84–95. New York: UNDP.

Humphrey, C., 1983. *Karl Marx Collective: Economy, Society and Religion in a Siberian Collective Farm*. Cambridge: Cambridge University Press.

Humphrey, C., 1998. *Marx Went Away – But Karl Stayed Behind*. Ann Arbor, MI: The University of Michigan Press.

Ilkhamov, A., 1998. '*Shikats, Dekhqon* farmers and others: farm restructuring in Uzbekistan'. *Central Asian Survey*, 17 (4): 539–60.

Ilkhamov, A., 2000. 'Divided Economy: Kolkhoz System vs. Peasant Subsistence Economy in Uzbekistan'. *Central Asia Monitor*, 4: 5–14.

IMF, 1998. *Republic of Uzbekistan: Recent Economic Developments*. IMF Staff Country Report No. 98/116. Washington, DC: IMF.

Kandiyoti, D., 1998. 'Rural Livelihoods and Social Networks in Uzbekistan: Perspectives from Andijan'. *Central Asian Survey*, 17 (4): 561–78.

Kandiyoti, D., 1999a. 'Rural Domestic Economy and Female Labour Supply in Uzbekistan: Addressing the Feasibility of Gender-Targeted Micro-Credit Schemes'. Final Report, DFID, ESCOR Unit Grant No. R6978 (mimeo).

Kandiyoti, D., 1999b. 'Poverty in Transition: An Ethnographic Critique of Household Surveys in Post-Soviet Central Asia'. *Development and Change*, 30 (3): 499–524.

Kandiyoti, D., 2002. 'How Far Do Analyses of Post-Socialism Travel? The Case of Central Asia'. In *Postsocialism: Ideals, Ideology and Practice in Eurasia*, ed. C. Hann, 238–57. London: Routledge.

Karimov, I., 1997. 'Development of Agriculture is a Source of Welfare of the People'. *Pravda Vostoka*, 26 December.

Kemp, M., 1998. 'Unveiling Uzbek Women: Liberation, Representation and Discourse, 1906–1929'. PhD thesis. University of Chicago, Illinois.

Khan, A.R., 1996. 'The Transition to a Market Economy in Agriculture'. In *Social Policy and Economic Transformation in Uzbekistan*, ed. K. Griffin, 65–91. Turin: ILO/UNDP.

Kitching, G., 1998. 'The Revenge of the Peasant? The Collapse of Large-Scale Russian Agriculture and the Role of the Peasant "Private Plot" in that Collapse, 1991–97'. *Journal of Peasant Studies*, 26 (1): 43–81.

Lerman, Z., 1998. 'Land Reform in Uzbekistan'. In *Land Reform in the Former Soviet Union and Eastern Europe*, ed. S.K. Wegren, 136–61. London: Routledge.

Lubin, N., 1981. 'Women in Central Asia: Progress and Contradictions'. *Soviet Studies*, 33 (2): 182–203.

Lubin, N., 1984. *Labour and Nationality in Soviet Central Asia*. London: Macmillan.

Massell, G., 1964. *The Surrogate Proletariat*. Princeton, NJ: Princeton University Press.

Poliakov, S., 1992. *Everyday Islam: Religion and Tradition in Rural Central Asia*. New York: M.E. Sharpe.

Pomfret, R., 1995. *The Economies of Central Asia*. Princeton, NJ: Princeton University Press.

Pomfret, R., 2000. 'Agrarian Reform in Uzbekistan: Why Has the Chinese Model Failed to Deliver?' *Economic Development and Cultural Change*, 48 (2): 269–84.

Razavi, S., ed., 2002. *Shifting Burdens: Gender and Agrarian Change under Neoliberalism*. Bloomfield, CT: Kumarian Press.

Rumer, B.Z., 1989. *Soviet Central Asia: A Tragic Experiment*. Boston, MA: Unwin Hyman.

Snesarev, G.P., 1974. 'On Some Causes of the Persistence of Religion-Customary Survivals among the Khorezm Uzbeks'. In *Introduction to Soviet Ethnography*, eds S.P. Dunn and E. Dunn, 215–38. Berkeley, CA: Highgate Road Social Science Research Station.

Standing, G., 1996. *Russian Unemployment and Enterprise Restructuring: Reviving Dead Souls*. London: Macmillan.

Spoor, M., 1993. 'Transition to Market Economies in Former Soviet Central Asia: Dependency, Cotton and Water'. *The European Journal of Development Research*, 5 (2): 142–58.

Spoor, M., 1995. 'Agrarian Transition in Former Soviet Central Asia: A Comparative Study of Uzbekistan and Kyrgyzstan'. *Journal of Peasant Studies*, 23 (1): 46–63.

TACIS/Government of Uzbekistan, 1996. 'Pilot Integrated Development Programme, Bulungur District, Samarkand, Uzbekistan'. Final Report BS6-Land Tenure. Tashkent: TACIS/Government of Uzbekistan.

Thurman, J.M., 1999. 'The "Command-Administrative" System in Cotton Farming in Uzbekistan, 1920s to Present'. Papers on Inner Asia No. 32. Bloomington, IN: Indiana University.

Tokhtahodjaeva, M., 1995. *Between the Slogans of Communism and the Laws of Islam*. Lahore: Shirkat Gah.

Trushin, E., 1998. 'Uzbekistan: Problems of Development and Reform in the Agrarian Sector'. In *Central Asia: The Challenges of Independence*, eds B. Rumer and S. Zhukov, 259–91. New York: M.E. Sharpe.

Verdery, K., forthcoming. 'The Obligations of Ownership: Restoring Rights to Land in Postsocialist Eastern Europe'. In *Property in Question*, eds C. Humphrey and K. Verdery. New York: Berghan Press.

World Bank, 1999. *Uzbekistan: Social and Structural Policy Review*. Report No. 19626. Washington, DC: World Bank.

8

Women's Land Rights and Rural Social Movements in the Brazilian Agrarian Reform

CARMEN DIANA DEERE

This article examines the evolution of the demand for women's land rights in the Brazilian agrarian reform through the prism of the three main rural social movements: the landless movement, the rural unions and the autonomous rural women's movement. Most of the credit for raising the issue of women's land rights rests with women within the rural unions. That women's formal land rights were attained in the constitutional reform of 1988 was largely a by-product of the effort to end discrimination against women in all it dimensions. The achievement of formal equality in land rights, nonetheless, did not lead to increases in the share of female beneficiaries of the reform, which remained low in the mid-1990s. This was largely because securing women's land rights in practice was not a top priority of any of the rural social movements. Moreover, the main social movement determining the pace of the agrarian reform, the land-less movement, considered class and gender issues to be incompatible. By the late 1990s, nonetheless, there was growing awareness that failure to recognize women's land rights was prejudicial to the development and consolidation of the agrarian reform settlements and thus the movement. The growing consensus among all the rural social movements of the importance of securing women's land rights, coupled with effective lobbying, encouraged the State in 2001 to adopt specific mechanisms for the inclusion of women in the agrarian reform.

Keywords: agrarian reform, social movements, women's land rights, Brazil

INTRODUCTION

From a gender perspective, the Brazilian agrarian reform stands out in terms of its relatively low share of female beneficiaries as compared with other Latin American countries. This is curious since Brazil in 1988 was among the first to stipulate explicitly that women could be potential beneficiaries and, along with

Most of the research for this paper was undertaken while the author was a Fulbright-Hays Scholar during 2000 at the Federal University of Rio de Janeiro. I am grateful to Paola Cappellin, Maria José Carneiro, and Anita Brumer for facilitating my research in Brazil, to Merrilee Mardon for research assistance, and to all the above for insightful comments on earlier versions of this article. I am also indebted to Magdalena León, with whom I conducted initial research in Brazil in 1998, for permission to use material in an earlier co-authored working paper.

Colombia, to introduce the possibility of joint adjudication and titling to couples of land distributed through the agrarian reform. Yet, in the mid-1990s, women constituted only 12.6 per cent of the beneficiaries in Brazil compared with 45 per cent in recent land distributions in Colombia. Further, a comparative analysis with Latin American countries that introduced gender-progressive agrarian legislation in the 1990s shows that these measures were least implemented in Brazil (Deere and León 2001). This raises the question of why it has been such a laggard in securing women's land rights.

One reason is that whereas in Brazil joint adjudication and titling to couples is an *option*, in most other countries it is now mandatory that lands distributed by the State be jointly titled. Given deep-seated cultural practices, supported by legal norms until recently,[1] that only husbands represent the household and manage its assets, it is not surprising that joint titling must be mandatory for this measure to be implemented in practice. Moreover, in most countries the attainment and implementation of gender-progressive legislation has depended on the existence of strong rural women's organizations and their persistence in demanding recognition of women's land rights (Deere and León 2001, chapter 6).

What is also curious about the Brazilian case is that rural women, beginning in the 1980s, began to participate in growing numbers in rural unions and in the nascent landless movement, as well as to form their own autonomous organizations (Deere and León 1999). Their demands for land rights were formally attained in the 1988 Federal Constitution, which established that in land to be distributed through the agrarian reform, 'land titles or use rights be given to men, to women, or to both, independent of their civil status' (Article 189, in da Luz 1996, 177). But, after 1988, there was relatively little follow-up with respect to implementing women's land rights.

It took 12 years until some of the rural social movements successfully championed women's land rights at the national level. In August 2000, the demand for the joint adjudication and titling of land to couples under the agrarian reform finally figured prominently in the largest national demonstration yet to be held of rural women. This march on the capital city of Brasilia, known as the *Marcha das Margaridas*, was coordinated by the Women's Commission of the national agricultural workers' union, CONTAG (Confederação Nacional dos Trabalhadores na Agricultura), in coalition with one of the regional organizations of autonomous rural women, the MMTR-NE (Movimento das Mulheres Trabalhadoras Rurais do Noreste) and other groups. As in other Latin American countries, once organized rural women began to demand land rights and consistently confront the State on this issue, the institute of agrarian reform, INCRA (Instituto Nacional de Colonização e Reforma Agraria) was forced to revise its regulations.

---

[1]   The 1988 Federal Constitution of Brazil established that 'the rights and obligations of the marital society are to be jointly exercised by the man and the woman' (Article 226, in CFEMEA 1996, 49). Most Latin American countries established the dual headed household through constitutional or civil code reform in the 1970s and 1980s (Deere and León 2001, Table 2.1).

The main question addressed in this article is why it took so long for organized rural women to demand effective recognition of their land rights. I argue that this is related to the multiple and often competing venues for participation which opened up to rural women in the 1980s and 1990s and the many priorities of these rural social movements. Moreover, it was not until the exclusion of women began to have real practical consequences for the consolidation of the agrarian reform settlements (the *assentamentos*) that women's land rights became an issue within the main social movement leading the agrarian reform, the MST (Movimento dos Trabalhadores Rurais Sem Terra), and for the State.

Recognition of the importance of women's land rights generally takes place for two reasons, what we have called elsewhere the 'productionist' and the 'empowerment' arguments (Deere and León 1998, 2001).[2] The productionist argument refers to the recognition that women's land rights are associated with an increase in the well-being of women and their children, as well as an enhancement of their productivity and, hence, the well-being of their community and society. The empowerment argument recognizes that women's land rights are critical to enhancing their bargaining power within the household and community, to ending their subordination to men and, hence, to achieving real equality between men and women. In Brazil, women gained formal land rights as a by-product of the process to achieve equality between men and women in all of its legal dimensions, through the expansion of women's rights in the 1988 Constitution. But the attainment of specific mechanisms of inclusion of women in the agrarian reform – to increase the share of women with effective land rights – was not achieved until the productionist arguments were better understood and internalized both by the State and all of the rural social movements.

Agrarian reform was once again on the Brazilian national agenda in the 1980s largely as a result of the actions of the landless movement, the MST. The movement was born in southern Brazil in the late 1970s around a series of land occupations. By the early 1980s – the period of transition to democracy from military rule – these occupations had spread nationally (Fernandes 1996, 66–7). The origins of the movement are found in the Christian-base communities that proliferated in rural areas and shantytowns, beginning in the 1960s, in concert with liberation theology. The land invasions which grew out of this consciousness-raising process were supported by the Pastoral Land Commission, the CPT (Comissão Pastoral da Terra), which was organized by the National Council of Catholic Bishops in 1975, and which increasingly publicized and gave coherence to these land struggles. The CPT also played a crucial role in bringing together landless workers from different states. After a series of regional meetings, the

---

[2]   These are a synthesis of Bina Agarwal's (1994) detailed development of the four principle arguments for women's land rights: to enhance their welfare, efficiency, equality and empowerment. For a summary of how women's land rights have evolved in the thinking of international institutions, the international women's movement and among governments, see Deere and León (2001, chapter 4).

first national meeting in 1984 resulted in the founding of the MST (Fernandes 1996, 70–8; Stedile and Fernandes 1999). The MST today is organized in 22 states and is the leading force in the struggle for agrarian reform (Hammond 1999).

The other main force behind agrarian reform has been the rural unions. These have quite a heterogenous membership, being composed of agricultural wage workers and tenants, as well as family farmers. They were consolidated on a national scale under the federated union structure of CONTAG during the period of military dictatorship (1964–84). In this period they were the main vehicle of State control as well as of assistance in rural areas, primarily through their provision of social services such as health care.[3] In the period of transition to democratic rule, local and state federations became main foci of contestation by the forces of the new unionism, led by the leftist oppositional national union, the Central Workers' Union, the CUT (Central Unica dos Trabalhadores) (Maybury-Lewis 1996). In the mid-1990s, CONTAG affiliated with the CUT. By then, both organizations were militant participants in the struggle for agrarian reform, often acting in concert with the MST, but also competing with it at times at the local, state and/or national level. The autonomous rural women's movement, today linked in the National Articulation of Rural Women Workers, ANMTR (Articulação Nacional das Mulheres Trabalhadoras Agricolas), has its roots in the activities of the Christian-base committees in the 1960s and 1970s as well as in the rise of the new unionism in the 1980s.

In the next section, I briefly summarize agrarian reform efforts up to the mid-1990s. I then trace the development of the rural women's movement and show how the demand for women's land rights within the unions and autonomous rural women's movement led to its inclusion in the 1988 Constitution. The next section considers the mechanisms of exclusion of women in the meagre agrarian reform efforts during the period of military rule, and how these were not ameliorated in the renewed reform efforts of the 1985–96 period. The subsequent section considers why none of the rural social movements, but particularly the MST, were very effective advocates for women's land rights in this period. The sixth section turns to developments since 1996, when all of the rural social movements began to internalize gender concerns and, specifically, women's land rights, to a much greater degree than in the past, resulting in the adoption in 2001 of specific mechanisms of inclusion of women in the agrarian reform. The main findings are summarized in the conclusion.

BACKGROUND

The struggle for agrarian reform in Brazil dates from the early 1960s. In this period, the labour and peasant movements were gaining strength, the latter organizing against the injustices of the traditional landholding system, the *fazenda*,

---

[3] The rural health care system is financed by a 1 per cent tax on farm sales. On the growth of union membership during the period of military rule, see Maybury-Lewis (1996).

or large estate with a dependent labour force working under non-capitalist labour relations. Under the regime of President João Goulart, the first labour legislation was passed, which extended to rural workers many of the rights and privileges of urban workers, including the right to organize into unions. In addition, an agrarian reform institute was created and legislation was introduced defining which lands could be expropriated for the purpose of agrarian reform. These measures were sufficient to provoke a military coup in March 1964, one which ushered in 21 years of military rule (Cardoso 1997, 18–19).

Given the high degree of mobilization around agrarian reform at the time, as well as pressure from the United States Government, which was championing agrarian reform under the Alliance for Progress,[4] the military government of General Castelo Branco was forced to adopt a mild land reform law in 1964, the *Estatuto da Terra*. This law provided for large landholdings (*latifundia*) to be expropriated with compensation when it was considered to be in the social interest.[5] However, farms considered to be 'rural enterprises', vaguely defined as those that 'exploit the land economically and rationally', were exempt from the reform (Hall 1990, 216–17). Among the intended beneficiaries of the reform were those who worked on the expropriated estate, including squatters, wage workers, sharecroppers and renters (Minc 1985, 90).

Little was accomplished with respect to land redistribution under military rule, since the military was beholden to the traditional landlord class, and its primary interest was in supporting the modernization of agriculture. Government policy in the 1970s centred on the modernization of the *fazendas* through the provision of abundant, subsidized credit. The larger the estate, the more credit it was eligible for, encouraging the growing concentration of land (Cardoso 1997, 19). Particularly favoured were the growing of soya for export and agribusiness interests in lumber and cattle ranching. The modernization policy also provoked a change in labour relations, with the resident labour force of tenants on the *fazendas* replaced by a temporary wage labour force. The military government's priority in terms of solving the problems of landlessness and rural conflict was focused on planned and spontaneous colonization of the Amazonian frontier, which coincided in purpose with the evolving doctrine of Brazilian national security.[6] For the millions dispossessed by the modernization policy, the main option was migration to urban areas and Brazil's major cities mushroomed in size.

---

[4] Under the Alliance for Progress, promulgated in 1961, shortly after the Cuban revolution, United States development assistance was made conditional on Latin American countries pursuing agrarian reform.
[5] *Latifundia* were defined as those 600 times larger than the regionally defined farm module. The size of these farm modules was determined by a combination of criteria, including the population density of the region, land quality, type of activities pursued, etc., and ranged from 2 to 12 hectares.
[6] In order to secure its borders, the military embarked on a very ambitious road-building project throughout the Amazon region. Spontaneous settlement of the North, West-central and Northwest of Brazil ended up being a much more important phenomenon than planned settlement (Hall 1990, 208–9; Cardoso 1997, 21). But through the 1980s, rural–urban migration significantly exceeded rural–rural migration.

Table 1. Distribution of farmland in Brazil, 1985

Farm size (ha)	Total number of farms (%)	Total area of farmland (%)
less than 10	52.9	2.7
10–100	37.3	18.6
100–1000	8.9	35.0
1000+	0.9	43.7
	100.0	100.0
	(5,793,004)	(374.9 million ha)

Source: Brasil (1990, 2–3).

During the whole period of military rule, 1964–84, only 185 estates were expropriated (Cardoso 1997, 22). Thus at the beginning of the democratic transition, land continued to be extremely concentrated, as shown in Table 1. One per cent of the farms, those larger than 1000 ha, held 44 per cent of the land. The Gini coefficient of land concentration had increased from 0.825 in 1940, to 0.853 in 1980, being among the highest in Latin America (Thiesenhusen and Melmed-Sanjak 1990, 396). In the mid-1980s, the number of landless and near-landless families was estimated to be of the order of between 6 and 11 million (Maybury-Lewis 1996, 28–9; Hall 1990, 207).

Upon the return of civilian rule in 1985, President Jose Sarney introduced a proposal for a National Agrarian Reform Plan of the New Republic (PNRA-NR) and created a new Ministry for Agrarian Reform and Rural Development (MIRAD). With the goal of stemming rural–urban migration and encouraging small-scale production, his administration set the goal of expropriating 43 million hectares of land and settling 1.4 million households over a period of four years (Suárez and Libardoni 1992, 110). The landed oligarchy quickly organized themself in opposition, creating the União Democratica Ruralista (UDR), which became a very effective anti-reform lobbying group in the national congress. The PNRA-NR was redrafted 12 times before it became law in October 1985. In the final version, many more properties were ineligible for expropriation than under the original legislation. The debates over the PNRA-NR overlapped with the drafting of Brazil's new constitution. The landlord's lobby, the UDR, was successful in making sure that the constitutional provisions for agrarian reform were left quite vague. For example, while land that does not serve a social function could still be expropriated, 'productive' farms, irrespective of size, were made exempt from expropriation (Hall 1990, 219–20).[7] Given this context, little progress was made in the late 1980s on agrarian reform. Under the Sarney Government, only 89,950 families were settled on 4.5 million hectares of land

---

[7]   A productive farm was defined as one on which 80 per cent of the surface is effectively utilized, where ecological and labour standards are respected, and where 'the use is considered to be of common benefit to land owners and workers'.

(Suárez and Libardoni 1992, 110). Many of the expropriated estates were ones that had been occupied by peasant groups in land occupations, particularly in the South. The main innovation of this period was that beneficiaries were provided with credit at subsidized terms through a programme known as PROCERA (Hall 1990, 225). But, by 1989, the reform effort was weakening and during the next administration came to a virtual standstill (Cardoso 1997, 23). All told, between 1964 and 1994 only 850 agrarian reform settlements were created, bene-fiting 143,514 families (Cardoso 1997, 23). The total amount of land incorpor-ated in these settlements (8.1 million hectares) represented only around 2 per cent of the total land reported in farms in the 1985 agricultural census.

PLACING WOMEN'S LAND RIGHTS ON THE AGENDA

The genesis of the rural women's movement is found in the context of the democratic opening of the 1980s and the consolidation of the feminist and women's movement in Brazil (Alvarez 1990). In rural areas, the Christian base communities and women's groups organized by the CPT in the previous decade often provided the formative experience that led rural women to question social injustice, often linked to health or education issues (Cappellin 1997, 646). But, given that the main organizational structures in rural areas were the unions, in the decade of the 1980s the rural women's movement developed around two central demands: the incorporation of women into the unions and the extension of social security benefits, including paid maternity leave and retirement, to rural women workers (Siqueira 1991, 58). These demands reflected the growing par-ticipation of rural women in the agricultural labour force and the discrimination that women faced both as wage workers and within the rural unions.

Through the mid-1980s, in the unions affiliated with CONTAG, it was gen-erally assumed that only one person per household could be a union member, generally the male household head. Moreover, women were rarely considered to work in agriculture, their work being 'invisible', whether as unpaid family workers or temporary wage workers. In the north-eastern state of Paraíba, for example, union leaders argued that women were not rural workers; that since they were a dependent of their husbands they had no need to join the unions because they had guaranteed benefits; and they even claimed that the unionization of wives was prohibited by law, although this was not the case (MMTR-NE 1987; Albuquerque and Rufino 1987, 328).

Since the unions were the main source of health care in rural areas, the exclu-sion of women from union membership meant that female household heads were at a severe disadvantage. Women were also at a disadvantage in terms of retirement benefits, since only one person per family was eligible for retirement benefits, the household head. Moreover, whereas workers received 50 per cent of the minimum wage upon retirement, their widows received a survivor's pen-sion equivalent to only 30 per cent (Suárez and Libardoni 1992, 122–3). But it was not until 1985, at the Fourth Congress of CONTAG, that rural women's issues were seriously addressed in a national forum of the labour movement.

The impetus came from the first official gathering of the Movement of Rural Women Workers (MMTR, Movimento das Mulheres Trabalhadoras Rurais) of the Sertão Central in the north-eastern state of Pernambuco. The roots of the MMTR in the Northeast can be traced to meetings held in Brejo, Paraíba and Serra Tablada in the Sertão Central of Pernambuco during 1982 and 1983, largely focused on the emergency situation provoked by a prolonged drought. But by 1984, when the MMTR-Sertão Central was officially founded, the main concern was how to increase the participation of rural women workers within the union movement (Federação dos Trabalhadores Agricolas de Pernambuco: FETAPE 1986). At this meeting a proposal was formulated to present to the CONTAG Congress in Brasilia that a priority of the organization should be the unionization of rural women workers and consideration of their concerns (Cappellin 1989, 256). The women's demands were backed by the male leaders of FETAPE, who accompanied the women to Brasilia.

Rural women union members in the South were also meeting regularly in the early 1980s, concerned principally with how to increase their numbers within the local and state union structure. In Rio Grande do Sul, for example, the first of what were to become annual meetings of women in the leadership of FETAG-RS (Federação dos Trabalhadores na Agricultura no Rio Grande do Sul), took place in 1981 (Prá and Britto 1988, 29). The First State Meeting of Rural Women Workers organized by FETAG-RS and the CPT in October 1985 was attended by some 10,000 rural women (Stephen 1997, 214). FETAG-RS's State Commission of Rural Women Workers grew out of this meeting, which also selected 48 women to attend the Fourth CONTAG Congress (FETAG-RS 1998, 6–7).

Although women represented only 1 per cent of the participants at this national congress (Portella and Camurça no date), CONTAG adopted the goal of incorporating women into the union structure and recognized that women experienced specific problems of discrimination, particularly wage discrimination. Local-level unions were instructed to begin encouraging women's participation and to train women to occupy leadership positions. They were also encouraged to elect women as delegates to departmental and national congresses (Siqueira 1991, 69–70). The need for rural women, particularly those in the family farming regime, to declare that their profession was that of rural women workers was also discussed, both as a means of raising their consciousness as well as facilitating their incorporation into unions and access to social security benefits (MMTR-NE 1987, Appendix; CONTAG 1988).

One of the factors which explains the opening of CONTAG to women members at this point in time was the growth of what is known as 'the new unionism' and the competition between CONTAG and the recently formed and more radical CUT (Central Única dos Trabalhadores) for new members. For the first time in many years, contested elections were taking place at the local and state level,[8] and

---

[8] On the heterogeneity within the union structure affiliated with CONTAG, see Maybury-Lewis (1996). By the end of the military dictatorship, the local syndicates and state federations were differentiated by either being assistencialist (concerned primarily with the delivery of social services), corrupt (*pelayo*) or combative. It was the latter who affiliated to the CUT.

women were coming to be viewed as a potential positive force for change within the traditional union structure.[9] By 1987 women represented approximately 29 per cent of the membership of the unions affiliated with CONTAG.[10]

During this same period the CUT, at its Second National Congress in 1986, organized the National Commission on the Question of the Working Woman, to address the concerns of both urban and rural women. The impulse for this latter development also came from the Northeast, from the state of Paraíba, where the first state-level Women's Secretariat had been created at the First State CUT Congress in 1985 (Cappellin 1989, 260). The Women's Secretariat had been a demand of the MMTR of Brejo, along with the demand for recognition of women's land rights, specifically, that land under the agrarian reform be jointly titled to couples (Albuquerque and Rufino 1987, 324–5).

The demand for women's land rights was also raised in the South in this period. In the text drafted in preparation for a rural women worker's congress in Rio Grande do Sul in 1986, organized by the group known as 'the Margaridas'[11] (after the slain Northeastern union leader, Margarida Alves), it was proposed 'that the property title distributed in the agrarian reform be made out in name of the couple irrespective of their legal marital status'. Moreover, 'if the family is the basis for selection of the beneficiaries, that the rights of female household heads (widows, separated women, single mothers) to the property and benefits of the agrarian reform be recognized' (MEMTR 1986, section 2.4).

During the term of President José Sarney, in 1985, the National Council on Women's Rights, the CNDM (Conselho Nacional de Direitos da Mulher), had been created under the Ministry of Justice, which included representatives of civil society, including many feminists. The CNDM, working in tandem with the growing rural women's movement, was largely responsible for the enhanced State attention to rural women's issues in the mid-1980s (Siqueira 1991, 63; Barsted 1994). EMBRATER, the rural extension service of the Ministry of Agriculture, organized the first National Congress of Rural Women in 1986, a congress building on a series of previous State and municipal-level meetings of rural women throughout the country.[12] At this congress, the demand for the

---

[9] Interview with researcher Paola Cappellin, of the Universidade Federal do Rio de Janeiro, and former advisor to the CUT on gender issues, 1 March 1999, Amherst, MA.

[10] This figure is based on a sample of 1398 local syndicates (with 4.1 million members) out of the 2913 syndicates affiliated with CONTAG. Its total membership at that time was estimated as approximately 9 million (FETAPE 1988).

[11] There were three different organizations of rural women in this state in this period, the Margaridas; the women affiliated with the dominant union structure, FETAG-RS; and the Organization of Farm Women (Organização das Mulheres da Roça) which eventually would become the MMTR-RS (Carneiro 1994; Brumer 2000). Some of the members of the Margaridas eventually joined one of the two latter groups. E-mail communications to the author from Loiva Rubenich, ANMTR, 14 December 2000, and Sonilda Pereira, FETAG-RS, 18 December 2000.

[12] My perusal of the available reports of these meetings suggests that they were held between 1984 and 1986 and that the initial themes were quite vague, focusing on 'the situation of women workers' and their recognition as agriculturalists. Land rights were only addressed immediately preceding the 1986 National Congress, when the theme 'women and the property question' was introduced at some of the state-level meetings. Files of Maria José Carneiro, researcher at CPDA, Federal Rural University of Rio de Janeiro, Rio de Janeiro.

distribution of agrarian reform land to female household heads and for the joint titling of agrarian reform land to couples was put forth by almost all of the regional working groups, but most forcefully by the women from the Northeast region. It recommended 'That there be equality in the right of access and ownership of land. When the agrarian reform comes that land be distributed without discrimination, to the men and women who want to work it, and that female households heads – separated and single mothers – not be excluded' (in EMBRATER 1986, 16).

Alongside the growth of the participation of women in the rural union movement, the 1980s were characterized by the growth of the autonomous rural women's movement, the MMTRs, in many states. The state-level MMTRs emerged in the mid- to late 1980s in both the South and the Northeast at approximately the same time. For example, founding meetings of the autonomous rural women worker associations were held in the following years: in 1984 in Santa Catarina; in 1985 in Paraná; in 1986 in Paraíba; in 1987 in Pernambuco and Espirito Santo; and in 1989 in Rio Grande do Sul (MMTR 1994, 16, 20–1; ANMTR 1997, 5–15). These meetings were usually preceded by municipal and regional-level meetings within a given state, sometimes these having taken place over a number of years, beginning in the early 1980s.

The state-level MMTRs were often formed by women who were members of unions affiliated to CONTAG or the CUT and who felt the need to create their own space to deal with gender issues and women's concerns. Although some women rose to leadership positions within the rural unions and in other movements, such as the MST, they often became frustrated when their gender-specific demands were considered irrelevant or less important than the class-based, economic demands which motivated these organizations.

The first national meeting of autonomous rural women was held in 1986 in Barueri, São Paulo, supported by the CUT and the MST, with the objective of creating a national organization of rural women workers. At the meeting, which was attended by women from 16 states, it was decided that such a national organization was premature, and that efforts should concentrate on creating regional networks (MMTR-NE 1987; MMTR 1994, 47; ANMTR 1997, 10). This meeting was a catalyst to the organization of both the MMTR-NE and the AIMTR-Sul (Articulação das Instancias das Mulheres Trabalhadoras Rurais dos 5 Estados do Sul). A history of the founding of the MMTR-NE gives credit to the 1986 São Paulo national meeting (which six women from the Northeast attended) as providing the impetus for the First Meeting of the MMTR-NE at João Pessoa in 1987 (MMTR-NE 1987). This latter meeting was attended by women from eight Northeastern states and, in each of these, the MMTRs were closely tied to the rural unions at the municipal level.[13] Two themes dominated

---

[13]   The close and over-lapping ties between members of the MMTR-NE and the rural unions are illustrated by the fact that of the 22 rural women workers attending the 1987 founding meeting, 20 belonged to a union; the other 14 women attending were advisors. A survey of the MMTR-NE membership carried out in that year (with 181 members responding from six states) revealed that 52 per cent were union members (MMTR-NE 1987, 9, 21–2).

the discussion: the need to increase women's participation in the unions and the demand for agrarian reform.

In the South, the AIMTR-Sul was created in 1988, formally linking women from the five Southern states.[14] Its objective was to provide a forum for the discussion of what were considered women's issues, among them, health, sexuality, recognition of the profession of rural women workers, and gender, and 'to give visibility to the problematic of rural women workers (their condition, work, lack of citizenship . . .)' (ANMTR 1997, 10). The AIMTR-Sul and its constituent organizations were the ones to take the lead in national campaigns focusing on obtaining rural women's social security rights and the recognition of the profession of rural women workers. The Movement of Women Farmers (MMA-SC) of Santa Catarina, for example, led the 1986 campaign for 100,000 signatures of rural women workers to place their rights on the constitutional agenda, delivering these to Brasilia in a major caravan (ANMTR 1997, 5).[15]

Before the adoption of the 1988 Federal Constitution, the issue of women's land rights had been raised in municipal-level meetings. For example, in the 25 municipal meetings held in Santa Catarina in 1986 one of the themes had been 'the struggle for land titles in women's names in the agrarian reform settlement projects' (ANMTR 1997, 5). Subsequently, land rights seemed to disappear as an issue and were not taken up by the state-level association. According to Lucy Choinaski, one of the founders of the MMA-SC and the first rural woman to be elected a congressional deputy, this was because the organization was largely made up of women who were in the regime of family agriculture and their primary concerns were other ones, such as health care, social security benefits, participation in the unions, etc. In the regime of family agriculture 'land is in men's name . . . it is the exception for daughters to inherit a land parcel . . . There was never a debate on this issue although women have been concerned and raise the question of women's ownership of land.'[16]

The demand for women's land rights was most persistently articulated by the women in CONTAG, where it was a major issue at the First National Seminar of Rural Women Workers in Brasilia in 1988. Moreover, the fact that women were being dispossessed from their land when they were widowed – whether as tenants, wage workers or in the agrarian reform settlements – was denounced in

---

[14]   The AIMTR included the following organizations: Movimento de Mulheres Trabalhadoras Rurais do Rio Grande do Sul (MMTR-RS), Movimento de Mulheres Agricultoras de Santa Catarina (MMA-SC), Comissão Estadual da Questão da Mulher Trabalhadora Rural do DETR-Paraná, Movimento Popular de Mulheres do Paraná (MPMP), Movimento de Mulheres Agricultoras de Mato Grosso do Sul, and the Movimento de Mulheres Assentadas de São Paulo.

[15]   Interview with Jaci Kuhn Sckeeren, member of the National Commission of the ANMTR, 23 June 1998, Brasilia.

[16]   Unpublished transcript made available to the author of interview by Maria Ignez Paulilo, researcher at the Federal University of Santa Catarina, 26 July 2000, Florianopolis, SC. The reference cited earlier to women's land rights as a demand of rural women in this state may be due to the fact that EMBRATER explicitly introduced this theme at the seminars held here preceding the 1986 First National Congress of Rural Women. See 'A mulher rural e suas reinvidicações', EMBRATER-SC (no date) files of Maria José Carneiro.

no uncertain terms (CONTAG 1988, 7). The constitutional convention was meeting at the time, and participants at the seminar lobbied vigorously for the constitutional article that would explicitly establish women's land rights in the agrarian reform (CONTAG 1988, 24). This constitutional article, as well as a number of others dealing with women's rights, was the result of a popular amendment to the Constitution, one resulting from a nation-wide signature campaign. It was the initiative of feminist activists and scholars who worked in tandem with the CNDM. Beginning in 1986, under the slogan 'for the constitutional process to be valid it must include women's rights', meetings and seminars on women's rights were held throughout the country. It was as a result of the interaction between the CNDM and the female leadership of the unions, as well as the growing movement of rural women, that women's land rights, specifically, were included on the constitutional agenda as part of the general expansion of women's rights in the 1988 Constitution.[17]

Besides the inclusion of women in the agrarian reform, other gains for rural women in the 1988 Constitution included the establishment of equal rights for urban and rural men and women with respect to labour legislation and social security benefits. It was stipulated that these benefits applied to permanent and temporary wage workers as well as family farmers, including unpaid family workers. These benefits include, besides the right to unemployment and disability insurance, 120 days of paid maternity leave for women. In addition, the age of retirement for rural women was set at 55 years and for rural men, at 60 years, or after 30 years of service for women and 35 years for men, conditions more favorable than for urban workers. Women who were unpaid family workers in peasant production would be eligible for retirement benefits directly and no longer only as a dependent of the male household head (CUT 1991, 10; Suárez and Libardoni 1992, 124–5).

The new constitutional rights acquired by rural women in 1988 required enabling legislation to be implemented. But with the election of President Collor in 1989, the CNDM went into a period of decline (Barsted 1994, 42). Moreover, he vetoed in 1991 the implementing legislation for paid maternity leave for women in family agriculture, arguing that in the case of 'special producers' there was no correlation between their payment of quotas and potential benefits (Cappellin 1992, 59). Since attaining effective social security rights was an issue that united most rural women (whether temporary or permanent wage workers, landless or in the family farming regime), it is not surprising that these rights would constitute the most important arena of struggle for the rural women's movement in subsequent years, to the detriment of the struggle for women's land rights (Deere and León 1999).

---

[17] Particularly important in terms of rural women's land rights was the lobbying effort which resulted from the 1987 seminar 'Rural Women: Their Identities in Research and in the Political Struggle' held at the Federal University of Rio de Janeiro (Lavinas 1987). Interview by the author and Magdalena León with researcher Heleithe Saffioti, 28 June 1998, São Paulo.

Table 2. Beneficiaries of the agrarian reform by sex and region, 1996 (per centages)

	Men	Women	No info.	Total
North	85.0	12.7	0.3	100
Northeast	85.3	13.4	1.3	100
Southeast	83.2	13.8	2.9	100
Centre-west	86.8	11.5	1.7	100
South	91.1	7.9	1.0	100
Total	85.6	12.6	1.8	100
	($n = 135,011$)	($n = 19,905$)	($n = 2841$)	($n = 157,757$)

Source: INCRA/CRUB/UnB (1998, 26).

WOMEN'S PARTICIPATION IN THE AGRARIAN REFORM

According to the First Agrarian Reform Census, as of 1996 only 19,905 women were direct beneficiaries of the reform, representing 12.6 per cent of the national total of 157,757. As Table 2 also shows, given the size of Brazil, there was considerable variation in women's participation by region, with the share of female beneficiaries being highest in the Southeast (13.8 per cent) and Northeast (13.4 per cent), and lowest in the South (7.9 per cent).

The relatively low share of female beneficiaries reflects the discrimination against women that prevailed prior to the 1988 constitutional reform and the fact that it was not eliminated by measures to establish women's formal equality with men. The 1964 Land Statute, the governing legislation on agrarian reform until 1985, gave priority to household heads with the largest families who wanted to dedicate themselves to agricultural activities (da Luz 1996, 123). These criteria discriminated against women since, following cultural norms, if a man resides in the household he is always considered its head, a norm supported by the 1916 civil code until also modified by the 1988 constitutional reform (Albuquerque and Rufino 1987, 324–5). The family size criterion was biased against female-headed households since, by definition, these are smaller than male-headed households given the absence of an adult male in the former. Moreover, in selecting beneficiaries, INCRA applied a point system whereby men between the ages of 18 and 60 were awarded one point, whereas women in this age group were awarded only 0.75 points, with the discrimination by sex maintained for children. This norm obviously discriminated against female-headed households as well as those households with large numbers of female children. The criteria regarding the length of experience in agricultural work discriminated against all women, since women's agricultural work – whether as unpaid family labour or temporary wage workers – has largely been invisible and undervalued, and it has been difficult for women to prove their agricultural experience (Albuquerque and Rufino 1987; Siqueira 1991, 63; Suárez and Libardoni 1992, 118–19).

The discrimination against women was such that INCRA functionaries assumed that women without a husband or partner were incapable of managing a farm unless they had a grown son, and it was not at all uncommon for women who found themselves widowed with young children to lose their right to remain in an agrarian reform settlement (Lavinas 1991, 6). Moreover, when a widow's eldest son was named the beneficiary, she sometimes lost access to land when he married and formed his own household (Rufino and Albuquerque 1990, 367).

The main consequence of the constitutional reform establishing that women could be beneficiaries of the agrarian reform was an INCRA norm (SEASC 01 of October 1988), which provided for equal weight to be given to male and female labour in the point system utilized to select beneficiaries (Suárez and Libardoni 1992, 119). The other beneficiary selection criteria, however, were not changed; thus female household heads continued to be discriminated against by the criteria favouring large families, and all women, by the criteria favouring agricultural experience. The share of female beneficiaries of the reform not only failed to increase after 1988, but actually fell slightly in the 1991–6 period, suggesting that the constitutional provisions guaranteeing women's formal land rights had little direct impact.[18]

In order to further understand why women formed such a low proportion of the beneficiaries and the variations by region, I carried out interviews with the leaders of the rural social movements and INCRA officials in seven states during 2000: four North-eastern states, two characterized by high female participation in the agrarian reform (Pernambuco and Paraíba) and two with low female participation (Ceará and Rio Grande do Norte); two Southern states with low female participation (Rio Grande do Sul and Paraná); and Rio de Janeiro, characterized by the highest share of female participation in the agrarian reform of all states.[19] In all states, the leaders of the social movements considered INCRA functionaries to play the determining role in the selection of agrarian reform beneficiaries, for it is INCRA that determines their eligibility and through a point system prioritizes those to be settled on each *assentamento*. In contrast, in interviews, INCRA officials stressed the role of the social movements as the key filter in determining this selection, particularly since the early 1990s when the pace of the agrarian reform has largely been determined by land occupations and the pressure of those within the encampments (*acampamentos*) which are subsequently formed. It is acknowledged that participation in the latter has become a precondition for beneficiary status.[20]

---

[18]   Women constituted 13 per cent of the beneficiaries of the agrarian reform settlements constituted before 1991; their share subsequently fell slightly, to 12.5 per cent. Calculated by the author from the 1 Censo da Reforma Agrária – 1996.

[19]   On the factors explaining the variation in women's participation by state, see Deere (2001).

[20]   Nonetheless, since 1998 it is official INCRA policy to try 'to break the monopoly in the determination of the beneficiaries by the social movements in certain regions of the country, which impedes the exercise of the democratic right of access to the agrarian reform' (INCRA 1998). During 2000, INCRA introduced a new modality for applying to become an agrarian reform beneficiary – by mail registration – with the forms available at all post offices throughout the country, as an attempt to weaken the role of the social movements in the agrarian reform.

As previously noted, it is INCRA policy to bestow land rights on only one person per household, generally, the household head. Through 2000, there was no general INCRA directive on joint adjudication and titling of land to couples. As INCRA officials often state, justifying this policy, 'the agrarian reform registry (*cadastro*) does not have space to put the name of the man and woman, there is only space for one name, that of the man'. As leaders of the social movements conclude from this, 'thus it is INCRA itself which maintains the policy of domination of women'.[21] According to INCRA officials, the goal of the agrarian reform is to benefit families and by benefiting families – as represented by the household head – they are benefiting all the members within them. Moreover, they tend to assume that the families to be benefited are predominantly nuclear families, where both parents are present. These assumptions have worked to the detriment of female-headed households as well as single young people.[22]

The First Agrarian Reform Census sheds light on this matter. As Table 3 shows, the great majority, 58.9 per cent, of the female beneficiaries were married

Table 3. Marital status of the agrarian reform beneficiaries by sex, 1996

	Women	Men	Total
Married	33.9	63.7	59.9
Consensual union	25.1	22.3	22.6
Sub-total	58.9	86.0	82.5
Single	13.3	9.6	10.1
Separated	9.3	2.2	3.1
Divorced	1.4	0.5	0.6
Widowed	16.7	1.5	3.5
Other	0.4	0.2	0.2
Sub-total	41.1	14.0	17.5
Total	100.0	100.0	100.0
	($n = 18,048$)	($n = 124,134$)	($n = 142,182$)

Source: Author's calculations based on the *1 Censo da Reforma Agrária-1996*.

[21] Interviews with Nina Tonin, MST coordinator in Rio Grande do Sul, 8 November 2000, Porto Alegre, and Isabel Greem, MST-Paraná, 14 November 2000, Curitiba. Also see Rua and Abramovay (2000, 198–201).
[22] These assumptions were most explicit in my interview with José Carlos de Araujo Vieira, INCRA Superintendent in Paraná, 13 November 2000, Curitiba. He was quite opposed to including single people as beneficiaries on the *assentamento*, irrespective of sex, saying that the goal of the agrarian reform was to 'strengthen the family'. Among the different social movements, the MST has most strongly defended the inclusion of young, single people (who are usually the most active participants in the land occupations and encampments), particularly in the context of the collective adjudication of land. Interviews with Dulcineia Pavan, MST International Relations Office, 30 June 1998, São Paulo, and Fátima Ribeira, MST coordinator in Rio Grande do Norte, 1 October 2000, Fortaleza.

or living in a consensual union.[23] Only 41 per cent are female household heads. Among this group, widows predominate (16.7 per cent of the total), followed by single (9.3 per cent), separated (9.3 per cent) and divorced women (1.4 per cent). In contrast, the overwhelming majority of male beneficiaries are married or living in a consensual union, 82.5 per cent; only 10.1 per cent are single, with the remainder widowed, separated or divorced.

The data on marital status suggest that female household heads have been severely under-represented as beneficiaries. Nationally, women represent 12.2 per cent of rural household heads (Brasil 1994, Table 6.11), whereas they constitute only 5.2 per cent of the household heads on the *assentamentos* censused in 1996. This under-representation suggests that female household heads have been particularly discriminated against, irrespective of the 1988 constitutional provisions. The problem seems to be that INCRA continues to prefer to title a son (even if legally under-age) than to title a female household head, with single mothers often being asked 'don't you have a son who is a little older?'[24] Moreover, if a male beneficiary dies, INCRA continues to cede the land rights to the eldest son rather than to the widow, and if a female household head with land rights gets married, these are sometimes transferred to her spouse (Rua and Abramovay 2000, 198–9). But in addition, the low proportion of female household heads among the beneficiaries suggests that the rural social movements did not champion their land rights very effectively, let alone prioritize these.

THE FAILURE TO PRESS FOR WOMEN'S LAND RIGHTS

Since its founding, the primary objective of the MST has been the struggle for agrarian reform and 'a more just and egalitarian society'. The movement recognized that to accomplish this, 'the participation of all rural workers' was necessary, '. . . encouraging the participation of women at all levels' (MST 1986, 44; Navarro 1996, 98). Women have been very visible in the MST-led land occupations, where they are estimated to be between one-third to one-half of the participants, and they are often in the front lines in confrontations with the police. Moreover, women usually play a very active and key role in the encampments that result from these. Nonetheless, once the *assentamentos* are constituted, few women participate as actively and, until recently, there have been few women in their leadership or of the MST (Miele and Guimarães 1998; Rua and Abramovay

---

[23] The main reason that married women appear on the registries as representing their family is because their husband or partner is for some reason ineligible to be a beneficiary of the reform (Rua and Abramovay 2000, 197). I only found evidence of married women demanding land rights in their own names in Pernambuco and Rio de Janeiro, usually in cases where they had been active in the land occupation while their husbands or partners had not and the latter had non-agricultural occupations (Deere 2001).

[24] Interview with Wellington Gurgel, acting Superintendent of INCRA-CE, 28 September 2000, Fortaleza. A notorious case was one in Paraíba where INCRA ceded land rights to the son of a well-known CUT activist rather than to her, even though she qualified as a beneficiary and was demanding land rights in her own name. Interview with Genero Ieno Neto, researcher at Unitrabalho, Federal University of Paraíba, and others, 23 September 2000, João Pessoa.

2000). As noted by women activists in the movement, 'It is still observed that once the land is won, a large number of women in the *assentamento*s return to their own private work, on the individual plot, in the home and with the children. Because of this it is necessary that women organize themselves and participate in the struggle of the working class at all levels.'[25]

In its initial years, the MST gave little concern to gender issues: 'According to the women on the *assentamento*s it is perceived that gender relations within the movement are considered to be of secondary importance when not considered a nuisance' (Lechat 1996, 108). Nonetheless, a National Commission of Women of the MST was organized in the latter half of the 1980s and it lobbied for women's groups to be created within the *assentamento*s and encampments; for a women's commission to be created within each state; and for the state-level leadership as well as that within the *assentamento*s to support the organization of women within the movement.[26]

Most of these proposals were adopted as norms at the various national meetings so that in September 1989, when the MST published the first edition of its *General Norms of the MST*, it included a chapter on 'The Articulation of Women'. Besides the objective of encouraging women's participation at all levels, other objectives included (i) the struggle against all forms of discrimination as well as *machismo*; (ii) the organization of women's groups to create the space for women to discuss their own specific problems; (iii) to encourage women's participation in all forms of organization of the MST, including within the union movement, where rural women workers participate irrespective of their class position; and (iv) to organize a national-level women's commission responsible for proposing policies for the movement (MST 1989a, chapter 8).

Training manuals for the 1989–1993 period stress the importance of increasing women's participation and that to do so it was important to 'create the conditions so that women and youth be able to participate in collective production and in all activities of the movement', the first implicit reference to some of the impediments that might limit women's more active participation.[27] But throughout this period, no particular attention was given to women's land rights. This lack of attention was due to several factors. The provisions for agrarian reform in the 1988 Constitution were considerably weaker than the legislation encompassed in the 1985 National Agrarian Reform Plan of the New Republic (PNRA-NR), legislation which the landlord's lobby, the UDR, successfully watered down in this intervening period. After 1988, the lobbying efforts of the MST and other progressive forces focused on attaining favourable implementing legislation for the limited range of expropriations allowed under the Constitution. In addition, under the Collor Government (1990–2), not one estate was expropriated

---

[25] Comissão Nacional de Mulheres do MST, 'Avançar na luta', *Journal Sem Terra* (São Paulo), No. 72, April, 1988, 18.
[26] Ibid.
[27] Item 48, Part III, 'Desafios da luta pela reforma agrária'; Item 80, 'Perspectivas para o MST – 1989/1993', in MST (1989b).

for being in the social interest, and actions under the subsequent Government of Itamar Franco (1992–4) were also minimal, leading the MST to step up its land occupations (de Medeiros 1989, 166–98).

The lack of attention by the MST to women's land rights, particularly to the joint adjudication and titling of land to couples, is also related to the fact that throughout this period a priority of the MST was the collective adjudication and titling of land, rather than its division and formal distribution to individual families: 'The titling of land should be collective, in the name of all the *assentados*, independently of whether production is carried out collectively or individually, thus guaranteeing usufruct rights, but that the land cannot be alienated.'[28] With the struggle for land rights defined as a collective issue, there was little room for discussion of the individual land rights of women.

Rather than being strengthened, the National Commission of Women of the MST apparently ceased to function after 1989 as women were told that if they were interested in gender issues they should also join other organizations, such as the MMTRs.[29] Gender issues were seen as divisive issues for the movement, particularly at a moment (during the Collor Government) when the struggle for agrarian reform was becoming even more contentious, and in some cases, violent. The primary concern was for the unity of the movement – a struggle that demanded unity from all family members.[30] The fear that gender issues would be divisive to the movement is evident in a 1993 document that states explicitly that the incorporation of women into the movement should be treated as a class issue and not as a gender issue.[31] According to Article 45 of the 1993 *Basic Document*, the movement should 'consider issues specific to women and their participation as an integral part of the demands of the organization, treating these as class rather than gender issues' (MST 1996, 5). But in Article 152 of this same document, it was reiterated that since it was an objective of the movement to encourage women's role in production and their participation in cooperatives, it was also necessary 'to struggle against the inequality and traditionalism which exists among the peasantry' (MST 1996, 6).

The movement went a step further in recognizing the specificity of gender subordination in its Agrarian Program of 1995, approved at the Third National Congress. A section was devoted to 'The Situation of Women in the Countryside', which included recognition that it was often women who suffered the most from the 'miserable living standards' in the countryside, including the double day. 'In addition, there is a generalized situation of prejudice and discrimination

[28]   Ibid., Item 105.
[29]   Interview with Dulcineia Pavan, MST International Relations Office, op. cit., and confirmed in interviews with members of the national-level Gender Collective, Nina Tonin, MST-RS, 8 November 2000, Porto Alegre, and Isabel Greem, MST-Paraná, 14 November 2000, Curitiba.
[30]   Interview by the author and Magdalena León with Nalu Faria and Miriam Nobre, SOF (Sempreviva Organização Feminista), 27 June 1998, São Paulo.
[31]   This debate over the relationship of gender and class analysis was also carried out within the union movement in the late 1980s and early 1990s, particularly the CUT, but resolved much earlier in favour of the need to integrate the analysis of gender, class and race. See Lavinas and Cappellin (1991).

due to the practice of machismo in rural areas that forces an inferior position on women' (MST 1996, 6). But the general objective regarding gender equality adopted at this congress was similar to previous statements: 'To struggle against all forms of social discrimination and to aim for the egalitarian participation of women' (MST 1996, 6).[32]

Turning to the rural unions in this period, rural women's paid maternity leave, together with the need for recognition of the occupation of rural women workers and the right to retirement benefits, remained among the main demands of rural women at state congresses of the federations affiliated with CONTAG in the early 1990s, at the First National Meeting of Rural Women Workers of CONTAG in 1991, and at the Fifth CONTAG Congress of that same year. The need to incorporate more women into the unions as well as in the leadership also remained important issues. New issues taken up in this period, reflecting the growing feminist discourse by women within the unions, included the problems of the double day and the demand for sexual freedom (Siqueira 1991, 70–1). Among the demands made by the agrarian reform commission at the Fifth CONTAG Congress (where women now constituted 10 per cent of the delegates), besides a strongly worded demand for the deepening of the agrarian reform, was that women be given land titles in their own names, or jointly with their spouse or partner, suggesting that women's land rights were not being ignored all together (Suárez and Libardoni 1992, 135–6).

In 1989, the CUT organized its first national meeting on the Working Women's Question, which included both urban and rural women. The next year it organized a Rural Women's Commission linked to its National Department of Rural Workers to better address what was considered to be the low participation of rural women in its affiliated unions and the general lack of recognition of rural women as workers (CUT 1991, 23–4). Among the main demands of rural women at the Second National Meeting of Women Workers of the CUT in 1991 were the implementation of retirement benefits for rural women, a call for recognition of the profession of rural women workers, and that women's names appear on agrarian reform land titles (Godinho 1995, 165), suggesting that they too continued to give importance to attaining women's effective land rights. But for neither the CUT or CONTAG in this period were women's land rights the foremost issue.

In partnership with the CUT's Rural Women's Commission, the AIMTR-Sul organized a major campaign around the 1991 population census to have rural women declare themselves as rural workers instead of as housewives or unpaid family workers in the questionnaire (Lavinas 1991, 4). This campaign was launched with a caravan of a thousand or so rural women from 15 states marching on Brasilia for International Women's Day celebrations in March 1992. Among their other demands were that Collor's veto of paid maternity leave for unpaid family workers be overturned. In addition, they demanded that (i) retirement

---

[32] See www.mst.org.br/historico/historia7.html (accessed 18 April 2001).

benefits be paid immediately to rural workers; (ii) child care centres be set up for rural women workers; (iii) priority attention be given to women's integral health care; (iv) an end be brought to violence against women; and (v) that the constitutional provision for agrarian reform be regulated (Cappellin 1992, 59; Suárez and Libardoni 1992, 132). The AIMTR-Sul also established an office in Brasilia to lobby for paid maternity leave and was eventually successful in getting the national congress to pass the Bill in 1993 (ANMTR 1997, 5).

In order to foster the participation of women in the unions, the CUT approved the adoption of a quota system in 1993, so that 30 per cent of national, state and regional leaders be women.[33] The first leadership under the new quota system was elected at its 1994 Congress, with nine women elected among the 32 national leaders (Godinho 1996, 52). A decision was also made at this congress to fuse the Rural Department of CUT with CONTAG, if CONTAG agreed to join the CUT, a move subsequently taken. This led to the Rural Women's Commission of the CUT being disbanded at the national level, leading to several years of chaos and a weakening in the work with rural women.[34]

In 1995, another national meeting was held in São Paulo to create a national-level network of rural women, the Articulação Nacional de Mulheres Trabalhadoras Rurais (ANMTR). This meeting brought together women from 17 states and this time they succeeded in creating a loosely structured, national organization. Among the resolutions passed at this meeting was to focus on actions to secure in practice the rights won in the constitution such as paid retirement and health care, and to carry out coordinated actions under one theme on 8 March, international women's day. Their primary activity has been a national campaign to obtain official documents for rural women under the slogan, 'To have personal documents and those of workers is but one step in the conquest of our citizenship' (ANMTR 1997, 26–7).[35] Of an estimated 18.5 million rural women workers, only some three million currently have their profession officially recognized, a precondition for them to be eligible for social security benefits (ANMTR no date). Several MST women leaders participated in the organization of the founding meeting of the ANMTR in late 1995. They consider that there

---

[33] A quota was considered necessary, for in 1989 women represented only 7 per cent of rural union leaders, and 60 per cent of the rural unions affiliated with the CUT had directorates which were all male. Moreover, in the national leadership there were only two women out of 32 members (Godinho 1996, 49).
[34] Interview by the author and Magdalena León with Lena Lavinas, researcher at IPEA and former advisor to the CUT on gender issues, 18 June 1998, Rio de Janeiro.
[35] The number of documents required for official transactions in Brazil is no small matter. Necessary personal documents include a birth certificate; a marriage certificate; an identity card; a voter registration card; and an employment card (*carteira do trabalho*). A birth certificate is required to obtain any of the other personal documents. In addition, in order to have one's profession registered and thus to be eligible for social security benefits, at least one of the following is required: a union card; a land title (or INCRA certification that one's name is on the registry of an *assentamento*); a rental contract for land; and registration in the sales declaration form of peasant producers or on the income tax registration form. ANMTR's campaign materials stress the importance of women having their name on land titles as both a means and an end of citizenship (ANMTR 1997, 6–20; ANMTR no date).

was a qualitative leap forward within the MST with respect to the discussion of gender issues after this meeting.[36] They organized the first national meeting of MST women militants shortly thereafter, leading to the founding of the National Collective of Women of the MST in May 1996. The Collective soon published a pamphlet, 'The Question of Women in the MST', with the sub-title, 'Participating without fear of being a woman'. This document clearly points to the gap in MST theory and practice, highlighting how women were not sufficiently represented in the leadership. Moreover, although a basic principle of the movement since 1989 had been to end the discrimination against women and to promote their participation, it concludes that this had not been achieved in practice (MST 1996, 3–5).

In this publication, women's land rights are directly addressed for the first time. Among the proposed actions is that the organization 'guarantee that women get land titles' and that in the associations and cooperatives on the *assentamento*s it be guaranteed that women participate on equal terms with men (MST 1996, 7). It was stressed that a major campaign was necessary if women's names were to be secured, along with their husbands or partners, in the *assentamento* registry and on land titles. Moreover, it was recognized that a pre-condition for women to be agrarian reform beneficiaries was that they have the required personal documents. Hence, they recommended that the movement strongly support and participate in the documentation campaign being organized at that time by the ANMTR (MST 1996, 9–10). But up to this point (1996, when the first agrarian reform census was undertaken), no other efforts had been taken by the MST to encourage women's participation as direct beneficiaries of the agrarian reform.

INCREASING THE PACE OF THE REFORM AND OF FEMALE BENEFICIARIES

The pace of the Brazilian agrarian reform stepped up in the mid-1990s, largely as a result of the actions of the landless movement. By mid-1999 there were 3958 *assentamento*s nationally, with 475,801 beneficiary families holding almost 23 million hectares of land.[37] Compared with the 1996 First Agrarian Reform Census figures, the number of *assentamento*s had increased by 2533 and beneficiary families by 316,023. While the pace of the agrarian reform under the Government of Fernando Henrique Cardoso compares favourably with previous administrations, the land area in agrarian reform settlements constitutes only around 6 per cent of the land reported in farms in the 1985 agricultural census, and the number of families that benefited equivalent to only between 5 and 10 per cent of the number of landless families in the mid-1980s. The majority of the *assentamento*s resulted

---

[36] Interview with Itelvina Maria Masioli, member of the MST National Directorate from Mato Grosso and one of two MST representatives in the national commission of the ANMTR, at a national seminar of the ANMTR, 23 June 1998, Brasilia.

[37] http://www.mst.org.br/bibliotec/assentam/assent4.html (downloaded 18 November 2000) which, in turn, is drawn from 'Banco de Dados da Luta pela Terra', UNESP/MST, as of June 1999.

from land take-overs led by the MST, but in this period many of the unions affiliated with CONTAG also engaged in land occupations, as did groups supported by the CPT in the Northeast.[38]

Preliminary data for eight states suggest that the increased pace of the agrarian reform has been accompanied by an increase in the share of women beneficiaries. Between 1996 and 2000, the number of agrarian reform beneficiaries more than doubled in five of the eight states, while substantial increases were reported in the other three. The share of female beneficiaries increased significantly in Rio de Janeiro (to 23 per cent) and substantially in Ceará, Rio Grande do Norte and Santa Catarina (states which had been at the low end of the spectrum in 1996) and Paraíba. The share of women remained about the same in Pernambuco and Rio Grande do Sul, and actually decreased in Paraná, which in both periods reported the lowest share of female beneficiaries. Before commenting on these state-level trends, it is relevant to first consider the changes that have taken place in the gender discourse of the MST.

Recall that it was only in 1996, when the National Women's Collective was constituted, that women's land rights were addressed by the MST. In 1999, this forum was reconstituted as the National Gender Collective, with an equal number of men and women as members, and the plan was for similar structures to be created at the state and sub-regional levels. According to one of its members, the mandate of the women's collective had never been very clear and what had become apparent was the need for a 'cultural revolution' in the relations between men and women: 'It has to be a problem of both men and women and in all of its dimensions.'[39]

Several factors explain the greater opening to gender issues by the MST at this time. For one, there was growing recognition within the leadership of the tendency for women to withdraw from active participation once the *assentamentos* were constituted. The exclusion of most women from land rights has meant their exclusion from participation in the associations and cooperatives that make the crucial decisions governing production plans and infrastructure and social investments, etc., on the *assentamentos*. As explained by one MST leader:

> The fact women's names are not on the land registry is a major problem
> . . . for she is not the landowner, and then, for example, what happens
> when technical assistance is to be given? The technician arrives and con-
> vokes the owners to a meeting. And who is the owner officially? It's the
> husband. So only he goes to the meeting to receive technical assistance.
> Only he goes to discuss the use of resources . . . And that's how women
> are excluded during all the key moments . . .[40]

---

[38]   As of August 2001, there were 1490 MST-led *assentamentos* with 108,849 families. Between 1990 and late 1999, some 368,325 families had participated in MST-led occupations and been registered on their encampments. In August 2001, there were 75,730 families residing in 585 MST encampments awaiting INCRA to distribute land to them. Drawn from http://www.mst.org.br/bibliotec.html (downloaded 7 December 2001).

[39]   Interview with Marina dos Santos, coordinator of MST-RJ, 28 August 2000.

[40]   Interview with Isabel Greem, MST-PR, op. cit.

It is increasingly recognized that this exclusion is not only prejudicial to women's personal development, but also to the well-being of the *assentamento* and of the movement. In some cases, the non-participation of women has been associated with a general apathy within the *assentamento* for collective endeavours, in turn, related to the general lack of participatory structures. In other cases, it became apparent that the exclusion of women from the land registry has generated practical problems, such as when, due to the absence of the husband for whatever reason, women were unable to get credit for production purposes.

Also, the problem of separations among couples has been gaining attention. The usual case is for the person with land rights, the husband, to remain on the land. The wife often has no choice but to leave with the children, for 'in separation, the women loses all rights'. Sometimes she has to start the process all over, going to another encampment in hopes of obtaining land even though she has already spent years in the struggle. While sometimes the man is willing to leave so that his wife and children can remain in their home, this presents difficulties; since the land is in his name, officially, he cannot again be an agrarian reform beneficiary.[41]

One of the first activities of the Gender Collective was the publication of a training pamphlet consisting of eight topics for sessions designed to reflect on gender relations (MST 2000). One of the topics is 'Women and Agrarian Reform', and includes the following point with respect to women's land rights:[42] 'In the struggle for land, the occupation, the encampment, mobilizations, the whole family participates, thus the conquest of land is a conquest of the whole family. There is nothing more just that when INCRA comes to do the land registry, that the name of both be registered . . .' (MST 2000, 57–8). This point implies that the joint adjudication of land to couples is now MST policy and was so confirmed by women in the MST leadership.[43] Nonetheless, this demand still does not form part of the MST's public discourse.

The ambigious position of the MST with respect to women's land rights was evident at the March 2000 mobilization of rural women workers jointly coordinated by the ANMTR and the MST. During 13–17 March, some 3000 rural women from 24 states camped out in Brasilia, in what was termed 'the first encampment of rural women'. Among the demands was the need to deepen the agrarian reform, but there was nothing concerning women's land rights.[44] This ambiguity was also apparent in the conclusions presented at the MST's Fourth National Congress in Brasilia in August 2000. Among the 12 main policies

---

[41] Group interview by the author and Emma Siliprandi with women militants in the MST Regional Sarandi, 9 November 2000, Pontão, RS, and interview with Isabel Greem, MST-PR, op. cit. Also see Rua and Abramovay (2000, 201–3).

[42] This section of the pamphlet is drawn from the 'Political Directives of the MST on the Participation of Women', which was approved by the National Coordination of the MST in January 1999; e-mail to the author from Gema Galgani, gender advisor to the MST-Ceará, 8 May 2001.

[43] Interviews with Fátima Ribeira, MST-RN, op. cit., and Nina Tonin, MST-RGS, op. cit.

[44] *Boletím Semanal da Secretaria Agrária Nacional do PT*, 18–24 março 2000, ano III, No. 145, Anexo 3, in www.pt.org.br/san/3milmulheres.htm

reaffirmed at the congress was 'to redeem and implement the gender question in our policies and in all activities of the MST and in society'.[45] But nothing specific was said about women's land rights. Nonetheless, one of the important recent changes within the MST is that women now constitute nine out of the 21 members of its National Directorate.[46]

What became apparent in my interviews is that the internalization of gender concerns is taking place within the MST at different paces in different states. In certain states, there is a notable change in the gender discourse taking place at the base, often associated with an increase in the number of women in leadership positions on the *assentamentos* or within the MST's sub-regional or state leadership. This evolving process may account, in part, for the increase in the share of female agrarian reform beneficiaries in states such as Ceará, Rio Grande do Norte, Santa Catarina and Rio de Janeiro. I do not think it is coincidental that women are the state coordinators of the MST in these states; moreover, in Ceará, women now constitute the majority of the MST state leadership. Also Ceará and Rio Grande do Sul are among the leaders in implementing some of the new policies outlined in MST (2000). The retrograde in my case studies is the state of Paraná, where the share of women agrarian reform beneficiaries has actually fallen since 1996, from 7.2 per cent to 6.8 per cent, in the period when the total number of beneficiaries more than tripled. The MST in this state is also a laggard with respect to gender issues. Only in October 2000 did the state directorate (including only two women out of 18) take up the discussion of gender issues and the state gender collective has yet to be created. Besides the lack of attention by the MST to women's land rights, the data on women's participation in the agrarian reform may also reflect the very conservative nature of this state, characterized by continued landlord dominance and much weaker social movements as compared with other Southern states.

Turning to CONTAG, not until 1997 (three years after it joined the CUT and the Rural Women's Commission of the CUT was disbanded nationally) did it organize a national commission on women. By then, there were on the order of two million rural women affiliated to rural unions (Abramovay and da Silva 2000, 355). That same year CONTAG held the First National Plenary of Rural Women Workers, where the main focus of discussion was whether a 30 per cent quota for women should be mandated in union elections, and securing rural women's social security benefits. Nonetheless, a demand of the meeting with respect to the agrarian reform was that women be included in the land registry on the *assentamentos* (CONTAG 1997, 14). At its Seventh Congress in 1998, the union adopted the 30 per cent female quota and created the position of Coordinator of the National Commission of Women as part of its Executive Directorate. All

---

[45] 'Linhas politicas reafirmadas no IV Congresso Nacional do MST', in www.mst.org.br/historico/congresso (downloaded 18 April 2001).
[46] Interview with Vilanisi Oliveira da Silva, MST Coordinator in Ceará, 27 September 2000, Fortaleza. Also see 'Entrevista-Fátima Ribeiro', *Jornal do Commercio* (Recife), 19 August 2001, p. 5.

told, 47 specific actions relevant to rural women were approved, including that in the land registry of the *assentamentos* the name of each member of a couple be included (CONTAG et al. 1998, 124).

The year 2000 yielded some progress in terms of advancing women's land rights. As part of the national coordination for the World March of Women,[47] CONTAG launched events in Brazil with the celebration of International Women's Day on 8 March. More than 36,000 women were reported to have participated in local events throughout the country and set the stage for the planned march on Brasilia, the Marcha das Margaridas, on 10 August (the anniversary of the assassination of North-eastern union leader Margarida Alves). The slogan of the march was 'Against hunger, poverty and violence'. In the flyers and pamphlets distributed prior to the march, a recurring theme was 'the valorization of the participation of women in the agrarian reform', but without land rights being made explicit.[48] In the 'Demands of the Marcha das Margaridas', prepared for the 10 August event by the coordinating committee, nonetheless, women's land rights did figure explicitly.[49] The first among nine major categories of demands was for state support of a national documentation campaign aimed at rural women. A second was access by rural women workers 'to the public policies of agrarian reform', specifically, 'That a norm be issued so that in the documentation of the *assentamento* the parcel be adjudicated in the name of the couple or in the name of the woman when she was single' (CONTAG et al. 2000, 6).

With an estimated 15,000–20,000 rural women converging on Brasilia, the coordinating committee was received by President Fernando Henrique Cardoso and INCRA President Orlando Muniz on 9 August, to whom they presented their list of 81 specific demands. It was reported in the press that 'According to Muniz, the institute is going to change its titling of rural properties so that these appear in the name of the couple and not just the man, correcting the distortion denounced by rural women workers . . . INCRA is going to study the other demands.'[50]

---

[47] The 2000 World March of Women resulted from a proposal from the women's movement in Quebec, Canada, to organize women world-wide between 8 March and 17 October (International Day in the Struggle against Poverty), culminating with a delegation presenting its demands before the World Bank, International Monetary Fund and the United Nations.

[48] See the pamphlet distributed by CONTAG, *Boletim Informativo* (no date) 'Marcha Das Margaridas: Contra a fome, a pobreza e a violencia – dia 10 de Agosto'.

[49] The Coordinating Committee for the march, besides CONTAG and its affiliated state federations and municipal-level unions, included the CUT, MMTR-NE, Movimento Nacional de Quebradeiras de Coco, Conselho Nacional de Seringueiros, Movimento de Luta pela Terra, União Brasileira de Mulheres and the NGOs Sempre Viva Organização Feminista (SOF), Associação Agroecologica Tijupa, FASE, and ESPLAR. Notably absent was the MST as well as the ANMTR. Tensions between CONTAG and the MST were high at this point over disagreement on the degree to which they should cooperate with government programmes, such as the proposed Land Bank. The ANMTR (in contrast to one of its constituent organizations, the MMTR-NE) usually follows the lead of the MST on such political questions.

[50] *Pagina Agrária (Boletim Semanal da Secretaria Agrária Nacional do PT)* # 165, 12–18 August 2000, in www.pt.org.br/san

The expedition of Resolution No. 6 of 22 February 2001 by the National Council on Sustainable Rural Development (CNDRS, Conselho Nacional de Desenvolvimento Rural Sustentavel) of the Ministry of Agrarian Development (MDA, Ministerio do Desenvolvimento Agrário) was the outcome of the negotiating process between the coordinating committee of the march and the interministerial group charged with following up on their demands. According to the Ministry, this resolution provides for a 'gender perspective in all the administrative procedures of the MDA', and there are to be changes in 'the selection norms to facilitate the access of women to the benefits of the agrarian reform'.[51]

Subsequently, the 'Affirmative Action Program to Promote the Equality of Opportunities and Treatment of Men and Women' was institutionalized within the Ministry.[52] The new office was charged with revamping all criteria and norms to facilitate rural women's access to land and to titles, credit, training, technical assistance and social security benefits. This objective was made more concrete by another directive, which established a target for 2001 of 30 per cent female representation in the distribution of credits within the family agriculture support programme, PRONAF (Programa Nacional de Fortalecimiento da Agricultura Familiar) and the Land Bank (Fundo do Terras e da Reforma Agrária) as well as in PRONAF training and extension programmes.[53] In addition, a goal of the Ministry became to progressively attain 30 per cent female representation in its administrative structure.[54]

With respect to INCRA, one of the first accomplishments of the Affirmative Action office was to redesign almost all of the forms utilized in the agrarian reform beneficiary selection process so that the name of both spouses or partners appear on the first page of the form as co-applicants or beneficiaries. (Formerly, the names of wives and companions appeared on the second page, heading the list of the dependents of the head of household.) In August 2001, I found that only one form remained to be changed, a crucially important one, the official 'List of Beneficiaries' on each *assentamento*. Following traditional practice, this listing still included only one person per household. During my visit to MDA/INCRA, steps were put in motion to assure that the name of the couple appear in this crucial record of beneficiaries.[55]

While a number of gender-progressive measures were thus adopted during 2001, it is worth noting that no specific mention has been made of female household heads. In order to end the discrimination to which these have traditionally been subject, other Latin American countries have found it necessary to employ

---

[51] Note that the resolution does not explicitly establish joint adjudication and titling of land, but rather focuses on nondiscrimination against women. It does provide for women to be considered as rural workers or agriculturalists in the land registry, rather than the traditional designation of housewives. See *Diario Oficial da Uniõ*, 5 March 2001, and www.desenvolvimentoagrario.gov.br/mulher/noticias (accessed 10 March 2001).

[52] MDA, Portaria No. 33, 8 March 2001 (photocopy).

[53] MDA, Portaria No. 121, 22 May 2001 (photocopy).

[54] MDA, Portaria No. 120, 22 May 2001 (photocopy).

[55] Interview with Lenita Nonan, Special Advisor to the Minister and Coordinator of the Affirmative Action Program, and MDA/INCRA staff, 8 August 2001, Brasilia.

positive action or reverse discrimination, making these an explicit priority in State programmes involved in the redistribution of assets. This has usually been accomplished by assigning them more points in beneficiary selection criteria, justified on the grounds that this favoured treatment is necessary to compensate for the discrimination to which they were previously subject (Deere and León 2001, chapter 6). Given the fact that the majority of female beneficiaries of Brazil's agrarian reform up through 1996 were wives or partners, rather than female household heads, the lack of specific attention to female household heads remains a lacunae in its policies to end gender discrimination.

Nonetheless, Brazil is the pioneer among Latin American countries in assigning rural women a target quota of 30 per cent in the credit being made available for the purchase of land under the market-assisted agrarian reform. The Land Bank is the subject of intense controversy, seen by its critics as a means of undermining the federal government's responsibility for agrarian reform.[56] It is questionable whether a programme that requires credit-worthiness as a pre-condition for participation and that expects farmers to be able to repay their mortgages on near commercial terms under neoliberal policies is the best way to guarantee gender equity in the acquisition of land. But this topic awaits further research.

CONCLUSION

This review of the issue of gender and land rights within the Brazilian rural social movements leads to the following conclusions. Most of the credit for raising the issue of women's access to land within the agrarian reform rests with women within the leadership of the rural unions, both CONTAG and CUT. Their efforts, combined with the organizational activity of rural women within the local, state and regional-level MMTRs, and those of the state (at the prodding of the CNDR), largely explain why women's land rights became an issue in the period preceding the constitutional reform. That they were successful in obtaining women's formal land rights in the 1988 Constitution is largely due to the coalition of women within the State and political parties working in concert with a unified urban and rural women's movement in support of attaining an expansion of women's rights in the Constitution. Women's formal land rights in the agrarian reform were achieved as a by-product of the effort to end discrimination against women in all its dimensions.

The achievement of formal equality in land rights, nonetheless, did not lead to increases in the share of female beneficiaries in the agrarian reform. INCRA did modify its most explicitly discriminatory practice, the assignment of fewer points to women than men in the beneficiary selection process. Other criteria, however, continued to discriminate against female household heads. Moreover, although joint adjudication and titling was now a legal possibility, the fact that it was an option rather than mandatory meant that it was simply not implemented.

---

[56] 'Cédula da Terra: mais uma mentira do governo', *Jornal Sem Terra*, December 1998, 10–11; also see 'Artigos reforma agrária', http://www.mst.org.br/bibliotec.htm (accessed 18 November 2000).

I have argued that the relatively low share of female agrarian reform beneficiaries in the mid-1990s also reflects the fact that attaining women's effective land rights was not a top priority of any of the rural social movements. While women's participation in rural unions continued to grow over this period, and women's land rights were on the agenda at most national meetings and congresses, land rights were one issue among many. The priorities of the autonomous rural women's movement were perhaps even more varied and diffuse than that of the unions. CONTAG, CUT and the MMTRs all gave greater attention to the pressing issue of the recognition of rural women's profession in the context of their attaining social security benefits, than to women's land rights. This is understandable given the fact that this was the issue that united all rural women, independent of their class position, uniting the heterogenous membership of the unions and autonomous women's movement. But it also created a vacuum in terms of the effective championing of women's land rights since, throughout this period, the main social movement determining the pace and content of the agrarian reform was the MST. Of all the rural social movements, as I have shown, it had the most muted discourse on gender, one that essentially considered class and gender issues to be incompatible. Taken together, these factors largely explain why women formed such a relatively low proportion of the beneficiaries of agrarian reform in the mid-1990s.

The expansion of the agrarian reform in the second half of the 1990s – a result associated with the territorial consolidation of the MST as a national organization, the radicalization of the unions on the agrarian reform issue and a surge in the number of land occupations – is associated with an increase in the share of female beneficiaries in certain states. I have suggested that this trend is partly attributable to the gradual opening within the MST to gender concerns, which itself reflects the slow, but incremental participation of women within the MST leadership at all levels, and the pressing need to consolidate the *assentamentos*.

As noted in the Introduction, recognition of the importance of women's land rights generally takes place for two reasons, the productionist and the empowerment arguments. The opening of the MST to gender concerns in the late 1990s is related to growing acceptance of the productionist argument; that is, that the failure to recognize women's land rights is prejudicial to the development and consolidation of the *assentamentos* and thus the movement. It is now recognized that joint adjudication and titling to couples is a precondition for women's participation in *assentamento* assemblies, associations and cooperatives, and that their participation in these leads to better results, both for the community and for women. There is also growing awareness that land rights strengthen women's bargaining position and thus their ability to defend and pursue their own practical and strategic gender interests. Given the MST's commitment to social and gender equality, there is thus growing acceptance of the empowerment argument: that is, that gender relations must change which, in turn, requires increasing women's bargaining power within the household and community as complementary and interactive measures. But this is a much slower process and one that has yet to reach fruition.

REFERENCES

Abramovay, Miriam and Rocicleide da Silva, 2000. 'As Relações de Gênero na Confederação Nacional de Trabalhadores Rurais (CONTAG)'. In *Trabalho e Gênero: Mudanças, Permanencias e Sesafios*, ed. Maria Isabel Baltar da Rocha, 347–75. São Paulo: editora 34.

Agarwal, Bina, 1994. *A Field of One's Own: Gender and Land Rights in South Asia*. Cambridge: Cambridge University Press.

Albuquerque, Ligia and Isaura Rufino, 1987. 'Elementos que Dificultam a Participação da Mulher no Processo da Reforma Agrária'. In *Anais do Seminario Mulheres Rurais: Identidades e na Luta Política*, ed. Lela Lavinas, 320–39. Rio de Janeiro: IPPUR/UFRJ.

Alvarez, Sonia, 1990. *Engendering Democracy in Brazil: Women's Movements in Transition Politics*. Princeton, NJ: Princeton University Press.

ANMTR, 1997. 'Primer Encontro Nacional 1995'. Mimeo. Passo Fundo, Rio Grande do Sul: Articulação Nacional de Mulheres Trabalhadoras Rurais.

ANMTR, no date. 'Proposta de Implementacão da Campanha da Documentação a Nível Nacional, Regional, e Municipal'. Internal memo. Passo Fundo, Rio Grande do Sul: Articulação Nacional de Mulheres Trabalhadoras Rurais.

Barsted, Leila de Andrade Linhares, 1994. 'Em Busca do Tempo Perdido: Mulher e Políticas Publicas no Brasil 1983–1993'. *Revista Estudos Feministas* (CIEC/Escola De Comunicação UFRJ), Special Number, October: 38–53.

Brasil, 1990. *Censos Economicos de 1985, Censo Agropecuarino*. Rio de Janeiro: IBGE.

Brasil, 1994. *Censo Demográfico 1991*. Rio de Janeiro: IBGE.

Brumer, Anita, 2000. 'Gênero e Agricultura: a Situação da Mulher na Agricultura do RGS'. Paper presented to the XXII International Congress of the Latin American Studies Association, 16–18 March, Miami.

Cappellin, Paola, 1989. 'Silenciosas e Combativas: as Contribuições das Mulheres na Estrutura Sindical do Nordeste, 1976/1986'. In *Rebeldia e Submissão: Estudos sobre a Condição Feminina*, eds Albertina de Oliveira Costa and Cristina Buschini, 225–98. São Paulo: Ed. Vertice and Fundação Carlos Chagas.

Cappellin, Paola, 1992. 'Mulheres Invisiveis'. *Teoria & Debate*, 19: 59–63.

Cappellin, Paola, 1997. 'Os Movimentos de Trabalhadoras e a Sociedade Brasileira'. In *História das Mulheres no Brasil*, ed. Maria Del Priore, 640–66. São Paulo: Ed. Contexto e Editora UNESP.

Cardoso, Fernando Henrique, 1997. *Reforma Agrária: Compromisso de Todos*. Brasilia: Presidência da República, Secretaria de Comunicação Social.

Carneiro, Maria José, 1994. 'Mulheres no Campo: Notas sobre sua Participação Política e a Condição Social do Gênero'. *Estudos, Sociedade e Agricultura*, 2: 11–22.

CFEMEA, 1996. *Guia dos Direitos da Mulher*. Rio de Janeiro: Rosa dos Tempos, 2nd edn.

CONTAG, 1988. *Primer Seminario Nacional da Trabalhadora Rural, Brasilia, dias 27, 28 e 29 de julho de 1988*. Brasilia: Confederação Nacional dos Trabalhadores na Agricultura.

CONTAG, 1997. 'Plenaria Nacional de Mulheres Trabalhadoras Rurais, 19–22 março 1997, Relatorio Preliminar'. Memo. Brasilia: Confederação Nacional dos Trabalhadores na Agricultura.

CONTAG, FETAGs, STRs, 1998. *Anais: 7 Congreso Nacional de Trabalhadores e Trabalhadoras Rurais, 30 março-1 avril 1999*. Brasilia: Confederação Nacional dos Trabalhadores na Agricultura.

CONTAG, FETAGs, STRs, CUT, MMTR-NE, MNQC, CNS, MLT, UBM, SOF, TIJUPÁ, FASE, ESPLAR, 2000. 'Pauta de Reivindicações da Marcha das Margaridas, Mobilização das Mulheres Trabalhadoras Rurais em adesão a Marcha Mundial de

Mulheres 2000'. Memo, 10 August. Brasilia: Confederação Nacional dos Trabalhadores na Agricultura.

CUT (Central Única dos Trabalhadores), 1991. *Mulheres Trabalhadoras Rurais: Participação e Luta Sindical*. São Paulo: Departamento Nacional dos Trabalhadores Rurais, Comissão Nacional da Questão da Mulher Trabalhadora.

da Luz, Valdemar, P., 1996. *Curso de Direito Agrario, Contem o Estatuto da Terra*. Porto Alegre: Sagra-DC Luzzatto, Eds, 2nd edn.

Deere, Carmen Diana, 2001. 'Gender, Land Rights and Rural Social Movements: Regional Differences in the Brazilian Agrarian Reform'. Paper presented at the International Congress of the Latin American Studies Association, 6–8 September 2001, Miami.

Deere, Carmen Diana and Magdalena León, 1998. 'Mujeres, Derechos a la Tierra y Contrareformas en América Latina'. *Debate Agrario* (Lima), 27: 129–54.

Deere, Carmen Diana and Magdalena León, 1999. 'Towards a Gendered Analysis of the Brazilian Agrarian Reform'. Latin American Studies Consortium of New England, Occasional Papers No. 16, April. University of Connecticut.

Deere, Carmen Diana and Magdalena León, 2001. *Empowering Women: Land and Property Rights in Latin America*. Pittsburgh, PA: University of Pittsburgh.

EMBRATER, 1986. 'I Congresso Nacional de Mulheres Rurais, Brasilia, DF, 25 al 28 de novembro de 1986, Conclusões'. Memo. Brasilia: Ministerio de Agricultura, Serviço de Extensão Rural.

Fernandes, Bernardo Macano, 1996. *MST: Formação e Territorialização*. São Paulo: Ed. Hucitec.

FETAG-RS (Federação dos Trabalhadores Agricolas do Rio Grande do Sul), 1998. *Revista da Trabalhadora Rural: FETAG/RS* (Porto Alegre), Ano 1, no. 1.

FETAPE, 1986. 'Relatorio, Quarto Encontro de Mulheres Trabalhadoras Rurais, Sertão-PE, em preparação ao Primer Encontro Estadual'. Mimeo. November. Serra Talhada: Federação dos Trabalhadores Agricolas de Pernambuco.

FETAPE, 1988. 'Relatorio, Quinto Encontro de Mulheres Trabalhadoras Rurais, Sertão Central'. Mimeo. December. Serra Talhada: Federação dos Trabalhadores Agricolas de Pernambuco.

Godinho Delgado, Maria Berenice, 1995. 'A Organização das Mulheres na Central Única dos Trabalhadores: a Comissão Nacional sobre a Mulher Trabalhadora'. Master's thesis, Pontificia Universidade Catolica de São Paulo.

Godinho, Delgado, Maria Berenice, 1996. 'Mais Mulheres na Direção da CUT'. *Textos para Debate Internacional* (CUT), 49–58.

Hall, Anthony L., 1990. 'Land Tenure and Land Reform in Brazil'. In *Agrarian Reform and Grass Roots Development: Ten Case Studies*, eds Roy Prosterman, Mary Temple and Timothy Hanstad, 205–34. Boulder, CO: Lynne Rienner.

Hammond, John, 1999. 'Law and Disorder: The Brazilian Landless Farmworkers' Movement'. *Bulletin of Latin American Research*, 18 (4): 468–89.

INCRA/CRUB/UnB (Instituto Nacional de Colonização e Reforma Agrária), 1998. *Primer Censo da Reforma Agraria do Brasil*. Brasilia: Ministério Extraordinario de Política Fundiaria.

INCRA, Gabinete do Ministro Extraordinario da Política Fundiaria, 1998. 'Cadastramento e Seleção Nacional'. Mimeo. June. Brasilia.

Lavinas, Lena, ed., 1987. *Anais do Seminario Mulheres Rurais: Identidades e na Luta Política*. Rio de Janeiro: IPPUR/UFRJ.

Lavinas, Lena, 1991. 'Produtoras Rurais: a Novidade dos Anos 90'. *Reforma Agraria* (Campinas, BZ), May/June: 4–9.

Lavinas, Lena and Paola Cappellin, 1991. 'Gênero e Classe: Mulheres Trabalhadoras Rurais'. *Mulheres Trabalhadoras Rurais* (Revista da CUT, Departamento Nacional dos Trabalhadores Rurais), 28–41.

Lechat, Noelle Marie Paule, 1996. 'Relações de Gênero em Assentamentos do MST (RS): a Participação da Mulher na Produção e Reprodução em Unidades Familiares e Coletivas'. In *Mulher, Família e Desenvolvimento Rural*, eds Clio Presvelou, F. Rodrigues Almeida and J. Anécio Almeida, 93–116. Santa Maria: Universidade Federal de Santa Maria.

Maybury-Lewis, Biorn, 1996. *The Politics of the Possible: The Brazilian Rural Workers' Trade Union Movement, 1964–1985.* Philadelphia: Temple University Press.

de Medeiros, Leonilde Servolo, 1989. *História dos Movimentos Sociais no Campo.* Rio de Janeiro: FASE.

MEMTR, 1986. 'Primeiro Congresso Estadual das Mulheres Trabalhadoras Rurais, Teses, Textos Básicos para a Preparação do Congresso'. Mimeo. Porto Alegre: Movimento Estadual das Mulheres Trabalhadoras Rurais.

Miele, Neide and Flávia Maia Guimarães, 1998. 'As Mulheres nos Assentamentos Rurais: O Antes e o Depois'. In *Qualidade de Vida e Reforma Agrária na Paraíba*, eds Genaro Ieno Neto and Thomas Bamat, 205–50. João Pessoa: UNITRABALHO-UFPB.

Minc, Carlos, 1985. *A Reconquista da Terra: Estatuto da Terra, Lutas no Campo e Reforma Agrária.* Rio de Janeiro: Jorge Zahar Ed.

MMTR (Movimento das Mulheres Trabalhadoras Rurais), 1994. *Uma Historia de Mulheres: Uma Historia da Organização do MMTR do Sertão Central de Pernambuco no Interior do Movimento Sindical.* Serra Tablada, PE: MMTR-OXFAM.

MMTR-NE, 1987. 'Primer Encontro das Mulheres Trabalhadoras Rurais do Nordeste, João Pessoa 4 a 7 de maio de 1987'. Mimeo.

MST, 1986. *Construindo o Caminho.* São Paulo: Secretaria Nacional do Movimento dos Trabalhadores Rurais Sem Terra.

MST, 1989a. *Normas Gerais do MST.* São Paulo: Movimento dos Trabalhadores Rurais Sem Terra.

MST, 1989b. *Caderno de Formação*, No. 17. São Paulo: Secretaria Nacional do Movimento dos Trabalhadores Rurais Sem Terra.

MST, 1996. *A Questão da Mulher no MST.* São Paulo: Coletivo Nacional de Mulheres do Movimento dos Trabalhadores Rurais Sem Terra.

MST, 2000. *Mulher Sem Terra.* São Paulo: ANCA (Associação Nacional de Cooperação Agrícola) and INCRA.

Navarro, Zander, 1996. 'Democracia, Cidadania e Representação: os Movimentos Sociais Rurais no Estado do Rio Grande do Sul, Brasil, 1978–1990'. In *Política, Protesto e Cidadania no Campo: As Lutas Sociais dos Colonos e dos Trabalhadores Rurais no Rio Grande do Sul*, ed. Zander Navarro, 62–105. Porto Alegre: Editora da Universidade UFRGS.

Portella, Ana Paula and Silvia Camurça, no date. 'Comentarios sobre a Trajetoria das Mulheres no Sindicalismo Rural'. Texto de Apoio 5, Seminario de Sensibilização, Projeto INCRA/FAO-TCP/BR/8922A, Brasilia.

Prá, Jussara Reis and Maria Noemi Castilhos Brito, 1988. 'Movimento de Mulheres no Sul do Brasil: 1975 a 1987'. Cadernos de Estudos, No. 1, Programa de Pos-Graduação em Antropologia Social. Porto Alegre: UFRGS.

Rua, Maria das Gracas and Miriam Abramovay, 2000. *Companheiras de Luta ou 'Coordenadoras de Panelas'?* Brasilia: Edição UNESCO Brasil.

Rufino, Isaura and Ligia Albuquerque, 1990. 'Posição da Mulher no Processo de Reforma Agrária'. In *Política Fundiaria no Nordeste: Caminhos e Descaminhos*, ed. Dirçeo Pessoa, 361–84. Recife: Fundação Joaquim Nabuco and Ed. Massangana.

Siqueira, Deis Elucy, 1991. 'A Organização das Trabalhadoras Rurais: o Cruzamento de Gênero e de Classe Social'. In *Technologia Agropecuaria e a Organização dos Trabalhadores Rurais*, eds D.E. Siqueira, João G.L.C. Teixeira and Maria Stela Grosso Porto, 57–90. Brasilia: UNB.

Stedile, João Pedre and Bernardo Mançano Fernandes, 1999. *Brava Gente: A Trajetória do MST e a Luta pela Terra no Brasil*. São Paulo: Ed. Fundação Perseu Abramo.

Stephen, Lynn, 1997. *Women and Social Movements in Latin America: Power from Below*. Austin, TX: University of Texas Press.

Suárez, Mireya and Marlene Libardoni, 1992. *Mulheres e Desenvolvimento Agricola no Brasil: Uma Perspectiva de Gênero*. Brasilia: IICA, Escritorio no Brasil.

Thiesenhusen, William C. and Jolyne Melmed-Sanjak, 1990. 'Brazil's Agrarian Structure: Changes from 1970 through 1980'. *World Development*, 18 (3): 393–415.

Index